BUSINESS LAW AND PRACTICE
SECOND EDITION

Liz Jones

Second edition published 2022 by
The University of Law,
2 Bunhill Row
London EC1Y 8HQ

First edition published 2021

British Library Cataloguing in Publication Data

A catalogue record for this book is available from the British Library.

ISBN 978 1 915698 00 1

Preface

This book is part of a series of Study Manuals that have been specially designed to support the reader to achieve the SQE1 Assessment Specification in relation to Functioning Legal Knowledge. Each Study Manual aims to provide the reader with a solid knowledge and understanding of fundamental legal principles and rules, including how those principles and rules might be applied in practice.

This Study Manual covers the Solicitors Regulation Authority's syllabus for the SQE1 assessment for Business Law and Practice in a concise and tightly focused manner. The Manual provides a clear statement of relevant legal rules and a well-defined road map through examinable law and practice. The Manual aims to bring the law and practice to life through the use of example scenarios based on realistic client-based problems and allows the reader to test their knowledge and understanding through single best answer questions that have been modelled on the SRA's sample assessment questions.

For those readers who are students at the University of Law, the Study Manual is used alongside other learning resources and the University's assessment bank to best prepare students not only for the SQE1 assessments, but also for a future life in professional legal practice.

We hope that you find the Study Manual supportive of your preparation for SQE1 and we wish you every success.

The legal principles and rules contained within this Manual are stated as at 1 June 2022.

Author acknowledgments

My thanks go to David Molyneux for his thorough and intelligent comments on the whole book and to Stephen Allinson for his expert input into the original draft of Chapter 8. I am also grateful to Jacqui Kempton, whose examples I used for some of the tax and accounts sections, and to David Stott and the editorial team.

Thank you to my amazing family, for putting up with my deadlines, and to Sarah Roberts, for ably holding the fort with Business Law and Practice while I wrote this.

This book is dedicated to the memory of my mum, Margaret Jones, 1946–2020.

BUSINESS LAW AND PRACTICE

The
University of
Law

The University of Law
133 Great Hampton Street
Birmingham B18 6AQ
Telephone: 01483 216041
Email: library-birmingham@law.ac.uk

Contents

Table of Cases

Table of Statutes

1 The Different Types of Business

SQE1 syllabus

This chapter, combined with **Chapters 2 and 6**, will enable you to achieve the SQE1 Assessment Specification in relation to Functioning Legal Knowledge concerned with the following:

- business and organisational characteristics (sole trader/partnership/LLP/private and unlisted public companies)

- legal personality and limited liability

- procedures and documentation required to incorporate a company/form a partnership/LLP and other steps required under companies and partnerships legislation to enable the entity to commence operating:

  - constitutional documents; and

  - Companies House filing requirements

Note that for SQE1, candidates are not usually required to recall specific case names, or cite statutory or regulatory authorities. In this chapter, statutory references are provided for information only.

Learning outcomes

By the end of this chapter you will be able to:

- identify and compare the different types of incorporated and unincorporated business operating in England and Wales;

- give basic advice on which type of business is appropriate for a particular client;

- identify the documents which must be submitted to create a new company;

- advise on what the applicant must decide before they are in a position to apply to register a new company;

- understand the role of solicitors, company formation agents and the Registrar of Companies in setting up a company; and

- understand the significance of a company's constitution, in particular the articles of association and their key provisions.

1.1 Introduction

Businesses are part of the fabric of our lives. Most of what we own will have been manufactured, transported and sold by a business. It is likely that almost everything we eat will have been grown, processed and sold by a business. Businesses are the means by which the UK creates economic wealth, and it is not surprising, therefore, that most solicitors will deal with businesses in practice.

Future corporate lawyers are aware that they will spend their working lives acting for businesses. They know that a comprehensive understanding of business law will be necessary to enable them to advise their clients. But knowledge of business law is also an important part of other practice areas. Solicitors may be acting for one party to a divorce who is alleging that their spouse has hidden money or assets through a complicated company structure or network of businesses. An understanding of business law would be essential to advise the client accurately and to fully understand the client's position. Alternatively, solicitors may be involved in criminal prosecution or defence in a fraud case. They will need an understanding of business law and accounts to understand the allegations against the client or the possible defences available. So a good grounding in business law is essential to almost every practice area, even for those who do not intend to represent business clients.

A client setting up a business has a wide variety of choices open to them. This chapter will describe the main forms of business medium and why a client might choose to operate using one form rather than another. The second part of the chapter will explain how to set up a company and will explore the company's constitution.

Part 1 Types of Business

1.2 Incorporated and unincorporated businesses

An incorporated business exists as a separate legal entity from its owners and managers. It is formed when the individuals who wish to set it up comply with various legal requirements in order to incorporate their business. A feature of incorporated businesses is that their owners are generally not liable for business debts. The most common form of incorporated business is the limited company, which is considered later in this chapter. Unincorporated business are businesses run by individuals who have not set up a separate legal entity to run the business and who have full personal liability for the debts of the business.

Below we consider the main types of business medium. We begin with unincorporated businesses (sole traders, partnerships and limited partnerships) and move on to incorporated businesses.

1.3   Sole traders

A sole trader is someone who runs an unincorporated business on their own as a self-employed person. A business operated by a sole trader is the most common form of business medium in the UK. A sole trader can operate in any trade or profession and can be anything from a dog walker to an architect. Sometimes sole traders are referred to as sole proprietors. Professionals who operate as a sole trader, for example, solicitors, are known as sole practitioners. The term 'sole trader' will be used in this book to refer to all of these types of business-person.

Operating as a sole trader does not mean that you work alone. A sole trader may have one or more employees, but the sole trader is the person who owns the business, benefits from the profits and bears any losses. Sole traders earn income from the money received from customers or clients and keep all the profit, once they have paid their expenses. They pay income tax as a self-employed person.

A sole trader is personally liable for all of the debts of the business. This means that the sole trader's business assets and personal assets are all treated the same for legal purposes. Imagine that a person operates a small café as a sole trader. If the business performs badly and the sole trader cannot pay the debts they owe to suppliers, the suppliers may take legal action against the sole trader. The defendant in such an action would be the sole trader. If the café business did not have enough money to pay the debt, the claimant could be paid from the sole trader's personal bank account and other personal assets. If the sole trader were unable to pay off all of the debts, they could be made bankrupt.

The idea that there is no limit to the sole trader's liability is known as the concept of unlimited liability. When the sole trader retires or dies, the business ceases, although the individual assets or even the business itself can be sold if a buyer can be found.

There is no dedicated piece of legislation governing businesses run by a sole trader. Of course the sole trader's activities will be governed by the law, but it will be in various pieces of legislation which can apply to individuals or businesses generally, for example, tax legislation or sale of goods legislation.

1.4   Partnerships

A partnership exists when two or more people run and own a business together. It is formed when the definition of 'partnership' set out in the Partnership Act 1890 ('PA 1890') is met. This provides that a partnership is formed when two or more people are 'carrying on a business in common with a view of profit'. A partnership is an unincorporated business but differs from a sole trader because it involves more than one person running the business.

Partnerships can carry on any trade or any profession, and a partnership can be as simple as two people running a gardening business, to as complicated as a multinational law firm with hundreds of partners and employees. Partnerships that satisfy the definition in the PA 1890 are usually just referred to as partnerships, but the term 'general partnership' can be used to distinguish these partnerships from limited partnerships and limited liability partnerships, which are covered below.

The PA 1890 provides a default partnership agreement for the partners. The partners may decide to enter into an agreement which disapplies some of the provisions in the PA 1890, but if they do not, the PA 1890 applies, and its provisions will be implied.

A partnership is not a separate legal entity. The phrase 'partnership assets' may be used to describe the assets which are used in the partnership business, but the partnership itself does not actually own the assets. They are owned by the partners. As with sole traders, partners are personally liable for all of the debts of the partnership. Their personal assets are at risk if there is not enough money in the business to pay creditors.

The partners will divide the profits or losses of the business between them. In a partnership made up solely of individuals, the partners are taxed separately as self-employed individuals, paying income tax on their share of the profits of the partnership (and if any of the partners are companies, they may be liable for corporation tax on their share of the profits instead). It is important to remember that partners are not employees; they own the business. Usually the partners will all work for the business, but sometimes there are one or more 'sleeping partners' who are not involved in day-to-day matters, only in making fundamental decisions about the business.

Chapter 6 covers the law on partnerships in much greater detail.

1.5 Limited partnerships

Limited partnerships ('LPs') are not widely recognised, but currently there are over 49,000 LPs in existence. An LP is similar to a partnership in that there must be at least one general partner who has unlimited liability for the partnership debts. Unlike a normal partnership, an LP is permitted to have a limited partner whose liability is limited to the amount they initially invested in the business. This limited liability is conditional. The limited partner must not:

- control or manage the LP;
- have the power to take binding decisions on behalf of the LP; or
- remove their contribution to the LP for as long as it is in business.

If the limited partner breaches any of these rules then they will lose the protection of limited liability and be treated as a general partner with unlimited liability.

The Limited Partnerships Act 1907 (LPA 1907) governs the formation and operation of LPs. They were originally created to encourage entrepreneurs to set up businesses by reducing some of the effects of unlimited liability which may arise from an ordinary partnership. Over time the limited company became the business format of choice, as it offered even greater protection. Nowadays, LPs have come back into fashion for specialist financial businesses, such as investment funds and venture capital funds.

Unlike ordinary partnerships, LPs must be registered with the Registrar of Companies, who also acts as the Registrar of LPs, before they can start trading.

Limited partnerships are not covered in **Chapter 6** because their significance to modern business practice is limited.

1.6 Companies

There are several different types of company. Companies can be private or public, and can be limited by shares or by guarantee. In this book we focus on private companies limited by shares and unlisted public companies limited by shares, which will be explained in the following paragraphs.

1.6.1 Private companies limited by shares

When we imagine a business, we often think of the company. A company in the UK is formed by registering certain documents with the Registrar of Companies in accordance with the requirements of the Companies Act 2006 ('CA 2006'). Whereas sole traders and partners can begin trading straight away, and may not even be aware that their business fits the definition of sole trader or partnership, steps need to be taken to set up a company before it can start trading.

Businesses run as companies perform a wide range of economic activities. Many large companies are household names, but many companies are much smaller, and most have only between one and four employees.

One of the main advantages of a company over most other forms of business medium is that the company has a separate legal personality. This means that the people who own and run the company are separate from the company itself. If somebody wishes to sue a company, the defendant will be the company itself, rather than the individuals who own and run it. The individuals who own the shares in the company will not usually be liable for its debts – their liability is limited to the amount they paid or agreed to pay for their shares. It is this huge benefit which has enabled companies to grow. It is important to take calculated risks when in business, in order to allow a business to expand. Directors of companies are able to take more risks because most of the time their personal assets are safe from creditors. It is hard to see how huge multinational companies such as Apple could have grown to such an extent if they were run as partnerships and the partners had personal liability for the business's debts.

1.6.1.1 Separate legal personality

Salomon v A Salomon and Co Ltd [1897] AC 22 is a landmark case confirming the full extent of the concept of separate legal personality. The claimant argued that because one person controlled the company and was entitled to all the benefits of it, the company did not exist as a separate legal person and its principal shareholder and director could be held personally liable for the company's debts. The House of Lords rejected this, holding that as long as a company is legally incorporated, it must be treated like any other independent person with rights and liabilities: using a company to manage risk and avoid liability for debts is acceptable.

There have been numerous cases since *Salomon v A Salomon and Co Ltd* where the claimant has tried to pierce the corporate veil, that is, look behind the company and impose liability on the individual(s) who own or run the company. The most recent authority on this is *Prest v Petrodel Resources Limited and others* [2013] UKSC 34, where the Supreme Court decided that the corporate veil could only be pierced when a person is under an existing legal obligation or liability or is subject to an existing legal restriction which he deliberately evades, or whose enforcement he deliberately frustrates, by interposing a company under his control. Even then, the corporate veil can only be pierced so as to deprive the company or its controller of the advantage that they would otherwise have obtained by the company's separate legal personality.

Any decisions where the court has ignored separate legal personality are rare and generally considered to be very specific to their facts.

1.6.1.2 Decision-making

The fact that the company is a legal person in its own right means that it needs humans to make decisions on its behalf. Those decisions are made either by the company's directors or by the company's shareholders (or by someone to whom the directors have delegated certain decisions). The directors of a company run the company. The shareholders of the company are the individuals who provide the money (in return for shares) to allow the company to operate. Often the directors and the shareholders are the same people, but when they are making decisions which affect the day-to-day running of the business, they must think and act like directors, and when they are making decisions reserved for shareholders alone, they must think and act like shareholders.

Shareholders tend to get involved only in the more important decisions affecting the company. This division of responsibility, and the fact that directors collectively make decisions at board meetings (or in writing) whereas shareholders make decisions at general meetings (or in writing), introduce a degree of formality which is usually not present in partnerships. You can read more about company decision-making in **Chapter 2.**

The CA 2006 uses the term 'member' instead of shareholder, because the term 'member' can apply equally to companies limited by guarantee and companies limited by shares. This book focusses on companies limited by shares and generally the term 'shareholder' rather than 'member' is used throughout.

1.6.2   Public companies limited by shares

A public limited company ('plc') is a company limited by shares which has complied with the requirements of the CA 2006 to enable it to be registered as a plc. Some of the biggest companies in the UK are public companies.

For a company to be a public company:

1. the constitution, which is the set of rules which govern the company, must state that it is a public company;

2. the words 'public limited company' or the abbreviation 'plc' (or the Welsh equivalent, for a Welsh company) must be included at the end of the company's name; and

3. the company's owners must invest a specified minimum amount of money for use by the company: the allotted share capital of the company must be at least the 'authorised minimum', currently £50,000 (ss 761 and 763 CA 2006). Each allotted share must also be paid up to at least a quarter of its nominal value, plus the whole of any premium on it (s 586 CA 2006).

1.6.2.1   Why operate as a plc?

The main advantages to being a public company are that they are more prestigious and, even more importantly, can raise money by offering shares to the public, unlike private companies, which are prohibited from doing so (s 755 CA 2006). Private companies can instead offer their shares to a person already connected with the company or certain other targeted individuals rather than to the public or a section of the public (s 756 CA 2006).

Public companies can apply to join the stock market in the UK. Fewer than a quarter of UK public companies have joined the stock market. The main stock markets in the UK are the London Stock Exchange's Main Market and the Alternative Investment Market, known as AIM. The stock markets allow companies to raise large sums of money by enabling investors to buy the company's shares quickly and easily. It is not possible to start a company as a publicly traded company; this is only an option if the business reaches a certain size, reputation or level of growth.

Generally, private companies are subject to less regulation than public companies because they do not offer shares to the public at large; instead, they raise finance either from people who already know the company or specialist investors who understand the risks involved. Publicly traded companies are more regulated than unlisted public companies and private companies to protect the public, who can easily invest in a company which is listed on the stock market and are at risk if the company does not perform well financially. Unlisted companies can also offer shares to the public, but because their shares are not listed, it is harder for unlisted public companies to find buyers.

Some of the requirements of the CA 2006 are different for public companies, and you will encounter examples of this in this book.

1.6.2.2   How to become a public company

Companies can be registered as a public company on original incorporation, or they can register as a private company and then re-register as a public company. Please see **1.16 and 1.17** for an explanation of both procedures.

1.7   Limited liability partnerships

A limited liability partnership (LLP) is formed under the Limited Liability Partnerships Act 2000 ('LLPA 2000'). Putting it very simply, an LLP can be likened to a cross between a partnership and a limited company. Like a company, it has a separate legal personality distinct from its owners. It also offers its owners protection from liability for the LLP's debts, like a limited company. However, the LLP is run with the informality and flexibility given by a partnership, and the partners are taxed as if the business were a partnership rather than a company. Many law firms are run as LLPs.

LLPs can be formed by two or more members carrying on a lawful business with a view of profit. They are formed by filing a series of documents with the Registrar of Companies at Companies House and paying the applicable fee. A more expensive same-day registration service is also available. Once the LLP is successfully registered, the Registrar will issue a certificate of incorporation. The LLP legally comes into existence on the date of incorporation on the certificate.

In the same way that partners in a partnership governed by the PA 1890 do not have to have an express partnership agreement because the PA 1890 provides a default contract, in an LLP the Limited Liability Partnerships Regulations 2001 provide a default contract for partners who have not agreed all or any of the terms of their partnership.

Individual members of the LLP must register with HMRC as self-employed.

In many ways, LLPs combine the best features of both companies and partnerships, and it may be surprising that they are not more widely used. This is largely because the business world, particularly outside the UK, is more familiar with the concept of a company so companies have a higher status.

Chapter 6 covers the law on LLPs in much greater detail.

1.8   Other types of business medium

There are many other types of business medium. Most of them are used for very specific purposes, and it is possible that a corporate lawyer may never come across any of these in practice, depending on the type of work they do and who their clients are. The detail is outside the scope of this book, but some of the more common ones are:

*   **Companies limited by guarantee,** which are usually used for organisations that are not seeking to make a profit, such as a professional society. Instead of buying shares, the shareholders guarantee the company's debts up to a specified amount, usually £1.

*   **Unlimited companies,** which are rare in practice, because most people who are happy to run a business with unlimited liability for its debts will choose to run it as a sole trader or partnership.

- **Community interest companies,** a form of limited liability company intended for businesses that wish to use their profits and assets for the public good and not for private profit.

- **Charitable incorporated organisations,** which provide the advantages of a corporate structure, such as reduced risk of personal liability, without the burden of dual regulation by both the Registrar of Companies and the Charity Commission.

- **Overseas companies.** Often overseas companies wish to operate in the UK and set up a regular physical presence here. The law governing this is set out in the Overseas Companies Regulations 2009, which were made under authority granted in the CA 2006. All overseas companies that set up a branch or any other place of business in the UK must register selected details of the establishment within one month of their opening.

- **Companies established by Act of Parliament or Royal Charter.** Historically, trading companies were sometimes established by special Act of Parliament, often to establish railways and public utilities in the UK. There are just 45 of these companies still in existence. Sometimes companies were formed by Royal Charter, such as the Royal Bank of Scotland. The right to form a company in this way does remain and is referred to in the CA 2006, but generally this method of establishing companies is more of historic interest.

- **Joint ventures.** A joint venture is a commercial enterprise undertaken jointly, by two or more parties. The parties retain their own identity but generally pool their resources for a specific purpose. An example of a well-known joint venture is Google and NASA developing Google Earth together. Sometimes the joint venture will be governed merely by a contract between the parties and sometimes the parties may set up a corporate structure which they will jointly control. So a joint venture is not a separate type of business medium in itself, but rather a description of a joint commercial enterprise which could take many forms.

1.9 What type of business is best?

Many people who wish to set up a business will be undecided as to which business format to choose, and may seek advice from their solicitor. Which business is best will depend on many factors, which are addressed below.

1.9.1 Liability

Liability is often the most important consideration for those wishing to set up a new business. As we have seen, shareholders benefit from limited liability for the company's debts, whereas partners are personally liable for partnership debts and risk losing almost everything they own if they operate as a partnership. How much of a concern this is depends on many factors, an important one being the nature of the business. For example, the biggest liability a law firm is likely to face is a claim for professional negligence, but this will usually be covered by insurance, so it is not as much of an issue as it first seems. This is why law firms have successfully operated as partnerships for many years, although many have now switched to the less risky medium of an LLP.

1.9.2 Tax

Tax is often an important factor in deciding on a business medium. Most businesses are set up to make money for their owners, and how much tax the owners will be required to pay is a key consideration. Whether an incorporated business or an unincorporated business is more advantageous depends on the financial circumstances of the business and its owners.

1.9.3 Formalities

As we have seen, it is possible to run a business as a sole trader or partnership without the owner or owners even realising which business medium they are using, because no formalities are required to set up a business as a sole trader or partnership. Setting up a company or LLP is more time-consuming and costly than operating as a sole trader or partnership and the parties will often seek legal or accountancy advice. It is worth noting, however, that it is advisable for partners to enter into a written partnership agreement. The partners require legal advice on this, which will incur a cost and take time.

After the business has been set up, an important advantage for an unincorporated business is that there are no formal requirements once it has been established (other than tax-related formalities required by HMRC), and no legal documents have to be prepared. Companies, in contrast, will have to complete minutes of meetings, maintain certain statutory registers and file certain documents with Companies House. Many companies will also have to have their accounts audited and file these at Companies House. These administrative requirements are time-consuming and will often involve the company incurring professional costs, such as accountants' fees or solicitors' fees.

Lastly, companies are subject to the detailed requirements and strict rules of the CA 2006, which governs how they make decisions and what decisions they are allowed to make. Sole traders and partnerships have freedom over decision-making in their businesses, although partners may (and should) choose to enter into a partnership agreement which sets out how decisions must be made.

Limited liability partnerships are also required to file certain documents at Companies House, but not as many as companies. Further, LLPs have freedom over how they make decisions, just like general partnerships.

1.9.4 Publicity of information

Sole traders and partnerships must disclose the identity of the sole trader or all of the partners, and an address for service of documents, but that is all. Companies and LLPs must reveal certain information to the public at large, including certain financial information. Companies must make public information regarding their directors, their shareholders and many of the significant decisions it has made by filing documents with the Registrar of Companies and keeping various company registers open for inspection on payment of a fee. This is explained more fully in **Chapters 2–5**.

People who wish to start a business but want to keep it private often choose to operate as a sole trader or partnership due to the lack of requirement for publicity.

1.9.5 Cost

Sole traders and partnerships can be set up without any legal or administrative cost, as these businesses trade straight away, although many partners will wish to enter into a partnership agreement. To form a company or an LLP, there is a charge, and the individuals setting up a company or LLP will often require legal advice.

Certain costs are the same regardless of the type of business chosen, for example wages, rent and utilities, but incorporated businesses (companies and LLPs), will usually cost more to run from an administrative point of view because of the extra legal and administrative burdens placed upon them.

1.9.6 Status

Many businesses or individuals would prefer to trade with a company than a partnership or sole trader because they are often used to companies being the business medium of choice for large, successful businesses. They may also feel reassured by the amount of information which is publicly available to those considering doing business with the company.

1.9.7 Finance

Lastly, both companies and LLPs can offer an additional form of security for loans, the floating charge, which is a charge over all of the business's assets and is not available to partnerships or sole traders. This makes companies more desirable clients for lenders such as banks. See **5.17.2** for a full explanation of fixed and floating charges.

It is for the client to decide which of the above factors is the most important for them and therefore which type of business is best. For some businesses, limited liability might not be such a big advantage, because the nature of the business is such that the owners do not anticipate incurring significant debts. Other clients may decide that whilst they want to run a company to benefit from the limited liability it offers, they do not want the business's affairs to be made public so opt for a general partnership instead.

⭐ Example – which business medium is best for the client?

Amal and Dev are surveyors and wish to set up their own practice. They will need to invest a large proportion of their savings into the new business. They are not concerned about information about their business being in the public domain. In terms of tax, it does not matter whether they set up a company or trade as a partnership. They will not need to borrow much money to start trading. They intend to take out professional indemnity insurance, and do not anticipate facing any significant liabilities which will not be covered by their insurance. They both dislike paperwork.

After considering your advice, Amal and Dev decide to set up a partnership. Whilst they are investing large sums of money into the business, they think the risk of facing any large liabilities is minimal, and the most likely liability, a claim for professional negligence, will be covered by insurance. For this reason, they do not feel that they need the benefit of limited liability for the business's debts. They would prefer to start a partnership and enjoy the benefits of having little paperwork to deal with rather than start a company unnecessarily.

Part 2 The Limited Company

Unless stated otherwise, all references in **Part 2** of **Chapter 1** are to private companies limited by shares, which account for over 96% of the corporate bodies registered at Companies House. Reference may occasionally be made to other types of company for completeness.

We have seen that private limited companies are a very popular business medium, and that one of their key features is that they have a legal personality separate from their owners. For the rest of this chapter, we will consider how to set up a company and discuss the main features of the company's constitution.

1.10 Forming a company

To incorporate a new company, the applicant must complete Companies House form IN01 and submit it, along with a document called a memorandum of association, and possibly the company's articles of association, to Companies House with the applicable fee. The application can be made either electronically or on paper. Companies House in Cardiff processes applications for companies to be registered in England and Wales. Companies

House in Edinburgh and Companies House in Belfast process applications for companies to be registered in Scotland and Northern Ireland respectively.

1.11 Who will make the application?

Applications can be made online, by post or through suitably enabled software provided by Companies House. The application method will depend on who is making the application. Some individuals make their own application to Companies House, and are likely to do so by post or online. It is highly unlikely that individuals wishing to incorporate a company would think it worth their while to obtain software from Companies House to make their application.

Many applicants ask their solicitor, accountant or a company formation agent to apply on their behalf. There is a list on the Companies House website of over 100 company formation agents who have the requisite software to complete an application to register a company online and are authorised by Companies House to submit electronic incorporations. They offer a range of packages, starting from a basic one for under £20, to packages including preparation of the first year's accounts and registering the company for VAT, for over £200. Solicitors and accountants may have the requisite software to make the application, or may just apply by post or online as an individual might if they were processing their own application. Alternatively, law and accountancy firms may already have a shelf company the client can use, to avoid the need to set up a company from scratch. Please see **1.18** for more information about shelf companies.

Although the application is addressed to the Registrar of Companies, it is a team of people at Companies House who actually process the applications. They will check that the paperwork has been completed correctly and fully, they will check the Disqualified Directors' Register to check that the proposed directors have not been disqualified from being directors, and they will check that the correct fee has been paid. The amount of the fee will depend on the application method and whether the applicant has requested a same-day service (which is only available by post or using authorised software).

If the person processing the application is satisfied that the requirements of the CA 2006 have been met, they will incorporate the company and issue a certificate of incorporation. The company comes into existence upon the certificate of incorporation being issued (ss 15(4) and 16(2) CA 2006). The certificate of incorporation must state, under s 15 CA 2006:

- the name and registered number of the company
- the date of its incorporation
- whether it is a limited or unlimited company and, if it is limited, whether it is limited by shares or by guarantee
- whether it is a private or public company
- whether the company's registered office is situated in England and Wales (or in Wales), in Scotland or in Northern Ireland.

The certificate will be signed by the Registrar or authenticated by the Registrar's official seal. The certificate of incorporation is conclusive evidence that the requirements of the CA 2006 as to registration have been complied with and that the company is registered under the CA 2006.

Companies must all be registered with HMRC for corporation tax. Companies formed following an online application will be registered for corporation tax automatically, but if the application was made by post, using a formation agent or using third party software, the applicant will have to make a separate application to HMRC, within three months of starting to do business, for the company to be registered for corporation tax.

Incorporating a new company is a common task for trainee solicitors in law firms. It is worth browsing the Companies House website at https://www.gov.uk/government/organisations/companies-house to see what information it contains and what services it provides.

1.12 Decisions to be made

The CA 2006 sets out the information that must be submitted in order for a company to be set up. The applicant can provide this information to Companies House by completing and submitting form IN01. The individuals setting up the company will have to make certain decisions about their proposed company so that they can fill in the IN01, and these matters are addressed below.

1.12.1 Company name

The IN01 requires the applicant to insert the company name. There are some restrictions on the words that can be used in the company name, which are summarised below.

1.12.1.1 Required ending

Private companies (apart from certain charities and certain companies limited by guarantee) must end in Limited or Ltd. If the company was registered in Wales, its name can end in cyfyngedig, or cyf, instead of Limited or Ltd (s 59 CA 2006). Public companies must end in plc or public limited company, or the Welsh equivalent cwmni cyfyngedig cyhoeddus, or ccc (s 58 CA 2006).

1.12.1.2 Similarity to existing names

The company name must not be the same as an existing company (s 66 CA 2006). The first step should be to look on the Companies House website at the name availability checker (https://find-and-update.company-information.service.gov.uk/company-name-availability) to ensure that a company with the proposed name does not already exist. As well as identical names, a company's name can be deemed the same as an existing company's name even if the names are not identical, under the Companies, Limited Liability Partnerships and Business (Names and Trading Disclosures) Regulations 2015 ('Names Regs 2015'). Schedule 3 explains when two names will be considered to be the same. Examples are that '£' is deemed to be the same as 'pound', 'two' and '2' are the same and 'Á' is deemed the same as 'A'. An illustration of the rules given on the Companies House website is that 'Easy Electrics For You Limited' is the same as 'EZ Electrix 4U Limited'.

Under the Names Regs 2015, an applicant can only register a 'same as' name if the proposed new company will be part of the same group as the company or Limited Liability Partnership (LLP) with the existing name and the applicant has written confirmation that the company or LLP has no objection to the applicant using the name. An example of two companies in the same group with 'same as' names is Web Services Limited and Web Services UK Limited.

Helpfully, the company name availability checker will list any 'same as' names as well as identical names.

1.12.1.3 Prohibited or restricted names

Certain names are prohibited or can only be used with permission. The rules are that:

- a company may not use a name which, in the opinion of the Secretary of State for Business, Energy and Industrial Strategy ('BEIS'), would constitute a criminal offence or be offensive (s 53 CA 2006). Examples are swear words or the name of certain terrorist groups;

- the approval of the Secretary of State for BEIS is needed to register a company which suggests a connection with a government department or authority (s 54 CA 2006);

- certain sensitive words or expressions must be approved by the Secretary of State for BEIS before they can be used in the company name or trading name, including words which refer to geographical areas, such as 'British'. This is to protect the public from potentially being misled as to where company operates. Other examples are words which denote regulated professions, such as 'dental' and 'university'. Schedule 2 of the Names Regs 2015 sets out the relevant body to be approached to request permission to use the name;

- certain letters, characters, signs, symbols and punctuation cannot be used in the company name (under the Names Regs 2015); and

- the name of the company cannot exceed 160 characters, including spaces.

1.12.1.4 Trading names

Companies can trade using a different name from their registered name. This is known as a trading name or a business name. The Names Regs 2015 and the CA 2006 contain similar restrictions to those governing choice of the company name. Form IN01 does not refer to a company's trading name; this is something that can be decided once the company is incorporated.

Unlike company names, there is no need to register business names.

1.12.1.5 Trademark infringement and passing off

If a company or trading name is too similar to another company's trademark and the owner of the trademark makes a complaint, the company name or trading name may have to be changed. For this reason, it is wise to carry out a trademark search on the Intellectual Property Office's website (https://trademarks.ipo.gov.uk/ipo-tmtext) before registering a new company or changing the company's name. The owner of the trademark could also bring a claim for trademark infringement.

Sometimes a client's company name or proposed name will be very similar to an existing company's name. Even if the existing company's name is not a registered trademark, the existing company may still take action against the client in the tort of passing off. The basis of this action is effectively that the client is suggesting an association with the existing company name, and benefiting from its good reputation, by registering a similar name.

1.12.2 Registered office

The company will need a registered office (s 86 CA 2006) and will need to insert the address of the registered office on the IN01. The registered office will be the address to which correspondence from Companies House will be sent, and also any official documents such as court documents. The registered office address is publicly available and cannot be kept private. Companies must have a registered office address in the same part of the UK in which the company is registered. It is fairly common, especially for small companies, to use the company's accountants' or solicitors' address as the registered office.

A board resolution is required to change the company's registered office (s 87 CA 2006), and the company must file form AD01 at Companies House. The change of registered office address takes place when the registrar changes it, but documents (including, for example, letters of claim) can still be sent to the previous registered office for 14 days after the change and they will be deemed to have been sent to the registered office.

The registered office is also the place where certain records must be kept, for example board minutes and minutes of general meetings. Many companies will also have their statutory books at the registered office. A company's statutory books are records which a company is required by statute to maintain, such as the register of members, the register of directors and the register of directors' residential addresses. Note, however, that companies can now elect to keep these records at Companies House instead.

1.12.3 First directors

The applicant will need to decide who the company's director or directors will be, and include their name and date of birth on the IN01 (although only the month and year will be shown on the public register for security). The directors will run the company day to day, whereas the shareholders, who own the company, will be involved in certain key decisions only. Every company must have at least one director (and public companies must have two or more (s 154 CA 2006)). Every company must have at least one director who is a natural person, that is, a human being (s 155(1) CA 2006) and directors must be 16 or over (s 157 CA 2006) if they are an individual.

1.12.4 Directors' residential and service addresses

A director's service address is the address to which any official documents for that director must be sent, and this address must be inserted on the IN01 for each director, as well as their residential address.

Usually directors will choose to use the company's registered office as their service address, rather than their residential (home) address. A director's residential address will not appear on the public register unless the director chooses to use their residential address as their service address. Even if they do not appear on the public register, directors' residential addresses are shared with specified public authorities (SPAs) and credit reference agencies (CRAs). If directors do not want their residential address to be available to SPAs or CRAs, they can make an application for it to be kept private. There must be a serious risk of violence or intimidation to the director or a member of the director's family in order for Companies House to accept the application, which may be the case if the company is engaged in controversial activities such as animal testing. The director will need to provide evidence of the serious risk of violence or intimidation, for example, a police incident number relating to a previous incident.

1.12.5 Company secretary

Private companies do not have to have a company secretary (s 270 CA 2006), but may choose to have one, and if they do, their name and a service address must be inserted on the IN01. The company secretary can also be a director. The company secretary will be responsible for administrative tasks such as filing documents at Companies House and keeping board minutes. Having a company secretary does not mean that directors have relinquished responsibility in any way: they are still liable if the company secretary fails to carry out his or her duties, for example if the company secretary fails to notify Companies House that a new director has been appointed.

1.12.6 First shareholder(s)

The company's first shareholders are called the subscribers, and their name(s), address(es) and details of their shareholding(s) need to be entered on the IN01. It is common practice for companies to be incorporated with two shareholders, each of whom owns one ordinary £1 share, but companies can be incorporated with only one shareholder. There is no maximum number of shareholders. When the company is up and running, the company can issue more shares to new or existing shareholders to raise money.

1.12.7 Statement of capital

When an applicant registers a company they need to provide information about the shares (known as a statement of capital) on the IN01. This includes:

- the number of shares of each type the company has and their total nominal value – known as the company's share capital; and
- the names and addresses of all shareholders – known as subscribers.

The applicant must also give information about what rights each type of share gives the shareholder. Please see **2.9.1 and 2.9.2** for a detailed explanation of some of the different types of shares a company can have. This information is known as 'prescribed particulars' and must include:

- what share of dividends they receive;
- whether they can exchange ('redeem') their shares for money;
- whether they can vote on certain company matters; and
- how many votes their shares entitle them to.

Shares all have a 'nominal value', which means the amount originally paid for them; for example, £1 shares will have been allotted for £1 and will always be called a £1 share, even if the company performs well and holders of the shares can sell the shares for more than £1 each in future. If a share is sold for its nominal value, another way of saying this is that it was sold at 'par value'.

Once the company has been incorporated (registered), the directors will hold the first board meeting (or make decisions unanimously in writing – see **2.2.6**) and may then decide to allot more shares, perhaps to the subscribers, and perhaps to other new shareholders instead of or in addition to the subscribers. The money which a company needs to operate will initially come from its shareholders. The shareholders will pay money to the company in return for shares and the company will use the money provided by shareholders to run the business. The shareholders' money will be used to, amongst other things, rent premises, buy stock and pay employees.

Of course, as the company grows, it will hopefully make more money, so the company will eventually be worth more than the amount the shareholders contributed. Further information about company finance can be found in **Chapter 4.**

1.13 The company's constitution

The company's memorandum of association and articles of association ('articles'), along with the certificate of incorporation, current statement of capital, copies of any court orders and legislation altering the company's constitution, shareholders' resolutions affecting the constitution and certain agreements involving shareholders, form the company's constitution (s 17 and s 29 CA 2006).

The company's articles can be described as the company's rulebook. They address such matters as the notice period for board meetings, the minimum number of directors required in order for a board meeting to be valid, whether the board of directors can refuse to register a new shareholder and the circumstances in which a director will be prevented from voting at a board meeting.

Historically, the memorandum was a detailed document which also contained a restriction on the number of shares a company could have and an often lengthy description of the company's objects, so that it was clear what the company was incorporated to do and therefore when it had exceeded its powers. Under the CA 2006, the memorandum was streamlined, and now consists of a statement that the subscribers wish to form a company and agree to become a shareholder and take at least one share each. The memorandum must be signed by the subscribers. The company's memorandum must be in the form set out in the

Companies (Registration) Regulations 2008 and a copy of the correct memorandum appears on the Companies House website.

Many people who wish to operate their business as a company will not know enough about how companies operate to make informed decisions about what should be included in the company's articles. For this reason, and to save companies time, a set of standard articles, called the Model Articles of Association ('Model Articles'), are set out in the Companies (Model Articles) Regulations 2008: schedule 1 contains the version for private companies limited by shares and schedule 3 contains the version for public companies. In this book, individual articles from the Model Articles for private companies limited by shares are referred to by 'MA' followed by the number of the article, for example 'MA 3'. A summary of the contents of the Model Articles for private companies limited by shares is set out in **Table 1.1** below.

Table 1.1 Contents of the Model Articles for private companies limited by shares

Article number	Subject
1–2	Defined terms and liability of members
3–6	Directors' powers and responsibilities
7–16	Decision-making by directors
17–20	Appointment of directors
21–29	Shares
30–35	Dividends and other distributions
36	Capitalisation of profits
37–41	Organisation of general meetings
42–47	Voting at general meetings
48–51	Administrative arrangements
52–53	Directors' indemnity and insurance

When applying to register a new company, the applicant can choose to adopt the Model Articles in their entirety to avoid drafting articles from scratch. The Model Articles will apply by default if the applicant does not provide a bespoke set of articles when applying to incorporate a company (s 20 CA 2006).

Many companies are happy with the majority of the Model Articles but wish to change certain aspects. An example of an article which is often excluded is MA 14, which prevents directors from voting when they have a personal interest in the subject matter of the vote. Many companies will disapply MA 14 because the company is a small one and if directors with a personal interest in a decision were not permitted to vote, the board would not be able to conduct its business effectively because there would not be enough directors able to vote at board meetings. In such a situation, the company would supply their own articles when submitting their application to register a new company. Other companies may wish to supply articles which differ significantly from the Model Articles and will draft and supply those with their application.

1.13.1 The Companies Act 1985 and Table A

The Companies Act 2006 came into full force on 1 October 2009. Any companies incorporated from this date onwards will almost certainly have the Model Articles, or an amended form of the Model Articles, as their articles. Those companies incorporated before October 2009 are likely to have Table A articles, unless they have modernised their articles by adopting the Model Articles or an amended version of the Model Articles. Table A was the standard set of articles drafted for those incorporating a company under the Companies Act 1985; it is essentially the precursor to the Model Articles and there are many similarities between Table A and the Model Articles. The reason for the differences is that Table A was drafted to be consistent with the Companies Act 1985, whereas the Model Articles were drafted to be consistent with the CA 2006. An example of a difference is that under the Companies Act 1985 (which is no longer in force), 21 days' notice was required for a general meeting of the shareholders where a special resolution was proposed, and this is repeated in Table A. Under the CA 2006, 14 clear days' notice is required of any general meeting, irrespective of the type of resolution which is proposed, and this is repeated in the Model Articles. In practice, it is important to be familiar with Table A as many of the companies which solicitors come across will have been incorporated before the CA 2006 came into force and will still have Table A articles.

1.13.2 Amending the articles

The shareholders can amend the articles by special resolution (s 21(1) CA 2006). A shareholders' special resolution is a decision of the shareholders which must be passed by a majority of at least 75 per cent of the shareholders (s 283(1) CA 2006). Please see **Chapter 2** for a full explanation of shareholders' resolutions.

When a company changes its articles, it must file a copy of the amended articles at Companies House within 15 days of the amended articles taking effect (s 26(1) CA 2006). It must also file a copy of the special resolution to amend the articles (s 29 and s 30 CA 2006). The special resolution must be filed at Companies House within 15 days after it is passed (s 30 CA 2006).

The CA 2006 contains some voluntary provisions and some mandatory provisions. Voluntary provisions are those that will apply unless they are excluded by the company's articles. These are easily identified because the section will state that the rule or obligation is 'subject to the company's articles'. Those rules or obligations which do not state that they are subject to the company's articles are mandatory and cannot be excluded by the company's articles.

In summary, there are three options open to those starting a company when it comes to submitting the company's proposed articles:

1. They can adopt the Model Articles in their entirety. If they choose this route, they do not need to file a copy of the Model Articles; they can just tick the relevant box on the IN01 form to indicate that the Model Articles will apply.

2. They can adopt the Model Articles with some amendments. The company's articles would state that the Model Articles apply in their entirety save for the provisions listed, followed by a list of the aspects of the Model Articles which they wanted to exclude and a list of replacement provisions.

3. They can supply entirely bespoke articles.

The applicant must indicate on the IN01 whether they are adopting the Model Articles or whether they have drafted their own articles. If they have drafted their own articles, they must submit a copy of them when they file the IN01.

1.14 People with significant control

The IN01 form requires the applicant to state whether, on incorporation, there will be someone who will count as a person with significant control. This can be an individual, or it can be a corporate body or a firm that is a legal person under the law by which it is governed (s 790C CA 2006). Control is deemed significant if the person:

- holds more than 25% of the shares in the company; or
- holds more than 25% of the voting rights in the company; or
- holds the right to appoint or remove a majority of the board of directors of the company.

The applicant must tick the relevant box on the form to show that the person holds:

- more than 25% but not more than 50% of the company's shares/voting rights;
- more than 50% but less than 75% of the company's shares/voting rights; or
- 75% or more of the company's shares/voting rights.

The reason for Companies House requesting information about persons with significant control is that shareholders with significant shareholdings may exert a great deal of influence over the company, usually because of their voting power. This may be something that third parties would like to know, just as they may be interested in the identity of the company's directors so that they can make informed decisions about whether to do business with the company.

The thresholds for each of the three categories of persons with significant control have been chosen because they reflect the percentage of shares needed to block or pass ordinary or special resolutions (although do not forget that not all persons with significant control will have the power to vote – they may instead have non-voting shares). Those in the first category can block special resolutions on their own, because they have more than 25% of the company's shares, and may also be able to block ordinary resolutions, if they have exactly 50% of the shares. Those in the second category can both block and pass ordinary resolutions on their own, because they have more than 50% of the shares, but they cannot pass special resolutions, because they have less than 75% of the shares in the company. Those in the third category can pass special resolutions alone, because they own 75% or more of the company shares. Clearly, they can also pass ordinary resolutions and block both ordinary and special resolutions. Shareholders' resolutions are explained in detail at **2.3**.

Once a company has been incorporated, it must keep a register of persons with significant control (see **2.7.4**).

1.15 The application

Once the applicant has inserted all of the required information on the IN01, they will have to complete the statement of compliance in Part 9 of the form, to confirm that the requirements of the CA 2006 as to registration have been complied with. They will then make the application. Assuming that the application has been made accurately, Companies House will issue a certificate of incorporation, and it is when this is issued that the company officially exists as a separate legal person.

1.16 Registering as a public company

A full explanation of how to register as a private company appears at **1.10 and 1.11**. In addition to those requirements, for a public company the applicant must also comply with the requirements in **1.6.2** and its articles must be in a form suitable for a public company. There is a set of Model Articles tailored to public companies (Sch 3 to the Companies (Model Articles) Regulations 2008 (SI 2008/3229)), which will apply unless the applicant provides bespoke or amended articles (s 20 CA 2006).

Provided that the above requirements have been met, Companies House will issue a certificate of incorporation proving the company's existence and status as a public company. However, before it commences trading, it must obtain a trading certificate as proof that it can trade and borrow, and crucially, that it has met the allotted share capital requirements set out at **1.6.2** (s 761 CA 2006). The application for the trading certificate is made to Companies House on form SH50.

1.17 Converting to a public company

Alternatively, companies may start life as a private company and then decide to become a public company.

To do this, they must pass a special resolution approving the re-registration of the company (s90(1)(a) CA 2006), altering the company's name so that it is in a form suitable for a public company (adding public company, plc or the Welsh equivalents) and altering the articles so that they are in a form suitable for a public company. At the time the shareholders pass the special resolution, the company must have satisfied the share capital requirements set out at **1.6.2**.

A trading certificate is not required, because Companies House will not re-register a private company as a public company unless it has satisfied the same conditions regarding its allotted share capital that it would have to show in order to obtain a trading certificate. The new certificate of incorporation is all the company needs to continue to trade.

1.17.1 Application for re-registration

The applicant must file at Companies House:

- the special resolution;
- an application for re-registration on Form RR01, which includes a statement of compliance;
- the fee for re-registration;
- the revised articles (s 94(2)(b) CA 2006);
- a balance sheet and a written statement from the company's auditors, and a valuation report on any shares which have been allotted for non-cash consideration between the date of the balance sheet and the passing of the special resolution.

1.17.2 Certificate of re-registration on incorporation as a public company

Provided that the above requirements have been met, Companies House will issue a certificate of incorporation proving the company's existence and status as a public company (s 96 CA 2006). The revised articles and change of name will take effect on the issue of this certificate.

1.18 What are shelf companies?

Many law firms, in the knowledge that their clients will often need a company forming very quickly, will have a team of people or a person who forms shelf companies for clients to use, often at short notice. The shelf company is a company which has already been set up, usually with two directors and two shareholders, each of whom owns one ordinary £1 share, which is formed and then left 'on the shelf' at the law firm until such time as a client needs a company quickly. This could be part-way through a transaction, and using an existing shelf company will be cheaper but, more importantly, quicker than even the Companies House same-day registration service. The directors and initial subscribers of the shelf company will be employees of the law firm.

Company formation agents and law stationers also have shelf companies for people to purchase and use at short notice.

⭐ *Example – a shelf company*

Danesh and George are paralegals employed by Bloggs LLP. They work in the corporate department and one of their responsibilities is to ensure that there are always several shelf companies available for clients to use at short notice. Each time one of them completes the paperwork to set up a new company, they will list Danesh and George as the company's first directors. Danesh and George will each take one ordinary £1 share in the company, so they will be the subscribers to the memorandum and the company's first shareholders.

Let's say that ABC Limited wishes to set up a company at short notice as part of a larger transaction involving a group of related companies. Danesh and George use an existing shelf company and arrange the company's first board meeting. At the meeting, they will appoint one or more new directors and, once these appointments have taken effect, Danesh and George will resign. Before the board meeting, Danesh and George will have signed a stock transfer form to transfer their shares to the client, and at the first board meeting, Danesh and George will vote to register the new shareholders. The company is now effectively under the control of the client, and the client can appoint more directors and perhaps a company secretary. It can also invest more money in the company in return for more shares. The shelf company has been transferred into a functioning company.

Board meetings and directors' and shareholders' decisions are explained fully in **Chapter 2**.

1.19 Post-incorporation steps

Following incorporation or the conversion of a shelf company, the directors will have to take steps to get the company in a position to start operating. They are likely to have a board meeting (or pass a directors' written resolution) to make decisions on the matters listed below.

1.19.1 Chairperson

The directors will need to decide whether to have a chair of the board. Under MA 13, the chair has a casting vote in the event of a board resolution being tied. This can be useful but also gives the chair more control than the other directors, which may not be desirable.

1.19.2 Bank account

There is no obligation for companies to have a bank account, but in practical terms, this will be necessary. The board will need to decide who can spend the company's money and how much they are allowed to spend at any one time, and complete a bank mandate letting the bank know who is authorised to make payments on the company's behalf.

1.19.3 Company seal

Companies do not need a seal but some choose to have one, usually to make their company documents look more official, and may adopt one by board resolution (s 45(1)). Under the CA 2006, the seal can be used to execute a document (s 44 CA 2006), but the Model Articles provide that where a company seal is used to execute a document, the document must also be signed by at least one authorised person in the presence of a witness who attests the signature (MA 49). Of course, the company may choose to disapply MA 49 and insert its own provisions with regard to the use of a company seal.

1.19.4 Changing the company name/adopting a business name

If the company is a shelf company, the directors will almost certainly want to change the company's name. Under s 77 CA 2006, a company changes its name by a special resolution of the shareholders or by other means provided for in the company's articles (the Model Articles are silent on this point). When a company changes its name, it must file form NM01 at Companies House, along with a copy of the special resolution and the applicable fee. Provided that the name is not already in use or restricted for one of the reasons explained at **1.12.1**, Companies House will issue a new certificate of incorporation, and it is when this new certificate is issued that the company's name is officially changed (ss 80-81 CA 2006).

Some companies operate using a business name and the board will need to agree a name by board resolution.

1.19.5 Accounting reference date

When a company is incorporated, its accounting reference date, which is the date up to which it must prepare its annual accounts, will be the last day of the month in which the company was incorporated (s 391(4)). So if a company is incorporated on 5 May, its accounting reference date will be 31 May. Often companies want to change this to tie in with how they wish to run the business. Many companies choose to align their accounting reference date with the tax year. Some prefer to make their accounting reference date 31 December so that their annual accounts are prepared in line with the calendar year. To change the accounting reference date, the company will have to pass a board resolution, and can either extend or shorten its accounting reference date. The company will then need to complete form AA01 and file it at Companies House (s 392 CA 2006).

The accounting reference date cannot be extended so that the accounting reference period lasts more than 18 months. Further, it cannot be extended less than five years after the end of an earlier accounting reference period of the company that was also extended.

1.19.6 Auditor

All companies must prepare annual accounts (s 394 CA 2006). Under s 477 CA 2006, companies which are classed as small companies under s 382 CA 2006 (see **2.5.5**) are exempt from audit provided that certain conditions are satisfied. Companies which need to file audited accounts will need to appoint an auditor. Please see **2.6.2** for more information on the auditor's role.

1.19.7 Service contracts

Service contracts are employment contracts for directors. These will set out the terms of the director's employment, including duties, responsibilities, working hours, salary, holidays and duration of the contract and any notice period. The board of directors can decide to award service contracts, but if the service contract is to be for a guaranteed term of more than two years, it must be approved by ordinary resolution of the shareholders. See **3.13** for more detail.

1.19.8 Tax registrations

Companies House will automatically notify HMRC of the registration of the new company, and HMRC will then send to the company's registered office address an introductory pack concerning the tax affairs of the company.

1.19.9 Corporation tax

The pack will include a form which must be completed and returned to HMRC. This will initiate the company's registration for corporation tax purposes.

1.19.10 PAYE and National Insurance

The company will normally have employees working for it (and the directors themselves will usually be treated as employees of the company). The directors should register the company with HMRC to arrange for the deduction of income tax from salaries under the PAYE scheme, and for the payment of National Insurance contributions by the employees. It is possible to do this online via the UK government's website.

1.19.11 Value added tax

Most businesses, except those with a very small turnover, must register for value added tax (VAT) with HMRC. Again, this can be done in most cases online on the UK government's website. The company will then be allocated a VAT number.

The directors will approve the applications for tax registration at the first board meeting, and they will then be submitted.

In 2018 a new Streamlined Company Registration Service was introduced which allows new companies to be registered and at the same time to register for tax with HMRC.

VAT is covered in more detail at **7.14**.

1.19.12 Insurance

The board will need to decide what insurance they wish to take out and to make arrangements for it to be put in place.

1.19.13 Shareholders' agreement

The shareholders may wish to enter into a shareholders' agreement at this early stage, although this is not an appropriate item for the board meeting, because it involves shareholders and not directors. Please see **2.8.2** for a full explanation of how shareholders' agreements work.

Sample questions

Question 1

A client wishes to set up a new business with a friend. She does not know whether she would like to trade as a partnership, limited liability partnership or company. The business is a clothing manufacturing business and eventually the client and her friend would like to attract business from multinational retailers. They want to make their business seem as professional as possible to attract business from other parts of the world. They will need to take out substantial loans in the future to expand. They do not envisage anyone joining them in running the business, but they will be taking on employees.

Which of the following best describes the type of business that the client should set up?

A   The client's best option would be to start a partnership because the process is informal, there is no obvious reason why the client and her friend would need their liability for the business's debts to be limited, and there would be no need for them to grant a floating charge.

B   The client's best option would be to start a company because the shareholders' liability for debts would be limited, they would be able to attract finance because companies can grant floating charges, and the company is a widely recognised business medium worldwide.

C   The client's best option would be to start an LLP because the partners' liability for debts would be limited, they would be able to attract finance because LLPs can grant floating charges, and the LLP is a widely recognised business medium worldwide.

D   The client's best option would be to start either an LLP or a partnership because there will only be two partners and there is no need to start a company and have the burden of the legal and administrative requirements it brings.

E   The client's best option would be to start a company or an LLP because this will enable them to run the business in a more organised way, whereas partnerships tend to be run more informally because no partnership agreement is necessary.

Answer

Option B is correct. In a trading business, having limited liability for the debt of the business is an advantage because of the risk of paying for materials and then not being paid for the manufactured goods and being in debt. In a partnership, the liability of the partners is unlimited. Accordingly, option A does not represent the best advice in the circumstances. Further, the client wants to attract finance so a company or LLP would be better than a partnership, because they can grant floating charges. The company has a higher status than an LLP and is more widely recognised worldwide, which would benefit the client because she has said they want to attract international business. Accordingly, the option of starting an LLP set out in options C to E does not represent the best advice to the client.

Question 2

A client wishes to set up a private company limited by shares (ordinary £1 shares only) and, following advice, wishes to adopt the Model Articles in their entirety.

Which of the following best describes the additional information that should be requested from the client before completing form IN01?

A   The identity, date of birth and address of the proposed company's first shareholders, directors and any company secretary, the address of the registered office, the name of the company and how many shares the first shareholders will have.

B   The identity, date of birth and address of the proposed company's first shareholders, directors and any company secretary, the address of the registered office, the name of the company, the number, type and nominal value of the shares and the contents of its articles of association.

C   The identity, date of birth and address of the proposed company's first shareholders, directors and any company secretary, the address of the registered office, the name of the company, the number, type and nominal value of the shares and whether the client wishes to appoint additional directors once the company is incorporated.

D   The identity, date of birth and address of the proposed company's first shareholders, directors and any company secretary, the address of the registered office, the name of the company and the contents of its articles of association.

E   The identity, date of birth and address of the proposed company's first shareholders, directors and any company secretary, the address of the registered office, the name of the company, any trading name of the company, the number, type and nominal value of the shares and the contents of its articles of association.

Answer

Option A is correct. All of this information is needed in order to complete form IN01 and the client has not yet provided it. The client wishes to adopt the Model Articles so they do not need to be asked about the contents of the proposed company's articles. Similarly, we already know the company will have ordinary £1 shares, so we only need to know how many shares the client wishes the company to have on incorporation. Lastly, the IN01 does not need the company's trading name: this is a business decision which can be made following incorporation, as can the decision to appoint more directors.

2 Company Decision-making, the Company's Officers and Shareholders

SQE1 Syllabus

This chapter, combined with **Chapter 1**, will enable you to achieve the SQE1 Assessment Specification in relation to Functioning Legal Knowledge concerned with the following procedures and processes:

- business and organisational characteristics (private and unlisted public companies)
- procedures and documentation required to incorporate a company and other steps required under companies legislation to enable the entity to commence operating:
  - constitutional documents; and
  - Companies House filing requirements
- corporate governance and compliance:
  - rights, duties and powers of shareholders of companies;
  - company decision-making and meetings: procedural, disclosure and approval requirements;
  - documentary, record-keeping, statutory filing and disclosure requirements; and
  - minority shareholder protection

Note that for SQE1, candidates are not usually required to recall specific case names, or cite statutory or regulatory authorities. In this chapter, statutory references and case law are provided for information only.

Learning outcomes

By the end of this chapter you will be able to:

- identify who makes certain company decisions;

- advise on the different methods directors and shareholders have for making decisions;

- advise on the rules governing the holding of directors' and shareholders' meetings;

- advise on the rules governing shareholders' written resolutions;

- advise on the rights granted to shareholders by the law;

- understand who the officers of a company are and their role; and

- understand the different types of shareholder and the role of shareholders in a company.

2.1 Introduction

Since a company cannot make decisions itself, its directors and shareholders do so on its behalf. The company's directors are responsible for the day-to-day running of the company and the shareholders are only involved in a limited number of decisions, most of which do not relate directly to the day-to-day running of the company. Putting it simply, the directors run the company and the shareholders provide the money to allow the business to operate and are responsible for some of the decisions the company can make. The directors' authority to run the company is set out in MA 3.

The decisions which are for shareholders to make fall into two categories:

1. The first category is **decisions which the shareholders alone make**. Two key examples of such a resolution are changing the articles of association of the company and changing the name of the company, both of which are special resolutions (ss 21 and 77 CA 2006). These decisions are explained at **1.13.2** and **1.19.4**. Once the shareholders have formally decided to do this, the directors cannot reverse the decision or decide not to go ahead: they must ensure that the correct paperwork is completed and that Companies House is notified.

2. The second category of decision reserved for shareholders is **decisions which give the directors permission** to enter into certain types of contract which carry particular risks for the company, or where the directors could potentially use their position as a director to benefit personally from the contract. An example would be where the company is buying a property from a director. Clearly there would be potential for the director to vote in favour of such a purchase to make sure that they received a high price for the property. Such a purchase would probably need shareholder approval to ensure that the transaction would benefit the company. The key point with this type of decision is that the shareholders give *permission* to the directors to proceed with the contract; the shareholders do not decide to enter into the contract themselves. They do not have the power to enter into contracts on the company's behalf; only the directors have the power to do this. Examples of this type of shareholders' resolution are in **Chapter 3**.

In this chapter we consider how shareholders and directors make decisions on the company's behalf, the role of the company's officers (its directors, the company secretary and the auditor), and the shareholders' role and rights. The focus of this chapter is private companies limited by shares, but many of the principles covered also apply to public companies limited by shares.

2.2 Decision-making

It is crucial for solicitors to understand who is responsible for making a particular company decision. This is set out in the CA 2006, and if the correct authorisation for a particular decision is not obtained there may be serious consequences. For example, a transaction entered into without the necessary approval may be voidable. We will firstly address how directors make decisions, and then move on to how shareholders make decisions.

2.2.1 Directors' decision-making

Directors make decisions collectively in board meetings. The decisions they make in board meetings are called board resolutions. The CA 2006 and the Model Articles set out various requirements which must be satisfied in order for a board meeting to be valid, which are explored below. As explained in **1.13.2**, companies can, and often do, amend the Model Articles and so it is important to consider the company's articles as a whole when considering the decision-making process.

Not all of the day-to-day decisions which need to be made by a company are made in board meetings. This would be an inefficient and unworkable way of operating. Under MA 5, the directors can delegate their powers as they see fit, so employees will be allowed to make decisions within their job description and certain directors will have specific areas of responsibility, for example, a human resources director, finance director or managing director.

2.2.2 Notice of board meetings

Rule (MA 9)

When a director calls a board meeting, they must give notice to the other directors.

Notice must be reasonable (*Re Homer District Consolidated Gold Mines, ex parte Smith* (1888) 39 Ch D 546). What is reasonable will depend on the facts. It may be reasonable to give a few minutes' notice of a board meeting if all of the directors work in the same building for a small company. The notice period will need to be longer for a multi-national organisation with directors in different time zones. There is no need for the notice to be in writing, but the notice must include the time, date and place of the meeting (MA 9(3)). If it is not intended that the directors should meet in the same place, the notice must state the method of communication – for example, Skype or an instant messaging service could be acceptable, as long as the directors can each communicate to the others any information or opinions they have on any particular item of the business of the meeting (MA 10(1)(b)).

2.2.3 Quorum at board meetings

Rule (MA 11)

A quorum of two directors must be present at all times during a board meeting.

The quorum is the minimum number of directors who must be present in order for the meeting to be valid. Requiring two directors to be present reduces the risk of one director turning up and making rash or fraudulent decisions without another director present to rein in that director or give an alternative point of view. If there is a quorum present at a board meeting, we say the meeting is *quorate*.

2.2.4 Directors' personal interests

Rule (MA14)

A director may not count in the quorum or vote if a proposed decision of the board is:

- concerned with an actual or proposed transaction or arrangement with the company
- in which a director is interested

The above rule is logical: directors are supposed to make their decisions based on what best promotes the success of the company, and directors with a personal interest in a matter could easily make decisions which benefit them rather than the company (for example, where a company is buying a property from a director). It is important to note that a director who is prevented from counting in the quorum or voting on a resolution by virtue of MA 14 can count in the quorum for the part of the meeting where other resolutions are being passed, and can also vote on other resolutions.

Rule (s 177 CA 2006)

Where a director has a personal interest in a proposed transaction or arrangement with the company, they must declare *the nature and extent of this interest* to the board.

The above rule is logical: it is important for the board to be aware of any potential bias the director may have when carrying out their role as a director as a result of their personal interest in something in which the company is involved. There are various exceptions to the obligation to declare an interest, and these are set out in s 177(6).

In summary, a director does not need to declare their interest in a proposed transaction or arrangement with the company:

1. if it cannot reasonably be regarded as likely to give rise to a conflict of interest;
2. if, or to the extent that, the other directors are already aware of it; or
3. if, or to the extent that, it concerns terms of a service contract that have been or are to be considered...by a meeting of the directors.

In practice, if there is any doubt at all, best practice is always to declare a personal interest, even if one of the exceptions may apply. This is because, if that director's actions are being scrutinised at a later date, it is useful for the director to be able to prove that they declared the interest.

It is important not to confuse the obligation to *declare* a personal interest under s 177 with the MA 14 *prohibition on counting in the quorum and voting* when the director has a personal interest in the subject of the resolution. The obligation to declare a personal interest *cannot* be disapplied by the company's articles: the director must always declare the nature and extent of their interest unless one of the exceptions above applies. However, a company can disapply MA 14 in its articles, enabling directors to count in the quorum and vote even when they have a personal interest in the subject of the resolution. Disapplication is common practice in the articles of small companies, where there are so few directors that preventing a director from voting or counting in the quorum would mean that a valid board meeting could not be held. If a company's articles have excluded MA 14, the directors would still be able to vote and count in the quorum, even when they have a personal interest in a resolution connected with an actual or proposed transaction or arrangement with the company. This does not affect the operation of s 177: the director(s) would still need to make a declaration of interest under this section (or, depending on the facts, s 182 – declaration of an interest in an existing transaction), unless one of the exceptions in s 177(6) applied (or, depending on the facts, s 182(6)).

2.2.5 Voting at board meetings

Rule (MA 7)

Board resolutions are passed by a simple majority, which means that over half of those present must vote in favour in order for the board resolution to be passed.

Voting is carried out by a show of hands and each director has one vote. If the board has appointed one of its directors to act as chair of the board, that director will have a casting vote (ie one extra vote) in the event of a tie. The chair will only need to use this casting vote if they are in favour of the resolution, because if there is a tie, the resolution will not be passed.

2.2.6 Unanimous decisions

Directors do not have to call board meetings to make decisions. It is possible under MA 8 to pass a board resolution in the form of a resolution in writing or any other method which shows that all eligible directors have indicated to each other that they share a common view on a matter. Directors' written resolutions are common in practice, as they remove the need for directors to spend time in a board meeting. It is important to remember that in order to use this method of making decisions, the directors must vote unanimously in favour of a resolution, or it will not be validly passed.

2.3 Shareholders' resolutions

Some company decisions are reserved for shareholders. There are two types of shareholders' resolution: ordinary resolutions and special resolutions. The difference between the two is the majority required in order for the resolution to be passed.

Rule (s 282 CA 2006)

For an ordinary resolution to be passed, over half of the votes cast at a shareholders' general meeting must be in favour of the resolution.

If the resolution is proposed as a written resolution instead, the voting mechanism is slightly different – please see **2.3.7**.

The term 'ordinary resolution' refers only to shareholders' resolutions. Whilst the same majority is required to pass ordinary resolutions and board resolutions, it is crucial to remember that the term ordinary resolution can only be used to describe shareholders' resolutions and cannot be used to describe board resolutions.

Rule (s 283 CA 2006)

For a special resolution to be passed, 75% or more of votes cast at a shareholders' general meeting must be in favour of the resolution.

There are two ways of passing shareholders' resolutions: in a general meeting or by written resolution. These methods of passing shareholders' resolutions are alternatives to one another and the board will choose which method is more appropriate in the circumstances. Both methods are covered in turn below.

2.3.1 General meetings

Shareholders' meetings (other than annual general meetings, or AGMs) are called general meetings. General meetings are called by the board of directors by passing a board resolution (s 302 CA 2006). The board will call a general meeting when they want the shareholders to pass a shareholders' resolution, or sometimes when the shareholders have requested that the board call a meeting in order that the shareholders can pass one or more resolutions (see **2.5.2**). Public companies must hold a general meeting every year but there is no such requirement for private companies (s 336 CA 2006).

Companies formed under the CA 2006 will hold general meetings only, and not AGMs, unless they decide to include a provision in their articles which requires or allows for an AGM. In this book, the term general meeting refers to both general meetings and AGMs.

In order for a general meeting to be valid, the notice requirements under the CA 2006 must have been complied with (s 301 CA 2006), and the quorum must be met.

2.3.2 Contents of the notice of general meeting

The CA 2006 sets out various rules regarding the notice of a general meeting. Firstly, the directors must give notice to every shareholder and every director (s 310), and to the auditor if there is one (s 502). It must be given in hard copy, in electronic form, or by means of a website, or a combination of these means (s 308). The notice must set out, pursuant to s 311(1) and (2):

- the time, date and place of the meeting (s 311(1));
- the general nature of the business to be dealt with at the meeting (s 311(2));
- if a special resolution is proposed, the exact wording of the special resolution (s 283(6)(a)); and
- each shareholder's right to appoint a proxy to attend on their behalf (s 325). A proxy is a replacement who will vote in accordance with the absent shareholder's wishes.

2.3.3 Notice period

Rule (s 307 and s 360 CA 2006)

The minimum notice required for a general meeting is 14 clear days.

What 'clear' means is that the day that notice is deemed received by the shareholders and the day of the general meeting itself are not counted for the purposes of the notice. Only the days between these two dates are counted in calculating the notice period. This means that there will be 14 days which are 'clear' of anything happening between the day notice is deemed received and the day of the meeting itself. Everybody makes sense of this in their own way, but by way of illustration, an example of the calculation is set out below.

⭐ *Example – calculating the notice period for a general meeting*

The board of ABC Limited wishes to hold a general meeting. The directors hand the notice of general meeting to all of the shareholders on Monday 1 March, and so notice is deemed received by the shareholders on that day. The day notice is given (1 March) is not counted when calculating the notice period. There must be 14 full days in between 1 March and the day of the general meeting. The earliest date the meeting can be held is Tuesday 16 March.

A simple way of double-checking the correct date for a general meeting is by checking that the general meeting is held on the day of the week after the day of the week the meeting was called. So if notice is handed out on a Monday, the general meeting will be on a Tuesday. If notice is handed out on a Thursday, the general meeting will be on a Friday.

A complicating factor is when the notice of general meeting is sent out by post or email. If notice is given in this way, it is deemed received 48 hours after the notice was posted or emailed. This means that 48 hours must be added on to the 14 clear days to allow for posting or receipt (s 1147(2) CA 2006). So using the example above, if the notice was posted on the Monday instead of being handed out, the general meeting would take place two weeks and three days later, on Thursday 18 March.

2.3.4 Quorum and voting

Rule (s 318 CA 2006)

Subject to the company's articles, the quorum of a general meeting is two.

Note that where a company has only one shareholder, the quorum is one.

At the general meeting, voting will be on a show of hands (MA 42) and each shareholder has one vote. Unlike with board meetings, shareholders are generally not prevented from counting in the quorum or voting if they have a personal interest in the matter. This is because the shareholders own the company and their interests are seen as being the same as the company's interests: if the company performs well, the shareholders get more of a return on their investment in the company, by way of increased dividends or an increase in the value of their shares. There are two key shareholders' resolutions where the votes of a shareholder with a personal interest in the matter are effectively *not* counted. In these situations, the shareholder is free to vote, but their votes will not be counted if it is their votes which make the difference as to whether the resolution is passed or not. The resolutions where this restriction applies are:

- a resolution to buy back some or all of a shareholder's shares (see **4.6**), because the shareholder in question could be voting in their own interests, not the company's, when voting; and

- an ordinary resolution to ratify a director's breach of duty under s 239 CA 2006, where the director in question is also a shareholder (see **3.19**), because they would almost certainly vote in favour of ratifying their breach of duty as a director.

You may be wondering what happens when a shareholder with a personal interest in a matter is also a director. In this situation (assuming the company has the Model Articles as its articles) they would be prevented from counting in the quorum and voting at the board meeting. However, at the general meeting, they would be acting as a shareholder, not a director, so could vote and count in the quorum (unless the resolution in question was one of the two resolutions described in the preceding paragraph).

Test your understanding – passing shareholders' resolutions

ABC Limited has three shareholders, Anna, Ben and Chiara. They are voting on an ordinary resolution. Given that a majority is required in order for the ordinary resolution to be passed, how many of Anna, Ben and Chiara must vote in favour of the resolution?

Answer: Two out of three must vote in favour in order for the resolution to be passed. If two out of three vote in favour, this will be a majority of over 66%, but one out of three votes in favour will not meet the required majority.

Let's say that Anna, Ben and Chiara are now voting on a special resolution. Given that 75% or more of the votes cast must be in favour of the resolution, how many of Anna, Ben and Chiara must vote in favour of the resolution?

Answer: All three shareholders must vote in favour of the resolution in order for it to be passed. Two out of three is not enough because it does not meet the required 75%.

2.3.5 Poll votes

A poll vote is where the shareholders vote in a general meeting on the basis of one vote for each share that they own, instead of the usual one vote per person. This means that the more shares a shareholder has, the greater power they may have when voting at a general meeting. This can be seen as a way of ensuring a fairer outcome for those shareholders who have invested more money in the company and therefore feel entitled to more of a say when it comes to voting on resolutions.

Under MA 44(2), a poll vote may be demanded by:

(a) the chair of the meeting;

(b) the directors;

(c) two or more persons having the right to vote on the resolution; or

(d) a person or persons representing not less than one tenth of the total voting rights of all the shareholders having the right to vote on the resolution.

The poll vote can be demanded before a general meeting, or during the meeting, either before voting takes place, or after the shareholders have already voted on a show of hands.

If a poll vote is called after the shareholders have already voted on a show of hands, the outcome of the poll vote, if different from the vote on a show of hands, will override the vote on a show of hands.

Often there is no point in calling a poll vote, because the shareholders or directors know that it will not change the outcome of the vote on a show of hands. Sometimes, though, calling a poll vote and voting on that basis instead will change the outcome. Those with more shares may be able to influence whether a resolution is passed or not by voting on a poll basis.

⭐ *Example – poll votes*

Let's return to ABC Limited. The company has issued a total of 1,000 shares. Anna has 500 shares, Ben has 200 shares and Chiara has 300 shares.

Anna and Chiara would like to pass a special resolution to change the name of the company. Ben does not want to change the company's name and will vote against it at the general meeting. This means that the resolution will not be passed on a show of hands, because Anna and Chiara between them have two votes and Ben has one. If Anna and Chiara vote in favour of changing the company's name, they will between them have a majority of just over 66%, not the required 75% to pass the special resolution to change the company's name.

Understandably, Anna and Chiara may be aggrieved if Ben, who only owns 20% of the company's shares, can prevent them from passing the special resolution to change the company's name. It is open to Anna and Chiara to request a poll vote. On a poll vote, the shareholders will vote again, but this time, votes will not be counted on the basis of one per person. Instead, each shareholder has one vote for each share they own. So in this example, Anna will have 500 votes, Chiara will have 300 votes and Ben will have 200 votes. If Anna and Chiara vote in favour of the special resolution, then, on a poll vote, it will be passed because between them they can meet the required 75% majority (they own 80% of the shares between them).

2.3.6   Short notice

Sometimes a company may want a decision to be passed very quickly. Waiting 14 clear days for a general meeting to take place is not always a practical, commercial way to operate for a company. For this reason, it is possible to hold a general meeting on short notice (s 307(4) CA 2006).

Rule (s 307(5)–(6))

For a general meeting to be validly held on short notice:

*   a majority in number of the company's shareholders;
*   who between them hold 90% or more of the company's voting shares

must consent.

This percentage is increased to 95% for public companies.

Once the requisite percentage of shareholders has consented, the general meeting can be held straight away, although it may be held at a later date, for example, seven days later instead.

Test your understanding – short notice of a general meeting

Let's assume that ABC Limited has issued a total of 1,000 shares. Anna has 500 shares, Ben has 200 shares and Chiara has 300 shares. Anna and Ben want to hold a general meeting on short notice, but Chiara does not. Will Anna and Ben's consent be enough for the general meeting to be held on short notice?

Answer: No. Anna and Ben do constitute a majority of the company's shareholders – together they are two out of three of the company's shareholders, so the first of the two criteria for valid consent to short notice are met. Unfortunately for them, they do not between them have the necessary 90% of the company's shares, so the general meeting cannot be held on short notice.

2.3.7 Written resolutions

Sometimes it may not be convenient for the shareholders of the company to attend a general meeting, or the board may deem that there is no need for the shareholders to spend time attending a meeting. Instead, they will propose that the shareholders pass a resolution or resolutions by way of a written resolution (permitted under s 288 CA 2006 for private companies, but not for public companies). This is an alternative to a general meeting. Instead of issuing a notice of general meeting, the board will instead hand out, post or email a written resolution or place the resolution on a website. This document will set out the text of the ordinary and/or special resolution(s) which the board is proposing and the shareholder will have to sign and return the written resolution if they would like to vote in favour of it. If the written resolution is sent out by post or email, each shareholder will receive their own copy to sign and return.

The written resolution must be circulated to every eligible member (s 291(2) CA 2006). 'Eligible member' means the shareholders who are entitled to vote on the resolution as at the circulation date of the resolution (s 289).

Section 291(4) of the CA 2006 sets out certain information which must be included on the written resolution, which is:

- how to signify agreement; and
- the deadline for returning the written resolution, otherwise known as the lapse date.

Unless the articles state otherwise, the lapse date is 28 days from circulation of the written resolution (s 297 CA 2006). Unlike with the notice of general meeting, the method of circulation of the written resolution is irrelevant for the purposes of calculating the lapse date. The lapse date is the 28th day following circulation of the written resolution, whether it is handed to the shareholders, posted or circulated by email. The deadline is generally interpreted as meaning midnight of the 28th day following circulation of the written resolution. If an eligible member signifies their agreement after the lapse date, their agreement will not be counted.

⭐ Example – lapse date

The company secretary of ABC Limited posts a written resolution to each of the company's shareholders on Monday 1 June. Anna receives her written resolution the next day. Ben and Chiara receive their written resolutions on Wednesday 3 June. The lapse date is Sunday 28 June. This is the 28th day with the circulation date counting as day one. It does not matter when the shareholders actually received the written resolution, and no time is allowed for deemed delivery.

2.3.8   When are written resolutions passed?

Rule (s 296 CA 2006)

Written resolutions are passed when the required majority of eligible members have signified agreement to the resolution.

Unlike at general meetings, where the default method of voting is one vote per person, with written resolutions each shareholder has one vote for each share that they own (ss 282(2) and 283(2) CA 2006). This means that whether a resolution is passed or not can sometimes depend on whether it was proposed as a written resolution or a resolution at a general meeting. This is because when voting at general meetings, each shareholder has one vote per person and only the votes of those who attend the meeting are taken into account. The position with written resolutions is different: for an ordinary resolution, over half of the votes of all of the company's eligible members are needed to pass the resolution. For special resolutions, 75% or more of all of the votes of all of the company's eligible members are required in order to pass the resolution. Sometimes this can lead to a different outcome from voting at a general meeting.

⭐ *Example – different outcomes, depending on voting methods*

ABC Limited now has four shareholders, Anna, Ben, Chiara and Deya. All of the shareholders have 500 shares each. Anna and Ben wish to change the company's name, which requires a special resolution. The board has called a general meeting in order that the shareholders can vote on this resolution. Anna and Ben attend the general meeting but Chiara and Deya do not.

The special resolution to change the company's name is passed because Anna and Ben both vote in favour – two votes to zero.

Imagine that the special resolution to change the company's name is proposed by written resolution instead. Anna and Ben sign and return their copies of the written special resolution to indicate that they are in favour of it. Chiara and Deya do not return their copies of the written resolution. Anna and Ben have between them only 1,000 of the company's 2,000 shares, so there are only 1,000 votes in favour of the special resolution out of a total 2,000 votes of all eligible members. The special resolution is not passed because the required 75% majority has not been met.

2.4   How can I tell who is responsible for making a decision?

Interpretation of the CA 2006 is required to ascertain whether the responsibility for a particular decision is that of the directors or shareholders. If the section states that a special resolution is required, then that is obviously a decision for shareholders. If the section states that a resolution of the members is required, but does not state what type of resolution, then an ordinary resolution of the shareholders is needed (s 281(3) CA 2006), unless the company's articles require a higher majority. If the section states that the company may decide something, it is by default a decision for the directors, who run the company day to day.

2.5   When the shareholders take matters into their own hands

Usually it is the board that decides whether to call a general meeting or circulate a written resolution, but sometimes shareholders want a general meeting or a written resolution and the board will not call a general meeting or circulate a written resolution, so the shareholders do have certain powers to take matters into their own hands.

2.5.1   Shareholders' request for the company to circulate a written resolution

Rule (s 292 CA 2006)

A shareholder or shareholders who have 5% or more of the voting rights in the company are entitled to require the company to circulate a written resolution.

Under s 292(5) CA 2006, the company's articles can reduce this percentage below 5% but cannot increase it to more than 5 per cent.

The shareholders who have asked the company to circulate a written resolution can require the company to circulate with it a statement of up to a thousand words on the subject matter of the resolution (s 292(3)). The company must then circulate a copy of the resolution and any accompanying statement to all eligible shareholders, within 21 days of the shareholders' request. The shareholders who requested the circulation of the resolution must pay the company's expenses in complying with the request (s 294 CA 2006).

2.5.2   Requisitioning a general meeting

The shareholders can require the directors to call a general meeting (s 303 CA 2006). The directors are required to call the general meeting once they have received requests to do so from shareholders representing at least 5% of such paid-up capital of the company as carries the right of voting at general meetings (s 303(2)(a). The request must state the general nature of the business to be dealt with at the meeting (s 303(4)(a)).

If the shareholders exercise their right to request the board to call a general meeting, the directors must call it within 21 days of the request (s 304(1)(a)). As described in **2.3.3**, the minimum period of full notice of a general meeting is 14 clear days, but of course the board will often give more notice. To prevent the board from trying to delay the general meeting to frustrate the shareholders' intentions, the notice period for the general meeting called in response to the shareholders' s 303 request must be no more than 28 days (s 304(1)(b)). So the maximum period of time from the shareholders requesting the board to call a general meeting and the general meeting itself is seven weeks. This is because the board must call the general meeting within 21 days of the shareholders' request, and the meeting must be held no later than 28 days from the date of the notice of general meeting.

2.5.3   Post-decision requirements

2.5.3.1   Filing at Companies House

The fact that a company's shareholders benefit from limited liability for the company's debts is a disadvantage for third parties entering into contracts with the company. If those third parties issue invoices and the invoices are not paid because the company does not have any money, there is little that the third party can do about this. To make it easier for third parties to make informed decisions about whether to enter into a business relationship with the company, companies must make a great deal of information public. The CA 2006 requires companies to notify the Registrar of Companies when certain decisions are made. The penalty for failing to comply with the notification requirements in the CA 2006 is a fine for the company and all of its officers. Clearly, then, it is an important part of a lawyer's job to ensure that the client receives the correct advice regarding filing and administration.

Companies House has produced forms which companies must fill in and send to the Registrar of Companies, and these will suffice as notification to the Registrar of Companies. In addition, copies of all special resolutions must be filed at Companies House (s 29 and s 30 CA 2006). Some ordinary resolutions must also be filed, and you will learn about these as you progress through this book.

A summary of the Companies House forms covered in this book is provided in **Appendix 1**.

Note that regulations introduced under the Corporate Insolvency and Governance Act 2020 temporarily extended the deadlines for the filing of most of the documents which must be filed at Companies House, including accounts and forms. The extension applied between the dates of 27 June 2020 to 5 April 2021 inclusive.

2.5.3.2 Internal administration

There are numerous internal documents, that is, documents which are not sent to the Registrar of Companies, but which the company must, under CA 2006, keep up to date. These include the register of members (see **2.7.2**) and register of directors (see **3.16**). The registers (known as statutory books) can be kept at the company's registered office or a Single Alternative Inspection Location (SAIL). A SAIL address is notified to Companies House on form AD02, while movement of company records to the SAIL address is notified on form AD03. A form AD04 is used to notify Companies House of company records moving from the SAIL address back to the registered office.

Companies must also keep board minutes for every board meeting which takes place (s 248 CA 2006), and minutes of every general meeting (s 355 CA 2006). Companies must keep these, along with a record of the outcome of any written resolutions, at the company's registered office (or SAIL) for ten years.

As an alternative to keeping statutory books at the company's registered office or SAIL, companies can elect to keep these records on the central register at Companies House instead.

2.5.4 Company decision-making in practice

In practice, solicitors regularly advise company clients on the legal requirements for making valid decisions. Trainee solicitors are often asked to prepare board minutes in advance of board meetings, and clients will use the draft minutes as a guide for conducting the meeting, and amend and finalise the minutes once the board meeting has been held.

When advising clients on company procedure, it is important to remind clients of their obligation to file certain documents at Companies House, maintain the necessary registers, and draft minutes and keep them for ten years at the company's registered office. Failure to do so is usually a criminal offence, the penalty for which is a fine for the company and every officer in default.

2.5.5 Companies' annual responsibilities

Every company must keep adequate accounting records (s 386(1) CA 2006). What is adequate is set out in s 386. Failure to do so is an offence under s 387 CA 2006.

It is the directors' responsibility to ensure that accounts are produced for each financial year (s 394 CA 2006). The accounts must give a true and fair view of the state of affairs at the company as at the end of the financial year (s 393(1) and s 396(2) CA 2006).

Under s 415 CA 2006, the directors of every company (apart from private companies classed as a small company or micro-entity under s 382(3) CA 2006 or s 384 CA 2006) must prepare a directors' report for each financial year to accompany the accounts. 'Small company' means a company with a balance sheet total of not more than £5.1 million, a turnover of not more than

£10.2 million, and no more than 50 employees in a particular financial year (s 382 CA 2006). 'Micro-entity' means a company with a balance sheet total of not more than £316,000, a turnover of not more than £632,000, and no more than ten employees in a particular financial year (s 384A CA 2006).

It is the directors' responsibility to circulate the accounts, directors' report and, if required, an auditor's report to every shareholder and debenture holder, and anyone else who is entitled to receive notice of general meetings.

Every company must file its accounts and, unless it is a small company or micro-entity, the directors' report, for each financial year at Companies House (s 441 CA 2006). The time limit for filing accounts and reports at Companies House is nine months from the end of the accounting reference period for a private company (s 442(2) CA 2006), and six months from the end of the accounting reference period for a public company. Newly incorporated companies have the option of filing the accounts and report three months after the end of the company's first accounting reference period instead (s 442(3) CA 2006).

Every company must file a confirmation statement, on form CS01, within 14 days from the company's confirmation date, which is the anniversary of its incorporation (s 853A CA 2006). The purpose of the confirmation statement is to make sure that the information held at Companies House, particularly regarding directors, shareholders and persons with significant control, is correct and up-to-date. It is a criminal offence to file the confirmation statement late, or not at all.

2.6 The company's officers

The company's officers are the directors, company secretary and auditor. You will know by now that the directors are responsible for running the company. The power to run the company comes from MA 3. Directors have numerous rights and responsibilities, and are also subject to some restrictions to make sure that they cannot exceed their powers and thereby harm the company. All of these rights, responsibilities and restrictions are explained fully in **Chapter 3**. This part of **Chapter 2** covers the other officers of the company, that is, the company secretary and auditor.

2.6.1 Company secretary

Private companies are not required to have a company secretary (s 270(1) CA 2006), but public limited companies must have one (s 271 CA 2006). In practice, small private companies formed under the CA 2006 do not usually have them.

Companies use company secretaries to deal with the company's legal administrative requirements. The company secretary is an officer of the company (s 1121 CA 2006). It is possible to have a corporate company secretary, in which case, the secretary will act through a human being authorised by the company appointed as company secretary. Sometimes companies have more than one company secretary, and they will act as joint company secretaries.

Company secretaries of private companies do not have to have any specific qualifications, and the role they are expected to fulfil will vary from company to company. Very large companies will have a full-time company secretary who may run an administrative department. In other, smaller companies, the company secretary may also be a director, and will just be the person responsible for ensuring that the company keeps up to date with its filings at Companies House. The company secretary will generally also be responsible for writing up the company's board minutes and minutes of general meetings.

The board of directors will decide the contractual terms upon which the company secretary will hold office. In smaller, private companies, there will be no remuneration: the individual's company secretarial duties will just be another task they are expected to do as well as carry out their role as a director.

In companies without a company secretary, if the CA 2006 requires a company secretary to do something, it can be performed either by the directors or someone authorised by them (s 270(3)(b)).

Company secretaries will normally have apparent authority to enter into contracts of an administrative nature, but not trading contracts, for example, borrowing money. For an explanation of apparent authority, see **3.12**.

The company's first company secretary will often be the person named on the IN01 form. Any company secretary appointed after incorporation will be appointed by board resolution. Often the power to appoint a company secretary will be expressly stated in the company's articles, although there is no such power in the Model Articles for private companies because these are more suited to small private companies that do not have a company secretary. However, the directors can use their powers under MA 3 to appoint a company secretary.

2.6.1.1 Removal from office

The company secretary can resign from their position, or the directors can remove the company secretary from office by board resolution. Sometimes there will be a written contract between the company and company secretary, which will set out the consequences of removal from office, and this may include compensation for breach of contract. It may also give rise to employment law claims.

There are a number of administrative and notification requirements set out in the CA 2006 with regard to company secretaries:

- The company must notify the Registrar of Companies on form AP03 (for a human secretary) or AP04 (for a corporate secretary) within 14 days of the appointment of a company secretary (s 276(1)(a) CA 2006).

- Every company that has a company secretary must keep a register of secretaries (s 275(1)) with certain specified particulars (s 275(2)), which are set out in s 277 (human secretaries) and s 278 (corporate secretaries).

- Section 279A of the CA 2006 permits private companies to elect not to keep their own register of secretaries, and instead ensure that the information is filed and kept up-to-date on the central register for the company at Companies House.

- When a company secretary resigns or is removed from office, the company must notify the Registrar of Companies within 14 days of their resignation or removal, on form TM02 (s 276(1)(a) CA 2006). The register of secretaries will then need to be amended to reflect the fact that the company secretary has left office.

- The company must notify the Registrar of Companies within 14 days of any change in particulars of the company secretary kept in the register of secretaries (s 276(1)(b) CA 2006), on form CH03 (for a human secretary) and form CH04 (for a corporate secretary). Again, the register of secretaries will need to be amended to reflect the changes.

2.6.2 The auditor

The company's auditor will be an accountant whose main duty is to prepare a report on the company's annual accounts, to be sent to its shareholders (s 495(1) CA 2006). The auditor's report must state whether, in the auditor's opinion, the accounts have been prepared properly and give a true and fair view of the company (s 495(3) CA 2006). Essentially, they must ensure that the shareholders, whose money is invested in the company, are not defrauded or misled by the directors. If the auditor's report is qualified in any way, this is a warning to the shareholders that there may have been some unethical business dealings, or even fraud.

The obligation for private companies to appoint auditors to review their accounts comes from s 485 CA 2006. Small companies are exempt from the statutory audit requirements (s 477 CA 2006). See **2.5.5** for the definition of 'small company'. Companies which do not trade, known as dormant companies, are also permitted to file abbreviated accounts and are exempt from audit (s 480 CA 2006).

If the company must have an auditor, the auditor must be someone who is qualified, that is, a certified or chartered accountant, and independent, that is, not connected with anyone involved in the company (ss 1212–1215 CA 2006). Usually companies appoint a firm of accountants to be the company's auditor, meaning that any qualified member of the accountancy firm can undertake the audit.

2.6.2.1 Appointment of the auditor

The directors of a private company usually appoint the company's first auditor (s 485(3) CA 2006), and after that the shareholders also have the power to appoint the auditor, by ordinary resolution (s 485(4) CA 2006). The terms upon which the auditor is to hold office, and the auditor's fee, are a matter of negotiation between the auditor and the company.

An auditor of a private company is usually deemed to be reappointed automatically each year (s 487). The exceptions to this are set out in s 487 and include a situation where the auditor was appointed by the directors, as the first auditor will have been, or when the company's articles of association require the auditors to be reappointed every year.

2.6.2.2 Auditors' liability

Case law has established that auditors do not owe a duty of care either to the shareholders or to potential new shareholders when conducting their annual audit. For liability to be imposed, there would also have to be proximity between the relevant parties.

Auditors can be sued for negligence by the company they are auditing. There are two criminal offences relating to auditors under s 507 CA 2006. The first is knowingly or recklessly including misleading, false or deceptive material in the auditor's report. The second is omitting certain statements from the report which are required to be included by the CA 2006.

2.6.2.3 Removal of the auditor

The shareholders can remove the auditor from office at any time by ordinary resolution (s 510 CA 2006). The shareholders must give special notice to the company of the proposal to remove the auditor (s 511 CA 2006). Special notice is explained at **3.14.1**.

The auditor can resign at any time by notice in writing sent to the company's registered office (s 516 CA 2006).

The consequences of removal of the auditor will depend on the terms of the contract between the company and the auditor. Whenever an auditor ceases to hold office, whether as a result of removal or resignation, they must deliver a statement to the company explaining the circumstances connected with ceasing to hold office (s 519 CA 2006). This can be useful in situations where the auditor suspects unethical behaviour by the company and it is a way of making questionable behaviour by the company public.

2.7 Shareholders

2.7.1 Becoming a shareholder

The two people who sign the memorandum of association as subscribers automatically become the first shareholders of the company, and must be entered on the company's register of members (s 112 CA 2006).

Once the company is up and running, a person or a company can become a new shareholder in one of two ways. Firstly, the new shareholder could obtain shares from an *existing* shareholder, by:

- buying some of the shares of an existing shareholder;
- receiving some of the shares of an existing shareholder as a gift; or
- receiving the shares by way of transmission when a shareholder dies or becomes bankrupt, and electing to become a shareholder rather than transferring the shares to a third party.

Alternatively, a company may allot new shares. This means creating new shares and selling them to new or existing shareholders.

Transfer, transmission and allotment are covered fully in **Chapter 4**.

2.7.2 Register of members

Every company must keep a register of members (s 113 CA 2006). Alternatively, it may elect to keep the information on the central register at Companies House instead (s 128B). All shareholders have the right to have their name on the register of members (s 113 CA2006) and a company must register the transfer (ie enter the new shareholder on the register of members or reflect an existing shareholder's increased number of shares) as soon as practicable and, as a long stop, within two months of the transfer being lodged with the company (s 771 CA 2006). When a company allots new shares, it must enter the new shareholder on the register of members or reflect an existing shareholder's increased number of shares as soon as practicable and, as a long stop, within two months of the allotment (s 554 CA 2006). If the company has elected to keep the information at Companies House, it must instead notify the registrar of the share registration as soon as practicable or, as a long stop, within two months.

If the company has only one member, there must be a statement to that effect on the register of members (s 123 CA 2006). It is a criminal offence if the register of members is incomplete or incorrect (s 113), including where there is no reference to the fact that it is a one-member company (s 123).

Where the company keeps its register of members at its registered office or SAIL, it must be available for inspection to shareholders free of charge and to anyone else for a fee (s 116 CA 2006). Again, failure to allow someone to inspect the register under s 113 is a criminal offence (s 118 CA 2006).

2.7.3 Share certificates

All shareholders have the right to receive a share certificate (s 769(1)(a) and s 776(1) (a) CA2006). This is important because the share certificate is prima facie evidence of the holder's title to the shares (s 768 CA 06). Companies must issue share certificates within two months of the allotment of shares (s 769 CA 2006) or within two months of a transfer of shares being lodged with the company (s 776 CA 2006).

2.7.4 The PSC register

You first encountered the concept of persons with significant control in **1.14**. As well as disclosing information about persons with significant control in the IN01, all private companies and non-traded public companies must keep a register of persons with significant control ('PSC register'). The purpose of the PSC register is to enable third parties to understand who holds power in the company. Any shareholder who owns more than 25% of the shares or controls more than 25% of the voting rights in the company must appear on the PSC register. This applies not only to individual shareholders but also to shareholders which are 'relevant legal entities' such as companies.

Companies must keep a PSC register even if there are no shareholders entered on it because there are no shareholders with significant control. People with significant control, like directors, can apply to keep their residential address private, so that it does not appear on the public register at Companies House. They can also apply to have their name private, so all that will appear on the register of persons with significant control is that there is a person with significant control but that they have successfully applied to have their personal information kept private. If their application is successful, the PSC register will state how many shares a person has, but not their identity or address.

Under s 790 CA 2006, private companies can keep the information regarding persons with significant control on the central register at Companies House instead.

There are a number of Companies House forms which must be completed when the information on the PSC register changes. The most significant ones are:

- Form PSC01 must be completed by any individual who is to appear on the PSC register for the first time.

- Form PSC02 must be completed by any relevant legal entity who is to appear on the PSC register for the first time.

- Any shareholder who already appears on the PSC register but whose details change must complete form PSC04, and any relevant legal entity who already appears on the PSC register but whose details change must complete form PSC05.

- Anyone ceasing to be a person with significant control must complete form PSC07.

The deadline for filing the forms is 14 days from the date the company made the change in its PSC register (s 790VA CA 2006).

2.8 Shareholders' rights

2.8.1 Articles of association

Under s 33(1) of the CA 2006, the company's constitution is a statutory contract between each shareholder and the company, and between each shareholder and every other shareholder. This gives the shareholders a remedy for breach of contract if one or more shareholders, or the company itself, does not abide by the terms of the constitution. We have seen that the company's constitution consists mainly of its memorandum of association and its articles of association. Given that under the CA 2006, the significance and length of the memorandum were greatly reduced, it is the articles of association which provide the terms of this statutory contract.

The effect of s 33(1) is that it allows shareholders to take action against other shareholders of the company where that shareholder's membership rights have been infringed. A shareholder's membership rights include their voting rights and their right to share in the company's profits by receiving dividends.

2.8.2 Shareholders' agreements

Whilst shareholders have rights under the company's articles of association, it is always open to them to enter into a shareholders' agreement as well. A shareholders' agreement will bind all of the parties to the agreement and provide a remedy if one of its terms is breached. It is important to remember that it only binds those shareholders who have entered into the shareholders' agreement. In contrast, the company's articles of association bind every shareholder, present and future. Despite this, entering into a shareholders' agreement does have its advantages. The main advantages are privacy and protection of minority shareholders. Anyone can look at the company's articles of association on the Companies House website, but a shareholders' agreement will be private. Under the company's articles, minority shareholders will have very little power but provisions to protect them can be included in shareholders' agreements. An example would be a clause stating that the shareholders who are party to the shareholders' agreement must not vote in favour of changing the company's articles unless all of the parties to the shareholders' agreement are in favour of this.

Examples of matters which are commonly included in shareholders' agreements are:

- restrictions on transferring shares;

- Bushell v Faith clauses (from *Bushell v Faith* [1970] AC 1099). They give shareholders weighted voting rights (ie more votes than they would normally be entitled to) when the resolution under consideration is a resolution to remove that shareholder from their office as director; and

- a non-compete clause, preventing the shareholder from involvement in a business which competes with the company.

Whilst there are many provisions which could be included either in the articles or in the shareholders' agreement, the key point is that shareholders can only take action under the articles where it relates directly to their rights as a member.

There are limitations as to what the shareholders' agreement can contain. For example, the shareholders' agreement cannot restrict shareholders from voting a particular way in board meetings if they are also a director, because this could lead to the shareholder being in breach of their directors' duties.

2.8.3 Voting rights

Shareholders' primary way of exercising control is by voting at general meetings. As we have seen, the default voting method at general meetings is a show of hands, with each shareholder having one vote. As well as being entitled to attend general meetings and vote, shareholders have the following rights with regard to exercising their power to vote:

1. Right to send a proxy to a general meeting on their behalf (see **2.3.2**).

2. Right to a poll vote (see **2.3.5**).

3. Right to receive notice of general meetings (see **2.3.2**).

4. Right to requisition a general meeting (see **2.5.2**).

5. Right to apply to the court to call a general meeting, if for some reason it is not possible for one to be held otherwise (s 306 CA 2006). An example would be where the other shareholders are refusing to attend a general meeting and so it is not possible to hold a meeting which is quorate.

6. Right for a shareholder or shareholders with 5% or more of the voting rights in the company (or 100 or more shareholders with the right to vote, as long as they have paid up an average of £100 or more on their shares) to require the circulation of a written statement of up to a thousand words with respect to any resolution or business to be dealt with at a general meeting.

7. Right for shareholders holding 5% or more of the company's shares to require the company to circulate a written resolution and accompanying statement (see **2.5.1**).

2.8.4 Other rights

Shareholders also have the following rights:

1. Right to receive dividends, as long as there are profits available for the purpose (s 830 CA 2006) and as long as the directors have made a recommendation as to its amount (MA 30(2)) and this has been approved by the shareholders.

2. Right to apply to the court for the company to be wound up, on the grounds that it is just and equitable to do so (s 122(g) Insolvency Act 1986 ('IA 1986')) – for example, because the management is in deadlock and there is no way of resolving the situation other than winding up the company.

3. Right to remove a director by ordinary resolution (see **3.14.1**).

4. Right to remove an auditor by ordinary resolution (see **2.6.2.3**).

5. Right to inspect, without charge:

   - the company's minutes of general meetings and all shareholders' resolutions passed otherwise than at general meetings;
   - all of the company's statutory registers (see, eg, s 116(1) CA 2006);
   - directors' service contracts and any directors' indemnities; and
   - any contracts relating to the company's purchase of its own shares.

6. Right to receive a copy of the company's annual accounts and reports.

7. Right to seek an injunction under s 40(4) of the CA 2006 to restrain the company from doing something prohibited by its constitution.

2.8.5 Types of shareholder

2.8.5.1 Corporate shareholders and groups of companies

When thinking about shareholders, it is natural to imagine human beings, but often a shareholder will be a company. As companies cannot act without an individual to act on their behalf, s 323 CA 2006 provides that a corporate shareholder may authorise a person to act as its representative at any company meeting.

Often several companies will be linked together because they form a network of companies where some of the companies own shares in the other companies. When a company owns shares in another company, it may be that one of the companies is classed as a subsidiary of the other. Under s 1159(1) of the CA 2006, a company is a 'subsidiary' of another company, its 'holding company', if:

(a) that other company holds a majority of the voting rights in it; or

(b) that other company is a member of it and has the right to appoint or remove a majority of its board of directors; or

(c) that other company is a member of it and controls alone, pursuant to an agreement with other members, a majority of the voting rights in it; or

(d) it is a subsidiary of a company that is itself a subsidiary of that other company.

Under s 1159(2) of the CA 2006, a company is a 'wholly-owned subsidiary' of another company if it has no members except that other and that other's wholly owned subsidiaries or persons acting on behalf of that other or its wholly owned subsidiaries.

Consider **Figure 2.1**. Assume that all companies have the Model Articles of Association with no amendments, and that there are no agreements in place and no resolutions have been passed affecting voting rights.

A Limited is called the holding (or parent) company, because it is at the head of this structure.

B Limited is a subsidiary of A Limited, because A Limited owns more than half of its shares. C Limited is a wholly owned subsidiary of B Limited, because B Limited owns all of the shares in C Limited. D Limited is not a subsidiary of B Limited, because B Limited owns only 33% of the shares in D Limited.

Large businesses often operate several companies linked in a group structure to divide up liability between the companies: if one company becomes insolvent and is wound up, the other companies can still operate (although the shares in the insolvent company will be

Figure 2.1 Groups of companies

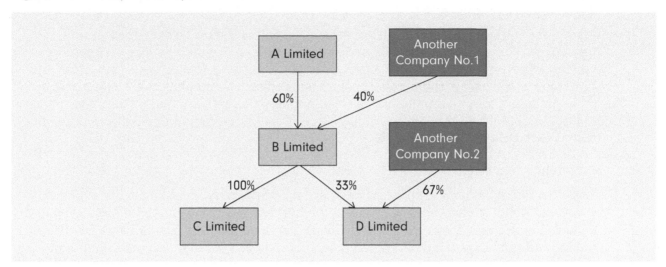

worthless). If the businesses were all run by one company and one part of the business failed, the risk is that the whole company would become insolvent and be wound up.

2.8.6 Public companies

The description of shareholders' rights above focuses on private limited companies. Shareholders in public companies have additional rights and responsibilities, particularly if the company is publicly traded. Those rights are outside the scope of this book.

2.8.7 Single-member companies

Many companies have only one shareholder. Typically this will be a company where one individual is both the sole director and the sole shareholder – a person running his or her business through the medium of a company. If the company is a single-member company, there must be a statement to this effect on the register of members (s 123 CA2006). Similarly, if the number of shareholders increases from one, there must be a statement stating that the company has ceased to have only one member, and the date on which that event occurred. It is an offence to breach s 123.

2.8.8 Joint shareholders

Sometimes shares will be held by two or more individuals jointly. If this is the case, the register of members needs to record both names but only one address (s 113(5) CA 2006). Breach of this section is an offence.

2.9 Types of share

There are a number of different types of share: ordinary, preference, redeemable and deferred shares are examples. Below we cover two of the most common, ordinary and preference shares.

2.9.1 Ordinary shares

Companies are usually formed with ordinary shares only. Ordinary shares generally give the shareholders the right to attend and vote at general meetings. Ordinary shareholders are also entitled to receive dividends if they are declared, that is, if the directors recommend the payment and the shareholders approve it. The amount of the dividend can vary depending the company's profits.

Sometimes companies will have different types of ordinary shareholder. There may be ordinary A shares and ordinary B shares, which have been created so that the shareholders can be treated differently in certain circumstances. For example, a company may wish to issue dividends to ordinary A shareholders but not the ordinary B shareholders. This is easier to manage if the ordinary shareholders are divided into different categories. The rights attaching to the shares will be set out in the company's articles of association and if they are not, all shares rank equally.

2.9.2 Preference shares

The other main category of shares is preference shares. Preference shareholders receive enhanced rights of some sort, over and above the ordinary shareholders, which, again, are set out in the company's articles of association. For example, they may have a guaranteed right to a dividend, and the ordinary shareholders will only receive dividends if there are any profits left after the preferential shareholders have been paid. The amount of the dividend is usually expressed as a percentage of the nominal value of the preference share. If the preference share is a 5% share, then the holder will receive a fixed dividend of 5p for each £1 preference share they own.

Preferential shareholders are often people who wish to invest in a company, and are willing to forego voting rights in return for greater financial returns. The other, ordinary, shareholders are often willing to grant the preferential shareholders enhanced rights on the basis that the preferential shareholders are not allowed to exert power by voting at general meetings.

 Example – preference shares

> *A company has five shareholders and wishes to expand. The company needs money to fund the expansion, but does not want to take the risk of committing to a loan. The board decides that the best way of financing the expansion is to issue more shares in the company in return for cash, but none of the existing shareholders can afford to pay for more shares. The board finds an investor who would like to invest £100,000 in the company in return for preferential rights to a dividend. The board and the investor agree that in return for investing £100,000, the investor will receive 5% preference shares. This means that if the company makes enough profit to pay dividends in a particular financial year, the investor will receive 5% of their initial investment by way of dividend, that is, £5,000. The other shareholders will only receive a dividend if there are any profits remaining after the investor has received their dividend.*
>
> *The other shareholders are happy with this arrangement because while they are likely to receive lower dividends, the company has received the money it needed to expand and flourish and the shareholders' voting power has not been affected because the preferential shares carry no right to vote at general meetings.*

It is useful to understand the terminology that is normally used to describe different types of preference shares.

Cumulative/non-cumulative: if a preference share is described as cumulative, this means that the preference shareholder has to be paid any missed dividends from previous financial years as well as the current financial year's dividend, as long as there are profits available to pay the dividends. This right ranks before payment of dividends to ordinary shareholders in the current financial year. Non-cumulative preference shares do not carry this right: if a dividend is not paid in a particular year, the shareholder loses the right to that year's dividend and does not have the right to receive it in the future.

Participating: participating shareholders have the further right to receive profits or assets, in addition to their other preference share rights. As an example, if the ordinary shareholders receive a dividend over a specified amount, this could give the participating preference shareholder the right to an additional payment, over and above their usual entitlement.

2.9.3 Protection of minority shareholders

Majority shareholders clearly have more power than minority shareholders in the form of more votes (on a poll vote or written resolution). However, there are legal mechanisms to protect minority shareholders, namely unfair prejudice actions and derivative claims, to ensure that they do have some recourse when they are unhappy with an aspect of the running of the company or their relationships with the other shareholders and/or directors.

2.9.3.1 Unfair prejudice petitions

Section 994 of the CA 2006 allows any shareholder to apply to the court for an order for a remedy where they feel that they have been unfairly prejudiced as a shareholder. The potential grounds for such a petition are that:

- the company's affairs have been conducted in a manner that is unfairly prejudicial to the interests of the members generally, or some part of its members (including the claimant); or
- an actual or proposed act or omission of the company is or would be so prejudicial.

The conduct must be prejudicial in that it causes harm to one or more shareholders, and it must also be unfair. Example of conduct which could result in an unfair prejudice action are:

- diverting opportunities to a competing business in which the majority shareholder holds an interest;
- awarding excessive pay to directors; or
- excluding a shareholder from management of the company, where, when the company was incorporated, the shareholders' negotiations led to the shareholders believing they would participate in management.

It is worth noting that removal of the auditor by the shareholders on the grounds of divergence of opinion on accounting or audit procedures is deemed to be unfairly prejudicial under s 994(1A) of the CA 2006.

If the court is satisfied that unfair prejudice has occurred, it may make such order as it thinks fit. The most common is an order that the other shareholders must buy the shares of the unfairly prejudiced shareholder, or an order for the company to buy back the unfairly prejudiced shareholder's or shareholders' shares. This is a logical remedy in the circumstances, because if the relationship between the shareholders or between the directors and the unfairly prejudiced shareholder has reached the point of legal action, it is likely that the unfairly prejudiced shareholder will want to cut all ties with the company. Other possible orders include a restriction on the company altering its articles of association without the leave of the court and an order that the unfairly prejudiced shareholder has permission to bring a derivative action (see **2.9.3.2**).

In order to ascertain whether a shareholder has been unfairly prejudiced, the court will apply an objective test. The court will ask whether a hypothetical bystander would believe the act or omission to be unfair. It is more difficult to succeed in an unfair prejudice action if the conduct about which the claimant is complaining is in accordance with the company's articles of association.

Unfair prejudice actions are expensive because they are time-consuming. The claimant will have to gather evidence, some of which it may be difficult to obtain, because it will be held by the company. The court will require a great deal of evidence before it will decide that the claimant has been unfairly prejudiced, and the parties may need an expert's report, for example a report from an accountant to show that a shareholder has been prejudiced and that the prejudice is unfair or to put a value on the shares.

2.9.3.2 Derivative claims

Derivative claims are governed by ss 260–264 CA 2006. A derivative claim is a claim instigated by a shareholder for a wrong done to a company which has arisen from an act or omission of a director.

When a company decides to issue proceedings, this is a board decision, because it relates to the day-to-day running of the company. The point of a derivative claim is to allow *shareholders* to instigate legal action instead of the board, because the board is neglecting to bring a claim or is refusing to do so. The claimant is still the company, but the shareholders and not the directors have instigated the claim. A derivative claim may only be brought in relation to a cause of action arising from an actual or proposed act or omission involving negligence, default, breach of duty or breach of trust by a director (s 260(3)). The defendant to a derivative claim is usually a director but can be another person.

Once the claim has been issued, the first stage of a derivative claim is for the shareholder to apply to the court for permission to continue the claim. First, the court will consider the application and the evidence in support of it without a hearing. The court will only allow the claim to continue if the application and evidence disclose a prima facie case for continuing. The reason for this first stage is to filter out spurious claims by disgruntled shareholders who are seeking to cause trouble because there has been a disagreement with the board. Clearly in some circumstances the shareholders will have a potentially legitimate claim, and the fact that the claimant has to apply to court for permission to continue ensures that only those claims will be allowed to proceed.

The court may dismiss the application at this first stage, on the basis that it does not disclose a prima facie case for continuing.

If the court decides that the application does disclose a prima facie case, the court may:

- give directions as to the evidence to be provided by the company; or
- adjourn the proceedings to enable evidence to be obtained.

The court will then list a full hearing to determine the shareholder's application for permission to continue the claim. Section 263(2) sets out the circumstances in which the court *must*, at the hearing stage, refuse permission to continue. They are:

- where the court is satisfied that a person acting in accordance with s 172 CA 2006 would not seek to continue the claim. In effect, this means that the court will not allow an individual who is not promoting the success of the company to continue the claim. A full explanation of this directors' duty to promote the company's success is at **3.16.2**;
- where the cause of action arises from an act or omission that has not yet occurred, but which has already been authorised by the company (see **3.16.5**); or
- when the act or omission has already occurred and was authorised before it occurred or has been ratified by the company (see **3.19**) since it occurred.

The court must also *take into account*, under s 263(3):

- whether the shareholder is acting in good faith in seeking to continue the claim;
- the importance that someone acting in accordance with s 172 (somebody who is acting in good faith to promote the company's success) would attach to continuing;

- whether any past or future action or omission was authorised, or if not, would be likely to be ratified;

- whether the company has decided not to pursue the claim; and

- whether the act or omission gives rise to a cause of action that a member could pursue in their own right.

In particular, the court is obliged to have particular regard to any evidence showing the views of those shareholders with no personal interest in the matter. This is because these individuals can be seen to be objective.

As explained above, the court must take into account any authorisation or ratification of a director's acts or omissions when deciding whether to let the claim continue. How such an action or omission is authorised or ratified will depend on the nature of it, but some can be authorised by board resolution, meaning that if over half of the directors authorise the act or omission or are likely to do so, the court is unlikely to give permission for the claim to continue. Other acts or omissions can be ratified by ordinary resolution, so if over half of the shareholders are happy with the board's actions or the actions of a particular director, the shareholders will ratify the breach and it is likely that the shareholder bringing the derivative claim will be refused permission to continue.

Following the hearing, the court may grant permission to the shareholder to continue the claim on terms the court thinks fit, or adjourn the proceedings. Only at this stage will the court give directions for the trial of the issues raised in the claim (ie the acts or omission giving rise to the cause of action).

The legal costs of making an application to continue a derivative claim are met by the applicant shareholder if permission to continue is refused. If permission to continue is granted, the company will meet all of the legal costs of the claim, as well as the other party's legal costs if the claim is unsuccessful.

Summary: shareholders' rights

Shareholding	What shareholders can do
100%	pass all resolutions
75%	pass or block a special resolution
over 50%	pass or block an ordinary resolution (shareholders can block an ordinary resolution with exactly 50% of the shares; it does not have to be over 50%, but they need over 50% of the shares to pass an ordinary resolution)
50%	block an ordinary resolution
over 25%	block a special resolution
10%	demand a poll vote
5%	circulate a written resolution requisition a general meeting circulate a written statement

(continued) .

(continued)

Shareholding	What shareholders can do
any shareholder	• vote (if they hold voting shares) • receive notice of general meetings • send a proxy to general meetings • receive a dividend (if declared) • receive a share certificate • have their name on the register of members • receive a copy of the company's accounts • inspect minutes and registers • ask the court for a general meeting • restrain a breach of directors' duties • bring an unfair prejudice petition • bring winding-up proceedings • instigate a derivative action

Sample questions

Question 1

The board of directors of a company wants to call a general meeting on short notice. There are five shareholders with the following shareholdings:

An accountant – 15,000 ordinary £1 shares

A financial adviser – 4,000 ordinary £1 shares

A doctor – 51,000 ordinary £1 shares

A teacher – 20,000 ordinary £1 shares

An estate agent – 10,000 ordinary £1 shares

Which of the following best describes which shareholders would need to agree in order for the general meeting to be held on short notice?

A   The doctor, because they hold a majority of the company's shares.

B   Any three shareholders, because between them they would constitute a majority in number of the shareholders.

C   The accountant, the doctor and the teacher and either the financial adviser or the estate agent, because between them they constitute the required majority in number holding between them at least 90% of the shares.

D   The accountant, the financial adviser, the doctor and the estate agent, because between them they constitute the required majority in number holding the majority of the shares.

E   All five shareholders, because they would all be needed in order for the required majority in number holding between them at least 95% of the shares.

Answer

Option C is correct. A majority in number of shareholders who between them hold 90% or more of the shares are required in order to agree to a general meeting being held on short notice (s 307(4)–(6) CA 2006). All of the other options are wrong either because they do not constitute a majority in number of shareholders or because those shareholders do not between them hold 90% or more of the shares.

Question 2

A private company has the Model Articles of Association with no amendments. It has six directors. A board meeting is scheduled for next week and the chair intends to propose a resolution to appoint a new director. Four directors (the chair, the finance director, the operations director and the HR director, referred to collectively as the 'Directors in Favour') are in favour of the appointment and the other two directors (the IT director and the director of planning) are against it.

Assume that at the board meeting everyone who attends will vote as indicated above and that none of the directors have a personal interest in the matter.

Which of the following best explains who should attend the board meeting in order for the resolution to be passed?

A   As long as any two directors attend the board meeting, the resolution will be passed.

B   As long as the chair and any one other director attend the board meeting, the resolution will be passed.

C   As long as the chair attends the board meeting, the resolution will be passed.

D   As long as any two of the Directors in Favour attend the board meeting, the resolution will be passed.

E   As long as the chair and one of the other Directors in Favour attend the board meeting, the resolution will be passed.

Answer

Option E is correct. In order for the resolution to be passed, the board meeting must be quorate and a simple majority of directors must vote in favour of the resolution (MA 7). The quorum for a board meeting is two (MA 11), so two of those directors in favour must attend, to ensure there is a quorum. If they did not, the directors who are against the resolution could fail to turn up and the meeting would not be quorate. The chair of the board has a casting vote (MA 13), so at the board meeting, either three directors or the chair and another director must vote in favour to ensure that there is a majority in favour of the resolution. Option E is the only combination which makes sure the quorum is met and that enough directors are present to outvote the IT director and the director of planning.

Question 3

A company has an entire issued share capital of 1,000 shares of £1 each. The original shareholders were a nurse, who had 950 shares and a dentist, who had 50 shares. Last week the nurse sold 500 of his shares to the dentist, and the rest of his shares to new shareholders: 200 shares to a local investor and 250 shares to a surgeon.

Which of the following best describes the amendments the company must make to the register of People with Significant Control ('PSC register') as a consequence of the sale described above?

A   The company will need to add the local investor and the surgeon to the PSC register.

B   The company will need to add the local investor and the surgeon to the PSC register and remove the nurse.

C   The company will need to add the dentist to the PSC register and remove the nurse.

D   The company will need to add the dentist to the PSC register.

E   The company will need to add the dentist, the local investor and the surgeon to the PSC register and remove the nurse.

Answer

Option C is correct. Only those with over 25% of the company's shares need to be on the PSC register. Before the transfers, the nurse had 95% of the company's shares and the dentist had 5% of the company's shares, so the nurse will have been on the PSC register and the dentist will not have been on it. Following the transfers, the shareholdings changed to the dentist (55%), the local investor (20%) and the surgeon (25%). The local investor does not have enough shares to appear on the register and neither does the surgeon, because they do not have over 25%. The dentist has enough shares to appear and must be added. The nurse should be removed because he has ceased to be a shareholder.

3 Directors

SQE1 syllabus

This chapter will enable you to achieve the SQE1 Assessment Specification in relation to Functioning Legal Knowledge concerned with the following:

Corporate governance and compliance:

- rights, duties and powers of directors of companies
- company decision-making and meetings: procedural, disclosure and approval requirements
- documentary, record-keeping, statutory filing and disclosure requirements
- appointment and removal of directors

Note that for SQE1, candidates are not usually required to recall specific case names, or cite statutory or regulatory authorities. In this chapter, statutory references and case law are provided for information only.

Learning outcomes

By the end of this chapter you will be able to:

- understand the director's role and different types of director;
- advise on the authority of directors to bind the company;
- advise on directors' statutory responsibilities;
- advise on how to terminate a directorship and the consequences of doing so;
- advise on the controls placed on directors by the CA 2006 and the circumstances in which directors' actions must be authorised by ordinary resolution if they are to be valid;
- advise on the fiduciary duties which apply to directors and how to assess whether they have been breached;
- advise on the potential claims against directors of an insolvent company; and
- advise on the circumstances in which directors may be disqualified and the effects of a disqualification order.

3.1 Introduction

The company's directors run the company day-to-day, by entering into contracts and making decisions regarding the trade or business of the company. Shareholders do not get involved in the day-to-day running of the business, although sometimes they are required to authorise a particular course of action the board of directors wishes to take. Of course, some shareholders are also directors, and those individuals will be involved in running the company day to day, but in their capacity as directors, not as shareholders.

3.2 Who can be a director?

All companies must have at least one director (s 154(1) CA 2006), and public companies must have at least two directors (s 154(2) CA 2006). Company directors do not have to be a natural person (human being), but every company needs at least one director who is a natural person (s 155(1) CA 2006) and who is sixteen years of age or older (s 157 CA 2006). The other director or directors can also be a natural person, but could also be corporate directors (that is, a director which is a company and not a natural person), or a combination of the two. If one or more of the directors is a corporate director, the company will send along an individual (a corporate representative) to board meetings to discharge its functions as a director.

The Small Business, Enterprise and Employment Act 2015 ('SBEEA 2015') inserts a new s 156A into the CA 2006, which will provide that every director must be a natural person. Under s 87 SBEEA 2015, the Secretary of State may make exceptions to the prohibition on corporate directors. The relevant provisions of the SBEEA 2015 are not in force at the time of writing, although it is expected that they will be in the near future, possibly in late 2022.

The directors' power to run the company is contained in MA 3. Directors exercise their powers by passing board resolutions at board meetings. Alternatively, under MA 7 and MA 8, they can exercise their powers unanimously without a meeting, as long as they indicate to each other that they share a common view on the matter. This could be a resolution in writing, or could be as informal as a text message from each director indicating their agreement to a resolution or course of action.

Under MA 5, the directors may delegate any of their powers as they think fit. This enables a company to work effectively – it would be cumbersome in many companies if all decisions had to be made by the board rather than a sole director or by a director rather than a more junior employee. Instead, all employees will be aware of the scope of their authority or job description and will exercise delegated powers as part of their work without even thinking about the fact that they are exercising a delegated power.

The company's shareholders cannot override or retrospectively alter a decision, but they do have prior veto over the directors' actions in certain circumstances. For example, if the directors want to enter into a substantial property transaction, the shareholders must first approve this by ordinary resolution (s 190 CA 2006 – see **3.22.1**).

3.3   Types of director

A director is described in s 250(1) of the CA 2006 as any person occupying the position of director, by whatever name they are called. So a person can be a director within the meaning of the CA 2006 even if they are not called a director. Under MA 19, the board has the power to decide what services the company's directors undertake. The board is also entitled to decide on directors' levels of remuneration and benefits.

Directors are either executive directors or non-executive directors ('NEDs'). Executive directors are those who have been appointed to the board of directors and also have an employment contract with the company. Directors' employment contracts are known as service contracts or service agreements. The service contract will set out that director's job title, duties and responsibilities. Many directors will simply have the job title of director and their service contract will set out what their role involves. Other directors may have a special function, for example finance director, human resources director or managing director. Often the directors appointed to special roles will have a background in that area. For example, finance directors usually have accountancy qualifications or some other experience of financial matters. The director who is in charge of the company will generally be called the managing director or chief executive.

Non-executive directors are appointed to the board and will be registered at Companies House as directors of the company, but they will not have service agreements with the company. They do not therefore receive a salary, but they will receive directors' fees for attending board meetings. They are more common in public companies, particularly publicly traded ones. This is because it is sometimes required by law to have NEDs to prevent poor decision-making by a board of directors who are too heavily invested in a decision to act objectively. Directors' duties apply to NEDs just as they do to employed directors (see **3.16**).

3.4   Chairperson

The directors may appoint a director to chair board meetings (MA12(1)), and can do so by passing a board resolution. This person is known as the chairman (MA12(2)) but many companies will just call this person the chair or the chairperson. The chair of the board will run the company's board meetings. The only additional power the chair has by virtue of their appointment as chair is a casting vote at board meetings (MA13). This means that if a vote is a tie, the chair can use their casting vote to ensure that the resolution is passed by a simple majority. If the chair does not want the resolution to be passed, they will not need to use their casting vote, because a tie means that there is no majority in favour of the resolution and it will not be passed.

If the board of directors does have a chair, this person will also chair general meetings, if they are present and willing to do so (MA39(1)).

The chair of a publicly traded company has a more important role than the chair of a private company. In a public company, unlike in a private company, the chair of the board acts as a figurehead in dealings with shareholders and anyone outside the company.

3.5 De facto directors and shadow directors

A de facto director is a person who acts as a director although they have never been appointed, or validly appointed. De facto directors, according to case law, can fall within the definition of director under s 250(1) of the CA 2006 or the IA 1986.

A shadow director is a person in accordance with whose directions or instructions the directors of the company are accustomed to act (s 251(1) CA 2006), but who has not been formally appointed as a director of the company. This could be a major shareholder, or, in extreme cases, a lender or a management consultant. It is not necessary for the whole board to act in accordance with a shadow director's directions or instructions; only a governing majority is necessary, and it is not necessary for the board to act in accordance with the shadow director's directions or instructions in relation to all matters for that individual to be classed as a shadow director.

The scope of the definitions of de facto director and shadow director is a complex topic, and there is some overlap between de facto directors and shadow directors. Putting it simply:

- de facto directors will generally be carrying out the job of a director even though they are not officially appointed; and

- shadow directors are more likely to be in the background and not carrying out the normal functions of director, but they will have a great deal of influence and control over the other directors' actions in practice.

Many sections of the CA 2006 refer to directors, and frequently these definitions will encompass shadow directors and de facto directors as well as legally appointed directors. If this is the case, it will be stated in the relevant section of the CA 2006.

3.6 Sole directors

The Model Articles provide that the quorum for directors' meetings is two (MA11). In companies with only one director, the director can still validly take company decisions because MA7(2) allows them to make decisions without calling a board meeting.

3.7 Alternative directors

If a director cannot attend a board meeting, sometimes they will appoint an alternative director to attend and vote in accordance with the wishes of the director who cannot attend.

There is no provision for alternative directors in the Model Articles; a company that wishes to allow its directors to send an alternative director must put a special article into its articles of association to that effect.

3.8 Appointment of directors

The company's first director or directors will take office on the certificate of incorporation being issued, and will be those individuals named in the statement of proposed officers on form IN01. Following incorporation, directors will be appointed in accordance with the company's articles.

Under the Model Articles, directors can either be appointed by the board or by ordinary resolution of the shareholders (MA 17). The quickest method of appointment is clearly by board resolution, because it means that the board does not have to call a general meeting or circulate a written resolution to appoint the new director. However, if the board is circulating a written resolution or calling a general meeting in order that the shareholders can pass other resolutions, the board may wish to add the ordinary resolution to appoint a director to the list of resolutions so that the shareholders have the opportunity to have a say in the matter.

3.9 Restrictions on being a director

A person cannot take office as a director if they are disqualified from doing so. Please see **3.22.7** for more information on directors' disqualification.

Under MA 18, a person will cease to be a director if a bankruptcy order has been made against them or a doctor gives a written opinion to the company stating that they have become physically or mentally incapable of acting as a director, and may remain so for more than three months.

3.10 Administrative requirements

When a new director is appointed, the company must notify Companies House within 14 days of the appointment (s 167(1)(a) CA 2006), and this will be done by filing form AP01 (for the appointment of an individual director), or form AP02 (for the appointment of a corporate director). The company must also enter the director on its register of directors and register of directors' residential addresses.

3.11 The shareholder/director divide

In smaller private companies, it is common for the directors and shareholders to be the same people. It is tempting to think that it is acceptable to merge the two roles when the same individual is both a shareholder and a director. But it is important to remember that when directors attend board meetings, they must act as directors and promote the success of the company without thinking of their personal interests as a shareholder. They must also adhere to their other duties (see **3.16**). When they attend general meetings, they can act as shareholders and vote to promote their own interests.

3.12 Directors' authority

Companies need directors to act on their behalf, and directors are agents of the company, with the company being the principal. Directors have both actual and apparent authority to bind the company into contracts with third parties.

Actual authority arises where a director has consent from the other directors to act in a certain way, for example to spend money. It can be express actual authority or implied actual authority to enter into the contract. The authority may be set out in the director's service contract, or it may have been given following a discussion between the board of directors. This is express actual authority. Implied actual authority arises where the board has not expressly permitted the director to act in a certain way, but the director has acted that way in the past and the board has not tried to stop the director or told them that they are not authorised to act in that way.

Apparent authority is where the director acts without the company's prior consent, whether express or implied, but still binds the company to the contract. Effectively the company is estopped from denying the director's authority. Apparent authority is based on a representation, by the company to the third party, by words or conduct, that the director is acting with the company's authority. It is important to note that it is not the director's actions which are significant for the purposes of ascertaining whether apparent authority exists; it is the company's actions or omissions which must be considered. The general theme of the recent case law on apparent authority centres around a director or other employee of the company having apparent authority in the absence of information from the company to correct this impression.

If a director does not have actual or apparent authority, the director is personally liable to the third party and the company is not a party to the contract or liable to the third party.

3.13 Directors' service contracts

The board of directors can decide on the terms of a director's service contract under a combination of their general powers to run the company (MA 3) and their specific power to decide on directors' remuneration (MA 19). Service contracts will cover such matters as salary, what authority the director has, the directors' responsibilities, benefits and notice period.

The exception to this is where the board is proposing to enter into a service contract with a guaranteed term of more than two years. These are considered long-term service contracts and must be approved by the shareholders by ordinary resolution (s 188 CA 2006). Note that if the company has the power under the terms of the service contract to terminate it with notice of two years or less, it will not fall under the definition of a guaranteed term of more than two years and will not need shareholder approval. It is the guaranteed term element of the contract that requires authorisation, not the overall length of the contract. A ten-year service contract with a notice period of one year does not need authorisation by ordinary resolution; a three-year fixed-term service contract with no provision for early termination does need authorisation by ordinary resolution.

The reason for the requirement for an ordinary resolution is a logical one: directors are often highly paid and it would be financially harmful to the company if it were locked into a long-term service contract with a director with no possibility of ending the contract. If a director had a service agreement with a guaranteed term of five years, and a salary of £100,000, the company's total liability to that director over the course of five years would be £500,000. If it became obvious after one year that that director could not carry out their job effectively, the company would still be obliged to pay another £400,000 to that director for the remainder of the term of the service contract. This is a situation which could clearly affect the value of the shareholders' investment in the company, and it is for this reason that they have the right to veto the guaranteed term element of the service contract.

In a company that has the Model Articles and that has only two directors, the directors will not be able to approve service contracts at board meetings, because the director in question will be prevented from counting in the quorum and voting by virtue of MA 14, because of their personal interest in the service contract. One solution to this is to change the company's articles permanently, by special resolution under s 21 CA 2006, allowing directors to vote even when they have a personal interest in the matter in question, or just to allow them to vote when the subject under discussion is their service contract. Alternatively, the shareholders could temporarily suspend operation of MA 14 by ordinary resolution under MA 14(3).

Under s 188(5), when the board proposes an ordinary resolution under s 188, it must keep a copy of the memorandum setting out the terms of the proposed service contract at the registered office for 15 days prior to the general meeting, and at the general meeting itself. If the ordinary resolution is proposed by written resolution, a copy of the memorandum must be circulated to the shareholders along with the written resolution.

If the company entered into a service contract with a guaranteed term of more than two years without the approval of the shareholders, the guaranteed term element of the service contract would be void, although the rest of the contract would be enforceable. The service contract would be capable of termination on reasonable notice.

Directors' service contracts (or a memorandum setting out their terms) must be available for inspection by the shareholders at the company's registered office during their term and until a year after termination of the service contract (s 228 CA 2006). Shareholders have the right under s 229 CA 2006 to inspect them without charge and within seven days of requesting to see them.

3.14 Ending the directorship

One way of a directorship ending is by resignation. If a director resigns, they must complete form TM01 (if they are an individual), or form TM 02, if the director is a company, within 14 days of resignation. Sometimes directorships end because the company dismisses the director. As we saw at **3.3**, the office of director and the service contract are separate matters. In the context of a directorship ending, removing a director will not terminate the director's service contract: this can only be terminated in accordance with its terms, unless the director is in repudiatory breach of their service contract and can be summarily dismissed on that basis. Similarly, ending a director's service contract does not mean that the director will automatically be removed from the office of director.

The director will have to notify Companies House of their resignation, or, if their service contract was well drafted, it will contain a clause giving the company power of attorney to complete the TM01 form on the director's behalf.

3.14.1 Removal of a director

The shareholders can remove a director by ordinary resolution passed at a general meeting (s 168 CA 2006). Special notice is required for a resolution to remove a director (s 168(2) 2006). Special notice is explained in s 312 CA 2006:

Special notice:

This means that the ordinary resolution to remove the director is not effective unless notice of the intention to pass it has been given to the company at least 28 days before the general meeting at which the resolution is proposed.

Once the company has received this special notice, it must inform the director in question forthwith, and, where practicable, give its shareholders notice of the resolution in the same manner and at the same time as it gives notice of the general meeting. Where this is not practicable, the company must give its shareholders notice at least 14 days before the general meeting, by advertisement in a newspaper having 'an appropriate circulation', or any other manner allowed by the company's articles. The director in question is entitled to speak at the general meeting, and also to require the company to send copies of any written representations the director wishes to make to the shareholders (s 169 CA 2006). The director can use this as an opportunity to argue that they should not be removed. The legal advice they have obtained and the evidence collected during the 28 days or more between notification of the proposed resolution and the meeting itself will help them to do this effectively.

Special notice seems like a tricky concept, but it is just a way of making sure that those who wish to remove the director tell the company that that is what they intend to do, so that the company can formally notify the director and give them time to seek advice and prepare for the general meeting. Often it will be in a situation where it is the shareholders, not the directors, who have called the general meeting. Sometimes it will be the other directors who want to propose the ordinary resolution, and in that case, to comply with the special notice requirement, the board would just have to make sure that they prepared a formal notice of the intention to propose the ordinary resolution, to keep at the registered office. They would then need to inform the director in question of the proposed resolution straight away ('forthwith').

If, after special notice has been given to the company, a general meeting is called for 28 days or less after the notice has been given, the notice is deemed to have been properly given (s 312(4)). This provision is designed to prevent the board from calling a meeting before the 28 days' special notice has expired in order to frustrate the shareholders' intention to dismiss the director.

Sometimes the board is unwilling to call a general meeting so that the shareholders can dismiss one of their number, and will refuse to call a meeting. In these circumstances, the shareholders may need to requisition a general meeting, which is explained at **2.5.2**.

3.14.2 Special provisions in the company's articles or a shareholders' agreement

Sometimes the company's articles contain a Bushell v Faith clause, named after the case in which the legality of the principle was first tested (*Bushell v Faith* [1970] AC 1099). Such clauses give someone who is both a shareholder and a director greater voting rights as a shareholder if the resolution in question is a resolution to remove that person as a director. For example, the articles may state that in such circumstances, the director has ten times more votes than usual.

Where some or all of the company's shareholders are also directors, the shareholders may also include a provision in a shareholders' agreement obliging them to vote against the removal of their fellow shareholders from their office of director. If a shareholder who was party to such an agreement voted in favour of the removal of another shareholder as a director, the dismissed director/shareholder in question would have a claim for breach of the shareholders' agreement.

3.15 Notification requirements

Companies benefit from limited liability, but in exchange for this, they must keep their business transparent, so that third parties can look into the company's affairs to decide whether or not they want to enter into contracts with the company. This is why companies are obliged to file so much information at Companies House. The notification requirements for directors in the CA 2006 are numerous. They are:

1. Companies must keep a register of directors, containing required particulars, under s 162(1) and (2). The particulars are set out in ss 163–164 and include the director's date of birth and address (for individuals) and the company's registered office. The register of directors must be available for inspection without charge by shareholders, or by other individuals following payment of a fee, at the company's registered office (s 1136). It is a criminal offence not to keep the register of directors or to breach the requirement to keep the register open to inspection (s 162). Note that the company can elect not to keep a register of directors at its registered office, and instead keep it on the central register at Companies House (s 167A and B).

2. Companies must keep a register of directors' residential addresses, for individual directors only (s 165(1)). The register of residential addresses is not open to inspection. However, as with the register of directors, the register of residential addresses can be kept on the central register at Companies House instead (s 167A).

3. Companies House forms CH01 and CH02 are used to notify a change in particulars for natural persons and corporate directors.

4. Forms AP01 (for human directors) and AP02 (for corporate directors) are used to notify Companies House of the appointment of a director, and they must be filed within 14 days of the appointment. (s 167). Forms TM01 (for human directors) and TM02 (for corporate directors) are used to notify Companies House of the resignation or removal from office of a director. These must be filed at Companies House within 14 days of the resignation or removal from office (s 167).

3.16 Directors' duties

Directors hold a great deal of power. They can commit the company to contracts worth billions of pounds, and, unless they are also shareholders, they will not suffer personally if the company loses money as a result of their decisions or actions. In order to make sure that directors are discouraged from and held to account for improper behaviour, they are subject to a number of directors' duties.

It is important to remember that the duties are owed to the company itself, not to the company's shareholders or its creditors. Therefore, when a claim is made against a director for breach of duty, the claimant will be the company itself. It is the board of directors who will decide to take legal action for breach of duty on the company's behalf. We saw in **Chapter 2** that derivative actions are an exception to this rule.

Directors' fiduciary duties were codified by the CA 2006 and we consider each duty in turn below.

3.16.1 Duty to act within powers – s 171 CA 2006

A director of a company must:

(a) act in accordance with the company's constitution, and

(b) only exercise powers for the purposes for which they are conferred.

When we refer to a company's constitution, we are generally referring to its articles of association, although various other resolutions and agreements are also classed as part of the company's constitution, including special resolutions (ss 17 and 29 CA 2006). So we must check the company's articles to ascertain whether there are any restrictions on the company's actions.

 Example – breach of duty under s 171(a) CA 2006

Eastham Limited's articles of association authorise directors to enter into contracts up to £5,000 without the agreement of the board. If a director wants to enter into a contract for more than £5,000, they must seek authorisation from the board before entering into the contract.

Jenny, one of the directors, enters into a contract worth £13,000 without authorisation from the board of directors, so she is in breach of duty.

Directors must promote the company's success (see **3.16.2**) and they are granted their powers for this purpose. Any director voting or acting to promote their own interests, rather than those of the company, would not be using their powers for the purpose for which they are conferred.

 Example – breach of duty under s 171(b) CA 2006

Rachel is sales director of Eastham Limited and has the power as sales director to enter into contracts for the sale and purchase of materials. She enters into a contract for the purchase of raw materials from a company owned by herself and her husband, even though she knows that another company is offering the same quality raw materials for a lower price. She is likely to be in breach of duty, because it seems that her motivation was to make money for the company she owns jointly with her husband, rather than to secure the best possible deal for Eastham Limited. In the language of the CA 2006, she was not exercising her powers for the purposes for which they were conferred.

3.16.2 Duty to promote the success of the company – s 172 CA 2006

A director must act in the way he considers, in good faith, would be most likely to promote the success of the company for the benefit of its members as a whole. This is a very wide-ranging duty, because arguably any breach of duty would also involve breach of this section as it would generally be seen to be inconsistent with promoting the success of the company.

When acting, directors must have regard, amongst other things, to the following six factors:

(a) the likely consequences of any decision in the long term,

(b) the interests of the company's employees,

(c) the need to foster the company's business relationships with suppliers, customers and others,

(d) the impact of the company's operations on the community and the environment,

(e) the desirability of the company maintaining a reputation for high standards of business conduct, and

(f) the need to act fairly as between members of the company.

The court will apply a subjective test to ascertain whether a director has breached this duty. This means that a director can act in a way which seems inconsistent with one or more of the six factors, but they will not be in breach if they considered, in good faith, that their actions were most likely to promote the company's success.

At first glance, this section may seem like a welcome move towards requiring companies to think of more than just how much its actions will benefit shareholders financially. However, the subjective nature of the test means that it is extremely difficult to establish that the section has been breached: if the court is satisfied that the director acted in good faith, even if the court believes that this belief was misguided or that disastrous consequences have resulted from the director's actions, the director will not be in breach of duty. Further, it is not entirely clear what success means in the context of s 172, but it seems that for a commercial company, success equates to an increase in share value.

⭐ *Example*

The board of directors of Eastham Limited unanimously agrees to purchase a new factory. They know that the factory will cause a great deal of pollution for the local community and they are aware that it will lead to redundancies, because it will give Eastham Limited more space to install machinery that will remove the need for as many factory workers. It will also be very noisy, which the board knows will affect local residents. However, the directors spend a long time giving thought to the six factors set out in s 172 and still believe that purchasing the factory will promote the success of Eastham Limited: it will make a great deal of money for the shareholders in the long run.

The directors are unlikely to be in breach of the duty to promote the company's success because it seems they have considered the six factors listed in s 172 and have still decided, in good faith, that the purchase will promote the company's success, even though it will damage the environment and the local community and will lead to employees losing their jobs.

3.16.3 Duty to exercise independent judgement – s 173 CA 2006

Directors must exercise independent judgement. This is not infringed by the director acting:

(a) in accordance with an agreement duly entered into by the company that restricts the future exercise of discretion by its directors, or

(b) in a way authorised by the company's constitution.

⭐ *Example*

HSD Limited ('HSD') owns 30% of the shares in J R McDonald Limited ('JRM'). JRM's articles of association give HSD the right, as a major shareholder, to appoint one of JRM's directors. HSD has chosen to appoint Aurelia to the board of JRM, as a non-executive director.

When Aurelia is carrying out her functions as a director of JRM, by voting or influencing the discussion in board meetings, she must not let any professional loyalty to HSD cloud her judgement. She must promote the success of JRM and make decisions independently, without HSD's interests as a shareholder influencing her.

3.16.4 Duty to exercise reasonable care, skill and diligence – s 174 CA 2006

Directors must exercise reasonable care, skill and diligence. This means the care, skill and diligence that would be exercised by a reasonably diligent person with:

(a) the general knowledge, skill and experience that may reasonably be expected of a person carrying out the functions carried out by the director in relation to the company, and

(b) the general knowledge, skill and experience that the director has.

⭐ *Example*

Felicity is the finance director of Eastham Limited, whose board of directors is interested in purchasing the entire issued share capital of a small rival company. Felicity worked in private practice for ten years as a partner of an accountancy firm before joining the board of Eastham Limited as finance director three years ago. Felicity is asked by the board to produce a report on the value of the target company so that the board can decide whether it is worth proceeding.

Felicity completes her report and Eastham Limited proceeds with the purchase. It later turns out that the target company was not worth as much as Eastham Limited had believed, but this was clear from the financial documents that Felicity used to prepare her report.

Is Felicity in breach of duty? Applying part 1 of the test, you would reasonably expect a finance director to have enough financial knowledge, skill and experience to assess the value of a company, or, if not, to realise that she would have to seek advice from someone more specialised. Applying part 2 of the test, we know that Felicity has ten years' experience as a partner in an accountancy firm and three years' experience on the board of Eastham Limited, which seems like extensive experience. Getting the valuation so wrong is clearly a potential breach of duty. You will see that the nature of the test is such that part 1 sets the minimum standard expected, and part 2 imposes a higher standard where the director's knowledge, skill and expertise is greater than the part 1 minimum standard.

3.16.5 Duty to avoid conflicts of interest – s 175 CA 2006

Directors must avoid situations in which they have, or can have, a direct or indirect interest that conflicts, or may possibly conflict, with the interests of the company. The duty to avoid a conflict applies in particular to the exploitation of any property, information or opportunity. It is immaterial whether the company could take advantage of the property, information or opportunity. It seems from case law that the fact that the company could have taken advantage of the property, information or opportunity but decided not to do so is also immaterial.

It is important to note that the duty does not apply to a conflict of interest arising in relation to a transaction or arrangement *with* the company – for this section to apply, it must relate to a contract in which the company is *not* involved. The same fact cannot therefore give rise to a breach of this section and s 177 or s 182 (see **3.16.7 and 3.20**), because s 177 and s 182 relate to a transaction *with* the company.

There is no breach if the situation cannot reasonably be regarded as likely to give rise to a conflict of interest. In addition, the duty is not infringed if the matter has been authorised by the directors (s 175(4) and (5)). This means that a board resolution authorising the breach or potential breach is enough to protect the director in question from a claim for breach of duty under this section. Note that the director in question will not count in the quorum for the vote to authorise the infringement and if they vote, their vote will not be counted, even if MA 14 has been excluded (s 175(6) CA 2006).

 Example

Sebastiano is a product designer on the board of directors of Eastham Limited. Eastham Limited is approached by a client to ask if they will design a new range of kitchen equipment. The board of Eastham Limited decides to decline the opportunity. However, Sebastiano approaches the client and offers to carry out the work himself, in his personal capacity. The client agrees and Sebastiano completes the work.

Sebastiano is in breach of duty, because he is exploiting an opportunity which was offered to the company. It is irrelevant that the company did not wish to proceed. However, if the other directors are happy for Sebastiano to carry out the work himself, it is always open to them to authorise his breach by board resolution.

3.16.6 Duty not to accept benefits from third parties – s 176 CA 2006

A director of a company must not accept a benefit from a third party conferred by reason of them either being a director, or doing (or not doing) anything as director.

There is no breach if the acceptance of the benefit cannot reasonably be regarded as likely to give rise to a conflict of interest.

⭐ *Example*

Amir is a director of Eastham Limited and enjoys occasional corporate hospitality, such as corporate boxes at local football matches, offered by a client. The client then offers him a week at his holiday home in the Caribbean, free of charge, and says 'I know you always do what you can for us when it's time to renew our contract'. Amir is aware that the client's comment is a thinly disguised signal that the client believes Amir will renew the contract between the client and Eastham Limited on favourable terms.

If Amir accepts the offer of the week in the Caribbean, he is likely to be in breach of duty, because he has accepted a benefit given to him because he is a director. This will apply whether or not he includes favourable terms in the contract in exchange for the week's holiday.

Normal corporate hospitality is not caught by this duty, provided that, viewed objectively, it cannot reasonably be regarded as likely to give rise to a conflict of interest. Amir's trips to the football matches would be highly unlikely to constitute a breach of this duty.

3.16.7 Duty to declare interest in a proposed transaction or arrangement – s 177 CA 2006

If a director of a company is in any way, directly or indirectly, interested in a proposed transaction or arrangement with the company, they must declare *the nature and extent of that interest* to the other directors. The declaration must be made before the company enters into the transaction or arrangement in question.

There is a great deal of flexibility regarding the way the declaration can be made. The section refers to the declaration being made at a board meeting or by a general notice in writing to the directors, but also states that the declaration does not have to be made in this way (contrast this with the notice requirement in s 182 (see 3.20).

There are exceptions to this duty to declare, which are:

- if the director is not aware of the interest, or of the transaction or arrangement in question (and a director is treated as being aware of matters of which he ought reasonably to be aware);

- if the interest cannot reasonably be regarded as likely to give rise to a conflict of interest;

- if, or to the extent that, the other directors are already aware of it (or ought reasonably to be aware of it); or

- if it concerns the terms of the director's service contract.

There must be a transaction or arrangement *with* the company for this duty to be breached. This means that the same fact cannot give rise to breach of s 177 (which requires a personal interest in a transaction or arrangement *with* the company) and s 175, where the duty does *not* apply to a conflict of interest arising in relation to a transaction or arrangement *with* the company.

⭐ *Example*

Matt is a director of Eastham Limited and is the sole shareholder and director of Ferry Holdings Limited, which owns several commercial properties. Eastham Limited is expanding, and the board of directors decides that Eastham Limited will buy some commercial premises from Ferry Holdings Limited. Before Eastham Limited proceeds with the purchase, Matt must declare his interest in the proposed transaction: there is clearly the potential for him to benefit from this transaction in his personal capacity. It is important that the board is aware of this so that they can take it into account when they make their decisions.

3.17 Declarations of interest and MA 14

It is important to understand the difference between s 177 CA 2006 and MA 14. When a company has disapplied MA 14, the obligation to declare an interest under s 177 remains. It cannot be disapplied by the company. See **2.2.4** for a full explanation.

3.18 Civil consequences of breach of directors' duties under ss 171–177 CA 2006

The consequences of breach of ss 171 to 177 are the same as would apply if the corresponding common law rule or equitable principle applied, so are enforceable in the same way as any other fiduciary duty owed to a company by its directors. The potential remedies for breaches of ss 171–173 and 175–177 are:

- an account of profits;
- equitable compensation for the loss suffered by the company;
- rescission of any contract entered into as a direct or indirect result of the breach;
- an injunction, to prevent further breaches/a continuing breach;
- restoration of property transferred as a result of the breach of duty.

Breach of s 174 is akin to negligence and so the remedy for breach of the duty to exercise reasonable care, skill and diligence is common law damages assessed in the same way as damages for negligence.

3.19 Ratification of breach

The shareholders can ratify a breach or potential breach of a director's duty by ordinary resolution (s 239 CA 2006). Where the ordinary resolution is proposed as a written resolution and the director in question is also a shareholder, they will not be an eligible member for the purposes of the written resolution. Where the ordinary resolution is proposed at a general meeting and the director in question is also a shareholder, their votes at the general meeting (and the votes of any shareholder connected with them) will not count.

If the director's breach is ratified in this way, this means that it is as if the director did not breach their duty at all, and the director will escape liability to the company for breach of duty. This mechanism is useful for directors who wish to take a course of action but fear that they will be sued for breach of duty if things go wrong: they can go ahead on the condition that the shareholders ratify their breach, in case a future board of directors, or a liquidator, if the company becomes insolvent, decides to pursue the director for breach of duty.

3.20 Declaration of interest in existing transaction or arrangement – s 182 CA 2006

Where a director of a company is in any way, directly or indirectly, interested in a transaction or arrangement that has been entered into by the company, he must declare the nature and extent of the interest to the other directors in accordance with this section. The declaration must be made as soon as is reasonably practicable.

This section does not apply if or to the extent that the director has already declared the interest under s 177 (duty to declare interest in a proposed transaction or arrangement).

In contrast to s 177, the declaration *must* be made at a meeting of the directors, or by notice in writing sent to all of the other directors, or by general notice of the interest given at a board meeting (ss 184 and 185 CA 2006).

There are exceptions to this duty to declare, which are:

- if the director is not aware of the interest, or of the transaction or arrangement in question (and a director is treated as being aware of matters of which he ought reasonably to be aware);

- if the interest cannot reasonably be regarded as likely to give rise to a conflict of interest;

- if, or to the extent that, the other directors are already aware of it (or ought reasonably to be aware of it); or

- if it concerns the terms of the director's service contract.

Failure to comply with the requirement to declare an interest in an existing transaction is a criminal offence punishable by a fine (s 183 CA 2006). This contrasts with s 177, where failure to comply is a civil matter.

 Example

Eastham Limited appoints Isabel as a director on 1 May. Two months before Isabel's appointment, Eastham Limited had entered into a contract for the purchase of raw materials from JKL Limited, in which Isabel owns 50% of the shares. There is clearly potential for Isabel to benefit from this contract and use her position as a director of Eastham Limited to secure good deals or other advantages for JKL Limited, thereby potentially increasing the value of her shares in JKL Limited.

Isabel must declare her interest in this existing transaction; otherwise she will be in breach of s 182 CA 2006.

3.21 Claims against directors of insolvent companies

3.21.1 Wrongful trading

In a claim against a director for wrongful trading under s 214 IA 1986, the court may order a director to contribute to the company's assets if:

- the company has gone into insolvent liquidation or insolvent administration;

- before commencement of the winding up of the company, the director knew or ought to have concluded there was no reasonable prospect that the company would avoid insolvent liquidation; and

- that person was a director of the company at the time.

There is a defence available to directors for wrongful trading: a director will not be liable for wrongful trading if they took every step with a view to minimising the potential loss to the company's creditors as they ought to have taken. There is a two-part test to apply to ascertain whether the director's conduct is caught by this defence. The test examines the facts that a director ought to have known or ascertained, the conclusions which they ought to have reached and the steps which they ought to have taken. The standard expected of a director is that of a reasonably diligent person having both:

- the general knowledge, skill and experience that may reasonably be expected of a person carrying out the same functions as are carried out by that director in relation to the company, and

- the general knowledge, skill and experience that that director has.

This is a similar test to the that set out in s 174 CA 2006 (duty to exercise reasonable care, skill and diligence), which we considered at **3.16.4**, and both tests enable the court to consider the director's conduct as a whole and what it would be reasonable to expect from that director in their role. The first limb of the test is objective because it considers the director's role in the company and what might reasonably be expected of a director carrying out that role. The second limb of the test is subjective in that it considers that particular director and their knowledge, skill and experience.

⭐ Example

Reena trained as an accountant and accepted the job of Finance Director of Chester Trading Limited six months ago, as soon as she had qualified as an accountant.

Harun also qualified as an accountant, and worked in a private accountancy practice for ten years before accepting the role of Finance Director of Northwich Electrical Limited three years ago.

Both Chester Trading Limited and Northwich Electrical Limited are in liquidation and the liquidators of both companies are considering wrongful trading actions against their respective finance directors.

When applying the two-part test to ascertain whether they have a defence to their conduct, Reena and Harun will both be expected to have the general knowledge, skill and experience of a finance director under the first limb of the test, irrespective of their actual experience. When applying the second limb of the test, more will be expected of Harun than Reena, because he has more accountancy experience, which is relevant to his role as Finance Director, and more experience as Finance Director of Northwich Electrical Limited.

Directors can take steps to minimise the likelihood of a successful claim for wrongful trading (and/or fraudulent trading – see below). Solicitors may be required to advise directors when a company is performing badly. Directors should:

- seek professional advice from solicitors and/or accountants at the first sign of problems;

- limit spending;

- check the company's accounts regularly;

- keep records of their own actions.

It is important to note that all directors should have a basic level of competence in running a company, but they will not be expected to be experts in every area.

Claims for wrongful trading are brought by a liquidator or administrator. Therefore, such claims can only be brought when a company is in insolvent liquidation or insolvent administration. As a remedy, the court may order the director to make a contribution to the company's assets, increasing the amount of money available to pay creditors.

3.21.2 Fraudulent trading under s 213 IA 1986

A director will be liable for fraudulent trading if, in the course of the company being wound up, it appears that the company's business has been carried on with intent to defraud creditors of the company or creditors of any other person, or for any fraudulent purpose. In such a case, the court may declare that any persons who were knowingly parties to the carrying on of the business in such a manner are liable to make such contributions (if any) to the company's assets as the court thinks proper.

Actions for fraudulent trading are brought by the liquidator or administrator, and, again, such claims can only be brought when a company is in insolvent liquidation or insolvent administration.

Successful claims for fraudulent trading are uncommon because the liquidator or administrator will need to show intention to defraud in order for the definition of fraudulent trading to be met, and it is usually difficult to find evidence of this. An example would be carrying on spending in the knowledge that the creditors will not get paid, but often the liquidator will not be able to prove the element of fraud. Given that the same facts will generally also give rise to a claim for wrongful trading, in cases where there is a reasonable basis on which to allege fraud it is common practice for liquidators to bring a claim for both wrongful and fraudulent trading, in the knowledge that if the claim for fraudulent trading fails, the claim for wrongful trading is likely to succeed.

Any director found liable for fraudulent trading also risks a criminal conviction under s 993 CA 2006.

3.21.3 Misfeasance

Misfeasance is breach of any fiduciary or other duty by directors. Under s 212 IA 1986, during the course of the winding up of the company, directors may be ordered to contribute to the company's assets by way of compensation in respect of the misfeasance. They may also be ordered to repay, restore or account for any money or property or any part of it that has been misapplied in breach of duty.

3.22 Controls on directors

So far, we have considered general duties imposed on directors. We will now consider specific controls placed on directors in certain circumstances. All of the controls that follow involve situations where directors could benefit personally at the company's expense, so the shareholders need to authorise their proposed action before it takes place. This gives the shareholders the opportunity to make sure that the transaction is in the company's best interests despite the involvement of a director in their personal capacity.

3.22.1 Substantial property transactions

Substantial property transactions are governed by ss 190–196 CA 2006. A substantial property transaction ('SPT') is where:

- a director, in their personal capacity, or someone connected with a director
- buys from or sells to the company
- a non-cash asset
- of substantial value.

If the board wishes to enter into an SPT, the shareholders' consent by way of ordinary resolution is required. Consent is required because substantial property transactions occur in circumstances where a director could gain something at the company's expense. A simple example would be where a director sold some office premises to the company at above market value. In this situation, the director would gain financially and the company would lose money. It is important to remember that the board of directors does not have to obtain the shareholders' consent for buying office premises. It is the involvement of a director, in their personal capacity, in this scenario which triggers the need for an ordinary resolution.

If the director or connected person is also a director of the company's holding company or a person connected with such a director, the transaction or arrangement must also be approved by ordinary resolution of the shareholders of the parent company (s 190(2) CA 2006).

We shall now consider each element of an SPT in turn.

3.22.1.1 What is a person connected with a director?

The definition of a person connected with the director is set out in ss 252–254 CA 2006, and is either a member of a director's family or a company in which the director or a person/persons connected with a director (or the director and persons connected with the director taken together):

- own/owns at least 20% of the body corporate's shares; or
- is/are entitled to exercise or control the exercise of more than 20% of the voting power at any general meeting of the company.

Members of a director's family are defined as:

- the director's spouse or civil partner;
- the director's child or stepchild;
- the director's parents;
- any person who lives in an enduring relationship with the director as their partner; and
- any children of a person who lives in an enduring relationship with the director as their partner.

3.22.1.2 What is a non-cash asset?

This is defined as any property or interest in property, other than cash (s 1163 CA 2006). So, for example, a loan would not be covered. Loans to directors are covered separately in the CA 2006 (see **3.22.2**).

3.22.1.3 What is classed as 'substantial'?

An asset can be classed as substantial in one of two ways (s 191 CA 2006):

- It will automatically be classed at substantial if its value is over £100,000.
- It will also be substantial if it is worth more than £5,000 *and* more than 10% of the company's net asset value.

The company's net asset value can be ascertained by looking at the company's balance sheet – it is the figure for 'net assets'.

To be substantial, an asset need only satisfy *one* of the two tests above, not both of them.

We will now turn to the possible situations which could constitute an SPT. In all of them, Zoe is a director of Tabley Limited and she has a daughter called Cara.

Figure 3.1 A transaction between the company and the director

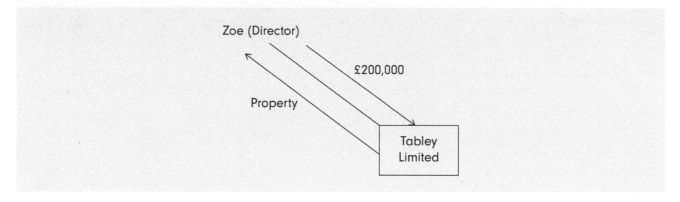

Figure 3.1 is the simplest type of SPT – a director (Zoe) is buying a non-cash asset (property) of substantial value (over £100,000) from the company of which she is a director. Clearly, Zoe could use her influence as a director to secure a good deal, and this is why shareholder approval is needed.

Figure 3.2 A transaction between the company and a family member of a director

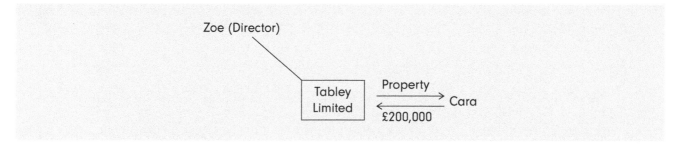

In **Figure 3.2**, Cara, Zoe's daughter, purchases a property from Tabley Limited for £200,000. This is an SPT because a person (Cara) connected to a director (Zoe) is buying a non-cash asset (property) of substantial value (over £100,000) from the company. Clearly, Zoe could use her influence as a director to secure a good deal for her daughter, and this is why shareholder approval is needed.

Figure 3.3 A transaction between the company (company A) and another company (company B) in which a director of company A has a shareholding of 20% or more.

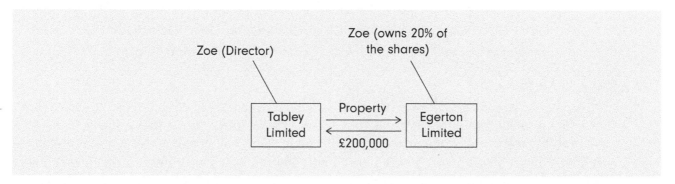

In **Figure 3.3**, Zoe owns 20% of the shares in Egerton Limited so it fits the definition of 'person connected with a director' here because it is a body corporate in which a director of Tabley Limited (Zoe) owns at least 20% of the shares. Zoe is likely to benefit financially if Egerton Limited secures a good deal in its purchase of a property from Tabley Limited, in terms of an increase in share value, however small, or increased dividends. This may mean that she votes in favour of the transaction because it benefits her personally, and not Tabley Limited, of which she is a director. The transaction falls within the definition of an SPT and so approval of the transaction by ordinary resolution is needed.

Figure 3.4   A transaction between the company (company A) and another company (company B) in which a director of company A has a shareholding, when added to the shareholding of another person connected with the director, of 20% or more.

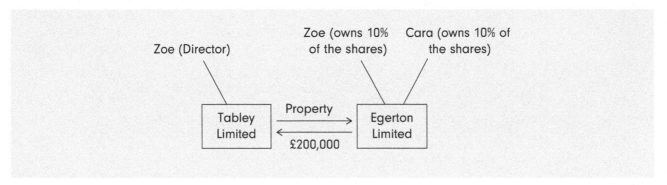

Figure 3.4 is the same as the previous example, but Zoe has only 10% of the shares in Egerton Limited. However, Egerton Limited is a 'person connected with a director' here because it is a body corporate in which a director of Tabley Limited (Zoe) and a person connected with the director (Cara, as Zoe's daughter) own at least 20% of Egerton Limited's shares. Note that Zoe does not need to own any of the shares in Egerton Limited for s 190 to apply here – it is sufficient for her daughter to own the shares instead, as long as she owns 20% or more of the shares.

There are some exceptions to the requirement for an ordinary resolution, the most likely one being for transactions with members or other group companies (s 192 CA 2006). An ordinary resolution is not needed to approve the following transactions:

- an SPT when the company in question is a wholly owned subsidiary of any other company;

- a transaction between a company and a person in his character as a member of the company;

- a transaction between a holding company and its wholly owned subsidiary; or

- a transaction between two wholly owned subsidiaries of the same holding company.

3.22.1.4   Effect of breach

If a company proceeds with a substantial property transaction without obtaining the necessary ordinary resolution, the transaction is voidable (s 195 CA 2006). In addition, the following individuals may be ordered to account to the company for any gain they have made and to indemnify the company for any loss or damage resulting from the arrangement or transaction:

- any director of the company (or of its holding company) with whom the company entered into the arrangement;

- any person with whom the company entered into the arrangement who is connected with a director of the company or of its holding company, *and* the director with whom any such person is connected; and

- any other director of the company who authorised the arrangement or any transaction entered into in pursuance of such an arrangement.

3.22.2   Loans to directors

Under s 197 CA 2006, a company may not make a loan to a director of the company or its holding company (or give any guarantee of security in relation to such a loan) unless the transaction has been approved by the company's shareholders by ordinary resolution.

If the director receiving the loan is also a director of the company's holding company, the holding company must *also* pass an ordinary resolution to authorise the loan.

Under s 197(3) of the CA 2006, a memorandum setting out the terms of the loan and the company's liability must be made available for inspection at the company's registered office for 15 days prior to the general meeting at which the ordinary resolution will be proposed, and at the general meeting itself. If the board wishes to propose the ordinary resolution by written resolution, a copy of the memorandum must instead be sent out with the written resolution and does not need to be available for inspection at the company's registered office.

The reason for the requirement for the ordinary resolution is clear. The board of directors could enter into risky loans to benefit members of the board at the company's expense if there was no requirement for an ordinary resolution.

There are a number of exceptions to the requirement for an ordinary resolution, and the most significant ones are:

- expenditure on company business. This covers expenditure for the purposes of the company or for the purposes of enabling the director to properly perform their duties. This exception is only available for a loan or loans up to a maximum of £50,000;

- expenditure on defending civil or criminal proceedings in relation to the company or an associated company;

- expenditure on defending regulatory proceedings or defending himself or herself in an investigation by a regulatory authority;

- minor and business transactions, as long as the transactions and any other relevant transaction or arrangement does not exceed £10,000.

If the company lends money to a director without the shareholders first passing an ordinary resolution, the transaction or arrangement is voidable at the instance of the company. The director who loaned the money from the company and any director who authorised the transaction or arrangement are liable to account to the company for any gain they have made, and are jointly and severally liable to indemnify the company for any loss or damage resulting from the transaction or arrangement. Of course, it is unlikely that the board will take steps to avoid the contract if the members of the board are the same as those who authorised it in the first place. The most likely circumstances where the contract would be avoided would be if the company became insolvent and an insolvency practitioner were appointed. The insolvency practitioner could investigate the company's recent transactions and may well decide that it would be in the company's best interests to avoid the contract and pursue the director for immediate repayment of the loan.

If the company enters into the loan without obtaining the necessary ordinary resolution, the transaction can be affirmed within a reasonable time by the company (or its holding company, if it is the holding company that has failed to obtain the ordinary resolution) by passing an ordinary resolution, meaning that the transaction is no longer voidable and the directors are no longer liable in relation to the initial failure to obtain the ordinary resolution.

3.22.3 Long-term service contract

The company may not enter into a service contract with a director for a guaranteed term of more than two years unless the shareholders have authorised the guaranteed term element of the service contract by ordinary resolution (s 188 CA 2006). See **3.13** for further details.

3.22.4 Payment for loss of office

When a directorship ends, the director will often receive payment. Sometimes the director will be legally entitled to a payment under the terms of their service contract. Sometimes the director will be entitled to compensation for unfair or wrongful dismissal or discrimination. The company must pay those sums because it is under a legal obligation to do so. However, any payments of £200 or more other than those to which the director is legally entitled can only be paid with the prior agreement of shareholders by ordinary resolution (s 217 CA 2006).

The requirement to obtain an ordinary resolution applies not only to payments to a director but also to:

- payments to past directors;
- payments to a person connected with a director;
- payments to any person at the direction of, or for the benefit of, a director or a person connected with a director.

The definition of 'payment' also includes a situation where the director is also selling their shares in the company and the price is in excess of the price other shareholders could have obtained.

As with loans to directors, a memorandum containing particulars of the payment for loss of office must be drawn up and made available at the company's registered office for not less than 15 days prior to the general meeting at which the resolution to approve the payment is proposed, and at the general meeting itself. If the resolution is to be passed by written resolution, the memorandum must instead be sent to all eligible shareholders, either with the written resolution or before the written resolution is circulated (s 217 CA 2006).

If the company makes a payment in breach of s 217, the money is held by the recipient on trust for the company and any director who authorises the payment is jointly and severally liable to indemnify the company that made the payment for any loss resulting from it (s 222 CA 2006).

3.22.5 Shadow director

It is worth noting that 'director' includes shadow director in those provisions of the CA 2006 which relate to payments for loss of office, loans to directors, substantial property transactions and long-term directors' service contracts (s 223 CA 2006).

3.22.6 Other liabilities

There are numerous other ways directors can be held liable in connection with their office. The most significant ways are listed below:

1. Failure to maintain company records is an offence punishable by a fine (s 1135 CA 2006). If the records in question are accounting records, the director(s) in default can be imprisoned for up to two years (s 389).

2. There are also specific offences relating to the failure to file certain documents at Companies House. For example, failure to file a special resolution or a memorandum setting out its terms at Companies House within 15 days of it being passed is an offence punishable by fine (s 30 CA 2006).

3. Liability for financial records (s 463 CA 2006). Directors face potential criminal and civil

liability for breaches of the law regarding their responsibility for the company's accounts and related reports, for example, compensation for loss resulting from any misleading or untrue statement in the directors' report.

4. Liability for breach of health and safety legislation, namely the Health and Safety at Work Act 1974. Directors can be imprisoned for up to two years and fined up to £20,000 for breaches of this legislation. If somebody dies due to management failure, directors can be liable for the common law offence of gross negligence manslaughter.

5. Bribery – the scope of the Bribery Act 2010 is wide and it is easy to see how seemingly innocent behaviour could be caught by it without the director in question realising.

6. Making political donations without shareholder approval.

7. Civil and criminal liability under environmental legislation, for example the Environmental Protection Act 1990.

3.22.7 Disqualification of directors

Under the Company Directors Disqualification Act 1986 ('CDDA 1986'), the court may disqualify a person from being a director for between two and fifteen years. Case law has established that the length of disqualification depends on the director's behaviour in relation to the current offence and previous behaviour. The grounds for disqualification are:

- Conviction for an indictable offence
- Persistent breaches of companies legislation
- Fraud on a winding up
- Summary conviction for failure to file a required notice or document
- Being an unfit director of an insolvent company
- Following an investigation and a finding of unfitness
- Fraudulent or wrongful trading
- Breach of competition law

Example tariffs from case law range from two years for breach of fiduciary duty and failure to file accounts and returns, to fifteen years for seeking money from investors in the knowledge that the company's assets heavily exceeded its liabilities.

The most common type of disqualification is for being an unfit director of an insolvent company. Factors to take into account include misfeasance, the extent of failure to comply with the CA 2006 and the extent of that director's responsibility for preferences or transactions at an undervalue.

Factors which count against the director are:

- using money meant for paying VAT, PAYE or national insurance contributions as the company's working capital (known as trading on Crown monies);
- paying excessive directors' remuneration; and
- recklessly trading while insolvent.

Factors which count in the director's favour include:

- employing qualified financial staff;
- taking professional advice; and
- a personal financial investment in the company.

None of the above factors are conclusive on their own.

3.22.8   Effects of disqualification

A director subject to a disqualification order cannot without the leave of the court be a director or in any way concerned in the promotion, formation or management of a company. Leave to be a director is rarely granted, but an example of where it may be granted is where the director is not dishonest, the business is profitable (and so unlikely to become insolvent) and there are other directors who could provide a check on the activities of the director in question.

Contravention of the disqualification order is a criminal offence and the director could be fined or sentenced to up to two years in prison. A director who is disqualified is personally responsible for the debts of the company if they are involved in the management of the company while disqualified (s 15 CDDA 1986).

Sample questions

Question 1

It is early 2023. The client had a flourishing business until December 2022. In December 2022, the client's managing director forgot to renew the fire insurance policy for the client's warehouse. Shortly afterwards the warehouse burned down, destroying nearly all of the client's stock. From then on, the managing director took every step she should have done with a view to minimising the potential loss to the client's creditors if it went into insolvent liquidation. However, the client has just gone into insolvent liquidation as a result of the fire.

In December 2022 the managing director was working both as managing director and buildings manager.

Assuming that the court accepts the facts stated above, which of the following best describes whether the managing director will be liable for wrongful trading?

A   No, she will not be liable for wrongful trading because she made an innocent mistake.

B   No, she will not be liable for wrongful trading because she has a defence.

C   Yes, she will be liable for wrongful trading because she was negligent and this resulted in the client going into liquidation.

D   Yes, she will be liable for wrongful trading because she should not have been carrying out two jobs at once.

E   Yes, she will be liable for wrongful trading but the client will incur liability instead as her employer.

Answer

Option B is correct. Liability for wrongful trading is personal to the director, and the employer is not vicariously liable. It may be that the managing director's mistake will result in liability being established for wrongful trading under s 214 IA 1986, but in any event the managing director will be able to use the defence under s 214(3). This is that she took every step she should have done with a view to minimising the potential loss to the client's creditors if it went into insolvent liquidation – and we are told in the question that she did do this.

Question 2

The client is a director of an electronical wholesale company and a shareholder in an electronical retail company.

If the client failed to mention their interest in the electrical retail company when the electrical wholesale company transacted with it, which of the following best describes their liability for breach of duty?

A   The client will not have breached their duties to the electrical wholesale company because their relationship with the electrical retail company cannot be regarded as giving rise to a conflict of interests.

B   The client is in breach of the duty to avoid conflicts of interest.

C   The client is in breach of duty, but the electrical wholesale company's directors may be able to authorise the breach as long the client is not counted in the quorum and does not vote when the decision is taken.

D   The client may be in breach of their duty to declare an interest in a proposed transaction or arrangement.

E   The client is in breach of duty, but this breach can be ratified by the shareholders by ordinary resolution.

Answer

Option D is correct. Options A and B are wrong because we do not know enough about the situation to be able to say for sure whether there is or is not a conflict of interest. If the client's shareholding in the electrical retail company is very small, the situation is unlikely to give rise to a conflict of interest, but we do not have enough facts to know whether this is the case. Option D is correct: the client should declare their interest unless it cannot be regarded as likely to give rise to a conflict of interest, and we do not know whether this is the case, so the client 'may' be in breach. Option C is wrong because it is not possible for the board to authorise a breach of the duty to declare an interest in a transaction. Option E is wrong because while the shareholders could ratify any breach by ordinary resolution, we cannot say for sure whether there is even a breach.

Question 3

The client is a manufacturing company with three directors, an IT director, a managing director and an operations director. The client has the Model Articles with no amendments and its net asset value is £95,000. The IT director has 49% of the shares in a distribution company. The IT director wishes to sell a van to the client for £6,000 and the distribution company wishes to purchase a warehouse from the client for £80,000.

Assuming that there are no agreements in place and no relevant resolutions have been passed, which of the following best describes what shareholders' resolutions the client would need to pass in order that the transactions described above could validly go ahead?

A   An ordinary resolution to authorise the sale of the warehouse.

B   Two ordinary resolutions, one to authorise the sale of the warehouse and one to authorise the purchase of the van.

C   An ordinary resolution to authorise the purchase of the van.

D   A special resolution to authorise the IT director's involvement in the purchase of the warehouse.

E   A special resolution to authorise the IT director's involvement in the purchase of the warehouse and two ordinary resolutions, one to authorise the sale of the warehouse and one to authorise the purchase of the van.

Answer

Option A is correct. The purchase of the van does not need to be authorised by the shareholders because its value is less than £100,000 and less than 10% of the client's net asset value of £95,000. The sale of the warehouse is a substantial property transaction ('SPT') and therefore does need to be authorised by the shareholders, by ordinary resolution under s 190. It is an SPT because:

- It is a transaction between the company and a person connected to the company (the distribution company, because the IT director owns over 20% of the shares in the distribution company);

- It involves a non-cash asset (the warehouse); and

- It is of substantial value (over £5,000 and over 10% of the client's net asset value of £95,000)

The IT director's involvement in the sale of the warehouse does not need to be authorised as a separate issue from the ordinary resolution to authorise the sale of the warehouse.

4 Equity Finance

SQE1 syllabus

This chapter, combined with **Chapter 5**, will enable you to achieve the SQE1 Assessment Specification in relation to Functioning Legal Knowledge concerned with the following:

*   funding options: debt and equity
*   distribution of profits and gains

Note that for SQE1, candidates are not usually required to recall specific case names, or cite statutory or regulatory authorities. In this chapter, statutory references are provided for information only, although you may need to recognise what is meant by a reference to s 172 CA 2006.

Learning outcomes

By the end of this chapter you will be able to:

*   understand the principle of maintenance of share capital;
*   advise a client on the procedure necessary to allot shares in a company;
*   advise a client on the mechanics for the transfer and transmission of shares; and
*   advise a client on how to buy back a company's shares out of profit or capital.

4.1 Introduction

Generally, companies obtain finance in one of two ways. Either:

- prospective shareholders pay money or give property to the company in return for shares, which is known as equity finance; or
- companies borrow money to fund expansion or just the day-to-day running of the company, which is known as debt finance.

This chapter addresses how shares are created and allotted to shareholders and how the ownership of shares changes: by transfer, transmission or buyback. The other main method of financing a company, debt finance, is addressed in **Chapter 5**.

4.2 Allotting, transferring and buying back shares: an overview

There are three ways shares can change hands: allotment, transfer (or transmission) and buyback. This chapter will explain all three concepts, but it is helpful to give an overview of all three at this stage, to provide an understanding of how each topic fits into the big picture.

Allotment is when a company decides to create shares and give them to an existing shareholder or a new shareholder in return for payment. The company will then issue a share certificate relating to the shares and enter the person on the register of members (or amend their existing entry to show their increased shareholding). The form of payment will usually be cash – money – but sometimes the consideration will be an object such as a property. The key point is that allotment is where a company creates new shares and receives consideration for them.

 Example

Figure 4.1 The effect of an allotment of shares

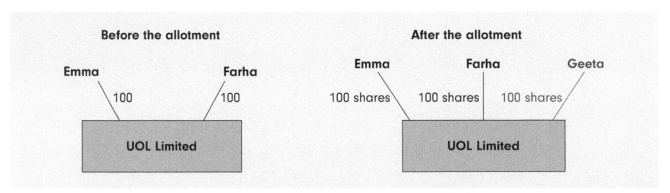

UOL Limited has two shareholders, Emma and Farha, each of whom owns 100 ordinary £1 shares. To raise money, UOL Limited decides to allot 100 ordinary £1 shares to Geeta for £1,000. Before the allotment, UOL Limited has two shareholders and 200 shares. After the allotment, UOL Limited has three shareholders and 300 shares.

Share transfer is where the shareholder sells or gives shares to another shareholder or to a new shareholder.

⭐ *Example*

Figure 4.2 The effect of a transfer of shares

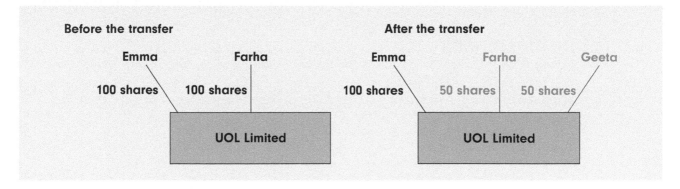

Before the transfer, there are two shareholders with 100 shares each, a total of 200 shares. After the transfer, there are three shareholders, with 100, 50 and 50 shares respectively, but there is still a total of 200 shares in the company. So, unlike allotment, the total number of shares remains the same – it is just the identity of the owners of the shares that has changed.

Buyback is where the company buys back some of its own shares from one or more shareholders. It may help to think of buyback as the reverse of allotment. Instead of new shares being created, the company 'reabsorbs' some of it shares so that the total number of shares in the company decreases. The shares that the company has bought back are cancelled.

⭐ *Example*

Figure 4.3 The effect of a buyback of shares

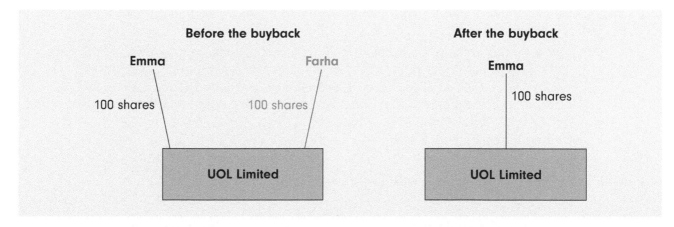

Before the buyback, there are two shareholders with 100 shares each, a total of 200 shares. After the buyback, there is one shareholder with 100 shares, a total of 100 shares in the company.

What is common to the three methods of shares changing hands is that they all involve the percentage shareholding of at least one of the shareholders changing. When shares are allotted, the number of shares in the company increases and so the existing shareholders' percentage shareholding will decrease, unless they have received some of the new shares. When shares are transferred, the transferor's percentage shareholding decreases and the transferee's percentage shareholding increases. When the company buys back some of its own shares, the remaining shareholders' percentage shareholding increases. As explained in **Chapter 2**, the percentage of shares which a particular shareholder owns is what gives that shareholder their power.

 Example – allotment

> *Currently, Emma has 25.1% of UOL Limited's shares, which enables her to block any special resolution. UOL Limited then allots 100 shares to Geeta. This increases the number of shares in UOL Limited from 1,000 to 1,100. This changes the position, as shown in* ***Figure 4.4***.

Figure 4.4   How allotment changes percentage shareholdings

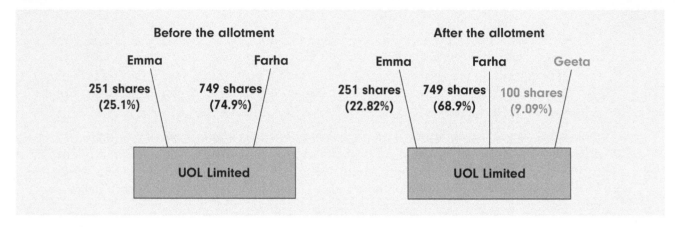

> *Emma now has only 22.82% of the shares, so she no longer has the power to block a special resolution. The share allotment has changed significantly the amount of power she has as a shareholder of the company.*

 Example – buyback

> ***Figure 4.5*** *illustrates what happens to shareholding percentages when buyback occurs. When UOL Limited buys back all of Geeta's shares, the number of issued shares is reduced from 1,000 to 900. Emma's percentage shareholding increases to over 50%, meaning that she can now block and pass ordinary resolutions on her own. Before the buyback, she was unable to pass an ordinary resolution on her own. Clearly this may be a cause for concern for Farha.*

Figure 4.5   How buyback changes percentage shareholdings

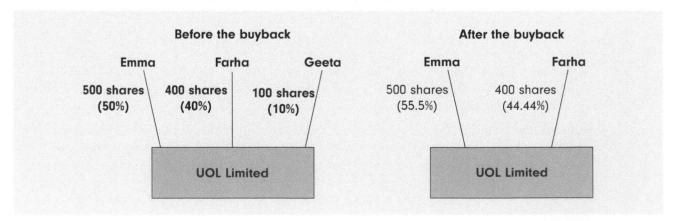

It is clear from the examples above that a shareholder, who has invested potentially a great deal of money in a company, might be aggrieved that they have lost power or that another shareholder has gained more power. It is for this reason that a number of restrictions are placed by statute on allotment and buyback. This chapter will explain the procedural steps the company must take in order to validly allot shares and buy back its own shares.

Share transfer is not as tightly controlled as allotment and buyback, because the percentage shareholding of a shareholder who is not involved in a share transfer will not change as a result of a share transfer. This is because with a share transfer, the total number of shares in the company does not change. However, shareholders often want to place restrictions on transfers, and we will consider the reasons for this at **4.4**.

We will now consider in detail allotment, transfer, transmission and buyback.

4.3 Allotment of shares

When a company is incorporated, there may only be one initial shareholder, or subscriber, but usually there are two, with one share each. The intention will almost certainly be to invest more money in the company. The board will therefore decide to allot more shares. The terms 'allot' and 'issue' are frequently used interchangeably, but they mean different things. A company *allots* shares when a person acquires the unconditional right to be included in the company's register of members in respect of the shares (s 558 CA 2006). This will be when the shares have been transferred and paid for and the board has passed a resolution to register the transfer. The shares are *issued* by the company when the name of the shareholder has been entered on the register of members.

When a company wants to raise equity finance by allotting shares, the board will decide the price and how many shares it wishes to allot, usually having taken the advice of the company's accountant or banker. Solicitors advise on the procedure necessary to lawfully allot shares, and prepare the necessary paperwork.

There are three questions to consider when working out the procedure needed to allot shares. These are:

1. Are there any constitutional restrictions on allotment?
2. Do the directors have authority to allot shares?
3. Are there any pre-emption rights?

These questions are considered and explained in turn below.

4.3.1 Are there any constitutional restrictions on allotment?

This question was more significant before the CA 2006 came into force on 1 October 2009. This is because in companies incorporated before October 2009, the company's memorandum of association always contained an upper limit, or ceiling, on the number of shares a company could have, called an authorised share capital ('ASC'). When the CA 2006 came into force, the ASC clause in the memorandum of association of existing companies was transferred to the company's articles (s 28(1) CA 2006). If such companies' articles have not been updated since the CA 2006 came into force, then the ASC will still be in the company's articles, but can be removed by ordinary resolution under transitional regulations passed under the CA 2006. It is important to note that this is an exception to the general rule that the company's articles can only be amended by special resolution, and a copy of the ordinary resolution must be filed at Companies House.

Any company incorporated under the CA 2006 will not have an ASC clause in its memorandum, but it may have a similar provision in its articles. Whereas it seems unnecessary to include such a restriction, only to have to remove it if the company wants to allot more shares, some companies may include an upper limit in their articles because the directors or shareholders are used to such a concept from other companies they have been involved in. So it is important to check the articles for any upper limit on the number of shares. If there is such a limit, the company can change its articles of association to remove the restriction. This will require a special resolution under s 21 CA 2006.

In summary, then:

- For companies incorporated prior to 1 October 2009, check whether they have updated their articles since that date. If not, the shareholders will need to pass an **ordinary resolution** to remove the ASC.

- For all companies, check the company's articles for a limit on the number of shares the company can have. If there is such a limit, change the articles by **special resolution**.

4.3.2 Do the directors have authority to allot shares?

The decision to allot shares can be either a board decision or a shareholder decision, depending on the type of company, the number of classes of share the company has, and the company's articles of association.

4.3.2.1 Private companies with one class of share

The directors of a private company which has one class of shares both before and after the allotment have authority to allot shares without the permission of the shareholders under s 550 CA 2006, as long as the company was incorporated under the CA 2006. All that is needed to allot the shares is a board resolution. See **2.9** for an explanation of the different classes (types) of share.

However, if the company was incorporated before the CA 2006 came into force, then the shareholders must pass an ordinary resolution to 'activate' s 550 (this, again, is set out in transitional regulations passed under the CA 2006). This is because before the CA 2006 came into force, directors did not automatically have authority to allot shares; the shareholders had to give permission. It could be detrimental to shareholders of companies incorporated before the CA 2006 came into force if the law were to allow directors to allot shares without shareholders being asked to give permission, when previously the directors of such companies did not have this right.

The company's articles of association may restrict the directors' power to allot shares under s 550. Companies can remove this power by amending the articles by special resolution.

4.3.2.2 Authority under s 551 CA 2006

The directors of public companies, or private companies with more than one class of shares before or after the allotment, must obtain the permission of the company's shareholders before they can allot shares. Section 551 CA 2006 provides that an ordinary resolution of the shareholders is needed before the company can allot the shares. The ordinary resolution must state the maximum number of shares the directors may allot and the date on which the authority will expire, which must not be more than five years from the date that the ordinary resolution is passed.

Once the authority to allot has expired, it may be renewed by ordinary resolution of the company for a further period not exceeding five years. Again, the resolution renewing the authority to allot must state the maximum amount of shares that may be allotted under the authorisation and the date on which the renewed authority will expire.

Alternatively, the authority to allot may be included in the company's articles of association from incorporation. Such an article must state the maximum number of shares that may be allotted under it, and must specify the date on which it will expire, which must be not more than five years from incorporation of the company.

It is important to note that s 551 is another exception to the general rule that the company's articles can only be amended by special resolution. This is made clear by s 551(8) of the CA 2006. Ordinary resolutions passed under s 551 must be filed at Companies House, even though they are ordinary resolutions (s 551(9), s 29 and s 30 CA 2006).

In summary, then:

- Private companies incorporated under the CA 2006 with one class of shares have authority to allot shares without shareholder approval; all that is needed is a board resolution.

- Plcs and private companies with more than one class of share may have authority to allot in their articles. If there is no authority in the company's articles, the shareholders will need to pass an **ordinary resolution** to allot shares.

4.3.3   Are there any pre-emption rights?

Pre-emption rights are rights of first refusal over shares which are being allotted. Under s 561 CA 2006, the company must not allot 'equity securities' to a person unless it has first offered them to existing holders of ordinary shares in the company on the same or more favourable terms. The company must offer existing shareholders the number of shares which will enable them to preserve their percentage shareholding in the company: the proportion of the new shares they are offered must equal (as nearly as practicable) the proportion of shares they already hold in the company.

The term 'equity securities' is defined in s 560 CA 2006, and it includes ordinary shares and rights to subscribe for, or to convert securities into, ordinary shares in the company. Ordinary shares generally give the owner the right to vote at general meetings. So if any ordinary shares, or shares which the owner can choose to convert into ordinary shares, are being allotted, this will dilute the voting power that the existing shareholders have. This is why existing shareholders of equity securities are given first refusal over the shares being allotted.

⭐ *Example – pre-emption*

UOL Limited has the following shareholders: Emma (600 shares, equal to 60% of the total shares in the company), Farha (300 shares, equal to 30% of the total shares in the company) and Geeta (100 shares, equal to 10% of the total shares in the company). The board proposes to allot 500 more shares to a third party in return for £1,000 cash. Pre-emption rights apply, so the existing shareholders must be given first refusal over the shares. How many shares must the board offer to each shareholder?

Answer: *Emma will be offered 300 shares (60% of the new shares), Farha will be offered 150 shares (30% of the new shares) and Geeta will be offered 50 shares (10% of the new shares). This will enable them to maintain the percentage shareholdings that they have already.*

When a shareholder is offered new shares in accordance with their pre-emption rights, s 562(4) of the CA 2006 states that the offer must state the period for acceptance (ie the deadline for accepting) and the offer must not be withdrawn within that period. Under s 562(5), the period for acceptance of the offer cannot be less than 14 days. If any or all of the shareholders do not take up the offer, then the directors can offer the shares to other buyers.

There are some exceptions to pre-emption rights. They do not apply in relation to the allotment of bonus shares (s 564), if the consideration for the allotment is wholly or partly non-cash (s 565) or if the shares are to be held under, allotted or transferred pursuant to an employee share scheme (s 566).

The exception where the consideration is non-cash is a logical one. If the proposed recipient of the shares owns something which the company needs, for example property, then it is important that the company allot the shares to that particular person and no other, so that the company receives the property that it needs. No other recipient of the shares can provide that property as consideration.

4.3.3.1 Pre-emption rights in the company's articles

The CA 2006 allows private companies to exclude pre-emption rights by provisions contained in its articles, either generally or in relation to particular allotments (s 567 CA 2006). This will override the statutory provisions contained in s 561. So before advising a client on how to disapply pre-emption rights, it is important to check the company's articles first, to check whether alternative provisions already exist. Any provisions in the company's articles could be removed by special resolution if the company no longer wants them to be included. Note that there are no pre-emption rights in the Model Articles.

Usually the reason for disapplying pre-emption rights is that the company wishes to include pre-emption rights which are more tailored to how it wishes to operate. For example, the board and the shareholders might agree that they would prefer the shareholders to have 21 days, not 14, to consider a pre-emption offer. Or they might decide that they would like pre-emption rights to apply even when the consideration for the allotment is non-cash.

4.3.3.2 Disapplication of pre-emption rights

Private companies can disapply the pre-emption rights contained in s 561 for a particular allotment by special resolution, so that the board can allot shares as it wishes and does not need to offer the shares to existing shareholders first.

It is worth noting that the company does not have to disapply pre-emption rights: it could just comply with them. But sometimes the board does not want to wait for all of the shareholders to respond to the offer, or might be keen for commercial reasons to make sure that the shares are allotted to a particular person.

Disapplication is always by special resolution, but the authority for this will depend on the type of company, the number of classes of shares the company has, and the wording of the authority to allot shares.

4.3.3.3 Private companies with one class of shares

Under s 569 CA 2006, the shareholders of a private company which has only one class of shares may pass a special resolution disapplying the existing shareholders' pre-emption rights. So companies which had authority to allot shares under s 550 can disapply any pre-emption rights by special resolution under s 569.

4.3.3.4 Public companies or private companies with more than one class of shares

When the company is a plc or has more than one class of shares, how pre-emption rights are disapplied will depend on the nature of those companies' initial authority to allot shares. We saw in **4.3.2.2** that companies which do not have automatic authority to allot under s 550 will need to pass an ordinary resolution under s 551 CA 2006 to give the directors authority to allot shares. If the ordinary resolution gave a general authority to allot (rather than authority in relation to a specific allotment) then s 570 allows the company to remove the pre-emption rights just by passing a special resolution. Disapplication will last as long as the directors' authority under s 551.

If the authority to allot shares contained in the s 551 ordinary resolution was in relation to a specific allotment, s 571 also allows companies to disapply pre-emption rights by special resolution. However, the special resolution must be recommended by the directors of the company (s 570(5) CA 2006) and before proposing a special resolution. Under s 571(6) the directors must make a written statement setting out:

- the reasons for making the recommendation;
- the amount the purchaser will pay; and
- the directors' justification of that amount.

The directors' written statement must be circulated to the shareholders along with the notice of the general meeting, or, if the resolution is proposed as a written resolution, it must be sent out with the written resolution (s 571(7) CA 2006).

It is an offence to knowingly or recklessly authorise or permit the inclusion of any matter that is misleading, false or deceptive in a material particular in the directors' written statement (s 572 CA 2006).

It makes sense, then, to pass an ordinary resolution giving general authority to allot, because when it comes to pre-emption, the pre-emption rights can be excluded by special resolution under s 570 (without the directors having to follow the recommendation procedure in s 571). Note that any company can use the procedure in s 571 in the unlikely event that it wishes to do so – it is not restricted to companies with more than one class of shares or public companies.

In summary:

- Pre-emption rights which differ from those set out in the CA 2006 are sometimes contained in the company's articles, so these should be checked first, and removed by **special resolution** if necessary.
- If the pre-emption rights under s 561 apply, because the company's articles have not changed the position, they can be disapplied by **special resolution**.
- Where the company is disapplying pre-emption rights under s 571 CA 2006, the directors must make a written statement justifying the disapplication of pre-emption rights.

4.3.4 Payment for shares

Under MA 21, all shares in a company must be fully paid, meaning that the buyer must pay for the shares when they receive them. If the company's articles do not include MA 21, then shares can be issued partly paid, but the shareholder must pay the remainder when contractually obliged to do so or if the company is wound up.

If the company performs well, the value of its shares will increase, so a share with a nominal value of £1, for example, may be allotted (or transferred) for £1.75 and we would say that the share was issued at a premium. The excess consideration of 75p would be recorded in a separate share premium account on the company's balance sheet (s 610 CA 2006). This money will then be treated as share capital and must be maintained (see **4.5** for an explanation of the principle of maintenance of share capital).

4.3.5 Allotment – administration

When a company has allotted shares, it must comply with various administrative and filing requirements, which are set out in **Table 4.1**.

The company will also need to prepare minutes of every board meeting and every general meeting (s 248 and s 355).

Table 4.1 Administrative and filing requirements on allotment of shares

Copies of resolutions to be sent to Companies House within 15 days	All special resolutions Any ordinary resolution removing the authorised share capital in a pre-CA 2006 company Any ordinary resolution to activate s 550 in a pre-CA 2006 company Any s 551 ordinary resolution granting directors authority to allot
Company forms to be sent to Companies House	Return of allotment and statement of capital (Form SH01) within one month of the allotment Possibly form(s) PSC01, PSC02, PSC04 and PSC07, for new persons with significant control/ a change of which percentage band a person is in/ a person ceasing to be a person with significant control
Entries in company's own registers	Amend register of members within two months Amend PSC register if necessary
Preparation and allocation of share certificates	Prepare share certificates within two months of allotment

4.4 Transfer of shares

The second of the means by which the ownership of shares changes is transfer of shares. With share transfer, a shareholder (the 'transferor') sells or gives shares to another existing shareholder or another person (the 'transferee') who is not an existing shareholder. The total number of shares in the company does not change but one or more of the shareholders' percentage shareholdings changes. There is nothing in the CA 2006 to prevent a shareholder from transferring the shares, and nor is there any obligation to offer the shares to existing shareholders first (pre-emption). However, it is not true to say that share transfer does not present any risks for the existing shareholders or that it should not give them cause for concern. Consider the diagrams in **Figure 4.6**.

Figure 4.6 How a transfer of shares can affect a shareholder's power

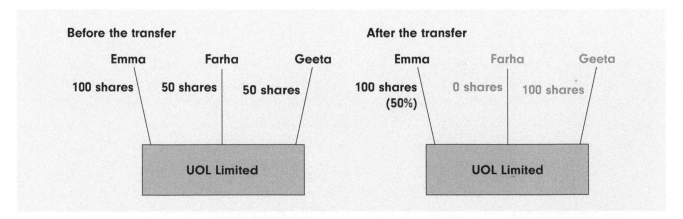

If Farha transfers her shares to Geeta, Geeta will now have equal power to Emma, and will be able to block ordinary resolutions, whereas before the share transfer, she could not. Often the company's articles will contain restrictions on transfer of shares to stop this sort of problem

occurring, or to stop a shareholder whom the other shareholders do not like and with whom they do not want to work from joining the company, because conflict between shareholders would probably mean that the company would not operate as smoothly. Solicitors often have to draft quite complex share transfer provisions in the company's articles, or interpret them should a shareholder want to transfer shares. It is common, in smaller companies, to state that share transfers to family members or other existing shareholders are permitted, but that any other transfer must be approved by the board of directors. Alternatively, shareholders may be allowed to transfer their shares to other people, but only if they have offered their shares to the existing shareholders first, at a fair value.

It is important to note that the articles cannot restrict a shareholder from selling the shares and cannot stop a particular purchaser from buying them. However, a person does not become a shareholder of the company until they are entered on the register of members (s 113 CA 2006). Model Article 26 gives the board discretion to refuse to register the transfer of shares, meaning that if a company has the Model Articles, every transfer must be approved by the board before the transferee can be entered on the register of members and therefore become a shareholder. If the transferee is never entered on the register of members, they will be the beneficial owner of the shares, but the transferor will remain the legal owner of the shares. If a general meeting is held after the share transfer but before registration of the transfer, it is the transferor of the shares, as their legal owner, who will be permitted to attend, and it is the transferor, as legal owner of the shares, who will receive any dividends paid. However, at the general meeting the legal owner of the shares must vote in accordance with the wishes of the beneficial owner of the shares and must also pay any dividends to the beneficial owner of the shares.

4.4.1   How are shares transferred?

The transferor must complete and sign a stock transfer form and give it to the transferee along with the share certificate relating to the shares (ss 770–772 CA 2006).

If the sale price of the shares is over £1,000, the buyer must pay stamp duty (currently charged at 0.5% rounded up to the nearest £5) on the stock transfer form. No stamp duty is payable if the shares are a gift. The minimum stamp duty is £5.

The transferee must then send the share certificate and stock transfer form to the company.

The company should then:

*   send the new shareholder a new share certificate in their name within two months (s 776 CA 2006);

*   enter their name on the register of members within two months (s 771 CA 2006); and

*   notify the Registrar of Companies of the change in ownership of the shares when the company files its annual confirmation statement (CS01).

4.4.2   Transmission

Transmission of shares is an automatic process whereby:

*   if a shareholder dies, their shares automatically pass to their personal representatives (PRs); or

*   if a shareholder is made bankrupt, their shares automatically vest in their trustee in bankruptcy.

Under MA 27, the trustee in bankruptcy and the PRs do not become shareholders of the company, but they are entitled to any dividends declared on the shares.

The trustee in bankruptcy and PRs of a deceased shareholder can choose to be registered as shareholders themselves (unless the directors are entitled to refuse to register them as shareholders and refuse to do so) and can then sell the shares. Alternatively, they can sell them directly in their capacity as representative.

4.5   Maintenance of share capital

Maintenance of share capital is one of the main principles of company law. The company's share capital is the money provided by shareholders in return for shares. A company's share capital is the foundation on which the company rests. It is a long-standing principle of company law that this fund cannot be reduced, because it is the fund which creditors look to for payment of debts owed to them. So paid up share capital cannot be returned to shareholders and their liability with regard to any capital they have not paid on their shares must not be reduced.

This principle has a number of consequences, which include:

*   dividends cannot be paid out of capital, just out of distributable profits; and

*   the company must not generally purchase its own shares.

There are exceptions to these rules. They are:

*   a company can buy back its own shares as long as the correct procedure is followed (s 690);

*   a company can purchase its own shares under a court order made under s 994 CA 2006 to buy out an unfairly prejudiced minority shareholder; and

*   a company can return capital to shareholders, after payment of the company's debts, in a winding up.

4.6   Share buyback

Why might a company buy back its own shares? Sometimes shareholders want to cut all ties with the company but cannot find a purchaser for the shares. Sometimes there are restrictions on share transfer, but not enough of the shareholders would support a special resolution to change the articles permitting the shareholders to transfer the shares as they wish. In situations such as these, the shareholders may be able to persuade enough fellow shareholders to vote in favour of an ordinary resolution authorising the company to buy back their shares.

If a company buys back its own shares, the shares in question are cancelled, and the company has to pay the outgoing shareholder for the shares, meaning that the company is financially worse off as a result of the buyback. Buyback will result in the reduction of profits available for declaring dividends, or of capital available for creditors in the event that a company cannot pay its debts. Further, if the company is wound up, there will be less money available for the company's shareholders once creditors have been paid. Directors must consider their duties under the CA 2006 when the company is buying back shares, and whether the buyback will be good for the company in the long run under s 172 CA 2006. The board will also need to make their decision with regard to the buyback with due skill, care and attention pursuant to s 174 CA 2006. However, companies can often justify buyback on the basis that it is better for the company in the long run to buy out a disgruntled shareholder than continue to work with them in an unproductive way, especially if that shareholder is also a director and their resignation was conditional on the company buying back their shares.

In some cases, the buyback may not be for good commercial reasons at all – perhaps one of the directors, who is also a shareholder, wants to retire and nobody wants to buy their shares so the company has agreed to buy them back. If this is the case, the board must be especially careful not to buy back shares where it would leave the company in a risky financial position.

4.6.1   How to buy back shares

There is a distinction between a buyback of shares on the stock market, called a market purchase, and buyback which is not on the stock market, known as an off-market purchase (s 693). In this book, we cover off-market purchases, because these are the purchases which private companies make.

It is because buyback is financially risky that the CA 2006 closely controls the circumstances in which a company may buy back its own shares. The requirements are:

1. Firstly, the company's articles must not forbid buyback (s 690(1)).
2. The shares must be fully paid (s 691(1)).
3. The company must pay for the shares at the time of purchase (s 691(2)).
4. The shares must usually be paid for out of distributable profits or the proceeds of a fresh issue of shares made for the purpose of financing the purchase (s 692(2)(a) CA 2006). What is meant by distributable profits is explained in s 830 CA 2006. They are the company's accumulated, realised profits less its accumulated, realised losses. They are shown on the bottom half of the company's balance sheet, under profit/loss reserve. Please see **12.9.4** for a full explanation of company balance sheets.
5. The shareholders must pass an ordinary resolution authorising the buyback contract (s 694 CA 2006).
6. A copy of the buyback contract, or a summary of it, must be available for inspection for at least 15 days before the general meeting and at the general meeting itself (or be sent with the proposed written resolution when or before it is circulated (s 696(2)).
7. Under s 702 CA 2006, a copy of the buyback contract, or, if the contract is not in writing, a written memorandum setting out its terms, must be made available for inspection at the company's registered office or SAIL as soon the contract has been concluded, for a period of ten years starting with the date of the buyback.

4.6.1.1   The buyback procedure

Table 4.2 summarises the procedure for a buyback out of profits.

Table 4.2   Procedure for a buyback out of profits

Timing	Procedure
Before board meeting	Check there is no limit in the company's articles on its s 690 power to buy back shares.
	Prepare accounts to ascertain available profits and confirm shares are fully paid.
Board meeting	Hold a board meeting to: • decide the method of finance • resolve to approve the draft terms of purchase • resolve to call a general meeting (GM)/propose a written resolution (WR)
	Contract or memorandum of terms made available to members If WR used: memorandum must be circulated with WR If GM: memorandum must be at registered office for at least 15 days before GM and at the GM
WR	**WR:** Circulate WR (ordinary resolution (OR) to authorise buyback contract) with contract. Holder(s) of shares being bought are not eligible to vote.

(continued)

Table 4.2 (*continued*)

Timing	Procedure
alternatively	
GM	**GM:** Pass OR to authorise buyback contract. Resolution is invalid if vote is passed on the strength of votes derived from the shares being bought, so such votes should not be cast. Contract must be available at GM.
After GM/WR	Keep minutes/written resolutions for ten years (s 355)
Completion of board meeting	Board resolves to enter into the contract and one or two director(s) are authorised to execute the buyback contract.
After completion	File return of purchase of own shares and notice of cancellation of shares within 28 days of completion Keep copy of contract at registered office for ten years Cancel the shares, update register of members and PSC register (if required).

4.6.1.2 Voting at the general meeting or by written resolution

As we saw in **Chapter 3**, personal interests do not generally prevent shareholders from voting, but an exception is where an ordinary resolution to approve a buyback under s 694 CA 2006 is proposed. Where the resolution is proposed as a written resolution, a shareholder who holds shares which are being bought back is not an eligible member for the purposes of the written resolution, so cannot vote, and at a general meeting the resolution will not be effective if that shareholder's votes made the difference between the resolution passing or not (s 695 CA 2006).

4.6.2 Practical considerations when buying back shares

An important consideration is whether the company has enough cash to pay for the shares. The company may well have accumulated enough profits for the buyback to be out of distributable profits, but this profit may have been used to, for example, purchase machinery. It will not necessarily be waiting in the company's bank account. So it is important to look at how much cash the company has to see if it can pay for the shares. It is also necessary to see what liabilities will need to be paid soon, to ensure that the company can both pay for the shares being bought back and meet any short-term liabilities out of the cash it has.

When deciding whether to propose a buyback, the directors of the company must also consider their directors' duties as explained at 4.6.

4.6.3 Buyback out of capital

Sometimes companies wish to buy back shares but do not have enough distributable profits to fund the buyback. Private companies are permitted to buy back their own shares out of capital, unless the company's articles forbid buyback out of capital (s 709 CA 2006). Public companies are not permitted to buy back shares out of capital. If private companies buy back shares out of capital, they must exhaust their distributable profits before using capital to fund the buyback. In other words, they cannot use the company's share capital to fund a buyback when they have distributable profits left. This means that where a company uses this method, the shares will be bought back partly using the company's profits and partly using its capital. For the payment to be lawful, the same conditions for a buyback out of distributable profits must be met (see **4.6.1**), as well as the following requirements specific to buyback out of capital:

1. The company's directors must make a statement of solvency, no sooner than one week before the general meeting, stating that the company is solvent and that it will remain solvent during the year following the buyback. The directors must think carefully before making such a statement, because if the company becomes insolvent and is wound up within one year of their statement of solvency, the seller of the shares and the directors of the company may be required to contribute to the financial losses of the company, and the directors may face criminal sanctions for making such a statement without reasonable grounds.

2. The statement of solvency must have annexed to it an auditors' report confirming that the auditors are not aware of anything to indicate that the directors' opinion is unreasonable (s 714 CA 2006).

3. The payment out of capital must be approved by special resolution (s 716). This is in addition to the ordinary resolution that the shareholders must pass under s 694 CA 2006 to approve the buyback contract. Where the resolution is proposed as a written resolution, a member who holds shares which are being bought back is not an eligible member (and so is not entitled to vote) (s 717(2) CA 2006). If the resolution is proposed at a general meeting, the shareholder whose shares are being bought back may vote, but the resolution will not be effective if it is that shareholder's votes that make the difference between the resolution passing or not (s 717(3) CA 2006).

4. A copy of the directors' statement of solvency and auditors' report must be available to members. If the special resolution is proposed by written resolution, the statement and report must be sent to the members along with the written resolution. If the resolution is proposed at a general meeting, a copy of the statement and report must be available for inspection at the meeting. If this requirement is not complied with, the special resolution is ineffective.

5. Within seven days of the special resolution being passed, the company must put a notice in the London Gazette, stating that the shareholders have approved payment out of capital in order that the company can buy back its own shares (s 719 CA 2006). It must specify the amount of capital to be used, the date of the special resolution and where the directors' statement and auditors' reports are available for inspection. It must also state that any creditors of the company may, within five weeks following the special resolution being passed, apply for an order under s 721 preventing the buyback out of capital. The company must also publish an equivalent notice in an appropriate national newspaper (one circulating throughout the part of the UK which the company is registered) or give notice to each of its creditors (s 719). The purpose of the notices is to let the company's creditors know that the company is planning to buy back shares out of capital so that they can apply to court to stop the buyback if they do not think the company can afford to do it.

6. The company must also file a copy of the directors' statement and auditors' report at Companies House before or at the same time as it places the notices in the London Gazette and the newspaper (s 719(4)).

7. The directors' statement and auditors' report must be kept available for inspection at the company's registered office from the time the company publishes its first notice until five weeks after the passing of the special resolution (s 720).

8. As long as none of the creditors object to the buyback out of capital, the directors hold a board meeting and will pass a board resolution to decide to enter into the contract to buy back the shares. The payment out of capital itself must be made no earlier than five weeks after the date of the special resolution to approve the buyback out of capital, and no later than seven weeks after the date of the special resolution (s 723(1)), so the board has a two-week window to enter into the contract.

4.6.4   Timeline – buyback out of capital

Figure 4.7 shows the timeline for a buyback out of capital and what must happen when.

Figure 4.7   Timeline for buyback out of capital

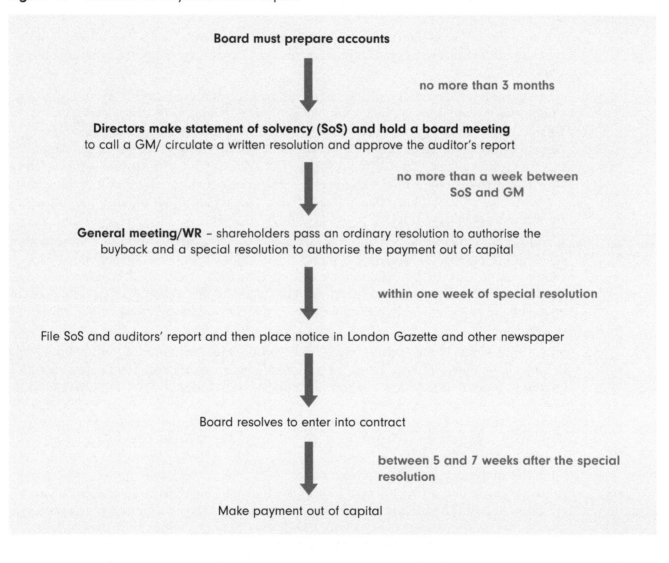

Table 4.3 shows the buyback out of capital procedure in more detail.

Table 4.3 Procedure for a buyback out of capital

Timing	Procedure	
Before board meeting	Check that there is no limit in the company's articles on its s 690 and s 709 powers.	
	No earlier than three months before the directors prepare the statement of solvency, prepare accounts to ascertain available profits and confirm that the shares are fully paid.	
Board meeting	Board meeting to: • decide method of finance • resolve to approve the terms of the statement of solvency and auditors' report • resolve to approve the terms of purchase • resolve to call a GM/propose WRs.	
	Contract or memorandum of terms made available to members If WR used: memorandum must be circulated with WR If GM: memorandum must be at registered office for at least 15 days before GM and at the GM	
	Statement of Solvency and Auditors' Report (SS and AR) must be signed no earlier than 1 week before GM/passing of WR	
WRs	**WR:** Circulate WR with contract, statement of solvency and auditors' report. Holder(s) of shares being bought back are not eligible to vote.	
alternatively		
GM	**GM:** Pass: • OR to authorise contract • special resolution (SR) to authorise payment out of capital Contract, statement of solvency and auditors' report must be at the meeting.	
	Resolution is invalid if vote is passed on the strength of votes derived from the shares being bought, so such votes should not be cast.	
After GM/WR	Keep minutes/WR	for 10 years
	Creditors' and dissenting members' right to object	lasts for 5 weeks after SR
	Keep SS and AR at the company's own registered office	for 5 weeks from date of SR
	Place notices in *London Gazette* and national newspaper/to creditors	within 1 week of SR
	File the SS and AR at Companies House	before first publication
	File SR	within 15 days of GM/WRs

(*continued*)

Table 4.3 (*continued*)

Timing	Procedure
Completion (board meeting)	Directors resolve to enter into contract and authorise 1 or 2 directors to sign. Payment out of capital takes place between 5 and 7 weeks after SR passed
After completion	File return of purchase of own shares (SH03) and notice of cancellation of shares within 28 days of completion
	Keep copy of contract at registered office for 10 years Cancel the shares, update register of members and PSC register

4.7 Dividends

The main reason for investing in a company is to make money. A shareholder can make money from their shares in two ways. Firstly, the value of the shares will increase as the company makes money, assuming that it is successful. Putting it very simply, if a company begins trading with 100,000 shares of £1 each, then makes profit in its first year so that the company is worth £150,000, each share is now worth £1.50, instead of £1. Secondly, shareholders will often receive dividends. A company can pay a dividend if it has profits available for the purpose (s 830 CA 2006). A company's available profits are its accumulated, realised profits less its accumulated, realised losses. They are shown on the bottom half of the company's balance sheet, under profit/loss reserve (see **12.18.1**). If, in a particular financial year, the company has not made any profit, it can use profits from previous years to pay a dividend if it wishes. Under MA 30, it is the directors who decide whether or not to recommend that a dividend be paid and how much it should be. The shareholders must then pass an ordinary resolution in order for this to be approved (or 'declared').

Sample questions

Question 1

A private company was incorporated in 2015 and has the Model Articles of Association with no amendments. The directors of the company propose to allot 1,000 ordinary shares for cash consideration. To date, no resolutions concerning the allotment of shares have been passed.

Which of the following statements best explains why the shareholders of the company do not need to pass an ordinary resolution to give the directors authority to allot the shares?

A   Because the company is allotting shares in return for cash so no authority is required.

B   Because the company is a private company with one class of shares so the directors already have permission to allot shares.

C   Because company directors can always allot ordinary shares without permission from the shareholders.

D   Because the shares to be allotted are not equity securities.

E   Because directors are permitted to allot up to 1,000 shares without shareholder approval.

Answer

Option B is correct. The company was incorporated after the Companies Act 2006 ('CA 2006') came into force and is a private company with only one class of shares – this must be the case because it has the Model Articles and no resolutions relating to allotment have been passed, so there cannot be any other types of share. No amendments have been made to the articles that might restrict the directors' authority to allot. The directors therefore already have authority to allot the shares under s 550 CA 2006. Option A is wrong because the fact that the shares are being allotted for cash does not change whether authority is required or not. Option C is wrong because sometimes directors do need permission to allot shares, depending on the company's articles, the type of share and company, and when it was incorporated. Option D is wrong because ordinary shares *are* equity securities. Option E is wrong because there is no such rule that directors can allot up to 1,000 shares without shareholder approval.

Question 2

A private company incorporated in 2015 has the Model Articles of Association with no amendments. It has two shareholders, a woman and a man, who are also the only two directors of the company. Each shareholder holds 50,000 ordinary £1 shares. The shareholders have agreed in principle that the company will buy back 25,000 shares from the man for £40,000. The company's distributable profits are £175,000 and its net assets are £800,000.

Assume that the shareholders have not passed any relevant resolutions.

Which of the following best describes what shareholders' resolutions would be required to effect the buyback described above?

A   One ordinary resolution, to authorise the buyback.

B   One ordinary resolution to authorise the buyback and one special resolution to authorise the use of capital.

C   One ordinary resolution to authorise the buyback and a second ordinary resolution to authorise the use of capital.

D   No shareholders' resolutions would be required because the company has the Model Articles of Association.

E   One special resolution, to authorise the buyback.

Answer

Option A is correct. This is clearly a buyback out of profits, not capital, because the company's distributable profits of £175,000 are enough to cover the agreed price for the buyback (£40,000). The net assets figure does not change the position. Accordingly, only one ordinary resolution is needed (s 694 CA 2006) to authorise the buyback. Options B and C are wrong because this is not a buyback out of capital. Options D are E are wrong because one ordinary resolution is required.

Question 3

A private company has four shareholders, a chemist, a translator, a software developer and a biologist, who are also the four directors of the company. The company has the Model Articles of Association with no amendments. It has an issued share capital of £100,000 ordinary £1 shares. The chemist owns 25,000 shares, the translator owns 50,000 shares, the software developer owns 15,000 shares and the biologist owns 10,000 shares. The software developer then sells 5,000 shares to each of the other three shareholders.

Which of the following describes the chemist, the translator and the biologist's percentage shareholdings following the transfer of the software developer's shares as described above?

A   The chemist owns 25%, the translator owns 50% and the biologist owns 10% of the company's shares.

B   The chemist owns 35%, the translator owns 65% and the biologist owns 12% of the company's shares.

C   The chemist owns 29%, the translator owns 59% and the biologist owns 12% of the company's shares.

D   The chemist owns 30%, the translator owns 55% and the biologist owns 15% of the company's shares.

E   The chemist owns 25%, the translator owns 50% and the biologist owns 15% of the company's shares.

Answer

Option D is correct. Each of the remaining shareholders obtains 5,000 more shares of the 100,000 in issue, giving the chemist 30,000, the translator 55,000 and the biologist 15,000 shares. So the chemist has 30,000/100,000, ie 30% of the shares, the translator has 55,000/100,000, ie 55% of the shares, and the biologist has 15,000/100,000, ie 15% of the shares.

5 Debt Finance

SQE1 syllabus

This chapter, combined with **Chapter 4,** will enable you to achieve the SQE1 Assessment Specification in relation to Functioning Legal Knowledge concerned with the following procedures and processes:

- funding options: debt and equity
- types of security
- distribution of profits and gains

Note that for SQE1, candidates are not usually required to recall specific case names, or cite statutory or regulatory authorities. In this chapter, statutory references are provided for information only.

Learning outcomes

By the end of this chapter you will be able to:

- understand the main types of loan and the advantages and disadvantages of each type of loan;

- understand the main terms in loan agreements;
- understand the advantages and disadvantages of debt and equity finance;
- understand the main types of security, including mortgages, fixed charges and floating charges;
- understand the key terms in a charging document;
- understand and advise on the priority of charges; and
- advise on the process for registering a charge and the consequences of failing to do so.

5.1   Introduction

This chapter concerns debt finance, which is when businesses obtain finance by borrowing money. Many of the principles in this chapter are applicable to sole traders, partnerships and companies, but some are only relevant to companies.

Sole traders and partnerships obtain money through their owners investing in the business or by way of a loan. Companies obtain most of the money they need from the same source as sole traders and partners: owner investment and loans. However, when companies' owners – shareholders – invest in the business, it is more complicated than just paying in some money. There is a procedure to follow for allotment of new shares, and this is covered in **Chapter 4**. This chapter focusses on loans as a source of finance, and covers the main types of debt finance in **Part 1** and taking security in **Part 2**.

Part 1   Types of Debt Finance

Debt finance is often required by businesses, either to help them to purchase items necessary to start trading, to enable them to expand or to help them through temporary cash flow difficulties.

There are two main types of debt finance: loans and debt securities. A loan is where a business borrows money from a bank or another lender, such as its owner(s) (for a sole trader or partnership) or its directors or shareholders (for a company). There are many types of loan. The main ones include a bank overdraft, a term loan and a revolving credit facility, all of which are explained below.

As an alternative to taking out a loan, or in addition, a company may issue debt securities to investors. These are IOUs which are issued by the company to the investor in return for a cash payment, and have to be repaid by the company at an agreed future date. What loans and debt securities have in common is that the company borrows money from a bank or from an investor which it will have to repay. In this book we will focus on loans.

5.2   Considerations prior to borrowing

Before a company borrows money, it must check that it is allowed to do so under its constitution. The Model Articles for private companies do not place any restrictions on borrowing. If the company was formed before 1 October 2009 and has not updated its articles, it is also important to check the company's memorandum to make sure that it contains no restrictions on the company borrowing money.

If there are any restrictions on borrowing money in the company's articles or memorandum, the shareholders will need to pass a special resolution under s 21 CA 2006 to change the articles to remove the restrictions (even for the memorandum, which will be treated as part of the company's articles (s 28 CA 2006)).

The directors must also have the authority to act on behalf of the company. For a company with the Model Articles, the directors' authority comes from MA 3. If the company has amended or bespoke articles, these must be checked to make sure there are no restrictions or, for example, a requirement that shareholders give prior approval before the company borrows over a certain amount.

Whereas equity finance is tightly controlled by the CA 2006, debt finance is largely governed by contract law. There is some legislation relevant to debt finance, but it is mainly relevant to debentures and the granting of security by companies.

Before a partnership borrows money, the partners should check that there is no restriction on doing so in their partnership agreement. If there is, the partners can generally only change this by unanimous consent.

The business will often have to offer the lender security over its property in return for the money. This means that if the business fails to repay the loan, or breaches the terms of the loan agreement, the lender may be able to take possession of some of the borrower's property in order to sell it and recoup the money the bank is owed.

First, we will look at the types of debt arrangements that a business may enter into.

5.3   Loans

When a business enters into a loan, it will negotiate with the lender over the terms of the contract. The terms will be agreed on the basis of usual market practice, the purpose and the length of the loan, the background and financial position of the business, the relative bargaining power of the parties and general economic conditions. Solicitors become involved once the commercial terms have been agreed, and the solicitor will negotiate the legal documentation. Secured loans involve the business giving security to the lender over some or all of its property so that the bank can recover what it is owed more easily if the business defaults on the loan. If the lender does not take security over the borrower's assets, the loan is said to be unsecured. Businesses pay higher rates of interest for unsecured loans, because the lender will require some financial advantage to compensate it for not taking security. There are many different types of loan, but in this book we concentrate on the three main types: an overdraft, a term loan, and a revolving credit facility. All three are governed by contract law, and which of the three a borrower chooses will depend on why it needs the loan and the typical features of each type of loan.

5.4   Overdraft facility

An overdraft facility is a contract between the business and its bank which allows the business to go overdrawn on its current account. Most small and medium-sized businesses rely heavily on overdraft facilities. They are a type of temporary loan used to cover everyday business expenses when there is no other source of money available. The maximum amount of the overdraft will be agreed with the bank in advance, but the amount used or owed by the business may vary on a day-to-day basis, and the business may move in and out of the overdraft facility day by day.

An overdraft is known as an uncommitted facility, meaning that it will usually be payable on demand. The bank may demand immediate repayment by the business at any time, without giving any notice. In practice, the bank will not demand repayment of the overdraft unless the business is in financial difficulties.

The business will have to pay a fee for the overdraft facility. The bank will also charge interest by reference to its base rate, which is the rate at which the bank is prepared to lend to its customers with the best credit rating. It is generally charged on a compound basis, which means that any unpaid interest is added to the capital (the amount borrowed) and interest is charged on the whole amount. This practice will be implied in overdraft contracts unless the parties have agreed otherwise.

The advantages of an overdraft for the business are that it is a flexible source of finance and relatively few formalities are required to arrange it. One disadvantage of an overdraft is that repayment may be demanded at any time by the bank. It is also a relatively expensive way to borrow, as it is usually unsecured and the banks charge high interest rates in return for offering such flexibility to the borrower.

5.5 Term loans

In a term loan, the business borrows a fixed amount of money, usually from a bank, for a specified period (ie term), at the end of which it must all be repaid. The borrower must also pay interest at regular intervals. Short-term loans are usually for up to one year and medium-term loans are usually for one to five years. Loans for over five years are deemed long term. Term loans are typically used by a business to purchase a capital asset, such as land, building or machinery.

Term loans may be secured or unsecured, although they are usually secured. They can be bilateral or syndicated. A bilateral loan is between two parties, the business and the bank. A syndicated loan is between the business and a number of different lenders, who jointly provide the money the business wants to borrow. Syndicated loans are common when the amount of the loan is high, and the risk of lending to the business is shared between a number of banks rather than just one. The contract for a term loan may be called a loan agreement, a credit agreement or a facility agreement. These terms are used interchangeably.

A term loan may allow the business to draw down, that is, take out, the loan all in one go, or to take it in instalments on, or by, agreed dates. The advantage of taking the money in instalments is that this will reduce interest payments.

The advantages of a term loan for a business are that it gives greater certainty than an overdraft, which is repayable on demand, and the borrower has greater control because the bank can only request repayment under the terms of the contract. The disadvantages are the time and expense in negotiating and agreeing all the legal documentation for such a loan and the fact that, once repaid, the money cannot then be re-borrowed by the business.

5.6 Revolving credit facilities

In a revolving credit facility, the bank agrees to make available a maximum amount of money to the business throughout the agreed period of the revolving credit facility. During the lifetime of the facility, the business can borrow and repay money. Interest is payable at regular intervals. The business is also able to reborrow amounts that it has already repaid, so long as it does not exceed the overall maximum figure, which is why it is called a revolving credit facility. Revolving credit facilities therefore share characteristics of both overdrafts and term loans. They are useful for businesses whose income is not evenly distributed throughout the year.

Revolving credit facilities may be secured or unsecured, although they are usually secured. They can be bilateral or syndicated. The contract for a revolving credit facility is usually called a facility agreement.

The advantages of a revolving credit facility for the business are that it is a very flexible means of borrowing money and it is possible to reduce the total amount of interest payable by reducing borrowings. The disadvantages of a revolving credit facility for the business are the time and expense in negotiating and agreeing all the legal documentation for the loan and the high fees that are charged.

5.7 Contractual terms

Both term loans and revolving credit facilities usually involve complex contracts which require a lot of negotiation between solicitors for the bank and the business. Set out below is an overview of some of the more important clauses which will be found in both types of loan. The term 'facility agreement' is used to cover both term loans and revolving credit facilities.

5.7.1 Payment of money to the borrower

The initial clauses of the facility agreement will set out:

(a) the amount of the loan;

(b) the currency (eg £, $ or €);

(c) the type of loan (if it is to be a term loan or revolving credit facility); and

(d) the availability period(s) during which the loan can be taken (for a revolving credit facility, this is almost the entire length of the facility).

Both a term loan and a revolving credit facility are 'committed' facilities. In other words, once the loan agreement has been signed, the bank must provide the business with the loan monies when it requests them.

5.7.2 Repayment and pre-payment

Unlike most overdrafts, the bank cannot demand repayment of a term loan or revolving credit facility whenever it wishes. It can do so only in accordance with the terms of the facility agreement.

The facility agreement will set out the agreed repayment schedule for the loan. It may provide for repayment:

(a) of the whole loan in one go at the end of the term (a 'bullet' payment); or

(b) in equal instalments over the term of the loan ('amortisation'); or

(c) in unequal instalments, with the final instalment being the largest ('balloon repayment').

Repayment in instalments will give the lender early notice should the business have difficulty in making repayments, because the business is likely to default on a payment if it is in financial difficulty. Repayments for a revolving credit facility will be towards the end of the facility period, whereas for a term loan they will be spread out more evenly throughout the period of the loan.

5.7.3 Interest rates

The interest rate payable for the loan is a matter of agreement between the parties. There is no statutory control of the interest rate applicable to companies. It will be expressly stated in the facility agreement. It may be fixed for the period of the loan, or it could be variable, that is, a 'floating' rate, where the interest rate is altered at specified intervals, for example three or six months, by reference to a formula which is intended to maintain the lender's profit on the loan. The reason for this is that the base interest rate for sterling is reviewed every month by a committee of the Bank of England, and may be altered up or down.

Lenders will often want to impose default interest if scheduled payments are missed. However, the law on penalty clauses could cause problems under the law of contract. Default interest clauses in a facility agreement must therefore be drafted very carefully.

5.7.4 Express covenants

The facility agreement will include a series of covenants given by the business to the bank. A covenant is a contractual promise to do or not to do something. The function of covenants is to try to ensure that the business conducts its business within agreed limits so that the lender has every chance of being repaid in full.

Many covenants relate to the provision of information on the business, and many relate to the financial performance of the business. There may be others dealing with non-financial matters.

The restrictions on the financial performance of the business are put in place to ensure that the business stays solvent and is not too dependent on debt. So, for example, the business will be required by the lender to pay all its debts as they fall due. The borrower will also usually be obliged to seek equity finance for new ventures, as opposed to further debt finance.

Covenants on the following matters are also commonly included, again to ensure that there will be sufficient money to repay the loan:

(a) **Limitation of dividends**. Companies must ensure that dividends and other distributions to shareholders do not exceed a specified percentage of the net profits.

(b) **Minimum capital requirements**. The business must ensure that current assets exceed current liabilities by a specified amount of money or a specified percentage.

(c) **No disposal of assets, or change of business**. The business must not dispose of assets without the lender's consent, or change the scope or nature of the business.

(d) **No further security over the assets**. The business must not create any further security over the whole, or any part, of the undertaking without the lender's consent (a 'negative pledge' clause, see **5.17.8**).

(e) **Provision of information on the business**, for example, annual accounts.

The final form of the covenants will depend on negotiations between the parties, but the lender has the money and the business needs the money, so the commercial strength is on the lender's side. However, the lender will give the business reasonable commercial latitude. One reason for this, when the borrower is a company, is the risk of the bank being found liable as a shadow director of the borrowing company.

As a matter of general commercial common sense, a lender will monitor the business's current account very closely. This will provide good information on how the borrower is progressing financially, and will give early warning of any problems.

5.7.5 Implied covenants

As with any contract, terms may be implied into the facility agreement, for example by trade usage such as the bank's right to charge compound interest. The court's power to imply terms is limited. A contractual term would be implied only if it were necessary to give business efficacy to the contract or if the term is so obvious that it 'goes without saying'. In any event, the court could not imply a term that was inconsistent with an express term of the contract. This should not be a problem with facility agreements drawn up by legal advisers.

5.7.6 Events of default

The facility agreement will contain 'events of default'. If the business breaches any of these terms, the lender may terminate the agreement if it so wishes. Such events include failure to pay any sum due, commencement of an insolvency procedure or breach of other obligations under the facility agreement.

5.8 Debentures

A debenture is not a separate type of debt finance. It has more than one meaning under the common law and the CA 2006, but is generally used to describe a loan agreement in writing between a borrower and a lender that is registered at Companies House. It gives the lender security over the borrower's assets. Only companies and LLPs can enter into debentures; sole traders and general partnerships cannot.

5.9 Secured debt

A lender with security may claim the secured assets of the business if the business fails to meet its obligations under the facility agreement. If the business becomes insolvent, secured creditors are therefore in a much stronger position than unsecured creditors, who generally do not have any rights of priority to the business's assets. Unsecured debts are governed by the equality (*pari passu*) principle, which means that the unsecured debts are all reduced pro rata if there are insufficient funds to pay all the business's debts. Most borrowing by a business will involve the business giving security over its assets. We examine taking security further in **Part 2**.

5.10 Companies: comparison between debt and equity finance

Whether to opt for equity or debt finance is a difficult decision for a company. **Table 5.1** shows some of the considerations to bear in mind.

Whether debt or equity finance, or a combination of the two, is the best option to raise new money for a company depends on a number of factors. In recent years debt finance has been the preferred source of new money by UK companies, partly because interest rates have been low for some time.

Table 5.1 Comparison of debt and equity finance

Corporate borrowers: comparison of debt and equity finance

	Equity finance	Debt finance
The relative risk of the investment	Buying shares in a company is generally perceived as a more risky investment than lending money to a company. If the company is in financial difficulties then it will not declare a dividend, as it can do so only if it has distributable profits, and even then the payment of a dividend is usually discretionary. The shareholder will also lose the capital value of their shares if the company goes insolvent – the shares they bought will be worthless.	With loans, the interest payments are a contractual liability of the company, and therefore will be paid before dividends. Also, a loan will often be secured over the company's property and there may be personal guarantees from the directors. This security means that a lender is much more likely to be repaid than a shareholder if the company becomes insolvent.
Involvement in the company	Shareholders, as owners of the company, have certain rights, such as the right to attend general meetings and vote. This enables them to influence the direction of the company.	A lender is merely a creditor of the company without any ownership rights, and therefore has no say in the way the company is run, provided the company sticks to the terms of the facility agreement.
Repayment of capital	Generally, companies do not repay a shareholder's capital unless the company is wound up, although shareholders may make money by selling their shares to a third party.	Loan capital must be repaid at some date in the future, possibly on demand. Consequently, the directors of the company must make provision for this and ensure that funds are available to repay the loan whenever it falls due, or the company will be in default.
Restrictions on sale	The transfer of shares is governed by the company's articles, and in a private company these usually restrict shareholders' freedom to sell their shares. For example, MA 26(5) gives the directors of a company discretion to refuse to register a new shareholder.	If a lender wishes to realise its capital earlier than the repayment date agreed, it may sell its debenture to a third party if it wishes. No restriction in the articles will affect its right to sell.
Capital value of the investment	The value of a private company's shares may increase or decrease, depending on the company's success. Many shareholders invest in shares hoping they will increase in value (known as 'capital appreciation') rather than because of income by way of dividend.	The capital value of a facility agreement generally remains constant, being the value of the loan. There is usually no possibility of capital appreciation or depreciation with this type of investment. The purpose of an investment in this form is the receipt of income in the form of regular interest payments by the company.

Table 5.1 (*continued*)

Corporate borrowers: comparison of debt and equity finance

Degree of statutory control	Equity finance is tightly controlled by the CA 2006 (see **Chapter 4**).	Debt finance is predominantly a matter of contract law, and may therefore be a more flexible way for the company to raise money.
Payment of income	The company is able to pay a dividend to its members only if there are sufficient available profits. Even if the company is sufficiently profitable, the directors usually have complete discretion as to whether a dividend should be paid (depending on the type of share).	Debt interest must be paid in accordance with the terms of the facility agreement, whether or not the company has profits available. If there are no profits, the company must use capital to make the interest payment. If the company fails to make a payment of interest, the lender may be entitled to enforce the terms of the debenture by the appointment of a receiver or an administrator.
Tax treatment of income payments	The payment of a dividend is not a deductible expense for the company. It is simply a distribution of profit, after it has paid corporation tax.	Payment of debenture interest, as it is incurred for the purposes of the trade, is a normal trading expense of the company, and so is deductible by it in computing trading profit before its corporation tax is assessed.
Cost	The cost of equity constitutes the likely returns to the new shareholder, including any dividends, capital appreciation and share buybacks. These returns are a cost to the existing shareholders, as their share of future dividends or capital growth is decreased by the presence of an extra shareholder. Dividends are not deductible for corporation tax purposes.	The cost of debt is the interest rate charged by the lender to the borrowing company. The rate depends on commercial factors such as the security offered by the company, how much is borrowed, how long it is borrowed for, the company's creditworthiness and general economic conditions. The tax system favours debt financing because interest, unlike dividends, is tax deductible. In assessing the cost of borrowing, the tax savings have to be taken into account.

(*continued*)

Table 5.1 (*continued*)

Corporate borrowers: comparison of debt and equity finance		
Existing capital structure	If the company already has a lot of debt (described as having a high 'gearing'), it may be able to obtain more finance only in the form of equity finance, by a fresh issue of shares. Gearing is the ratio of borrowings to shareholder funds (in effect, share capital and retained profits). High gearing means a greater burden of borrowings and the greater possibility of insolvency.	
Existing restrictions	The articles may restrict the company's ability to borrow.	The terms of existing facility agreements may restrict the taking of new loans or debt, at least without the existing lender's consent.

Part 2   Security

We looked in Part 1 at how a business can raise funds by borrowing money, known as debt finance. In this chapter, we look at how a business creates security over its assets, the different types of security, the process of registering security and the problems that result from a failure to do so.

5.11   Why grant security?

Ideally a business will repay the borrowed amounts to the lender in full and on time. Often the lender will require security over the borrower's assets in return for loaning money.

If the business fails to repay the loan as agreed then the lender can seize the secured assets, sell them and pay itself out of the proceeds of sale. Taking security is therefore advantageous for the lender, and often a prerequisite for a loan, as it lowers the risk of its not being repaid, even if it does not entirely eliminate that risk.

The business may benefit too from giving security, as the lender will usually allow the business to borrow money at a rate that is lower than would otherwise be the case. The downside for the business is that it must accept restrictions on the use of the asset or assets it has given as security. The reality is, however, that the business's need for the loan will outweigh any restrictions imposed. The type and extent of security and the terms on which it is granted are generally determined by agreement between the parties after negotiations.

5.12 Terminology

There is no consistency in the use of terminology for describing the security which a company may grant. The CA 2006 uses 'charge' as an umbrella term for most types of security, and in s 859A(7) specifically states that 'charge' includes 'mortgage'. In contrast, the Law of Property Act ('LPA') 1925 uses the term 'mortgage' as the umbrella term for security in that Act, defining this to 'include any charge or lien on any property'. The IA 1986 defines 'security' as 'any mortgage, charge, lien or other security'.

It is important, therefore, to check very carefully at the outset which legislation you are working with, and thus the precise meaning of the rules you are applying.

5.13 When sole traders, partnerships and LLPs borrow money

Most of the remainder of this chapter is relevant only to companies (and to a certain extent LLPs). Sole traders and general partnerships cannot grant floating charges, only fixed charges. These must be registered at HM Land Registry if they are over land.

LLPs can grant floating charges as well as fixed charges and the registration process is similar to that for companies.

5.14 When a company borrows money: initial considerations

As well as ensuring that the company has the power to borrow, the directors must make sure that the company has the power to grant security over its assets before entering into any security contracts on the company's behalf; otherwise they will be acting outside their authority and in breach of duty.

A company formed under the CA 2006 has unrestricted objects, unless specifically restricted by the company's articles of association (s30(1)). The Model Articles for private companies do not place any restriction on granting security. A company will therefore have an implied power to grant security for any borrowing. If the company has amended Model Articles or bespoke articles, these should be checked for any restrictions.

For a company formed before 1 October 2009, the objects of the company were set out in its old-style memorandum of association, and on that date became part of its articles. If the company's articles have not been updated to take account of the CA 2006, the memorandum must be checked to see that there is no restriction on the company granting security.

For both types of company, if there are any restrictions preventing the company from granting the security, the company's shareholders must first pass a special resolution under s 21 CA 2006 to amend the company's articles.

The directors should also ensure that they have the necessary authority to enter into any security contract on the company's behalf. For a company with Model Articles for a private company, the directors' authority is contained in MA 3. If the company has amended or bespoke articles, they must be checked for any restrictions on the directors acting in this situation.

5.15 When a company borrows money: initial considerations for the lender

The lender should make sure that there are no restrictions on the company granting security, and that the directors have the authority to act on behalf of the company in the transaction and that the people it is dealing with have actually been properly appointed as directors of the company. It should do this by inspecting the articles of the company, searching the company's records at Companies House and requesting copies of relevant board resolutions.

The lender should also search the company's records at Companies House to see if any charges have been registered already against the company's property, and ensure that there is sufficient value in that property to provide adequate security for the proposed loan. Under s 859I of the CA 2006, the Registrar of Companies must include a certified copy of the instrument creating the charge in the register, which is open to inspection by any person.

From the register, the lender will be able to discover:

(a) the date of creation of any existing charge;

(b) the amount secured;

(c) which property is the subject of the charge; and

(d) who holds that charge (ie who can enforce the charge).

If the lender is proposing to take a charge over land held by the company, it should also conduct a search at Land Registry to check the company's title to the land and to see if any pre-existing charges have been registered. Similarly, if a charge is to be taken over intellectual property rights such as a trademark, the lender should check the company's title to the intellectual property at the Intellectual Property Office.

A lender should also conduct a winding-up search by telephone at the Companies Court to check that no insolvency proceedings have been commenced against the company.

5.16 What assets may be secured?

Virtually all assets that a company (or LLP) might own may be offered as security for its borrowings. For example, they may grant security over:

(a) land, whether freehold or leasehold, and fixtures and fittings;

(b) tangible property, such as machinery, computers and stock;

(c) intangible property, such as money in a bank account, debts owed, any shares they own in other companies and intellectual property rights.

5.17 Types of security

The main types of security for a company or LLP are mortgages, fixed charges and floating charges.

5.17.1 Mortgages

This is the highest form of security. A lender would seek to take a mortgage over high-quality assets owned by the borrower, such as land, buildings, machinery, aircraft and ships, and even shares it owns in other companies. A mortgage, with the exception of land, involves the transfer of legal ownership from the mortgagor (the company/LLP) to the mortgagee (the lender); and although the mortgage gives the lender the right to immediate possession of the property, this is held in reserve and exercised only if the borrowed money is not repaid (ie if the borrower defaults). The title will be transferred back to the borrower when money has been repaid. A separate mortgage must be created over each asset. A mortgage taken over land is actually a charge by deed expressed to be by way of legal mortgage. The rights of the mortgagee over land include the rights to take possession of the land and to sell it.

5.17.2 Charges

This is a form of security which does not transfer legal ownership from the chargor (the borrower) to the chargee (also known as the charge holder) (the lender) and does not give the chargee the right to immediate possession of the property. A charge does, however, give the lender important rights over the asset should the borrower fail to repay the money borrowed. These are explained below. There are two different types of charge a company or LLP may grant: a fixed charge and a floating charge.

5.17.2.1 Fixed charges

A fixed charge may be taken over property such as machinery and shares owned by the company/LLP in other companies. The chargor must create a separate fixed charge over each asset. The effect of the charge is that the lender has control of the asset. For example, the chargor will not be permitted to dispose of the asset (eg, sell it) without the charge holder's consent. The charge holder will also require the chargor to keep the asset in good condition.

If the chargor gets into financial difficulties and goes into receivership or liquidation, the fixed charge holder will have the right to sell the asset and be paid out of the proceeds of the sale (to repay the outstanding amount of any borrowings) before any other claimants, such as unsecured creditors of the chargor, can claim the proceeds. This right of first claim over the proceeds makes a fixed charge a significant form of security for a lender.

It is also possible to create more than one fixed charge over the same asset. The effect is that the holder of the fixed charge which was created first will be able to sell the asset and pay itself out of the proceeds (see **5.17.6** for an explanation of priority of charges). The second fixed charge holder will then be able to pay itself out of the remainder.

5.17.2.2 Floating charges

Some assets belonging to a company/LLP, such as stock, are not suitable for a fixed charge because the company/LLP needs to sell them as part of doing business. If these assets were subject to a fixed charge, the company/LLP would need the charge holder's consent each time it wanted to sell any of them. Clearly this would be both unworkable and unwarranted, as selling its stock is what the company/LLP must do on a daily basis in order to operate its business and make money.

A floating charge is the solution to this problem. It secures a group of assets, such as stock, which is constantly changing. It is possible to create more than one floating charge over the same group of assets.

The three basic features of a floating charge are:

(a) they consist of an equitable charge over the whole or a class of the company/LLP's assets, such as stock;

(b) the assets subject to the charge are constantly changing; and

(c) the company/LLP retains the freedom to deal with the assets in the ordinary course of business until the charge 'crystallises'.

The assets subject to the floating charge are therefore identified generically, such as 'stock' or 'the undertaking', rather than specifying individual items as with a fixed charge, such as a particular building. Note that it is possible to take a floating charge even over all of the company/LLP's undertaking, which would be over all of the assets which make up the business run by the company/LLP.

It is the company/LLP's freedom to deal with the assets in particular which distinguishes the floating charge from other types of security.

A further characteristic of the floating charge is that on the occurrence of certain events, the floating charge will automatically *crystallise* over the assets charged. This will happen if:

(a) the chargor goes into receivership;

(b) the chargor goes into liquidation;

(c) the chargor ceases to trade; or

(d) any other event occurs which is specified in the charge document (the contract for the floating charge made between the chargor and the lender).

All of these events will prevent the chargor repaying, or make it less likely that it will be able to repay, the outstanding borrowings. On crystallisation the chargor can no longer deal with the assets covered by the charge. In effect the floating charge turns into a fixed charge. Think of a floating charge as something hovering, or floating, over the chargor's assets. It is not attached (fixed) to any particular asset until an event happens to cause it to crystallise, at which point it will descend on the assets and attach itself to them.

5.17.2.3 Book debts

Book debts are money owed to the company/LLP by its debtors. As an asset, book debts may be charged. As book debts vary over time, they are suitable for charging by way of a floating charge, and case law has established that book debts could also be secured by a fixed charge where the charge holder had control over both the debts and the proceeds once they were paid. This might arise, for example, where the charge holder allowed the company/LLP to collect the book debts, but then the company/LLP had to pay over the money to the charge holder to settle part of the debt owed to the charge holder. If, on the contrary, the company/LLP was able to use the proceeds from the book debts for its business purposes then this would indicate a floating charge.

5.17.2.4 Advantages of floating charges

One advantage of a floating charge from the chargor's viewpoint is that it allows it to deal with the secured assets on a day-to-day basis. Another is that, as a form of security which can attach to assets unsuited for a fixed charge or mortgage, it allows the chargor to maximise the amount that it is able to borrow. It is also advantageous that a floating charge may be taken over the whole of a company/LLP's business.

5.17.2.5 Disadvantages of floating charges

As a general rule, a fixed charge will take priority over a floating charge over the same assets.

 Example – priority of charges

Say that a fixed charge was granted over a factory owned by the borrowing company to a first lender. A second, different lender was then granted a floating charge by the same company over the whole of its undertaking (which would include the factory). If the company became insolvent and the factory was sold, the fixed charge holder (the first lender) would have priority over the proceeds of sale; only if there was money left over after the first lender's debts had been paid off in full would that go to the floating charge holder (the second lender).

A disadvantage of a floating charge from the viewpoint of the holder (the lender) is that the chargor is allowed to deal with the assets. The company could sell its existing stock and not purchase new stock to replace it, meaning that the lender does not have a charge over anything. So a floating charge over stock would be of little value in those circumstances. One solution to this problem is for the lender to take fixed charges over other assets of the business too. The more assets a charge holder takes a charge over, the better chance it has of being paid.

A further disadvantage is that certain other creditors have the right to claim money from the proceeds of sale of the assets covered by the floating charge if the company/LLP becomes insolvent before the charge holder itself gets the money. These include so-called 'preferential' creditors, who take priority over the holder of a floating charge but not over the holder of a fixed charge (see **8.17**).

In certain circumstances, under s 245 IA 1986 a liquidator or an administrator of an insolvent company may apply to have a floating charge set aside. If done, this would have the effect of removing the floating charge holder's priority over unsecured creditors of the company (see **5.17.6**).

5.17.3 Other security

There are other types of security or security-like agreements into which a company/LLP may enter. These include the following:

- personal guarantees: sometimes directors or partners in an LLP will give a personal guarantee for a loan, in case the lender is unable to recover the loan in full from the company/LLP. The individuals who give personal guarantees risk losing their personal assets if the business fails.

- a pledge, which arises where an asset is physically delivered by the debtor to the creditor to serve as security until the debtor has paid their debt. The creditor has the right to sell the asset to settle the debt owed, provided they give sufficient notice (which may be agreed in advance by the parties).

- a lien, which gives a creditor the right to physical possession of the debtor's goods or assets until the debt is paid. For example, a garage mechanic has the right to retain a business's van until any repairs have been paid for. There is no right to sell the assets to settle the debt owed.

- Retention of title: on a sale of goods, the buyer does not get full title to the goods until they pay the full price to the seller. If the buyer defaults then the goods are repossessed by the seller.

5.17.4 Key terms in a charging document

5.17.4.1 Security

This is one of the most important clauses in a charging document. It will state that the borrower charges the property to the lender and what the type of security is. The security might be in the form of a fixed charge or a floating charge, or might be a combination of the two, for example a fixed charge on anything owned by the borrower over which it is possible to take a fixed charge, and a further floating charge over the whole of the borrower's undertaking. The specific assets subject to each charge will also be listed.

5.17.4.2 Representations and warranties

The borrower will have to make a series of contractual statements relating to the assets which it is charging. This will be done with the intention of getting the borrower to reveal all relevant information about the assets. For example, the borrower will have to warrant that the property is free from any other charge. If there is another charge already over the asset then the borrower must disclose this or it will breach the contract and also give the lender the right to terminate the loan agreement.

5.17.4.3 Covenants

The borrower will have to make a series of covenants (contractual promises) relating to the assets it is charging. The covenants will seek to ensure that the value of the assets is maintained by the borrower, for example by stipulating that the borrower will conduct proper maintenance and arrange adequate insurance.

5.17.4.4 Enforcement and powers

The agreement will set out the circumstances in which the security becomes enforceable, for example if the loan payments are not made on time, if provisions of the charging document are breached or if the borrower gets into financial difficulty.

It will also set out the lender's powers, including the power to sell the assets which are the subject of the charge, to recover the debt due.

If the lender is a qualifying floating charge holder (QFCH), the lender will be empowered to appoint an administrator without petitioning the court (see **Chapter 8**).

5.17.4.5 Procedural matters for companies issuing debentures

It will usually be the directors' decision to borrow money in the company's name, and it is they who will negotiate with the lender the terms on which the loan is to be made and any security provided. A board resolution will usually be sufficient to authorise both the borrowing by the company and the grant of any security.

However, there may be problems over the ability of the directors to vote and count in the quorum on the resolution to borrow and grant security, particularly if the directors have been asked to guarantee the loan personally. The articles may prevent any director who has a personal interest (possibly all directors) from being involved in the decision to borrow. It may therefore be necessary to call a general meeting or to circulate written resolutions, either to suspend any prohibition in the articles by ordinary resolution, to allow the directors to count in the quorum or vote, or to change the articles by special resolution.

Once the directors have resolved to enter into the loan and grant security, the documents will be executed in accordance with the CA 2006 (see **5.17.11** for an explanation of how documents are validly executed).

5.17.4.6 Registration

A new and fundamentally different registration regime was introduced for charges created by a company on or after 6 April 2013. Whereas before then it was compulsory to register most charges, now the CA 2006 has introduced a voluntary system of registration. The company or a person 'interested in the charge' may decide to register it. However, because of the consequences of a failure to register a charge in the required time period (for example, the security may become void), in practice there is a huge incentive to register. The lender's solicitors will almost certainly register the charge to ensure that it is valid.

5.17.4.7 The registration process

Once the company has formally entered into the agreement containing the charge with the charge holder, the process outlined in **Figure 5.1** will take place.

Figure 5.1 Registering a charge

Within 21 days of creation of the charge, the company or any person 'interested in the charge' (which includes the charge holder) must file at Companies House a statement of particulars (usually form MR01), a certified copy of the instrument creating the charge (CA 2006, s 859A) and the fee.

Once the documents have been delivered, assuming everything is in order, the Registrar of Companies must register the charge (CA 2006, s 859A(2)) and include the certified copy of the charge on the register (CA 2006, s 859I(2)).

The Registrar must also give the person who delivered the documents a certificate of registration, which is conclusive evidence that the charge is properly registered (CA 2006, s 859I).

Form MR01 and the certified copy of the charging document will be put on the company's file, which is available for public inspection.

If the required documents are correctly delivered on time, the charge will be fully valid against another creditor of the company, or an administrator or a liquidator of the company.

A copy of the charging document and Form MR01 should be kept available for inspection (CA 2006, s 859P) at its registered office or SAIL (CA 2006, s 859Q). Failure to do this is a criminal offence, but it does not affect the validity of the charge.

If a fixed charge is taken over land then this must also be registered at the Land Registry, otherwise a buyer could acquire the land without being subject to the fixed charge, even if they actually knew of its existence.

5.17.4.8 Failure to register at Companies House

Failure to register the charge renders the charge void against a liquidator or an administrator of the company, and also against the company's other creditors (s 859H(3) CA 2006).

This means that the company is still obliged to repay the debt, and it is repayable immediately (s 859H(4)), but the lender cannot enforce the security – it is as if the security was not granted. The liquidator or administrator must ignore the original charge in determining how much creditors get and in what order, if the company goes insolvent. This would be disastrous for the original charge holder, of course, as it would lose its priority over the proceeds of sale of the asset and be treated the same as the other, unsecured, creditors. If the failure to register was due to the solicitor's mistake, it could well lead to a claim for negligence.

5.17.4.9 Late or inaccurate delivery

If the 21-day period for delivery of the required documents to Companies House is missed (note that weekends and bank holidays are included in the 21 days), or if the details supplied on the form are inaccurate, the same consequences apply as are explained at **5.17.4.8**, ie, the charge is void as against a third party.

There is a limited power under s 859F of the CA 2006 for the court to extend the 21-day period if the failure to deliver the required documents was accidental or due to inadvertence, or if it would not prejudice the position of other creditors or shareholders of the company. If an application is successful, the charge will have priority only from the date of actual registration, and it may therefore lose priority due to the delay if other charges have been registered in the meantime.

In addition to the court's power to order an extension of time, it has power under s 859M to allow rectification of any statement or notice delivered to the Registrar for any inaccurate details, and to order the replacement of a document on the register under s 859N if, for example, the charging document was defective or the wrong document was sent.

5.17.4.10 Redemption of the loan

When the loan secured by a registered charge is repaid by the borrower to the lender, a person with an interest in the registration of the charge (such as a director of the company) may, but is not obliged to, complete, sign and send Form MR04 to the Registrar of Companies at Companies House. In practice, this will be done to ensure the company's file is up to date. The Registrar will include a statement of satisfaction on the company's file.

If any entries were made against land at the Land Registry, these should now be removed.

5.17.4.11 Release of charge/sale of property

Sometimes the lender may decide to release the borrower's property from the charge or allow it to sell the asset covered by the charge. If this happens, a person with an interest in the registration of the charge (such as a director of the company) must complete, sign and send Form MR04 to the Registrar of Companies at Companies House. The Registrar will include a statement, either of the release of the charge or that the property no longer belongs to the company, on its file.

If any entries were made against the land at the Land Registry, these should now be removed.

5.17.5 Remedies of the debenture holder

See **Chapter 8** on administration.

5.17.6 Priority of charges

We have seen that more than one charge may attach to the same asset. Consequently, the priority of creditors over the proceeds of sale of that asset should the company become insolvent (in other words, which creditor gets its money first) is a very important matter. The order of priority is fixed by law.

It is a complex area, but to simplify considerably, provided the charges are all registered properly under s 859A of the CA 2006:

(a) A fixed charge or mortgage will take priority over a floating charge over the same asset, even if the floating charge was created before the fixed charge or mortgage.

(b) If there is more than one registered fixed charge or mortgage over the same asset, they have priority in order of their date of creation, not their date of registration.

(c) If there is more than one registered floating charge over the same asset, they have priority in order of their date of creation, not their date of registration.

⭐ *Example*

Eastham Limited has granted security to four different lenders, as described below:

1. *A fixed charge over its factory, dated 1 May 2020 and registered on 15 May 2020.*

2. *A floating charge over its whole undertaking, dated 1 November 2020 and registered on 1 April 2021.*

3. *A floating charge over its whole undertaking, dated 1 March 2021 and registered on 15 March 2021.*

4. *A fixed charge over its factory, dated 2 May 2021 and registered on 16 May 2021.*

The order of priority of charges as is follows:

1. *The lender with the fixed charge dated 1 May 2020 will rank first, meaning that it will be able to obtain possession of the factory and sell it to recover the money it is owed.*

2. *The lender with the fixed charge dated 2 May 2021 will rank second. It 'jumps over' the floating charges because it is a fixed charge. This means that it will be entitled to any money (up to the amount it is owed) left from the sale of the factory, after the first lender has taken what it is owed.*

3. *The lender with the floating charge dated 1 March 2021 will rank third, because the floating charge created on 1 November 2020 was not registered within 21 days, meaning that it is void as against third parties. Even if the court were to extend the time for registration beyond 21 days, the November charge would have priority only from the date of actual registration. It is entitled to any money left from the sale of the factory after the fixed charge holders have taken what they are owed. It will also be entitled to the company's other assets, because the charge was taken over the whole of the company's undertaking.*

4. *The floating charge dated 1 November 2020 is likely to be void for lack of registration. Even if the court extended the period for registration (which is rare), this charge would will rank last, and the lender would be entitled to any money left from the sale of the company's assets once the other floating charge holder had taken what it is owed by the company. If the court did not extend the period for registration, the charge would be void and this lender would join the pool of unsecured creditors.*

Lenders generally only want to enforce their security when a company is in financial difficulties, and often the company will be insolvent and will not have enough money to repay the debts secured by the charges.

5.17.7 Subordination

It is possible for creditors to enter into an agreement between themselves to alter the order of priority of their charges. This is known as subordination and the agreement is known as a deed of priority; it is executed by the creditors concerned and sometimes the company. This might happen, for example, if the holder of a fixed charge allowed a bank to have priority for its floating charge. Why would the bank do this? Perhaps the bank would only advance new funds to allow the borrower to continue to trade if the bank could have priority.

5.17.8 Negative pledge

A floating charge ranks behind a later fixed charge or mortgage over the same asset, provided that later fixed charge or mortgage is properly registered. In order to prevent this from happening, it is usual to include in the floating charge documentation what is called a 'negative pledge' clause. This clause prohibits the company from creating later charges with priority to the floating charge (ie fixed or mortgage) without the floating charge holder's permission. If a subsequent lender takes a charge over the same asset and has actual knowledge of the negative pledge clause then the subsequent lender's fixed charge will be subordinate to the original floating charge.

In practice, the existence of a negative pledge clause is disclosed by completing a section of Form MR01, sent to Companies House, and the clause itself will be included in the certified copy of the charging document which is delivered to the Registrar.

It is important to note that constructive knowledge by the subsequent charge holder, for example merely because the existence of the negative pledge clause was revealed on Form MR01, is not enough. However, if the subsequent charge holder conducts a search of the company's records at Companies House (as will usually be the case as part of checking the company's suitability) then it will come across the certified copy of the charging document containing this clause. The subsequent charge holder will therefore have the required *actual* knowledge and will not have priority over the floating charge. It is also possible that the subsequent charge holder will be liable for the tort of inducing breach of contract.

In order to protect itself from being in such a situation, the agreement for the subsequent charge should contain a covenant (contractual promise) by the company to the effect that there are no earlier charges which are subject to a negative pledge clause. If this is not true, the company will be in breach of that agreement and it may be terminated immediately.

5.17.9 Execution of documents

It is important that companies use the correct execution clause when signing or executing a document or it may be invalid. This is important with every contract or deed, not just loan agreements and security documents. The formalities for executing documents are set out in ss 43–46 CA 2006.

5.17.10 Contracts

Contracts can be entered into by a company using the company seal or on behalf of the company by a person acting under its authority, express or implied (s 43 CA 2006). This will often be a director, but could also be another employee if entering into contracts is part of their role.

5.17.11 Deeds

Under s 44 CA 2006, a company can execute a deed by:

- affixing its seal; or
- by the signatures of:

- ○ two authorised signatories (a director or company secretary); or
- ○ a director of the company in the presence of a witness who attests the signature.

Finally, the document must be delivered as a deed, which means that it must be clear on the face of it that it is intended to be a deed.

The position with regard to the company seal is more complicated if the company has the Model Articles: MA 49 states that if a company wishes to use its seal to execute a document, the document must also be signed by at least one authorised person (director, company secretary or other authorised person) in the presence of a witness who attests the signature.

Sample questions

Question 1

A private company has the Model Articles of Association with no amendments. The company proposes to borrow £500,000 from a bank. The loan agreement will be signed as a contract by the company. The company does not have a company seal or a company secretary.

Which of the following best describes the minimum execution formalities required in order for the loan agreement to be binding on the company?

A   The loan agreement must be signed by two directors, whose signatures must be witnessed.

B   The loan agreement must be signed by the company by a person acting under its authority express or implied.

C   The loan agreement must be signed by two authorised signatories, whose signatures must be witnessed.

D   The loan agreement must be signed by two directors or one director in the presence of a witness who attests the director's signature.

E   The loan agreement must be signed by the company by two directors acting under its authority express or implied.

Answer

Option B is correct. This is the minimum required for a contract as set out in s 43 CA 2006. The other options involve two signatories or one signatory and a witness, which is unnecessary for a contract.

Question 2

A bank has loaned money to a company on two occasions, and both times requested a charge over the company's assets. The company has also granted security to another lender, a building society. Details of the security are set out below:

1 May 2019: The bank lent the company £250,000, secured by way of a fixed charge over the company's factory. The charge was not registered.

1 June 2020: The bank extended the company's overdraft facility. In return, the company executed a debenture in favour of the bank in which it granted it a floating charge over the company's whole undertaking, to secure all monies outstanding to the bank at any time. The charge was correctly registered at Companies House.

20 January 2022: The building society was granted a fixed charge over the company's factory to secure a loan of £50,000. The charge was correctly registered at Companies House.

Will the building society's charge take priority over the bank's charges?

A   Yes, because it was correctly registered at Companies House and the bank's charges were not.

B   Yes, because the bank's fixed charge is void and the building society's charge, because it is fixed, takes priority over the bank's floating charge.

C   No, because the bank's second charge secures all monies outstanding to the bank at any time and was created before the building society's charge, so the bank will take priority.

D   No, because the bank's charges were created first and one of them was registered so the building society's charge must take second place to the bank's charges.

E   No, because the bank's second charge secures all monies outstanding to the bank at any time and therefore the bank will take priority.

Answer

Option B is correct. If a charge is not registered, it is still valid and enforceable between the chargor and chargee, but void against the liquidator and third parties. Fixed charges always rank ahead of floating charges, even if the floating charge was registered first. Fixed charges rank in order of date of creation, as long as they are registered.

Question 3

A company has the Model Articles of Association with no amendments and an issued share capital of £100,000 ordinary £1 shares. There are two shareholders, a woman and a man. The woman owns 50,001 shares and the man, with whom the woman sometimes has a difficult working relationship, owns 49,999 shares. The company is seeking finance – it needs £200,000 to expand its business (the import and distribution of road bikes). The company will either borrow the money or issue 50,000 new shares to the man's wife for £200,000.

Which of the following best describes which is the better option in this case?

A   A loan would be better because interest rates are currently low.

B   A loan would be better because allotting more shares would make it difficult for the woman to pass or block ordinary resolutions.

C   A loan would be better because allotting more shares would make it more difficult for the woman to pass special resolutions.

D   Allotting more shares would be better because the company will not have to pay interest.

E   Allotting more shares to the man's wife would be better because the current shareholders already know her.

Answer

Option B is correct. Currently the woman can block and pass ordinary resolutions alone, because she has 50.001% of the shares. The allotment of more shares would dilute her voting power to less than 50% of the shares, so she could neither pass nor block an ordinary resolution without either the man or his wife voting in the same way. Option C is wrong because she will not be able to pass special resolutions alone after the allotment but cannot do so before the allotment either. Options A, D and E sounds plausible but these are weak arguments compared with option B.

6 Partnership

SQE1 syllabus

This chapter, combined with **Chapter 1**, will enable you to achieve the SQE1 Assessment Specification in relation to Functioning Legal Knowledge concerned with the following:

- business and organisational characteristics (partnership/LLP)

- procedures and documentation required to form a partnership/LLP and other steps required under companies and partnerships legislation to enable the entity to commence operating:
  - constitutional documents
  - Companies House filing requirements.
- partnership decision-making and authority of partners:
  - procedures and authority under the Partnership Act 1890
  - common provisions in partnership agreements

Note that for SQE1, candidates are not usually required to recall specific case names, or cite statutory or regulatory authorities. In this chapter, statutory references are provided for information only, apart from the references to s 36 Partnership Act 1890, which you may need to recognise in an assessment.

Learning outcomes

By the end of this chapter you will be able to:

- advise on whether a partnership exists;
- understand the default contractual terms set out in the Partnership Act 1890 and when it is advisable to vary them;
- advise partners or an individual partner on the extent of their liability for debts incurred by the firm or by just one of the partners;
- understand the nature of limited liability partnerships and the legislation governing them; and
- understand the default contractual terms which govern limited liability partnerships in the absence of contrary agreement and when it is advisable to vary them.

Part 1   General Partnerships

6.1   Introduction

You were introduced to the most common forms of business medium in **Chapter 1**. **Chapters 2** to **5** expanded on the company as a business medium, and now we turn to partnerships. In practice, you will encounter many partnerships, and are likely to work for a firm which operates either as a general partnership or a limited liability partnership, both of which are explained in detail in this chapter. The first part of this chapter concentrates on general partnerships, governed by the Partnership Act 1890 ('PA 1890'). When you hear or see a reference to a partnership, this will almost certainly mean a general partnership; people almost always use the term 'limited liability partnership' or 'LLP' when they are instead referring to limited liability partnerships.

6.2 What is a partnership?

Under s 1 PA 1890, a partnership comes into existence when two or more persons are 'carrying on a business in common with a view of profit'. Often the partners are unaware that they are in a partnership, because as far as they are concerned, they have merely started a business with somebody else, and have not addressed their minds to the legal definition of their business. Other partners in other partnerships will be well aware that they are part of a partnership, will have sought legal advice prior to commencing business, and will almost certainly have a partnership agreement which has been drafted with their particular circumstances in mind. Partners can be individuals or companies, and the partnership does *not* have a separate legal personality from that of the partners.

Section 2 of the PA 1890 contains rules for determining the existence of a partnership, but none of the guidelines set out in the section are conclusive. For example, it states that the sharing of gross returns does not in itself create a partnership, and that the receipt by a person of a share of the profits of a business is prima facie evidence that they are a partner but that this does not in itself make that person a partner. Factors which help to determine whether two or more people are carrying on a business in common are:

* Do the individuals all take part in decision-making?

* Whose names are on the title deeds of any property?

* How are profits shared?

It is important to remember, though, that there is no one factor which will determine whether a partnership exists or whether a certain person is one of the partners. It is a matter of looking at all the facts, taking into account all of the guidance set out in s 2, and reaching a decision on the particular circumstances, with an understanding of how businesses generally function. It is also important that the s 1 definition is met – the partners need to 'carry on a business in common'. Agreeing to work together in partnership is not sufficient if working together does not constitute carrying on a business in common (ie embarking on a business together).

★ Example – is there a partnership and who are the partners?

Three companies, Aarons Limited, Butlers Limited and Collins Limited have agreed to combine their know-how and existing technology to develop, produce and distribute dictation software. They have not signed an agreement but they have been working together on the early developmental stages of the project. Each company has its own area of responsibility. Aarons Limited made a capital contribution at the outset and has contributed know-how in the early stages of development, although its day-to-day involvement and particular expertise will only be required in the later phases of development. Representatives from each company meet on a quarterly basis to discuss progress and to take decisions affecting future development strategy. The parties propose to share any profits of the new venture which may arise in proportion to their initial capital contributions.

There seems to be a partnership in existence because the parties are carrying on business in common: they appear to share responsibility for the business and for decisions which affect the business. This is with a view to a profit because the parties have agreed how they will share any profits. But are all the companies partners? At the outset, Aarons Limited was almost certainly a partner, because it contributed capital, shared decisions, had its own agreed area of responsibility and agreed to share the profits of the new venture with the other partners. Despite not having day-to-day input, Aarons Limited does continue to be involved in decisions by virtue of the quarterly meetings. This indicates that it is involved in the management of the business, albeit on a part-time basis. It would be worth enquiring who owns any partnership assets, who has the right to examine the accounts for the venture, the responsibility for sharing losses and the right to veto the introduction of a new partner. The answers to these questions will help to shed light on whether the companies are all partners.

6.3 Partnership Act 1890

Partnerships are governed by the PA 1890, which provides a default contract. This default contract will govern the relationship between the partners unless they have agreed any specific terms, which will usually override the provisions of the PA 1890. Note that any agreement between the parties does not have to be written: an oral agreement is just as valid as a written agreement, but a written partnership agreement is of course more desirable because it leaves less scope for disagreement. Agreements can also be implied by conduct, in circumstances where a partner has acted in a certain way over a period of time and the other partners have not objected.

The PA 1890 is over 130 years old and does not reflect modern business practice, and never has included default terms to suit every partnership. It is likely, then, that when partners enter into a partnership agreement, they will want its terms to override many of the provisions in the PA 1890.

Whilst most of the PA 1890 can be overridden by agreement, some sections cannot. The most significant examples to note are ss 1 and 2, which govern when a partnership comes into existence, and ss 5–18, which cover the relationship between the partners and third parties, and in particular, liability for debts.

6.4 Why operate as a partnership?

Partnerships can be started with no formality. As soon as two people run a business together, they are likely to be in a partnership, even if they are not aware of it. In contrast, companies are heavily regulated by the CA 2006 and other legislation, and must adhere to various accounting and administrative requirements. This is the 'flipside' of benefiting from limited liability for the company's debts. Partners do not enjoy limited liability for the partnership debts, but do not have to adhere to extensive administrative and accounting requirements and make so much information public. Partners do not have to enter into a written agreement if they do not want to, and this lack of formality and the lack of accounting requirements mean that partners can concentrate on their trade rather than spending time and money on legal and administrative matters. There may also be tax advantages to running a partnership, depending on the business of the partnership and the partners' individual circumstances.

The advantages and disadvantages of different forms of business medium are explored at **1.9**.

6.5 Starting a partnership

No formalities are required to start a partnership. However, it is always beneficial to seek legal advice when starting a partnership. The partners need to be made aware of the default terms which govern the relationship between them, as set out in the PA 1890, if they do not make alternative provision. Partners are likely to want a written agreement including contractual terms which better reflect the way the partnership will be run, or which ensure a fairer distribution of the partnership's wealth, than the PA 1890 provides.

It is crucial for solicitors to understand the provisions of the PA 1890. This is so that they can advise on the terms which will be implied into the contract between the parties if they have not agreed any terms themselves. Often, partners will have agreed certain terms but not all of the terms which they needed to include in order for the partnership to run smoothly, or perhaps they have agreed terms but have misunderstood each other during negotiations so it is not clear exactly what has been agreed. For this reason, it is always better to ensure that the parties' understanding of what has been agreed is set out in writing in the partnership agreement. When solicitors are instructed to draft a partnership agreement, they need to ensure that it fully reflects the client's wishes *and* needs. It is impossible to do this without knowing which terms will be implied into the contract by default.

Below, we consider the clauses that solicitors should consider including in a partnership agreement for a client. This includes an explanation of what the PA 1890 will provide in the absence of partners agreeing certain terms. Sometimes the partnership agreement will just repeat what the PA 1890 states on a particular point, but it is still worth including the provision in the agreement because it is useful for partners to have a complete document setting out all of their rights and obligations, rather than having to look at both the partnership agreement and the PA 1890.

6.6 The partnership agreement

6.6.1 Name

The partnership will need a name, even if it is just the names of the partners. It is a good idea to insert the name of the partnership and any trading name into the partnership agreement, so that it is clear what the parties have agreed. Partnership names must not:

- include 'limited', 'Ltd', 'limited liability partnership', 'LLP', 'public limited company' or 'plc';
- be offensive;
- be the same as an existing trademark; or
- contain a 'sensitive' word or expression, or suggest a connection with government or local authorities, without permission.

6.6.2 Place and nature of business

The partners will need a place of business. Often they will rent premises, or may even buy them, although this would be a big step to take before the partners even know whether the business will be successful. The agreement may set out the partnership's place of business, area of geographical operation and the nature of business.

6.6.3 Commencement and duration

A partnership begins when the definition in s 1 PA 1890 is satisfied, not when the parties decide that it has commenced. In that sense, it seems pointless to include a commencement date in a partnership agreement. However, it is useful to insert a date to make it clear when the parties believe that the particular rights, responsibilities and obligations contained in that particular agreement will commence. Solicitors should advise clients that if they begin to work on partnership business, even just planning rather than actually trading, before the commencement date shown on the agreement, the partnership may come into existence on the earlier date. The terms set out in the PA 1890 will apply until the commencement date set out in the partnership agreement.

Some partnership agreements are fixed term, so it will be clear from the terms of the contract when the partners expect the partnership to end. Often partners will enter into a fixed term partnership agreement when the purpose of the partnership is to achieve a specific aim, and, once that has been achieved, the partnership will end. If the partners instead carry on in business after the expiry of the fixed term, and do not enter into a new agreement, they are presumed to be partners on the same terms as before (s 27 PA 1890). Most partners, however, will want their business to continue indefinitely, or as long as there are two partners. You can read about how such partnerships come to an end at **6.6.12**.

6.6.4 Work input

Under the PA 1890, partners may take part in the management of the business, but they are not required to do so. This means that the partnership agreement should set out each partner's working hours, or state that they must work full-time for the business, so that it is clear what is required of each partner. In the absence of such a provision, it might be difficult for the other partners to argue that one partner should be working more. A common clause in partnership agreements is to state that a partner must devote the whole of their time and attention to the business. It is also advisable to state that partners must not engage in any other business whilst they are a partner, so that they are not distracted by other commitments. Non-compete clauses are common, although one will be implied by default under the PA 1890 in the absence of express agreement (see **6.7**).

The agreement should set out holiday entitlement, sickness and maternity and paternity provisions. Such matters are not included in the PA 1890, so there is no default position regarding these matters.

6.6.5 Roles

The partnership agreement should set out each partner's role. The partnership can only function effectively if each partner is aware of the full scope of their duties and responsibilities. Sometimes there may be restrictions on what partners are allowed to do. For example, under the partnership agreement, they may only be able to authorise financial transactions up to a certain value. If any partner breaches a restriction setting out the scope of their authority, they will be in breach of the partnership agreement. Failure to carry out their duties as set out in the partnership agreement may also be a reason for expulsion. Therefore, if the parties wish to include the right to expel one of the other partners on the basis of breach of the partnership agreement, they should set out clearly details of their role, duties and responsibilities.

6.6.6 Decision-making

With three exceptions, all decisions in a partnership must be taken by majority (s 24 PA 1890). The three exceptions are:

- changing the nature of the business (s 24 PA 1890);

- introducing a new partner (s 24 PA 1890); and

- changing the terms of the partnership agreement (s 19 PA 1890, and also the general contractual principle that contracts can only be varied with the consent of all the parties).

All of these three decisions can only be made unanimously.

Clearly it would be cumbersome to have a partnership vote for every decision the partnership needs to make. Therefore, responsibility for certain decisions will be delegated to the appropriate partner or employee.

Partners may decide that in their partnership, there should be more types of decision which can only be taken by unanimous agreement. Whilst they may believe that this reduces the risk of their fellow partners making rash decisions which they are powerless to stop, it can also make decision-making more cumbersome and more likely to result in deadlock, so it is important to weigh up whether it would be helpful in the long run to include more decisions which must be taken unanimously.

6.6.7 Financial input

The partnership will need money to start operating. It will need to buy or rent premises, and perhaps buy stock, and it will probably need money for utility bills and salaries. The partners will usually all contribute a sum of money to enable the partnership to start operating. These initial contributions are classed as capital. The partners may also take out a bank loan to finance the partnership.

The agreement should set out the amount of the partners' initial capital contributions and whether they will be obliged to contribute more capital in the future.

6.6.8 Shares in income and capital profits and losses

Under the PA 1890, the partners share equally in the capital and profits of the business. The initial capital of the business is the money the partners contribute to the business, and capital profits are one-off gains, such as an office building increasing in value. Income profits are generally those profits which are recurring in nature, such as trading profit, or rent received by a partnership that owns properties.

Clearly, however, equal shares may not reflect what is fair or what the parties have agreed. Often, if the parties have contributed different amounts to the partnership's capital, they will decide that they should own the partnership capital in those same proportions. They will need to decide whether they should also own any capital profits in the same proportions as their initial contributions. Any clause setting out that the partners share capital in unequal proportions will vary the default position set out in the PA 1890 (although case law has established that it can sometimes be inferred from a course of conduct that the partners own capital profits in unequal shares). The partnership agreement might provide for interest to be paid on capital contributions, to encourage investment and to reward the partners for contributing capital to the partnership.

The partnership agreement should also state the proportions in which income profits (after any salaries and interest payable on capital) are to be shared. Often the partners' share of income profits will depend on their working hours: a partner who spends more time working for the partnership will take more of the income profits. If the partners do not agree how they will share income profits, under the PA 1890, they are deemed to share them equally.

There should also be a provision in the agreement stating what happens if the partnership makes a loss. If this happens, will any salaries and interest on capital still be awarded? Will the partners share the losses equally or not? Under the PA 1890, the default position is that the partners will share losses equally.

6.6.9 Drawings and salaries

Partners are not employees. They own the business, and the income profits which partners receive are known as drawings. The partnership agreement should set out how much each partner is allowed to 'draw down' in any given period, usually a month. In the absence of agreement, as we have seen, partners are entitled to share equally in income profits. In some partnerships, some partners also receive a salary to reflect the work they do for the business, while other partners may not receive a salary at all, but share in any surplus profit.

6.6.10 Ownership of assets

The partners must ensure that the partnership agreement sets out how the assets the partnership uses are owned. Buildings and land will all have title deeds showing the legal owners of the property (although there may be a dispute as to who the beneficial owners are); other assets, such as stock and machinery, will not. Sometimes the partnership will use an asset belonging to one of the partners. That partner may always view the asset as belonging to them, but, perhaps as a result of some miscommunication or different view of what is fair, the other partners may believe that, over time, it has become partnership property. Such issues may arise when a partner leaves a partnership and the assets are being valued, or perhaps when a partner is trying to calculate their tax liability or whether they can benefit from a certain tax relief.

6.6.11 Expulsion

Under the default provisions of the PA 1890, no majority of partners may expel another partner unless the partners have expressly agreed to this (usually in a written partnership agreement) (s 25). This effectively means that it is impossible to expel a partner without an express agreement allowing the other partners to do so, since no partner is likely to agree to their own expulsion. Partnership agreements will often therefore contain an expulsion clause, allowing the partners to expel one of their number if they have conducted themselves in a certain way. This will sometimes be linked to poor performance.

6.6.12 Dissolution

Dissolution of a partnership can be described as the partnership ending. That does not necessarily mean that the partners will stop trading. It just means that the contractual relationship between those partners will come to an end. Even if all but the outgoing partner carry on in business together on the same terms, the original partnership is technically dissolved.

It is better for the partners to provide for dissolution in the partnership agreement, by setting out under what circumstances a partner can retire or when the partnership will come to an end. This gives partners more control than relying on the default position in the PA 1890, which is that any partner may end the partnership at any time by giving notice of their intention to do so to all of the other partners.

A partnership which continues indefinitely until notice is given under the PA 1890 is known as a partnership at will. Under the PA 1890, there is no requirement for the notice to be of a certain length of time, or for the notice to be in writing (unless the partnership agreement is a deed). The effect of this is that a partner can end the partnership with immediate effect by merely saying to the other partners that they wish the partnership to end. This is clearly an impractical and unworkable way to run a business, so it is important that solicitors advise clients to include a notice period and also stipulate that notice must be given in writing.

A partner leaving a partnership is known as retirement, and it just means leaving the partnership – it is nothing to do with a partner stopping work altogether or claiming a pension.

When any business starts trading, it takes some time for the business to get up and running and it will often make a loss initially. If a partner were to leave a partnership during these early stages, it would often be disastrous for the business. For that reason, it is also advisable to include a provision stating that notice to retire from the partnership cannot be given in, say, the first year of trading. This gives the partnership the chance to become established.

Under the PA 1890, a partnership is dissolved:

- when a partner retires (although the partnership agreement can provide that the other partners carry on in business, which is explained further below) (s 26);

- on expiry of a fixed term (s 32); or

- by the death or bankruptcy of any of the partners (s 33); or

- if the partners give notice of dissolution to a partner who has (by order of the court) granted a charge over their share of the partnership property, for a debt owed by them alone and not the partnership as a whole (s 33).

Sections 32 and 33 can be disapplied by the partnership agreement, and, as we have seen, partnership agreements can contain notice provisions which remove the partners' right to dissolve the partnership with immediate effect.

Partnerships also dissolve automatically if something happens which makes it unlawful for the business of the firm to be carried on (s 34 PA 1890). An example would be losing a licence which is needed in order for the partnership business to operate. This section cannot be disapplied in the partnership agreement.

Finally, the partners can also apply to the court under s 35 PA 1890 for an order that the partnership is dissolved if:

- a partner becomes permanently incapable of performing their part of the partnership contract;
- a partner's conduct is calculated to be prejudicial to the business;
- a partner wilfully or persistently breaches the partnership agreement;
- the partnership can only be carried on at a loss; or
- the court thinks that, for other reasons, it is just and equitable to order that the partnership be dissolved.

Clearly it would be better to include clear provisions allowing partners to expel one of their number rather than relying on s 35.

6.6.13 The effect of dissolution

Automatic dissolution of the partnership is undesirable. It means that, unless the partners all agree otherwise, the partnership must end, all the assets must be sold (or the partnership sold as a going concern), and the outgoing partner has to receive their share. In fact, an outgoing partner can insist on the business being sold under s 39 PA 1890, so the other partners do not necessarily have the option of continuing in business and just paying the outgoing partner for their share. For this reason, it is important to ensure that the partnership agreement states that in the event that a partner leaves, the remaining partners will continue in partnership. This is called partial dissolution – the partnership is technically dissolved, but will continue seamlessly with one less partner.

There should also be specific provisions setting out whether the other partners must buy the outgoing partner's share, or whether they merely have the option to do so, how the partnership share of the outgoing partner should be valued, and when that should be paid. It is useful to include a provision stating that the outgoing partner will be paid in instalments, so that it is more likely that the other partners will be able to afford to buy them out. Finally, there should be a provision containing an indemnity in favour of the outgoing partner if their liabilities were taken into account when their partnership share was valued. Please see **6.13**, particularly the example, which shows how an outgoing partner's share is calculated.

If the partnership agreement does not address the issue of payment for the outgoing partner's share, the outgoing partner is entitled to either interest at a rate of 5% per annum on the value of their partnership share until they receive their share from the other partners, or such sum as the court may order representing the share of profits made which is attributable to the use of their share.

⭐ Example – dissolution

The partners in RST partnership are Raoul, Samina and Ted. Raoul has told the other partners that he wants to leave the partnership. There is a partnership agreement, but the partners drafted it themselves without legal advice and it does not address dissolution. Raoul and the other partners are on reasonably good terms, but Raoul needs his money out of the partnership very soon so that he can start a new business. Unfortunately, Samina and Ted cannot afford to buy Raoul out of the partnership straight away. They will need up to a year to raise the money. Raoul needs his money before then so will insist (under s 39 PA 1890) on all of the partnership's assets being sold. This means that Samina and Ted will lose their business as they will have to sell it to a third party, given that they cannot afford it themselves. It would have been better to include a provision in the partnership agreement allowing Samina and Ted time to buy Raoul out of the partnership in instalments.

6.6.14 Goodwill

Goodwill can be described as a business's reputation and the value of its clients and contacts. When a business is sold as a going concern, part of the purchase price will be for the business's goodwill, because the business is up and running and can continue as before, retaining its clients and reputation. Goodwill is difficult to value, but commonly, two years' profit is taken as the value for goodwill. If the partnership's assets are sold individually to be used elsewhere, goodwill will not be part of the equation. Clearly, it is a huge advantage to partners who wish to sell a partnership business if they can sell it as a going concern, because part of its value will be goodwill. Partners can increase the likelihood of the partnership being sold as a going concern when the partnership is to be completely dissolved by including terms in the partnership agreement that build in some time for partners to find a buyer rather than having to sell the assets individually to raise money quickly.

6.6.15 Distribution of proceeds of sale

Under s 44 PA 1890, when a partnership business is sold, the proceeds of sale of the business or its assets are applied as follows (unless the parties have decided otherwise by agreement):

- First of all, creditors of the firm must be paid in full. If there is a shortfall, the partners must pay the balance from their private assets. They will share the losses in accordance with their partnership agreement.

- Secondly, partners who have lent money to the firm must be repaid the amount outstanding on the loan, including interest.

- Thirdly, partners must be paid the share of the partnership's capital to which they are entitled.

- Lastly, any surplus is shared between the partners in accordance with the terms of their partnership agreement.

All of the partners, unless they are bankrupt, have authority to act in winding up the business's affairs (s 38 PA 1890). If any of the partners are bankrupt or deceased, the trustee in bankruptcy or personal representative can also make such an application.

6.6.16 Restraint of trade

It is usual for partnership agreements to contain a restraint of trade clause which seeks to restrict outgoing partners in their business dealings once they have left the partnership. There is no implied restraint of trade clause in the PA 1890. A restraint of trade clause will only be enforceable if it protects a legitimate business interest, for example, business contacts, goodwill or confidential information, and is no wider than is reasonable to protect that interest, in term of duration, geographical area and scope.

A restraint of trade clause is a blanket description which includes non-compete clauses, non-solicitation clauses and non-dealing clauses. Non-compete clauses seek to prevent former partners from competing with the partnership business. Non-solicitation clauses prevent former partners from soliciting business from the partnership's clients (ie approaching them directly) or offering employment to their employees. This does not stop customers or employees from approaching the former partner and entering into a contract as a result. Non-dealing clauses are more restrictive, and prevent the outgoing partner from entering into contracts with clients, former clients or employees of the partnership that they have just left, whether as a result of the former partner approaching the employee or client or the other way round.

6.6.17 Dispute resolution

It is useful to include a provision stating that in the event of a dispute between the partners, the partners must use arbitration or another form of alternative dispute resolution rather than more formal court methods to resolve certain matters. Usually, those matters would be those regarding the interpretation or the application of the agreement, rather than factual disputes over the running of the business. This may mean the partners can resolve any disputes more quickly and cheaply than through the courts.

6.7 Partners' responsibilities under the PA 1890

Partners have certain rights and responsibilities towards each other because of the partnership relationship.

Under common law, partners owe a duty of the utmost fairness and good faith towards one another. Specific duties falling under this principle are contained in ss 28 to 30 PA 1890. Partners:

- must be completely open with one another regarding any relevant information regarding the partnership;

- must account to the firm for any private profits they have earned without the other partners' consent from any transaction concerning the partnership; and

- must not compete with the firm: this is classed as carrying on any business of the same nature as and competing with that of the firm. If the partner does so without the other partners' consent, that partner must account for and pay over to the firm all profits made by them in that competing business.

Section 24 PA 1890 also provides that the partners must:

- bear a share of any loss made by the business, in accordance with the terms of their partnership agreement; and

- indemnify fellow partners who have borne more than their share of any liability or expense connected with the partnership.

If there is a partnership agreement, this will undoubtedly contain other duties and responsibilities which the partners can enforce against one another.

6.8 When is the firm liable to third parties?

6.8.1 Contracts

Contracts may be made by all of the partners acting together (eg they all sign a lease of business premises) or by just one of the partners.

6.8.2 Actual authority

Under s 6 PA 1890, the firm is bound by any contract or deed entered into by partners (or employees, but here we will concentrate on partners) in the firm's name, provided that the partner's actions were authorised by the partners. An action may be authorised in various ways:

- The partners may have acted jointly in making the contract;

- Express actual authority: the partners may have *expressly* given one of the partners permission to enter into a particular transaction or type of transaction, or instructed them to enter into a particular contract on behalf of the firm. For example, one of the partners may have the responsibility, under the partnership agreement, for purchasing raw materials. That partner is then acting with actual authority when purchasing raw materials, and the firm is bound by any contract that the partner makes within the scope of that authority.

- Implied actual authority: the partners may have *impliedly* accepted that one or more partners have the authority to represent the firm in a particular type of transaction. If all the partners are involved in running the business without any limitations, it will be implied that each partner has authority, for example, to sell the firm's products in the ordinary course of business. Alternatively, authority may be implied by a regular course of dealing by one of the partners to which the other partners have not objected.

6.8.3 Apparent authority

The firm may be liable for actions which were not actually authorised but which may have appeared to an outsider to be authorised. This liability derives from application of the principles of agency law, based on the fact that each partner is an agent of the firm and of their fellow partners for the purposes of the partnership business. Even if between the partners there is an express or implied limitation on the partner's authority, the firm will be liable to third parties under s 5 PA 1890 when:

1. the transaction is one which relates to business of the kind carried on by the firm;

2. the transaction is one for which a partner in such a firm would usually be expected to have the authority to act;

3. the other party to the transaction did not know that the partner did not have authority to act; and

4. the other party deals with a person whom they know or believe to be a partner.

Points 3 and 4 concern the knowledge or belief of the third party who has dealt with the partner. Whether 3 and 4 are satisfied is a subjective test. Points 1 and 2 are an objective test of what would appear to an outsider to be the nature of the firm's business and what authority you would expect a partner in such a firm to have.

⭐ Example – apparent authority

Ursula, Verity and Wendy are in partnership, running a restaurant serving traditional British food like pies and fish and chips. Their partnership agreement states that they may each spend up to £1,000 on the partnership's credit card without authorisation from the other two partners. The partners have discussed expanding their food offering on several occasions, but each time they have agreed not to change what they offer, as it would weaken their brand. Wendy then goes to a trade fair and sees a top-of-the-range pizza oven at a very good price of £3,999. She purchases it, arranging for delivery to the partnership premises the following week. The oven is delivered and when Ursula and Verity return from holiday a week later, they find out about the oven and tell Wendy and the seller that they do not want the oven. The seller says that it is too late to cancel and refuses to take the oven back. Did Wendy have authority to purchase the oven?

Clearly Wendy did not have actual authority to purchase the oven. The partnership agreement only allows her to spend £1,000 alone, and during discussions the partners did not agree to the purchase and specifically decided not to branch out into other types of food. She may have apparent authority because:

- *the transaction almost certainly relates to business of the kind carried on by the firm, as the oven is used for cooking, although there could be an argument that it is for a different type of food that the restaurant did not serve; and*

- *arguably you would expect a partner at a trade fair to be able to spend money, although query whether £3,999 is too much for any partner to spend alone; and*

- *we do not know what the seller thought, but it is unlikely that the seller knew that Wendy did not have authority to act, as Wendy would be unlikely to disclose this; and*

- *we do not know whether the seller knew Wendy was a partner. We would need to ask the seller, or ask Wendy what she told the seller. Perhaps Wendy signed a contract describing herself as a partner, or gave the seller a business card? Perhaps, when Wendy gave the address for delivery, she said that it was her partnership address?*

We would need more information to know whether Wendy had apparent authority, but there is a strong argument that she did.

6.9 Personal liability

Where a partner has acted with apparent authority, the firm will be liable to the third party under the contract. In addition, the partner who has made the firm liable by virtue of their apparent authority is liable to indemnify their fellow partners for any liability or loss which they incur, because the partner has breached their agreement with their partners by acting without actual authority.

6.9.1 Liability in tort

Sometimes the firm (as well as the partner in question) is liable for a partner's act which is tortious in nature, for example, negligence. Under s 10 PA 1890, the firm is liable for any wrongful act or omission of a partner who acts in the ordinary course of the firm's business or with the authority of their partners.

6.9.2 Partners' liability for partnership debts

Given that partners have unlimited liability for partnership debts while they are partners, it is important to be aware of any circumstances in which they can escape liability or circumstances in which they may be unexpectedly liable. This will depend primarily on when the debt was incurred.

6.9.2.1 Before leaving the partnership

Each partner is liable jointly with the other partners for debts incurred by the partnership while they were a partner (s 9 and s 17 PA 1890). The Civil Liability (Contribution) Act 1978 allows the court to order a person to contribute towards the judgment debt of another person and also provides that recovering a judgment sum from one person does not bar the claimant from suing another person who is jointly liable for the same damage. These provisions effectively mean that partners are jointly and severally liable for the partnership's debts: a claimant can sue any or all of the partners, and collect the total damages awarded by a court from any or all of them, leaving the defendant(s) to seek a contribution from any the other partner(s).

Personal liability, as we have seen, is the big difference between companies and partnerships. It means that entering into partnership can sometimes be a risky business, because partners' personal assets are not safe from creditors. In practical terms, the situation is not as risky as it seems. Consider one of the most obvious examples of a business which is usually a partnership: the law firm. Whilst many law firms have become limited liability partnerships, most are still general partnerships, governed by the PA 1890 and any agreement between the parties. Yet the partners are happy to assume the risk of being a partner. This is because the main potential source of liability for solicitors is a professional negligence claim. Most of the time, these claims will be covered by professional indemnity insurance, and the partners will not be required to contribute much, if any, of the amount owed, because it will be covered by their insurance. A manufacturing business, in contrast, may have to buy millions of pounds worth of raw materials and manufacture a new product. If there is a sudden decrease in the need for such manufactured items in between the business purchasing the raw materials and manufacturing them, the business will be in debt. This would be catastrophic for the partners if the business were run as a partnership.

6.9.2.2 Novation agreements

In a novation agreement, a retiring partner will be released from an existing debt, by entering into a contract with the creditor and the other partners, and possibly an incoming partner. Under this contract of novation, the creditor will release the original partners from their liability under the contract and instead the firm as newly constituted will take over the liability. This is clearly advantageous to the retiring partner whilst disadvantageous to any incoming partner. An incoming partner will usually agree to this only as part of the package of terms on which they join the partnership.

It may be that a partner retires and no new partner joins. In this case, in order to ensure that the novation is contractually binding, either there must be consideration for the creditor's promise to release the retiring partner from the liability or the contract must be executed as a deed. Such agreements are rare since they reduce the number of people the creditor can sue if the partnership does not pay the debt, so the creditor will only agree to it if it benefits them in some other way.

A novation agreement must not be confused with an indemnity in relation to existing debts. Such an indemnity is an agreement between the retiring partner and the other partners. Since the firm's creditors will not be party to this agreement, they are not bound by it and can still sue the retired partner. It would then be for the retired partner to claim from the indemnifying partners to meet the liability.

It is not common for creditors to enter into novation agreements, so it is important not to overstate it as being a potential solution to a partner's continuing liability. Such agreements are most common in relation to ongoing liabilities such as loans, and almost unheard of for one-off debts.

6.9.2.3 After leaving the partnership

Once a partner has left the partnership, they will, as we have seen, remain liable for debts incurred while they were partner (unless there is a novation agreement releasing them from liability in relation to one or more of the debts). However, they will escape liability for any debts entered into *after* they had left the partnership as long as they comply with the requirements of s 36 PA 1890.

6.9.2.4 What does s 36 require?

Under s 36 PA 1890, anyone with whom the firm has dealt before must be given actual notice of the partner in question leaving. This means that they must be informed directly, rather than being notified by way of a notice in the newspaper or some other method of notification. If notice is not given, a person dealing with the firm is entitled to treat all apparent members of the firm as still being members.

Anyone who has not had dealings with the firm before the partner in question left must also be notified of the partner's retirement. This is done by placing a notice in the *London Gazette* (or the *Edinburgh Gazette* or *Belfast Gazette* for firms whose principal place of business is in Scotland or Northern Ireland rather than England and Wales). This notice in the Gazette acts as 'notice to the whole world' of the partner's departure.

Whenever solicitors are advising on liability for debts of the partnership, the first question should be 'When was the debt incurred?' This is because, in general, if the debt was incurred whilst the partner in question was still a partner, they will remain liable; if the debt was incurred after they left, they will escape liability as long as they have complied with s 36 PA 1890.

If the reason for ceasing to be a partner is death or bankruptcy (rather than retirement or expulsion), no notice of the event is required. The estate of the deceased or bankrupt partner is not liable for partnership liabilities incurred after the death or bankruptcy.

6.9.3 Holding out

When a creditor of a partnership has relied on a representation that a particular person was a partner in the firm (known as 'holding out'), they may be able to hold that person liable for the firm's debt (s 14 PA 1890). This would be the case even if the person had never been a partner or had retired before the contract was made. The holding out may be oral, for example, where the person is described as a partner in conversation, in writing (eg by leaving that partner's name on the firm's headed notepaper or by referring to them on the firm's website) or by conduct (eg that person representing the firm in a previous course of dealing). The representation may be made by that person or, provided it is made with the person's knowledge, by another person.

Any creditor who can establish that someone held themselves out or allowed themselves to be held out as a current partner, that they relied on the holding out and that they gave credit to the firm as a consequence will be able to sue that person for the debt owed by the firm. The flowchart in **Figure 6.1** should help you to ascertain whether a partner is liable or not.

⭐ *Example – complying with s 36 and holding out*

Hayley, Lucy and Liz set up in partnership in 2010. Hayley is emigrating and is leaving the partnership today. Lucy and Liz have written to every existing contact of the firm this morning to notify them of Hayley's retirement from the partnership. They have also placed an advertisement in the London Gazette *today, stating that Hayley has left the partnership.*

Unless Hayley holds herself out as being a partner in the future, or allows Lucy or Liz to do so, she will not be liable for debts of the partnership incurred after her departure. This is because Lucy and Liz have placed the required notice in the London Gazette *and have also notified existing contacts that Hayley has retired from the partnership.*

Examples of holding out are:

* *Hayley telling people she is a partner; or*

* *Hayley being aware of Lucy and Liz telling people that she is still a partner and not doing anything about it; or*

* *Hayley not objecting when Lucy and Liz fail to remove reference to her being a partner from the firm's website or headed paper.*

Note that Hayley should double check that Lucy and Liz have written to all existing contacts and also that the advertisement in the London Gazette *has been placed. This is because, whilst the PA 1890 does not stipulate who should place the notice and inform existing clients of the partner's retirement, it is Hayley who will suffer if it is not done. She could be liable in relation to any future contracts of the firm if the s 36 requirements are not complied with.*

Figure 6.1   Partners' liability for debts

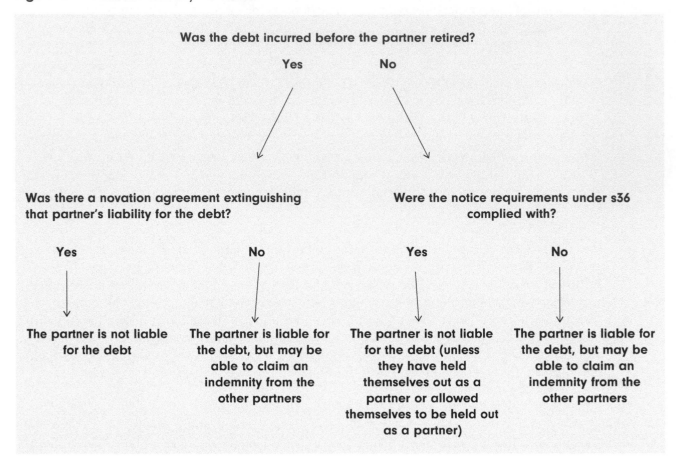

6.10   Enforcing the firm's liabilities

Any person who is seeking to enforce a liability of the firm will need to know who can be sued. There is a range of potential defendants.

- The claimant can sue the partner (or partners) with whom they made the contract because there is privity of contract between them. This will only be a problem for the partner if they acted without authority when they entered into the contract.

- The claimant can sue anyone who was a partner at the time when the debt was incurred. That partner can then claim an indemnity from their partners (under s 24 PA 1890 or possibly under the partnership agreement) so that the partners share the liability between them.

- The claimant can sue the firm (ie all of the partners), in the firm's name. Anyone who was a partner at the time when the debt was incurred is jointly liable to satisfy the judgment (under ss 9 and 17 PA 1890 and the Civil Liability (Contribution) Act 1978).

Clearly the best option is to sue all of the partners in a firm rather than just one partner. The judgment can then be enforced against the partnership assets and also, if necessary, against partners' personal assets. Under the Civil Liability (Contribution) Act 1978, the court may order another partner to pay a just and equitable amount by way of contribution to the debt, so if the claimant does sue just one party, the others can be made to contribute some or all of the amount of the judgment.

⭐ *Example – suing the partners*

Jess, Sue and Rahimah ('the partners') started an outdoor adventure business in 2015.

In March 2022, the partners entered into a contract with Outdoor Pursuits UK Limited ('the company') for the purchase of climbing equipment. The equipment was delivered in April 2022 and the partners received an invoice for £12,000, which the partners did not want to pay because they did not think the equipment was of good enough quality.

In May 2022, Jess left the partnership and sold her partnership share to David.

It is now September 2022 and the company is issuing proceedings in respect of the unpaid debt. The company has the following options:

1. *It can sue Jess, Sue and Rahimah, because they were the partners at the time the contract was entered into so there is privity of contract between them and the company.*

2. *It can sue any one of Jess, Sue and Rahimah, because they were the partners at the time the debt was incurred. That partner can then claim an indemnity from their partners (under s 24 PA 1890 or possibly under the partnership agreement) so that the partners share the liability between them.*

3. *It can sue the firm (ie Sue, Rahimah and David), in the firm's name. Anyone who was a partner at the time when the debt was incurred – here, this would be Sue, Jess and Rahimah – is jointly liable to satisfy the judgment (under ss 9 and 17 PA 1890 and the Civil Liability (Contribution) Act 1978).*

6.11 Insolvency

Although a partnership is not a legal person in its own right, an insolvent partnership can be wound up as an unregistered company or may use the rescue procedures available to companies, such as a voluntary arrangement with creditors or an administration order of the court. The individual partners may be made bankrupt if an obligation is enforced against their personal assets and there is still not enough to meet the partners' liabilities.

6.12 Tax

Partners may need to pay VAT, National Insurance and either income or corporation tax, depending on whether the partner is question is a company or an individual.

6.13 Liability between the partners

The partnership agreement, if there is one, should set out a mechanism for valuing an outgoing partner's share. Usually, when a partner leaves the partnership, they will 'leave in' the partnership bank account a sum of money to pay their share of any outstanding debts. If the remaining partners and the outgoing partner are sued by a creditor in respect of a debt incurred before the partner left the partnership, the outgoing partner may have to pay the third party because they always remain liable to third parties. However, they may have a contractual right to be reimbursed by the remaining partners, if such a right is included in the agreement. Alternatively, they could try to claim an indemnity under s 24(2) of the PA 1890 on the basis that they have incurred liabilities in the ordinary and proper conduct of the business of the firm.

Example – calculating an outgoing partner's share

PQR Partnership was set up by Priya, Quentin and Rukhsana five years ago. Each partner contributed £30,000 to the partnership, so at the outset the partnership was worth £90,000.

Quentin is leaving the partnership and the partners are calculating the value of Quentin's partnership share. The partnership's assets (cash in the bank, property, stock, etc) are worth £210,000. Given that the partners own a third of the partnership each, Quentin is entitled to £70,000 worth of the partnership's assets. However, Quentin is also responsible for a third of the partnership's debts. The partnership currently owes £60,000 to various creditors. Therefore, Quentin is not entitled to a payment of £70,000: he is entitled to £50,000 (total assets of £210,000 less liabilities of £60,000 equals £150,000. A third of this is £50,000).

Quentin will therefore receive £50,000 upon leaving the partnership. If, at a later date, a third party sues Quentin, Priya and Rukhsana for a debt incurred when Quentin was still a partner, Quentin will understandably be aggrieved if he pays any of it. This is because he left £20,000 in the partnership to satisfy all outstanding liabilities. However, this is not the third party's concern. As far as the third party is concerned, Quentin, as a partner, is a party to the contract and is therefore liable. Quentin will have to pay the amount owed to the third party if he is sued, but will then be able to claim against Priya and Rukhsana for an indemnity on the basis that Quentin left £20,000 in the partnership to satisfy his share of the outstanding liabilities on the day he left.

6.14 When a partner cannot pay

If a partner cannot pay a judgment debt owed to a third party, the third party can enforce the debt in the usual way. This may involve obtaining a charge over the partner's property or properties, and then applying for an order for sale of those properties in order to satisfy the outstanding debt. Alternatively, the third party may seize assets belonging to the partner.

If a partner cannot pay their fellow partners, the other partners have the same enforcement options as a third party. There may also be other consequences. For example, the partnership agreement may give the other partners the right to expel that partner.

Part 2   Limited Liability Partnerships

6.15 Introduction

Limited liability partnerships ('LLPs') were introduced by the Limited Liability Partnerships Act 2000 ('LLPA 2000'). They can best be summarised as a hybrid between a company and a partnership, offering the advantage of both limited liability for the LLP's debts and fewer administrative requirements than a company. Limited liability partnerships are corporate bodies, with a separate identify from their members. They are common in the world of professional services such as solicitors, accountants and surveyors. They are also commonly used in joint ventures.

In addition to the LLPA 2000, the Limited Liability Partnerships Regulations 2001 ('LLP Regulations 2001') are relevant in that they provide a default contract for an LLP, in the absence of the members (partners) agreeing terms which they would usually do in a formal LLP agreement. Finally, the Limited Liability Partnerships (Application of the Companies Act 2006) Regulations 2009 stipulate that certain sections of the CA 2006 also apply to LLPs. Some of those provisions are described in this chapter.

6.16 Legal requirements

6.16.1 Members

An LLP must have at least two members on incorporation. There is also a requirement to have two designated members, who are responsible for filing documents at Companies House. If the LLP only has two members, then these two members will have to be designated members to fulfil the requirement for two designated members. Generally, the original two designated members will be the subscribers to the incorporation document, but they can cease to be designated members at a later date if that is what the members decide. Sometimes the members decide that all of the members of the LLP will be designated members.

If at any time the number of members reduces to one, and this carries on for more than six months, that person is jointly and severally liable for any of the LLP's debts incurred during the period from the six-month point onwards.

6.16.2 Incorporation

An LLP is started by filing form LL IN01 at Companies House, along with the applicable fee. This is very similar to form IN01, the equivalent form for a company. There is no requirement for the LLP to file any LLP agreement.

Companies House will then issue a certificate of registration.

6.16.3 Name

The LLP's name must end 'LLP', 'limited liability partnership' or the Welsh equivalents. Unless the partnership's name consists wholly of the names of all of the partners, there are similar restrictions on LLPs' names to those that apply to companies (see **1.12.1**), in particular the restrictions imposed by the Companies and Business Names (Miscellaneous Provisions) Regulations 2009 and the Company, Limited Liability Partnership and Business (Names and Trading Disclosures) Regulations 2015.

The LLP must have its name on the outside of its place of business and its stationery must state its name, place of registration and registration number (and the address of the registered office).

Under the LLP Regulations 2001, an LLP can change its name at any time, with the consent of all of the members. Alternatively, the procedure for change of name can be set out in the partnership agreement.

6.17 Registered office

An LLP must have a registered office, which is its address for service of official documents, and the registered office address must appear on its stationery.

6.18 Designated members

Designated members have powers similar to directors in a company, and also have duties and responsibilities as members of the LLP.

Under the LLPA 2000, CA 2006 and Insolvency Act 1986, designated members are responsible for various administrative and legal matters, including:

- signing and filing the annual accounts with the Registrar;
- appointing, removing and remunerating the auditors;

- filing the annual confirmation statement;

- sending notices to the Registrar of Companies, for example concerning a member leaving or joining the LLP; or

- winding up the LLP.

Designated members must carry out all of their functions consistently with the core fiduciary obligation every member owes to the LLP itself. Designated members also owe a duty of reasonable care and skill to the LLP.

6.19 Effect of limited liability

If an LLP is insolvent, the company liquidation regime under the Insolvency Act 1986 applies to both the LLP and its members. This means that members may be liable for misfeasance, fraudulent trading or wrongful trading and may be required to contribute to the assets of the insolvent LLP. The Company Directors Disqualification Act 1986 applies to members of an LLP as well as to company directors, so, depending on their conduct, a member of an LLP could be disqualified from being a director or a member of an LLP.

6.20 Duties and responsibilities of members

The LLPA 2000 provides that the mutual rights and duties of the LLP's members are governed by agreement between members or between the LLP and its members. If there is any matter which the parties have not agreed, the LLP Regulations 2001 will apply.

Members also owe fiduciary duties to the LLP, as its agents. They include a duty of good faith, a duty to account for any money received on behalf of the LLP and a duty to the other members to render true accounts and full information on matters concerning the LLP.

6.21 Authority of members

Members of an LLP are agents of the LLP, under s 6 LLPA 2000. Limitations can be placed on a partner's actual authority in the partnership agreement, or orally. However, LLPs may still be liable to a third party, even if a partner has acted without actual authority, because of the principle of apparent authority, in the same way as in a general partnership.

6.22 Owning property and granting charges

Limited liability partnerships can own property and the LLP itself is the legal owner, rather than the individual members. They can also issue debentures and grant both fixed and floating charges, just like companies. This contrasts with general partnerships, which can only grant fixed charges.

Limited liability partnerships must keep a register of charges, along with a copy of every charge requiring registration, at its registered office. The register should include all charges affecting the LLP's property and floating charges. Any creditor or member of the LLP must be allowed to inspect the register without paying a fee. Limited liability partnerships are required to register charges with the Registrar of Companies, and which form to use depends on the nature of the charge.

6.23 Change in membership

Whether a new member can join an LLP, and the mechanism for agreeing to a new member joining, is governed by the LLP agreement.

If a new member joins an LLP, the LLP must deliver a notice to the Registrar of Companies, notifying them of the new member, within 14 days of appointment. This can be done by filing form LL AP01 (for an individual member) or LL AP02 (for a corporate member) at Companies House. The form is very similar to the form notifying Companies House of a new director of a company. It requires the member to give both a service address, which can be the LLP's place of business, and a residential address, along with full name, former names and date of birth. When a member leaves an LLP, the LLP is required to file form LL TM01 (for an individual member) or LL TM02 (for a corporate member) at Companies House within 14 days.

6.24 The LLP agreement

The LLP Regulations 2001 provide a set of default rules, just as the PA 1890 does for general partnerships. Many of its provisions mirror the PA 1890, covering such matters as sharing in income and profits, decision-making, expulsion and non-competition. However, its default terms will not suit every partnership, so a written partnership agreement is always advisable. Some common terms found in LLP agreements are discussed in the paragraphs that follow.

6.24.1 Capital and profits

The default position under the LLP Regulations 2001 is that the members of the LLP share equally in the capital and profits of the LLP. Of course, members can enter into an agreement which varies this default position. There is no default provision regarding losses, because those are borne by the LLP itself, as with a company. All that members of an LLP risk financially is losing their capital contributions, and, if they have loaned any money to the LLP, not being repaid.

6.24.2 Management and decision-making

The default rules in the LLP Regulations 2001 provide that every member may take part in the management of the LLP. They also state that members are not entitled to remuneration for taking part in management. Of course, again, members can agree to depart from these rules. They are free to create whatever management structure they want. There is no LLP equivalent to the Model Articles provided for companies – members of an LLP have a blank slate as far as management structure and rules are concerned, and there is no distinction between owner (shareholder) and manager (director) as with companies.

As with general partnerships, ordinary matters of the LLP can be decided by a majority of the members. Changing the nature of the business and changing the terms of the contract between the members can only be done by unanimous consent. The same practical considerations apply to LLPs as to general partnerships when members are considering whether to make more decisions ones which must be taken by unanimous consent: will it reduce financial risk? Will it make decision-making more cumbersome? Of course, members of LLPs do not have the constant worry of being personally liable for the LLP's debts in quite the same way as partners in general partnerships, so tend not to be as preoccupied with personal financial risk.

6.24.3 Leaving the LLP

Under the LLP Regulations 2001, members can leave the LLP by giving reasonable notice to the other members. Members cannot be expelled, so, if the members wish there to be a right of expulsion, this must be included in the LLP agreement. If the members wish the bankruptcy of one of their number to automatically cause termination of that person's membership of the LLP, they must stipulate this in the LLP agreement. Legislation does not provide for this otherwise.

When a member leaves an LLP, the LLP must notify Companies House on form LL TM01 within 14 days of the member leaving.

6.25 Advantages and disadvantages of an LLP

The obvious advantage of an LLP is the fact that its members have limited liability for the debts of the LLP. Additionally, they are able to grant fixed and floating charges over their assets, unlike general partnerships. They also benefit from having a great deal of leeway with regard to their management structure: they can decide how they wish to structure their organisation. Finally, they can appoint an administrator.

The main disadvantages of an LLP are the administrative and accounting requirements. Limited liability partnerships must file accounts with the Registrar of Companies and must file other information, such as notice of termination of membership, with Companies House. These documents are then available for public inspection. Limited liability partnerships are also subject to potential clawback provisions on insolvency (see **Chapter 8**).

Sample questions

Question 1

A man and a woman ('the partners') have recently set up a market-stall bakery. The man contributed more capital. The partners agreed that the man would work 8.00am–5.00pm and the woman would work 8.00am–4.00pm, but this was the only aspect of running the business that they expressly agreed. The business satisfies the definition of a partnership under the PA 1890.

Which of the following statements best describes how the partners will share the partnership's income and capital profits?

A   Capital profits will be shared equally but the man may successfully argue that it is an implied term that income profits will be shared according to how many hours each partner works for the partnership.

B   Capital profits will be shared equally but income profits will be shared according to how many hours each partner works for the partnership.

C   Income and capital profits will be shared according to how many hours each partner works for the partnership.

D   Income and capital profits will be shared according to the partners' initial capital contributions.

E   Income profits will be shared equally but the man may successfully argue that it is an implied term that the partners own the capital in accordance with their initial capital contributions.

Answer

Option E is correct. Section 24(1) of the PA 1890 provides that all capital and income profits and losses are shared equally, and that it does not depend on the hours the partner works – so options A, B and C are wrong. However, it has been established by case law that it can be inferred from a course of conduct that the partners own the capital profits in unequal shares. Option D is wrong because whilst a court may decide that the partners should share profits according to their initial capital contributions, this would depend on whether the relevant partner's argument was successful rather than it being an established legal rule.

Question 2

A client is leaving a partnership today. The other partners have removed her name from the letterhead and other documentation and will no longer refer to her as a partner. The client seeks advice on whether she will remain liable for existing and future debts of the partnership.

Which of the following best describes the best advice to the client regarding her liability going forward?

A   She will remain liable for existing partnership debts (unless she enters into a novation agreement with the partnership and its creditors) but will not be liable for future debts as long as she complies with the notice requirements in s 36 PA 1890.

B   Once she has left the partnership, the client will no longer have any liability for any existing or future debts of the partnership.

C   She will remain liable for both existing partnership debts and future partnership debts unless she enters into a novation agreement with the partnership and its creditors.

D   Once she has left the partnership, the client will no longer have any liability for any existing or future debts of the partnership as long as she complies with the notice requirements in s 36 PA 1890.

E   Now that the client's name has been removed from the partnership's letterhead and related documentation, she will no longer have any liability for any existing or future debts of the partnership.

Answer

Option A is correct. Partners cannot escape liability to third parties for debts the partnership entered into while they were a partner unless there is a novation agreement (s 17 PA 1890). This means that options B, D and E are wrong. The notice requirements in s 36 PA 1890 constitute notice to all existing and future contacts that the partner has left the firm, and complying with s 36 is sufficient notice that the partner has left the firm so will not be liable for any debts the partnership enters into after that date (unless there is evidence of holding out). For this reason, option C is wrong.

Question 3

Two individuals are going into business together as photographers for events such as weddings and large parties. They do not know which business medium to choose. They will have professional indemnity insurance and know that they do not want to expand the business beyond northwest England. They are happy to deal with small amounts of paperwork and do not mind paying administrative costs associated with running a business. Their solicitor advises them that a limited liability partnership ('LLP') would be a good option for them.

Which of the following best describes why an LLP would be advisable rather than a company or general partnership?

A   Because in an LLP, there is no paperwork but the partners will benefit from the advantage of limited liability for the firm's debts, which is always advisable.

B   Because a photography business may face large liabilities, so they must have a business which benefits from limited liability.

C   Because in an LLP, there is no paperwork and while the partners have unlimited liability for the LLP's debts, this is not significant here because the partners will have insurance, and this will cover liability for any of the LLP's debts.

D   Because it combines the advantages of limited liability with small amounts of paperwork, and because they will not be expanding overseas, they do not need the advantage of the medium of a company being well-known.

E   Because it combines the advantage of the prestige of an LLP with small amounts of paperwork and limited liability for the LLP's debts for anyone who is not a designated member.

Answer

Option D is correct. A photography business's most likely liability is a claim for professional negligence (eg photos that are not of the required standard), which will be covered by insurance (so option B is wrong). However, given that the individuals are happy with small amounts of paperwork and administrative costs, they might as well operate as an LLP and take advantage of the benefit of limited liability for the firm's debts. Companies are better known overseas but they will not be expanding overseas. Option A is wrong because it does not represent the best advice to the client: it omits the point about not needing the advantage of the medium of a company being well-known and in addition it is not true to say that there is no paperwork for an LLP. Option C is also wrong because it refers to there being no paperwork in an LLP. Option E is wrong because designated members also have limited liability for the firm's debts. In addition, there is no significant prestige attached to an LLP.

7 Trading: Calculating Profits and Paying VAT

SQE1 syllabus

Candidates are required to apply relevant core legal principles and rules appropriately and effectively, at the level of a competent newly qualified solicitor in practice, to realistic client-based and ethical problems and situations in the following areas:

- **finance**: records, information and accounting requirements
- **corporate governance and compliance**: documentary, record-keeping, statutory filing and disclosure requirements
- **value added tax**:
  - key principles relating to scope, supply, input and output tax
  - registration requirements and issue of VAT invoices
  - returns/payment of VAT and record keeping

Learning outcomes

By the end of this chapter you will be able to:

- calculate a business's trading profits;
- understand the tax reliefs that may be available to an unincorporated business for trading losses; and
- understand the UK system of value added tax.

7.1 Introduction

So far you have learnt how to set up a business, and the legal considerations in running one. However, businesses also need to know how they are performing financially and keep detailed records to enable them to assess the financial position of the business. In addition, they must pay tax: income tax and capital gains tax for sole traders and partners, or corporation tax for companies, and VAT for most businesses. We consider VAT at **7.14**, and income tax, capital gains tax and corporation tax are explained in **Chapters 9–11**.

This chapter explains how to assess a business's trading profit. This is the first step in working out how profitable a business is, and is also an important part of a business's income tax or corporation tax calculation, depending on whether the business is unincorporated or a company. This is because for sole traders and partners, the first step in an income tax calculation is to work out total income, and their income from their business *is* their trading profit, because, as the business's owners, this is what they receive from their business (although there may be other income too, for example, rental income, which will need to be added on to trading profits to produce total income).

For companies, the first step in a corporation tax calculation is to calculate income profits. Again, a company's trading profits will form part of its income (and may be its only income, although there may be other sources of income, for example, rental income). So when you have fully understood the calculation of trading profits, you will be able to move on to considering income tax and corporation tax.

Sometimes a business makes a loss, not a profit. Various trading reliefs may be available so that this loss can be set off against past or future profits, and the business will be able to claim a tax rebate for past or future gains. These reliefs are explained at **7.12** in so far as they relate to sole traders and partnerships. Reliefs available to companies are explained in the corporation tax chapter, at **11.4**.

Finally, we will turn to VAT and how the VAT system operates, a key issue for many businesses, and closely linked to the issue of trading.

7.2 Calculating trading profits

Businesses can make two kinds of profit, income and capital. Income profits are generally those profits which are recurring in nature, such as rent or trading profit, whereas capital profits are one-off items, such as an office building increasing in value. Income profits made by sole traders and partnerships form part of their total income for the purposes of income tax (or corporation tax for corporate partners). Companies' income profits are charged to corporation tax, as are its capital profits.

Trading profits are calculated in broadly the same way for both income tax and corporation tax, but under different statutes. So the principles are the same but the authority is different, being the Income Tax (Trading and Other Income) Act 2005 (ITTOIA 2005) for income tax and the Corporation Tax Acts 2009 and 2010 for corporation tax. The principles in the following paragraphs relate to both companies and unincorporated businesses.

7.3 The accounting period of a business

A business must prepare accounts for an accounting period, usually of 12 months, to show the profit or loss made by its trade during those 12 months. Trading profits or losses are calculated by subtracting deductible expenditure and capital allowances from chargeable receipts:

Chargeable receipts LESS deductible expenditure LESS capital allowances = trading profit/loss

7.4 What are chargeable receipts?

Essentially, chargeable receipts means money received for the sale of goods and services. The receipts must derive from the business's trade and be income (ie recurring) rather than capital in nature. Case law provides various definitions of trade, none of which is consistently applied, but the most useful one is perhaps 'operations of a commercial character by which the trader provides to customers for reward some kind of goods or services'.

Likewise, there is no statutory definition of income and how it differs from capital. It is generally accepted that if a business buys something to sell on at a profit, the proceeds of sale will be income. If, however, the business sells something which it has *used in* its trade – for example, its office premises – and makes a profit, this will instead be classed as a capital profit.

7.5 What is deductible expenditure?

Deductible expenditure must be of an income nature, and incurred 'wholly and exclusively' for the trade. Lastly, its deduction must not be prohibited by statute. Examples of expenses prohibited by statute are client entertainment and leasing cars with emissions over a certain level.

7.6 What is income in nature?

If the reason for incurring the expenditure is so that the business can sell the item at a profit (eg, stock), it is income in nature. Alternatively, if the expenditure has the quality of recurrence (for example, utility bills), again, it will be income in nature.

Expenditure on items to help the business to trade, for example, the office building, will be capital in nature and therefore not deductible.

7.7 What does 'wholly and exclusively for the purposes of trade' mean?

Case law has applied the definition 'wholly and exclusively' strictly: for example, in one case, eating in a restaurant when working away from home was not seen as an expense *'wholly and exclusively* incurred for the purposes of trade', because that person would have needed to eat something anyway. The cost of the meal therefore had a dual purpose. In fact, despite this principle, which has been clearly established in case law, HMRC allows some expenses to be apportioned so that part is deductible; for example, where a taxpayer works from home, part of the cost of heating and lighting the home will be deductible for tax purposes (and a right to apportion an identifiable proportion of an expense where that proportion is incurred wholly and exclusively for the purposes of the trade is now included in ITTOIA 2005).

The following items are commonly deductible:

- salaries (as long as they are not excessive given the services that the person carries out);
- rent on commercial premises;
- utility bills;
- stock;
- contributions to an approved pension scheme for directors/employees; and
- interest payments on borrowings.

7.8 Capital allowances

Capital items, such as plant and machinery, cannot in principle be deducted from chargeable receipts when calculating trading profits, because they are not income in nature. However, clearly, such items are expensive and a business which needs to heavily invest in such items could have severe cash flow problems. In addition, such assets almost always decrease in value over time, so businesses are faced with a situation where they have spent a great deal of money on an item which is necessary for the business but which may be valueless several years later.

To encourage businesses to invest in essential machinery to help them to grow, they are entitled to a capital allowance, which allows them to deduct a proportion of the cost of most capital items from chargeable receipts. This will ultimately result in the business paying less tax overall. The main types of capital asset for which a capital allowance is permitted are plant and machinery.

7.9 What is plant and machinery?

There is no statutory definition of plant and machinery. Case law is helpful: it has been held that plant includes whatever apparatus business people use to carry on their business. This includes all goods and chattels which they keep for permanent use in their business, but not stock in trade. Examples of plant and machinery are manufacturing equipment, tools, computers and other office equipment.

The value of most capital assets reduces over time. Each financial year, the business is entitled to a writing down allowance ('WDA'). The WDA is 18% of the value of the business's plant and machinery, valued at the start of the financial year. Each financial year, the plant and machinery the business owns will be valued, and 18% of its total value will be deducted from chargeable receipts when calculating trading profits for that accounting period.

The reduced value of the plant and machinery is known as the 'written-down value' of the asset.

 Example – capital allowances

Three years ago, Queensbury Limited ('Queensbury') purchased an item of machinery to use in its ceramics business for £100,000. It owns no other machinery or plant. Starting with the year in which it purchased the machinery (and ignoring the annual investment allowance for the sake of simplicity), Queensbury will be entitled to the following capital allowances:

> *Year 1: 18% of £100,000 = £18,000 WDA, leaving the asset with a written-down value of £82,000.*

> *Year 2: 18% of £82,000 = £14,760 WDA, leaving the asset with a written-down value of £67,240.*

> *Year 3: 18% of £67,240 = £12,104 WDA, leaving the asset with a written-down value of £55,136.*

Now let's consider how the WDA is treated in the trading profits calculation. We will assume that Queensbury's chargeable receipts less deductible expenditure are £500,000 every year.

In year 1, Queensbury's trading profit would be £500,000 less the WDA of £18,000, leaving a trading profit of £482,000.

In year 2, Queensbury's trading profit would be £500,000 less the WDA of £14,760, leaving a trading profit of £485,240.

In year 3, Queensbury's trading profit would be £500,000 less the WDA of £12,104, leaving a trading profit of £487,896.

The WDA, then, effectively allows Queensbury to deduct all or most of the value of the machinery from its trading profit over the course of several years, meaning that it pays little or no tax on this expenditure.

7.10 Pooling

Usually, of course, businesses own more than one item of plant and machinery. It would be extremely complicated to try to work out the capital allowance available for each and every item of plant and machinery every year, and to carry out a calculation every time an item is sold. For this reason, all plant and machinery is generally pooled, and the WDA is calculated each year on the basis of the value of the whole pool. If an asset is sold, the proceeds of sale are deducted from the value of the whole pool, not the individual item. This means that no balancing allowances or charges should be needed until the whole pool is sold, often when the business stops trading.

7.11 Annual investment allowance

In addition to the writing down allowance, businesses are entitled to an annual investment allowance ('AIA'). The AIA allows businesses to deduct the whole cost of plant and machinery purchased in that particular accounting period from chargeable receipts (not just 18% of the value of those assets, as with capital allowances). This, again, encourages businesses to invest and to not hold back from buying equipment they need.

The amount of the AIA has varied considerably since it was introduced in 1997. It rose to £1 million in 2019 and 2020, and at the time of writing it is due to remain at £1,000,000 until 31 March 2023. An AIA of £1,000,000 means that the first £1,000,000 of 'fresh' qualifying expenditure on plant and machinery incurred in an accounting period will be wholly deductible. Note that a group of companies will receive only one AIA for the group in each accounting period. However, the AIA can be allocated within the group as the group sees fit.

Super-deduction – for companies only

In response to the Covid-19 pandemic, the Government has introduced temporary capital allowances for companies investing in *brand new* qualifying plant and machinery. These companies will receive a super-deduction of 130% (which is uncapped) instead of the normal deduction (which was of 100% of the cost of the asset, capped at £1 million).

For the super-deduction to apply, the purchase contract for the asset must have been entered into after 3 March 2021 and the expenditure must be incurred between 1 April 2021 and 31 March 2023.

The normal AIA of 100% of the cost of the asset, capped at £1 million, is still in force in addition to the super-deduction, and will be relevant for assets which do not fit within the dates set out in the previous paragraph or which are second-hand or refurbished rather than brand new.

The super-deduction ends in April 2023.

Example – when the cost of the plant and machinery is less than the AIA

Let's assume now that Queensbury has an existing pool of machinery with a written-down value of £200,000, and buys some machinery second-hand for £150,000.

Queensbury is entitled to the following capital allowances for the accounting period:

AIA – the whole of the £150,000 cost of the machinery will be covered by the AIA, so £150,000 will be deducted from chargeable receipts.

The written-down value of the pool at the start of the accounting period was £200,000, so for this accounting period Queensbury will be entitled to a WDA of 18% of £200,000, which is £36,000.

*Queensbury's capital allowances for the accounting period are therefore £150,000 + £36,000 = **£186,000**. This £186,000 will be deducted from chargeable receipts to give total profit.*

 Example – when the cost of the plant and machinery is more than the AIA

Let's assume that Queensbury's machinery, from the example above, cost £1.2 million, not £150,000.

Queensbury would be entitled to the AIA of £1,000,000, but this would not cover all of the cost of the new machinery – it cost £200,000 more than the AIA. Queensbury would be entitled to a WDA of 18% on the balance of £200,000. The calculation would be as follows:

Calculation of capital allowances	£
AIA – first £1,000,000 spent on new machinery:	1,000,000
WDA:	
On remaining value of new machinery	200,000
Written-down value of pool	200,000
Total	400,000
400,000 x 18%	72,000
Total capital allowances for the accounting period	<u>**1,072,000**</u>

 Example – when the super-deduction applies

Let's assume that Queensbury's machinery was new, not second-hand, and cost £1.2 million. Queensbury would be entitled to the super-deduction of 130%, which is 1.3 x 1,200,000 = £1,560,000. In addition, Queensbury would be entitled to the WDA of £36,000, making capital allowances of £1,596,000 in total.

 Example – a basic calculation of trading profit

Sue is a sole trader, running a business making organic beauty products. Her total sales for the accounting period which has just ended were £185,000. There was deductible expenditure of £113,000, comprising:

Raw materials	£65,000
Wages	£30,000
Rent	£10,000
General overheads (telephone, electricity, advertising etc)	£8,000

Sue's business has a pool of plant and machinery which had a written-down value of £30,000 at the start of the accounting period. During the accounting period, Sue bought a new sterilising machine for £10,000.

Calculation of trading profit:	£
Chargeable receipts (sales)	185,000
Less	
Deductible expenditure	113,000
Less	
Capital allowances:	
On the machine – entire £10,000 (within AIA)	10,000
On the pool – £30,000 x 18% writing down allowance	5,400
Trading profit	56,600

The written-down value of the pool of plant and machinery carried forward to the next accounting period will be £24,600 (£30,000 less the £5,400 WDA claimed for this accounting period).

The calculation of trading profit that we have just examined applies just as much to companies as it does to sole traders and partnerships, as we have seen. However, companies pay corporation tax and are entitled to certain trading reliefs aimed at companies. Partners and sole traders can also claim trading loss reliefs, but they are different from those for companies. Trading loss reliefs for companies are covered in detail in **11.4**. Reliefs for unincorporated businesses are explained below.

7.12 Relief for a trading loss: unincorporated businesses

Carrying out a trading income calculation for a sole trader or partner may reveal a loss. The taxpayer may be able to claim relief for such trading losses. The reliefs effectively allow the taxpayer to deduct a trading loss from other income, resulting in them paying less tax overall.

Where the taxpayer is eligible for more than one relief, they may choose which relief to claim. If, after claiming as much relief as is available under one provision, there are still some unabsorbed losses, the taxpayer can claim relief for the balance of the loss under another provision if they are eligible.

Sometimes the loss is set against total income, and sometimes it is set against a particular component of income. Some of the reliefs are also subject to a cap for any one tax year.

Partners will decide individually which relief(s) they wish to claim in relation to their share of the partnership's losses: it is an individual decision, and the partners may all make different decisions, depending on their personal circumstances.

The reliefs are explained below. It is important to remember that the taxpayer must apply for the relief – they are not applied automatically by HMRC.

7.12.1 Start-up loss relief (also known as early trade losses relief)

This relief is available when the taxpayer suffers a loss in any of the first four tax years of the new business. The loss can be carried back and set against the taxpayer's total income in the three tax years immediately prior to the tax year of the loss. This relief is particularly useful for anyone who starts a new business but, before that, had an income from a former business or from their employment. It enables the taxpayer to claim back from HMRC some of the income tax they paid in their previous business or employment in the three tax years prior to the tax year of the loss (some or all of which they may have paid at the higher rate).

The loss must be set against earlier years before later years. Further, the claim for this relief must be made on or before the first anniversary of 31 January following the end of the tax year in which the loss is assessed.

7.12.2 Carry-across/one-year carry-back relief for trading losses generally

Trading losses in an accounting period are treated as losses of the tax year in which the accounting period ends. There are four options for this relief. The losses can be:

1. set against total income from the same tax year; or

2. set against total income from the tax year preceding the tax year of the loss.

Alternatively, they may be:

3. set against total income from the same tax year until that income is reduced to zero, with the balance of the loss being set against total income from the tax year preceding the tax year of the loss; or

4. set against total income from the tax year preceding the tax year of the loss until that income is reduced to zero, with the balance of the loss being set against total income from the tax year of the loss.

When the taxpayer claims this relief, they must set their loss against *total* income, often reducing it to zero, which means that the taxpayer then loses the benefit of their personal allowance. Again, the claim for this relief must be made on or before the first anniversary of 31 January following the end of the tax year in which the loss is assessed.

As a result of the Covid-19 pandemic, the Government introduced a measure allowing individuals to carry back losses for three years rather than one. This measure has now ended.

7.12.3 Set-off against capital gains

This relief allows the taxpayer to set trading losses against chargeable gains in the same tax year, and applies when a taxpayer has claimed carry-across relief but not all of the loss has been absorbed. The taxpayer must claim this relief on or before the first anniversary of 31 January following the end of the tax year in which the loss is assessed. This loss relief is unusual in that it allows loss relief against chargeable capital gains as well as against income.

7.12.4   Carry-forward relief

A taxpayer may carry forward their trading loss for a tax year and set it against *subsequent profits which the trade produces* in subsequent years, taking earlier years first. Losses can be carried forward indefinitely until the loss is exhausted, so if several years go by before the trade makes a profit against which to set the losses, this is no bar to claiming the relief.

Whilst losses can be carried forward indefinitely, the taxpayer must notify HMRC of its intention to claim the relief no more than four years after the end of the tax year in which the loss was incurred.

A taxpayer can use all of carry-forward, carry-across and carry-back reliefs in relation to the same loss, until the loss is wiped out.

 Example – using trading reliefs (start-up, carry-forward, carry-across and carry-back)

*Mary set up Cuisine2Go as a sole trader in the tax year 2021/22, and it is now summer 2023. Mary's accounting period ended on 5 April. She used to work full-time as a solicitor specialising in wills and probate, but reduced her hours when she set up Cuisine2Go. She also has a rental property. Her income from Cuisine2Go, along with her salary and rental income from the past few years, is shown in **Table 7.1** below. Cuisine2Go made a loss of £67,000 in its first year of trading and Mary wants to know if she can claim any reliefs to reduce her total income and pay less tax overall.*

Table 7.1   Mary's income

Tax Year	Cuisine2Go £	Salary £	Rental income £	Total income £
2018/19	-	44,000	8,000	52,000
2019/20	-	45,000	8,000	53,000
2020/21	-	46,000	8,000	54,000
2021/22	(67,000)*	23,000	9,000	32,000
2022/23	10,000	24,000	9,000	43,000
2023/24 (est.)	40,000	25,000	9,000	74,000

*Note that brackets are used to show that a figure is a minus figure, like here, or that it is to be deducted.

Option 1: start-up loss relief

*Mary could use start-up loss relief. She can set any loss made in the first four years of trade of Cuisine2Go against income from the preceding three years. She cannot choose which year to start in – she must go back to three years before Cuisine2Go started trading and work towards the present year by year until the loss is used up. This will reduce her 2018/19 total income to zero and her 2019/20 income to £38,000, meaning that she would get a tax rebate for tax paid in 2018/19 and 2019/20. This is shown in **Table 7.2**.*

Table 7.2 Start-up loss relief

Tax Year	Cuisine2Go £	Salary £	Rental income £	Total income £
2018/19	-	44,000	8,000	**Reduced to zero**
2019/20	-	45,000	8,000	**Reduced to £38,000**
2020/21	-	46,000	8,000	54,000
2021/22	**Loss used up**	23,000	9,000	32,000
2022/23	10,000	24,000	9,000	43,000
2023/24 (est.)	40,000	25,000	9,000	74,000

Option 2: carry-across and one-year-back relief

*Mary could use carry-across relief to reduce her total income for the tax year 2021/22 to zero. This uses £32,000 of her £67,000 loss. Mary can then carry back the remaining £35,000 of her £67,000 loss to reduce her total income for the tax year 2020/21 to £19,000. She has now exhausted all of her losses. This is shown in **Table 7.3**.*

Table 7.3 Carry-across and one-year-back relief

Tax Year	Cuisine2Go £	Salary £	Rental income £	Total income £
2018/19	-	44,000	8,000	52,000
2019/20	-	45,000	8,000	53,000
2020/21	-	46,000	8,000	**Reduced to £19,000**
2021/22	**Loss used up**	23,000	9,000	**Reduced to zero (so Mary will get a tax rebate for this tax year)**
2022/23	10,000	24,000	9,000	33,000
2023/24 (est.)	40,000	25,000	9,000	34,000

Alternatively, Mary could choose to apply the loss against the 2020/21 total income first, and the rest against the 2021/22 total income. She will pay the same amount of income tax whichever of these two options she chooses.

Can you see the disadvantage of using start-up, carry-across and carry-back relief?

Mary will lose the benefit of her personal allowance in the tax years where total income is reduced to zero, because losses must be set against total income, not just enough of the income to take total income down to £12,570, the level of the personal allowance.

Option 3: carry-forward relief

Mary can set her £67,000 loss against the first profits produced by Cuisine2Go and continue to carry the losses forward until they are exhausted. However, if she does not make a profit in future years, this relief will not give her much financial help. The advantage of this relief, however, is that she will retain the benefit of her personal allowance as the relief can only be used against her Cuisine2Go profits, not her total income.

If the business performs really well, her total income will be higher, meaning she is likely to pay a higher rate of tax. Using this relief enables her to reduce her income overall so that she may avoid entering the higher rate tax band.

7.12.5 Carry-back of terminal trading loss

Any loss incurred by a taxpayer in the final 12 months of trading can be carried across and set against trading profits in the final tax year, and then carried back and set against trading profit in the three years preceding the year of the loss, starting with the year preceding the year of the loss and moving back year by year until the loss is fully absorbed or the three-year limit is reached, whichever is first. There is no cap on the amount which can be relieved under this provision. You may be wondering how a loss can be set against a profit from the same trade from the same year – if there is a profit, how can there also be a loss? This is because the rules allow other sources of income which are connected to the trade but not actually profits of the trade to be treated as trading profits for the purposes of this relief.

Using this relief may result in the taxpayer receiving a tax rebate, because their trading profits from previous years will be reduced and it is likely that their tax liability will reduce as a consequence. It is important to note that this relief can only be applied to trading income, not to non-trading income or capital gains.

A claim for carry-back of terminal trading loss must be made no more than four years after the end of the tax year to which the claim relates.

7.12.6 Carry-forward relief on incorporation of business

If a taxpayer incorporates their business by transferring it to a company wholly or mainly in return for shares, any trading losses which have not been relieved can be carried forward and set against any income they receive from the company, such as their salary or dividends. To be classed as 'wholly or mainly in return for shares', 80% or more of the consideration for the business transferred must be shares in the company. The taxpayer can set the losses against more than one form of income until the loss is fully absorbed, for example, against both salary and dividends. They can also set the loss against these types of income in the order they choose, and they will naturally choose the order that offers the biggest tax advantages, which will depend on that taxpayer's particular financial circumstances.

There is no cap on the amount that can be relieved under this provision.

Whilst losses can be carried forward indefinitely, the taxpayer must notify HMRC of its intention to claim the relief no more than four years after the end of the tax year in which the loss was incurred.

7.12.7 Cap on reliefs

Start-up relief and carry-across/carry-back relief are all subject to a cap of the greater of £50,000 or 25% of the taxpayer's income in the tax year in relation to which the relief is claimed.

However, the cap does not usually have a significant impact because the cap only relates to income from sources *other than* the trade which produced the loss.

7.13 What next?

Now that you understand how to calculate trading profit and the reliefs that may apply in the event of loss, you can use this knowledge to move on to income tax, capital gains tax and corporation tax in **Chapters 9–11**. Calculating trading profit is also an important part of your introduction to business accounts, which we consider in **Chapter 12**.

We now turn to VAT, an important consideration for businesses.

7.14 Value added tax ('VAT')

Generally, VAT is charged every time a business supplies goods or services. The current rate of VAT is a flat rate of 20%. The business charges the customer VAT at 20% on the value of the goods or services, known as 'output tax'. The business deducts from the amount it collects in output tax any VAT it has itself paid ('input tax') on goods or services received, and pays the difference to HMRC as illustrated in **Table 7.4**.

Table 7.4 Charging and paying VAT

	Value of goods (£)	VAT charged to buyer (£)	VAT paid to HMRC (£)
A manufacturer buys raw material for £200 plus VAT from a producer	200	40	
Producer pays to HMRC			40
Manufacturer sells finished article to a retailer for £1,000 plus VAT	1,000	200	
Manufacturer pays to HMRC			160 (200–40)
The retailer sells the finished article to a consumer for £2,000 plus VAT	2,000	400	
Retailer pays to HMRC			200 (400–200)
Total VAT paid to HMRC			**400**

VAT does not cost the business anything, because the business recoups any VAT it has paid from the VAT it charges. The consumer takes the burden, because they pay £2,000 plus £400 VAT for the product. The £400 VAT has been paid to HMRC in three stages.

Under the Value Added Tax Act 1994, VAT is 'charged on any supply of goods or services made in the United Kingdom where it is a taxable supply made by a taxable person in the course or furtherance of any business carried on by him'. Tax is charged on the 'value of the supply'. An explanation of each element of this is set out below.

7.14.1 Supply of goods and services

Any transfer of the whole property in goods is a supply of goods, and this will include intangible goods such as an interest in land or a supply of electricity.

Anything done for consideration which is not a supply of goods is a supply of services. An example is the provision of legal advice.

7.14.2 Exempt supplies

Some supplies are exempt from VAT, including supplies of residential land, postal services, education and health services.

7.14.3 Taxable person

A taxable person is a person who makes or intends to make taxable supplies and who is or is required to be registered under the Value Added Tax Act 1994. Currently, a person must be registered if the value of their taxable supplies in the preceding 12 months exceeded £85,000.

7.14.4 Course of business

'Business' includes any trade, profession or vocation (s 94 Value Added Tax Act 1994). A supply in the course of business includes the disposal of a business or any of its assets.

7.14.5 Value of supply

Value added tax is charged on the value of the supply of goods or services. This is what the goods or services would cost if VAT were not charged. For example, some furniture may be advertised as costing '£400 plus VAT'. The value of the supply is £400. A price is deemed to include VAT unless stated otherwise.

7.14.6 Tax payable to HMRC

Anyone registered for VAT must submit a return to HMRC and pay the VAT it owes within one month from the end of each quarter in respect of taxable supplies made in that quarter. They will pay the VAT they have charged (output tax), less any VAT they have paid in the course of their business (input tax). If input tax exceeds output tax, the person will receive a rebate. HMRC may allow or require a taxpayer to make monthly returns in certain circumstances.

7.14.7 Zero-rated and exempt supplies

Zero-rated and exempt supplies are similar because the customer does not pay any VAT. However, a person who makes zero-rated supplies (for example, books, certain food and water) can reclaim the VAT they have paid from HMRC. A person who makes only exempt supplies cannot register and will not be able to reclaim any VAT.

7.14.8 VAT registration

Anyone making taxable supplies of more than £85,000 in any 12-month period must register and charge VAT, and those making less than this can choose to register but are not obliged to. However, only those registered for VAT can reclaim input tax they have paid, so sometimes a business will voluntarily register so that they can reclaim input tax. They will have to work out whether being able to reclaim input tax is worth losing the advantage of being able to undercut VAT-registered rivals when competing for business.

This means that sole traders and companies may need to register. In addition, and unlike the position for other taxes, a partnership can be registered for VAT in the name of the partnership itself. HMRC will issue each person registering with a VAT number which applies to all businesses operated by that person.

7.14.9 Tax invoices

A person making a taxable supply to a taxable person must provide a tax invoice, an invoice showing information such as the VAT number, the value of supply and the rate of tax charged.

The person charging VAT must have tax invoices in respect of all of the input tax they are reclaiming.

7.14.10 Penalties

Failure to comply with VAT legislation can lead to a range of criminal and civil penalties, as well as being required to pay any unpaid tax with interest.

Summary

Calculating trading profits

Chargeable receipts LESS deductible expenditure LESS capital allowances (including AIA) = Trading profit/loss.

Table 7.5 summarises the types of relief available to unincorporated businesses when they suffer a trading loss.

Table 7.5 Reliefs for a trading loss for sole traders and partnerships

Relief	Time of loss	Loss set against	Losses set against profits/income from which time periods?
Start-up relief by carry-back	The first four tax years of trading	Total income	The three tax years preceding the tax year of the loss
Carry-across and/ or carry-back one-year relief	Any accounting year of trading	Total income and (if this is exhausted) chargeable gains	The tax year in which the accounting year of the loss ends and/or the preceding tax year
Carry-forward relief	Any accounting year of trading	Subsequent profits of the same trade	Any subsequent tax year until the loss is absorbed
Terminal relief by carry-back	The final 12 months of trading	Previous profits of the same trade	The final tax year and then the three tax years preceding the final tax year
Carry-forward relief on incorporation	Up to incorporation	Subsequent income received from the company	Any subsequent tax year until the loss has been absorbed

VAT

1. Generally, VAT is charged every time a business supplies goods or services, at a rate of 20 per cent on the value of the goods or services.

2. Anyone making taxable supplies of more than £85,000 per annum must register and charge VAT, and those making less than this can choose to register but are not obliged to.

Sample questions

Question 1

A company had total sales in the accounting period ending 31 March 2023 of £2,400,000. The company incurred the following costs during the accounting period:

Costs	£
Stock	335,000
Salaries	333,000
Electricity/gas/telephone and rates	98,000
Rent	19,000
Insurance	6,000

The company sold some warehouse premises in June 2022 for £610,000. It purchased them in January 2010 for £360,000.

Which of the following best describes the company's trading profit for the accounting period?

A   £88,779

B   £2,400,000

C   £791,000

D   £1,609,000

E   £250,000

Answer

Option D is correct. Trading profit is calculated by subtracting deductible expenditure from sales. The sale of the warehouse is irrelevant for the purposes of calculating trading profit. Here, the listed deductible expenditure adds up to £791,000. Sales of £2.4 million less deductible expenditure of £791,000 = £1,609,000.

Question 2

A large trading company has an accounting period which ends on 31 March. In May 2022 it buys brand new plant and machinery costing £1,000,000. At the start of that financial year it had a pool of plant and machinery worth £500,000. Assume that the company always claims the maximum capital allowances available and that the rates for capital allowances remain the same as for the previous financial year.

Which ONE of the following statements best describes the capital allowance the company can claim in the accounting period ending 31 March 2023?

A   £1,000,000

B   £1,300,000

C   £90,000

D   £270,000

E   £1,390,000

Answer

Option E is correct. In the accounting period ending 31 March 2023, the company can claim the super-deduction of £1,300,000 (130% x £1,000,000) in relation to the brand new machinery.

It can also claim 18% of the existing pool of £500,000, that is, £90,000.

This gives total capital allowances for the accounting period of £1,300,000 + £90,000 = £1,390,000.

8 | Insolvency

SQE1 syllabus

Candidates are required to apply relevant core legal principles and rules appropriately and effectively, at the level of a competent newly qualified solicitor in practice, to realistic client-based and ethical problems and situations in the following areas of insolvency (corporate and personal):

- options and procedures – company voluntary arrangement (CVA)/individual voluntary arrangement (IVA), bankruptcy, administration, fixed asset receivership, voluntary and compulsory liquidation

- clawback of assets for creditors – preferences, transactions at an undervalue, fraudulent and wrongful trading, setting aside a floating charge

- order of priority for distribution to creditors.

Learning outcomes

By the end of this chapter you will be able to:

- understand the scope and aims of corporate and insolvency law;
- assess when a company or individual is or may be insolvent;
- understand the process of liquidation and bankruptcy and the distribution of the company's or individual's assets;
- advise on the alternatives to liquidation and bankruptcy; and
- advise on the potential claims designed to maximise the assets available to creditors on liquidation or bankruptcy.

8.1 Introduction

Insolvency is the inability of a company to pay its debts (corporate insolvency) or the inability of an individual to pay their debts (personal insolvency). The aims of corporate insolvency law are to save companies in financial difficulties, control company directors, and protect companies' creditors. The aims of personal insolvency law are to protect creditors and to encourage entrepreneurship by allowing individuals who are bankrupt but have behaved honestly to be discharged from bankruptcy after one year. Corporate and personal insolvency law are both governed largely by the Insolvency Act 1986 ('IA 1986') and the Insolvency Rules 2016 ('Insolvency Rules'). The first part of this chapter explores corporate insolvency; the second part explores personal insolvency.

Part 1   Corporate Insolvency

8.2 What is corporate insolvency?

Sections 122 and 123 of the IA 1986 set out the test for insolvency. A company is insolvent, in that it is deemed unable to pay its debts, when:

1. a creditor has served a statutory demand for an outstanding sum of £750 or more, and the company does not pay or come to an arrangement with the creditor within 21 days of service of the statutory demand;

2. a creditor has obtained judgment against the company, and has tried to enforce that judgment, but the debt still has not been paid in full or at all;

3. it can be proved to the court that the company is unable to pay its debts as they fall due (the 'cash flow test'); or

4. it can be proved to the court that the company's liabilities exceed its assets (the 'balance sheet test').

⭐ *Example – balance sheet and cash flow insolvency*

Table 8.1 *illustrates balance sheet and cash flow insolvency.*

Table 8.1 Balance sheet and cash flow insolvency

ASSETS	£	£	£
FIXED ASSETS			
Premises			150,000
CURRENT ASSETS			
Stock	15,000		
Debtors	20,000		
Cash	15,000		
		50,000	
Amounts Falling Due within 1 Year			
Creditors	125,000		
Provision for Tax	20,000		
		(145,000)	
Net Current Assets			(95,000)
Total Assets less Current Liabilities			55,000
Amounts Falling Due after more than 1 year			
Bank Loan			(60,000)
NET ASSETS			(5,000)
CAPITAL AND RESERVES			
Share Capital	100,000		
Profit and Loss Reserve	(105,000)		
SHAREHOLDERS' FUNDS			(5,000)

The company's liabilities exceed its assets, because its net assets figure is -£5,000. This means that the company appears to fail the balance sheet test. In addition, it has creditors owed £125,000 and a tax bill due in the next year, but only £15,000 cash in its bank account. Based on the information on the balance sheet, then, it has also failed the cash flow test: if a creditor owed more than £15,000 demanded payment today, it does not look as if the company could pay. However, remember that the balance sheet is just a snapshot – perhaps tomorrow all of the company's debtors will pay, giving it more cash to use to pay debts, and perhaps a new product it is considering selling will prove really popular, and its fortunes may turn around, however unlikely it seems when the company is insolvent. For this reason, the cash flow and balance sheet tests are not exact; they just give an indication of the company's financial situation. The court will take into account all available evidence, not just the cash flow and balance sheet tests.

8.3 Why do we need to know if a company is insolvent?

The main reason for needing to know whether a company is insolvent is that insolvency is almost always a prerequisite to a creditor commencing insolvency proceedings. For example, a creditor must be able to show that the debtor is insolvent before the creditor will be able to apply for the company to be wound up (see **8.6**). Another important reason is that certain remedies against directors of the company, which could result in a director being held personally liable to the company, depend upon whether the company is insolvent or was insolvent at the time of the director's actions.

8.4 Possible outcomes for an insolvent company

If a company is insolvent, it may go into liquidation, but other options include administration or a company voluntary arrangement ('CVA'). Liquidation, administration and CVAs are explained in detail below.

Creditors may force (or in the case of a CVA, encourage) the company to enter into any of these processes. There are a number of routes which, in addition, may be open to *secured* creditors. Depending on the terms of the security, they may be able to:

- appoint an LPA receiver;
- appoint an administrator out of court; or
- for security created before 15 September 2003, appoint an administrative receiver.

These options are all explained at **8.34**.

In addition, the Corporate Insolvency and Governance Act 2020 ('CIGA 2020'), which became law in June 2020, created two new insolvency rescue regimes, the moratorium and the restructuring plan.

8.5 Liquidation

Liquidation, also known as winding up, is the process whereby the business stops trading, its assets are sold and the company ceases to exist. When liquidation proceedings begin, a liquidator is appointed. The directors' powers cease, and the liquidator runs the company. The liquidator may review the company's past transactions, to see if any of them can be challenged. The purpose of this is to obtain more money that can be paid to the company's creditors. The liquidator will then distribute the assets of the company to the creditors in an order set down by statute, and the company will be dissolved at Companies House within a few months.

There are three types of liquidation:

1. Compulsory liquidation, where a third party commences insolvency proceedings against an insolvent company;

2. Creditors' voluntary liquidation (CVL), which is commenced by the company itself when it is insolvent, usually in response to pressure from creditors;

3. Members' voluntary liquidation (MVL), which is commenced by a solvent company, because it wishes to cease trading or because it is dormant and it wishes to bring its affairs to an end in an orderly manner.

We will now consider each of these three types of liquidation in turn.

8.6 Compulsory liquidation

Compulsory liquidation is commenced by a third party (in nearly all cases a creditor) presenting a winding up petition at court. The third party is known as the petitioner. The most common ground on which the petitioner will seek compulsory liquidation is on the basis that the company is unable to pay its debts (s 122 IA 1986). The petitioner may do this by establishing one or more of the grounds set out in s 123 IA 1986 (see **8.2**). A winding up petition is the first stage in a company's liquidation. When the company's assets are sold, the proceeds will be used to pay creditors, and this is why creditors issue winding up petitions – in the hope that they will get paid.

Unpaid creditors do not ordinarily have access to detailed, up-to-date financial information about the company. Usually, all they will be able to find out is the contents of the company's last set of filed final accounts, which may be a year old. Therefore, it is usually difficult for unpaid creditors to show that a company is unable to pay its debts as they fall due or that its liabilities exceed its assets, unless the company has admitted this in correspondence. Creditors will usually prove a debtor's insolvency by issuing a statutory demand and, if the statutory demand remains unpaid after three weeks, issuing a winding up petition against the company. Alternatively, they may obtain a judgment against the company, as the test of whether a company is insolvent is the inability to pay debts as and when they fall due. Clearly an unsatisfied judgment demonstrates that.

Generally, the petitioner will be prevented from proceeding with a winding up petition if the company can show that there is a genuine and substantial dispute in relation to the money owed. If the petitioner has already obtained judgment, it will be a difficult task for the company to argue that there is a dispute, unless it succeeds in having the judgment set aside. However, the IA 1986 makes it clear that the court 'may' still wind up the company if the company is unable to pay its debts. The court therefore has ultimate discretion in this area.

If the company indicates that it will be able to pay the debt within a reasonable period of time, the court may adjourn the hearing to a later date. If the court orders that the company should be wound up, the Official Receiver ('OR') will automatically become the company's liquidator. The OR is a civil servant and court official, and is employed by the Insolvency Service. The OR can appoint a private insolvency practitioner, depending on the nature of the case and the creditors' wishes, as long as the company has sufficient assets to pay the insolvency practitioner's fees.

8.7 Creditors' voluntary liquidation

This process is initiated by the company, through discussion and agreement between the company's directors and shareholders, and the creditors then take over at an early stage. Whilst it is technically voluntary, usually the directors will feel pressurised to enter into a CVL by the creditors. They will also be conscious of the risk of facing personal claims for misfeasance and fraudulent or wrongful trading if they continue to trade and then the company goes into liquidation.

8.8 Members' voluntary liquidation

A members' voluntary liquidation is only available if the company is solvent, and if, during an MVL, the liquidator realises that the company is insolvent, they must convert the MVL to a CVL. Members' voluntary liquidations are often used when companies are dormant, for example, where there is a group of companies and some of the companies within the group are no longer used. It is also common procedure when the directors in an owner-managed company all want to retire or cease trading. For an MVL to take place, the directors must first swear a statutory declaration that the company is solvent.

8.9 The process of liquidation

Liquidation as a process is fairly straightforward, and is similar in many respects whether the liquidation is compulsory or voluntary. It can take anything from a few months to a few years for the process to come to a conclusion. The effect of liquidation is that the directors lose their powers and, in a compulsory liquidation, their appointments are terminated. The liquidator takes over the running of the company. The liquidator's powers include:

(a) carrying on the company's business;

(b) commencing and defending litigation on the company's behalf;

(c) investigating the company's past transactions;

(d) investigating the directors' conduct;

(e) collecting and distributing the company's assets;

(f) doing all that is necessary to facilitate the winding up of the company.

As part of the liquidation process, the liquidator will sell the company's assets and distribute the money to the company's creditors. After they have completed their work, which includes preparing final accounts, the liquidator will apply to be released. The Registrar of Companies dissolves the company three months later.

Actions that a liquidator may take in relation to directors' conduct are discussed in **Chapter 3.** In this chapter, we will focus on two of the other main functions of the liquidator: preserving and increasing the assets of the company, and distributing those assets to creditors.

8.10 Preserving and increasing assets

Liquidators and administrators are under a duty to maximise the assets available to creditors. They have the power to investigate the company's affairs generally, and to investigate the directors' actions prior to liquidation or administration. There are a number of claims that liquidators and administrators may bring, the purpose of which is to increase the assets available to creditors. The claimant will be the company, and any money awarded to the company will then be available to pay to creditors. The key potential claims are:

(a) avoidance of certain floating charges (s 245 IA 1986);

(b) preferences (s 239 IA 1986);

(c) transactions at an undervalue (s 238 IA 1986);

(d) transactions defrauding creditors (s 423 IA 1986); and

(e) extortionate credit transactions (s 244 IA 1986).

Each of these five potential claims are examined in turn below. These claims are distinct from any order the liquidator or administrator may seek requiring a director to contribute personally to the company's assets, which we looked at in **Chapter 3**.

8.11 Avoidance of certain floating charges

Some floating charges may be voidable as a preference (see **8.12** below), but here we are concerned with invalid floating charges, which are automatically void under s 245 IA 1986. Essentially a charge is automatically void where, at the 'relevant time' before the onset of the company's insolvency, a charge was granted without the company receiving fresh consideration in exchange for granting security.

The relevant time means:

- if the charge was created in favour of a person who is connected with the company, during the two years ending with the onset of insolvency; or

- if the charge was created in favour of any other person, during the twelve months prior to the onset of insolvency.

The onset of insolvency means, in the case of a compulsory liquidation, the date of presentation of the winding up petition. For a CVL, the onset of insolvency is the date that the company formally enters into liquidation, and for administration, the onset of insolvency is when the company files a notice of intention to appoint an administrator (or the date it actually goes into administration, if that is earlier). If the floating charge was given to someone unconnected with the company, the company must have been insolvent at the time the floating charge was given or have become insolvent as a result. If the floating charge was given to someone connected with the company, it is not necessary to show that the company was insolvent when the charge was granted or became insolvent as a result.

A person 'connected' with the company is defined in ss 249 and 435 IA 1986. The definition includes:

- a director or shadow director of the insolvent company; or

- someone who is, in effect, a close relative or business associate of a director or shadow director; or

- an associate of the company – which broadly means a company in the same group as the company or which is controlled by a director of the insolvent company.

Generally the liquidator or administrator will write to the charge holder saying that they believe the charge is invalid. If the charge holder tries to enforce the charge, the liquidator or administrator will seek an injunction on the basis that the charge is invalid.

⭐ *Example – avoidance of a floating charge*

In September 2021, a company borrowed £250,000 from a director's husband, James, to upgrade its IT system in the wake of customer complaints and a downturn in business. In March 2022, the company borrowed a further £50,000 from James to complete the upgrade. James insisted that the company grant him a floating charge to secure its liability to him, both in respect of the existing loan of £250,000 and the new loan of £50,000. The new loan and the floating charge relating to both loans were entered into in April 2022. A winding up petition was presented at court by a creditor of the company in July 2022.

The charge was clearly created well within the relevant time, for a person connected to the company, of two years ending with the onset of insolvency (which is the presentation of the winding up petition). However, only the second payment of £50,000 was given at the same time as the charge and therefore, if properly registered, the charge would be valid under s 245 as to this amount, but invalid as to the first payment of £250,000 the previous January.

8.12 Preferences

A liquidator or administrator can challenge a transaction where the company, at the relevant time, has given a preference to someone else. A preference is where the company puts the other person in a better position, in the event that the company went into insolvent liquidation or administration, than they would have been in otherwise.

The relevant time means:

*   if the preference was given to a person who is connected with the company (see **8.11**), during the two years ending with the onset of insolvency; or

*   if the preference was given to any other person, during the six months ending with the onset of insolvency.

The onset of insolvency is defined at **8.11**.

The company must have been insolvent at the time of the preference, or have become insolvent as a result of giving the preference. The liquidator or administrator will produce financial information such as the company's balance sheet, along with evidence of court proceedings against the company or correspondence to show the company was insolvent at the time or became insolvent as a result of the transaction. Unlike with transactions at an undervalue (see **8.13**), there is no presumption of insolvency if the preference was given to a connected person.

There must also be a desire to prefer the other party, rather than just an intention to prefer them.

Re MC Bacon and a desire to prefer

Re MC Bacon Limited [1990] BCLC 324 is a leading UK insolvency law case, concerning transactions at an undervalue and voidable preferences.

MC Bacon Limited ('MCB') had an overdraft facility of £300,000 with its bank. It 1986 it lost a major customer, leading to business difficulties. The bank was of the opinion that MCB had reasonable prospects of trading out of its difficulties, so requested a fixed and floating charge over the company's assets in exchange for its continued support. The charge was granted in May 1987, and four months later the bank appointed an administrative receiver.

A liquidator was appointed three days later. The liquidator argued that the debenture should be set aside because it was a voidable preference or a transaction at an undervalue (see **8.13**).

The court held that the transaction was not a voidable preference under s 239 because the company was not influenced by a *desire* to put the creditor in a better position than it would have been in on liquidation. The company decided to enter into the charge not because of a desire to prefer but rather because it would not survive if it lost the financial support of the bank and therefore had no choice if it wished to continue.

Further, the transaction was not a transaction at an undervalue under s 238 (see **8.13**) because it was not entered into for a consideration the value of which, in money or money's worth, was significantly less than the value, in money or money's worth, of the consideration provided by the company: the mere creation of security does not deplete the company's assets and therefore couldn't fall within the definition.

Two of the most common scenarios where a preference may be a possibility is where one creditor is paid before one of the other creditors, or where an unsecured creditor is given security. If a preference is given to a person connected to the company, the desire to prefer is presumed, but this can be rebutted.

If the preference is proven, the court may order the release of any security given by the company, the return of any property transferred as part of the transaction, or the payment of the proceeds of sale of property forming part of the transaction to the company.

8.13 Transactions at an undervalue

A liquidator or administrator can challenge any transaction which the company has entered into at an undervalue at the relevant time. An undervalue is where the company makes a gift to the other person, or enters into a transaction and receives consideration which is significantly lower in value than the consideration provided by the company.

The relevant time means during the two years ending with the onset of insolvency.

The company must have been insolvent at the time of the transaction, or have become insolvent as a result of the company entering into the transaction. Insolvency is presumed where the transaction was with a person connected to the company, but this presumption can be rebutted (unlike with preferences).

There is a defence if the transaction was entered into in good faith, for the purpose of carrying on the business, and where, when the transaction was entered into, there were reasonable grounds for believing that it would benefit the company. An example would be where the company could not find a buyer for a property at full price and had to sell it quickly to the only buyer showing any interest in it, just to obtain some money, even though the buyer was not willing to pay market value.

⭐ *Example – preference and transaction at an undervalue*

Elm Wood Limited ('the company') is a company which specialises in manufacturing and supplying luxury mobile offices for people's gardens. In January this year, the board realised that the company was in financial difficulties, owing money to several creditors. The next month, the company sold one of its mobile offices to Matthew, a director of the company, for £12,000. The market value of the mobile office was £30,000, but the board knew that Matthew could not afford to pay any more and decided to let him pay what he could. A month later, the company responded to pressure from its bank to pay off the £10,000 outstanding and overdue for payment on a loan. Two months after that, the company went into liquidation.

Can the liquidator challenge either of these transactions?

The sale of the mobile office to Matthew is likely to be a transaction at an undervalue because:

* *the company received significantly less consideration for the sale of the mobile office than the consideration it provided;*

- *the transaction was within the relevant time, because the transaction occurred during the two years prior to the date of commencement of winding up; and*

- *insolvency is presumed, because Matthew, as a director, is connected to the company.*

It does not seem as if the defence is relevant on the facts.

The repayment of the bank loan probably cannot be challenged. There is evidence of intention to prefer the bank, but it seems that this was a response to ordinary commercial pressure, so there was no desire to prefer.

8.14 Extortionate credit transactions

A liquidator or administrator has the power to challenge an extortionate credit transaction made in the three years ending with the day on which the company went into administration or liquidation. For a transaction to be extortionate, it must require grossly exorbitant payments to be made, or must otherwise grossly contravene ordinary principles of fair dealing. Such claims are rare, because it is very difficult to prove that the payments were grossly exorbitant or grossly contravened ordinary principles of fair dealing.

8.15 Transactions defrauding creditors

A transaction defrauding creditors is a transaction at an undervalue (see **8.13**) which the company entered into in order to put assets beyond the reach of someone making a claim against it, or to prejudice the interests of that person in relation to any claim they might make. Challenges to transactions defrauding creditors are brought at the discretion of the court. The other party to the transaction may be ordered to return any property which was the subject of the transaction to the company, or discharge any security that was given by the company as part of the transaction.

There is no time limit for bringing a claim under this section. However, it is often very difficult to show intention to put assets beyond someone's reach or to prejudice their interests. Therefore, the claim is usually only made when the liquidator or administrator cannot bring a claim relating to a transaction at an undervalue because the time limit has expired (although the longer the passage of time, the longer such a claim can be to prove). Note that creditors can also bring such a claim, as a 'victim' of the transaction.

8.16 Distributing a company's assets during liquidation

There is a distinct order of payment of different creditors in an insolvency process and it is important to understand that.

Fixed charge holders, as opposed to floating charge holders, will receive the amount they are owed when the asset which was the subject of the fixed charge is sold. Any surplus is paid to the liquidator. If, instead, there is a shortfall, the fixed charge holder can join the pool of unsecured creditors and try to obtain some kind of contribution towards the outstanding debt.

⭐ Example

A company is in liquidation. One of its creditors, a bank, has a fixed charge over the company's office building, to secure a loan for £100,000. The office is sold for only

£75,000, which is £25,000 less than what the bank is owed. The bank will join the pool of unsecured creditors in relation to the shortfall of £25,000.

During liquidation, the liquidator sends a standard form to unsecured creditors, which they are required to fill in with details of the debt owed to them. This process is known as proving the debt. Once the liquidator has the forms, they can decide whether to approve or reject the creditors' claims. The acceptance procedure for small debts is more straightforward, a small debt being a sum that does not exceed £1,000, and these claims are effectively admitted more or less automatically.

Once the liquidator has sold the company's assets, and collected as much money as they can and paid the holders of valid fixed charges, they will make payments in the following order, which is set out in the IA 1986:

(a) the expenses of the winding up (the fees payable to the liquidator and their professional advisers);

(b) preferential debts, which rank and abate equally;

(c) money which is the subject of floating charges, in order of priority; and

(d) unsecured creditors, who rank and abate equally.

Any money remaining is distributed to the shareholders. 'Rank and abate equally' means that all of the creditors in a particular category will share the available money between them. They will not receive equal amounts: instead, they will receive the same percentage of the outstanding debt that they are owed. In most insolvent liquidations, unsecured creditors do not receive more than a few pence in every pound they are owed. This is because, usually, most of the assets are subject to security, and the charge-holder will take their money first, with the remainder being available for unsecured creditors.

⭐ *Example*

A company is in liquidation and has two unsecured creditors. One is owed £10,000 and the other is owed £5,000. However, only £7,500 is available for unsecured creditors. Each creditor will therefore receive £7,500/£15,000 = £0.50 for every pound they are owed.

The first creditor will get £10,000 x 0.50 = £5,000, and the second £5,000 x £0.50 = £2,500. The amount the creditor receives is known as a dividend.

8.17 Preferential debts

Preferential debtors are paid before all other unsecured creditors in insolvent liquidation. The most common preferential debt is wages/salaries of employees for work carried out in the four months immediately preceding the date of the winding up order, up to a maximum of £800 per employee. In addition, employees' accrued holiday pay is a preferential debt.

As of the beginning of December 2020, HMRC became a secondary preferential creditor (ranking behind employees), but only in relation to taxes which companies collect *on HMRC's behalf,* such as PAYE and VAT. It is not a preferential creditor in relation to other taxes which a company owes directly to HMRC, such as corporation tax. This change will have a huge impact on other creditors, as HMRC is often one of the largest creditors in insolvent liquidations.

8.18   Ring fencing

Ring fencing is the statutory procedure brought into force in 2003 setting aside a portion of the available money for *floating charge holders* (where the security was created on or after 15 September 2003) for the benefit of unsecured creditors (*not* secured creditors). The amount that should be set aside is:

- 50% of the first £10,000 of money received from the property which is subject to floating charges; and

- 20% of the remaining money

up to a limit of £800,000. Note that this limit was increased from £600,000 with effect from 6 April 2020. The previous limit of £600,000 still applies to any charges created before 6 April 2020, unless a floating charge created on or after 6 April 2020 ranks equally or in priority to the pre-April 2020 charge, in which case the limit of £800,000 will apply to both charge holders.

 Example – distribution of assets with no secured creditor involved

Table 8.2 shows an insolvent company's debts and how a liquidator would share assets of £100,000 among creditors.

Table 8.2   Sharing the assets of an insolvent company

Debts	
Owed to HMRC	£45,000
Costs of liquidation	£10,000
Owed to preferential creditors	£15,000
Owed to business creditors	£120,000
Total	**£190,000**
Sharing of assets	
Funds available to liquidator	£100,000
Less costs and expenses (paid in full)	(£10,000)
Less preferential creditors (paid in full)	(£15,000)
Amount remaining for unsecured creditors	£75,000

Unsecured creditors amount to £45,000 + £120,000 = £165,000

75,000/165,000 = approximately £0.46.

Unsecured creditors receive approximately 46p for every £1 they are owed.

8.19　Alternatives to liquidation

Companies that wish to avoid liquidation have a number of options:

(a)　administration (under Sch B1 IA 1986);

(b)　company voluntary arrangements (under Part I IA 1986);

(c)　schemes of arrangement (under ss 895–901 CA 2006);

(d)　restructuring plans (under Part 26A CA 2006);

(e)　a free-standing moratorium (under Part A1 IA 1986); or

(f)　informal agreements with creditors.

Below, we focus on administration and CVAs. Schemes of arrangement are not strictly an insolvency procedure (although they are similar to CVAs, because they involve coming to an agreement with creditors). They can be entered into at any time during the company's life, not necessarily when it is insolvent. They necessitate two court hearings and meetings of creditors and shareholders, and are therefore expensive and more difficult procedurally than CVAs. They tend to be used to restructure large companies with complicated structures, often before they are taken over.

Restructuring plans are similar in form to schemes of arrangement and are a brand new procedure brought in by the CIGA 2020. The company will propose a plan to its creditors or members. The main difference between a scheme of arrangement and a restructuring plan is that it is easier for a restructuring plan to be sanctioned by the court even if a group of creditors or members has voted against it.

A company's directors may also seek a free-standing moratorium by making a filing at court. The moratorium is designed to give a company in distress breathing space to attempt to rescue the company. Again, this is a completely new procedure introduced by the CIGA 2020. The fact that it is so new means that it not possible to analyse its impact in practice.

Informal agreements with creditors are not statutory and are not binding, so they carry the risk that any of the creditors may choose to wind up the company instead of going ahead with what was previously informally agreed. For this reason, they are often not a feasible or recommended option.

8.20　Administration

Administration is the process whereby an administrator (an independent insolvency practitioner) is appointed to run the company and make whatever changes are necessary to improve its financial performance. Alternatively, the administrator will aim to get the company into a position where it can be sold as a going concern. The main advantage of administration is that while the administration is under way, there is a statutory moratorium (not to be confused with the new, stand-alone moratorium procedure brought in by the CIGA 2020). This means that it is not possible for anyone to commence or continue with legal action against the company, enforce a judgment, or issue a winding up petition without the administrator's consent. This gives the administrator time and space to investigate the company, assess its viability and maximise the amount of money available to creditors.

 Example – The Jamie Oliver Restaurant Group Limited

The Jamie Oliver Restaurant Group Limited went into administration in May 2019. Changes in consumer preferences and saturation of the market were two possible reasons for the Group's demise. All but three of the Group's restaurants closed. The other three continued to trade in the short term, and the administrators, employed by KPMG, eventually found buyers for the Group's remaining sites.

8.21 The duties of the administrator

The administrator must perform their duties in the interests of all of the company's creditors as a whole, and have as a primary objective the wish to rescue the company as a going concern. If this is not practicable, they must try to achieve a better result for the company's creditors as a whole than would be likely if the company were wound up. If this is not practicable, they must realise (sell) property to pay one or more secured or preferential creditors.

8.22 Commencing administration

There are two ways of commencing administration. The first, known as the court route, is by court order, following an application to court and a court hearing. The second, called the out-of-court route, involves the company, its directors or the holder of a qualifying floating charge, or even an unsecured creditor, filing certain documents at court. These two routes are explained below.

8.23 The court route

The court can make an administration order only if it is satisfied that the company is likely to become unable to pay its debts, and the administration order is reasonably likely to achieve one of the three purposes of administration set out in **8.21**. The purpose of the administration most commonly seen is that the administration would achieve a better result for the company's creditors than liquidation.

As soon as reasonably practicable after applying for administration, the applicant must notify any person who has appointed or is entitled to appoint an administrative receiver of the company, and any qualifying floating charge holder ('QFCH') (see **8.25**) who is entitled to appoint an administrator.

8.24 The out-of-court route – appointment by the company or its directors

The purpose of this procedure is to make it easier to rescue a company.

The first stage of this route is to serve notice of intention of administration on:

* the court; and
* any QFCH; and
* any lender who is entitled to appoint an administrative receiver.

The directors must also file at court a statutory declaration that the company is unable to pay its debts, and is not in liquidation. This means that if a compulsory winding up petition in relation to the company has already been presented at court, directors cannot use the out-of-court route, and must instead apply to the court for an order that the company go into administration in place of the winding up petition being allowed to proceed. The moratorium comes into effect as soon as the notice of intention to appoint is filed at court.

8.25 Out-of-court route – appointment by QFCH

A qualifying floating charge is a floating charge where the charge document states that paragraph 14 of schedule B1 to the IA 1986 applies to it and:

- the charge document purports to empower the holder of the floating charge to appoint an administrator; or

- the charge document purports to empower the holder of the floating charge to appoint an administrative receiver within the meaning of the IA 1986;

and the charge document relates to the whole or substantially the whole of the company's property (or does so when added to other security held by the same lender). The out-of-court route allows lenders with floating charges to easily appoint administrators. If there is another QFCH who would have priority, the lender must notify them in advance to give them the opportunity to appoint the administrator if they wish. The floating charge must be enforceable, meaning that the charge holder must be entitled under the loan agreement to enforce the security. This is usually because of late payment, but there will almost certainly be other events of default set out in the charge document. The administrator has a duty to all of the company's creditors. Contrast this with receivers (see **8.34.1**), who have a duty only to the party which appointed them. Administrative receivers have a primary duty to those who appointed them, but also secondary duties to others.

The lender must file the notice of appointment at court, along with certain documents. The notice of appointment must include a statutory declaration by the lender stating that:

- the lender is a holder of a QFC in relation to the company's property;

- the floating charge is enforceable; and

- the appointment complies with the IA 1986, Sch B1.

The administration begins when the above documents are filed at court.

8.26 The process of administration

Once administration has started, as stated above, a moratorium comes into effect. The administrator will put forward the proposals for the company to the creditors. The creditors can ask for more information on the amended proposals, especially if the administrator has been appointed by the directors, and the creditors view them with some suspicion. Creditors can suggest amendments to the proposals.

The administrator's proposals will be approved if a majority in value of the creditors, present and voting, vote in favour of them, provided that those who vote against the proposals do not constitute more than 50% in value of the creditors who are unconnected to the company.

8.27 The effect of the administration order

Once the administration order has been made, the company is managed by the administrator and the directors' powers cease, even though they remain in office. The administrator is in control of the company's assets, although they do not own them, and the administrator carries out the proposals approved by the creditors. Throughout the administration, the moratorium described above continues.

8.28 The administrator's powers and duties

The administrator's statutory powers (under the IA 1986 and the Insolvency Rules) include:

(a) removing and appointing directors;

(b) paying creditors, but only with the court's permission if the payment is to an unsecured creditor;

(c) calling a meeting of creditors or shareholders;

(d) dealing with property that is subject to a floating charge;

(e) dealing with property that is subject to a fixed charge (with the permission of the court);

(f) investigating and applying to have the company's past transactions set aside or challenged (see **8.10**); and

(g) commencing fraudulent or wrongful trading proceedings against directors.

The order of distribution of assets is very similar to liquation (see **8.16**). In addition to their specific powers, the administrators have the power to do anything necessary or expedient for the management of the affairs, business and property of the company.

8.29 The end of the administration

There are numerous ways in which administration may be ended. Administration ends automatically one year from the date the administration took effect, but this can be extended. It can also be ended earlier, including by application to the court if its objective has been achieved or if the administrator believes its objective cannot be achieved, or by application to the court by a creditor. The creditor may then present a winding up petition if that is the wish.

8.30 Pre-pack administration

A pre-packaged administration (often called a 'pre-pack') is an arrangement whereby a company goes into administration and the administrator sells its assets and business straight away, often to the management of the insolvent company. The sale is effectively agreed before the company appoints an administrator, and it is a perfectly legal way of securing a sale of the business as a going concern. The justification for this route is that more jobs are likely to be saved, but the unsecured creditors are not consulted and are unlikely to receive very much in payment of the debts they are owed. Recent legislation places additional, more onerous requirements on pre-packs involving connected parties, partly to address the concerns of unsecured creditors, who have traditionally viewed pre-packs with suspicion.

8.31 Company voluntary arrangement

A company voluntary arrangement (CVA) is a further alternative to liquidation (and also to administration and administrative receivership, although anyone entitled to appoint a receiver or administrator will need effectively to support the CVA if it is to succeed, as it cannot interfere with the rights of secured creditors). A CVA can also develop out of administration as an exit route from that process.

What is a CVA?

A CVA is a written agreement which binds all of the parties to it, as long as the statutory procedures are followed. You will sometimes hear the term 'statutory contract' to describe the written agreement. The parties are usually the company and all of its creditors. In a CVA, the company's creditors usually agree to wait longer to receive what they are owed, or accept payment of only part of the debt, or both.

Company voluntary arrangements are generally used when the company's business is potentially fundamentally sound, but it is undergoing a temporary cash flow difficulty. Its aim is to prevent liquidation. Compared with administration, it is comparatively cheap and simple to undertake and is available to liquidators, administrators and the company itself of course. The advantage for creditors is that they are likely to be paid more in a CVA than they would receive if the company went into liquidation or administration. This is one of the main reasons why creditors may be persuaded to support it. Unfortunately, sometimes CVAs fail and the company goes into liquidation in any event.

In a CVA, the proposals put forward for payment of creditors must be approved by:

- 75% or more in value of the company's creditors; and

- 50% or more of *non-connected* creditors.

The chair of the CVA meeting (generally the Insolvency Practitioner who is seeking to be appointed as the supervisor of the process) decides if creditors are connected or not. Secured creditors are not allowed to vote in the CVA, apart from in relation to any part of the debt owed to them that is unsecured. Once the proposal is approved, it is binding on all unsecured creditors in relation to past debts, but not future debts.

The CVA does not affect the rights of secured and preferential creditors, unless they agree to it. Small companies used to be entitled to a moratorium of 28 days after filing the CVA proposal at court but this is no longer the case. However, companies could use the moratorium created by CIGA 2020 (see **8.33**) as well as entering into the CVA, and the moratorium would give the company the breathing space it needed to give the company the chance to enter into the CVA.

An insolvency practitioner will supervise the arrangement of the CVA and monitor its implementation and continuation.

8.32 Restructuring plan under CIGA 2020

This is a restructuring tool brought in by CIGA 2020 which has many features of schemes of arrangement, but there are certain key differences. The restructuring plan is court-supervised and is an 'arrangement' or 'compromise' between the company and all of its secured and unsecured creditors and shareholders. Companies do not need to be insolvent to apply for a restructuring plan but they must have encountered or be likely to encounter financial difficulties.

The directors will usually prepare a restructuring plan and apply to court for approval to call meetings of the company's creditors and shareholders. Creditors and shareholders are also allowed to do this but, in practice, the directors will do it because they have the detailed information needed for the meetings.

Implementation of the plan involves two court hearings and creditors can make representations at the first hearing. At the second hearing, the court will decide whether to sanction the proposed plan. Between the two hearings, the creditor and shareholder meetings will be held. Creditors and shareholders are divided into classes, and each class will be deemed to have approved the plan if 75% by value of that class vote in favour. This differs from schemes of arrangement, which require an overall majority in number to approve the scheme.

The key feature of the restructuring plan is the 'cross-class cram down provision', which is what really provides flexibility. It enables a dissenting class of creditors to be 'crammed down' so that they cannot block otherwise viable plans, and it must be sanctioned by the court. The court will only sanction it where it is satisfied that no member of the dissenting classes would be any worse off under the plan than they would be if the court were not to sanction the plan.

8.33 Moratorium under CIGA 2020

This measure was introduced in response to the Covid-19 pandemic, but it is a permanent measure. In this moratorium, the company is protected from actions by creditors relating to pre-moratorium debts, but it must pay debts incurred during the moratorium in full. During the moratorium, the company's directors remain in control, but a qualified insolvency practitioner acts as an independent monitor who has oversight of the moratorium and can terminate it in certain circumstances.

It is a requirement of the moratorium that the company must be unable to pay its debts or likely to become unable to pay its debts. A moratorium is not possible if the company has already entered into a moratorium during the previous 12 months. There are also certain companies which are not eligible for the moratorium, including banks, often known as the financial services exception.

The moratorium is only available for English companies with no outstanding winding up petitions against them. To obtain the moratorium, the directors must file the relevant documents at court, and the proposed monitor must also confirm that it is likely that the moratorium will result in the rescue of the company as a going concern. Whilst most pre-moratorium debts are suspended during the moratorium, certain debts are excluded from this payment holiday, including employees' wages or salary arising under a contract of employment, the monitor's remuneration or expenses, and goods or services supplied during the moratorium.

The moratorium lasts 20 business days beginning with the business day after the moratorium comes into force. This is the date of filing of the documents at court or the court order. However, it can be extended for a further 20 business days by filing certain documents at court. The moratorium can be extended by the directors for a period of up to one year if the creditors who are not going to get paid because of the payment holiday consent to this.

8.34 Options for secured creditors

Creditors who lend money to companies usually take security. These creditors may be able to appoint a receiver to take possession of the property which is the subject of the charge and deal with it for the benefit of the charge holder, as opposed to creditors generally. This will usually involve selling the property. Once the property is sold, the receiver has no further interest in the property. Normally the trigger for going into receivership is that the company has breached the charge holder's loan agreement, for example by defaulting on repayments. The charging document itself will state when a receiver can be appointed, and the company does not need to be insolvent. There are effectively two types of receivers to be considered in the insolvency arena, and they are explained below.

8.34.1 Law of Property Act (LPA) receivers

The term 'LPA receiver' is used to describe a receiver appointed by a *fixed* charge holder. These receivers were once appointed under the Law of Property Act 1925 ('LPA'), and this is why they are often called LPA receivers. However, now, the power to appoint the receiver is usually in the charge document. The aim of appointing an LPA receiver is usually to sell the charged property so that the creditor can be repaid. If the sum realised is not enough to pay what the creditor is owed, the creditor will become an unsecured creditor for the remainder. Conversely, if the sale realises more than the amount owed to the creditor, the surplus will be returned to the company and will be available for unsecured creditors.

Law of Property Act receivers do not have to be licensed insolvency practitioners.

8.34.2 Administrative receivers

Administrative receivers are appointed by floating charge holders, when the floating charge is over the company's whole undertaking. Subject to some exceptions, they are only used for floating charges created before 15 September 2003. Charges created on or after 15 September 2003 use the administration route instead (see **8.20**).

8.34.3 Appointing an administrative receiver

The loan agreement will list the events which trigger the lender being able to appoint an administrative receiver. Examples of trigger events are failure to make a payment, the company being unable to pay its debts, breach of the loan agreement or presentation of a petition to wind up the company.

The administrative receiver runs the company and sells the charged assets. They will use the proceeds to pay their own costs and pay the charge holder what they are owed under the loan secured by the charge. In theory, the administrative receiver then resigns, and the directors take over the management of the company once more. Unfortunately, liquidation will more often than not follow administrative receivership. This is because, if the company has reached the point where it cannot pay the charge holder other than by the charged assets being sold, it generally means that the company does not have much money – particularly now that some assets have been sold – and will not be able to carry on as a going concern.

8.34.4 Summary: the different liquidation processes

Compulsory Liquidation	Voluntary Liquidation	
	Creditors	Members
Petition filed at court and served on company. **Start of winding up**	Directors agree by a majority that the company is insolvent and needs to be placed into liquidation.	Directors make statutory declaration of solvency.
Company cannot dispose of assets	Members pass special resolution to liquidate company and may consider nominating a liquidator. Directors' powers effectively cease. **Start of winding up**	Members pass special resolution to start liquidation and ordinary resolution to appoint liquidator. Directors' powers cease. **Start of winding up**

(continued)

(*continued*)

Compulsory Liquidation	Voluntary Liquidation	
Petition advertised in the *Gazette*		
Court hearing. If winding-up order made, Official Receiver appointed as liquidator and directors' powers cease.	Directors must, before the end of 7 days beginning with the day after the day the company passes a resolution for CVL: • make out a statement in the prescribed form as to the affairs of the company • send the statement to the company's creditors • seek nomination from the company's creditors for a person to be the liquidator. Creditors considering the appointment of a liquidator must hold a virtual meeting/seek approval by the new deemed consent procedure. There is no physical meeting unless it is requested by the creditors.	
Official Receiver advertises order in the *Gazette* and notifies Registrar of Companies.	Once the resolution to wind up the company has been passed by the shareholders, the liquidator must file a copy at Companies House and it must be advertised in the *Gazette*.	Once the formalities of the meeting are concluded, the appointment will be published in the *Gazette* and the Registrar notified.
Liquidator investigates and reports to creditors.		
Creditors may appoint alternative liquidator if the majority are in favour of that.	Creditors may appoint alternative liquidator if the majority are in favour and a resolution is passed to that effect.	Creditors may appoint alternative liquidator if the majority are in favour and a resolution is passed to that effect.
Liquidator collects in assets and realises if necessary, and then distributes in the statutory order.		
Final accounts sent to creditors and/or members.		
Final return filed with court and Registrar of Companies.	Final return filed with Registrar of Companies.	
Company dissolved after three months.		

Part 2   Personal Insolvency

8.35   Introduction

Individuals may find themselves insolvent because they have cash-flow problems: perhaps they have borrowed too much, and cannot pay it back. They may lose their job and be unable to pay their debts. Alternatively, they may be part of an unsuccessful unincorporated business which fails and absorbs all of their money. In this part of the chapter, we will first examine when a person is insolvent and how this is proven. We will then consider the options available to an insolvent person whose creditors are chasing them for payment.

8.36   When is a person insolvent?

An individual is insolvent under s 267 IA 1986 when:

*   A debt is payable now but the debtor does not currently have enough money to pay; or

*   A debt is payable in the future and there is no reasonable prospect that the individual will be able to pay.

⭐ *Example – individual insolvency*

Kate has £500 in her bank account and earns £1,500 a month net of tax. She has no other source of funds. After she has paid for essentials such as rent, food and bills, she generally has around £300 left each month. Last month, she bought some furniture, and was given six months to pay. The cost of the furniture was £4,000. Is Kate insolvent?

Yes, Kate is insolvent. Kate does not owe the money yet, but given her financial circumstances, there is no reasonable prospect that she will be able to pay for the furniture when the time comes: she only has £300 a month to put towards the cost, and this only equates to £1,800 over six months – not the £4,000 she needs.

8.37   Proving insolvency

Section 268 of the IA 1986 sets out three ways a creditor can prove that an individual is insolvent:

1.   By serving a statutory demand on the debtor for a liquidated sum of £5,000 or more, and waiting three weeks to see whether the debtor pays or applies to court to set aside the statutory demand.

2.   By serving a statutory demand on the debtor in respect of a future liability to pay a debt of £5,000 or more, and waiting three weeks to see whether the debtor either:

   a.   shows a reasonable prospect of being able to pay the sum when it falls due; or

   b.   applies to court to set aside the statutory demand.

3.   By obtaining a court judgment for a debt of £5,000 or more, and attempting execution of the judgment without success.

8.38 Options for the insolvent person

The debtor does not have to wait until a creditor petitions for their bankruptcy. They can always try talking to their creditors to come to an agreement regarding the payment of the debt. If this does not resolve matters, they can apply for their own bankruptcy, to show that they are trying to take control of the situation themselves rather than 'burying their head in the sand'. Finally, they could enter into an individual voluntary arrangement ('IVA') or apply for a debt relief order. These options are explored at **8.54**. Note that the new Debt Respite Scheme may be available to give the debtor breathing space from creditor action for up to 60 days (see **8.54.4**).

8.39 What is bankruptcy?

Bankruptcy is the process whereby the debtor's assets pass to a trustee in bankruptcy, whose job it is to pay as many of the debts as possible to the debtor's creditors. The debtor is known as the bankrupt, and is subject to restrictions on their activities and spending during the bankruptcy process, and possibly afterwards. After one year (or possibly longer, see **8.52**), the bankrupt is discharged, meaning that the bankruptcy ends and the bankrupt is free from almost all their debts, even though the bankrupt has not paid all of their debts in full. The relevant legislation is contained mainly in the IA 1986, the Enterprise Act 2002 and the Insolvency Rules.

Student loans are not part of this process: they must be paid in full, even after the bankrupt has been discharged.

8.40 The bankruptcy procedure

Bankruptcy begins by a creditor presenting a petition at court, or by the debtor applying for their own bankruptcy online.

8.40.1 A petition brought by a creditor

A creditor is entitled to present a bankruptcy petition at court if they are owed £5,000 or more. This must be a liquidated, that is, fixed, sum, rather than, for example, the creditor claiming that they are owed unspecified damages which the court would need to assess. The creditor must also show that the debtor is unable to pay their debt or has little prospect of being able to pay their debt, which is presumed if the creditor has used one of the methods set out in **8.37** to show that the debtor is insolvent. Creditors owed less than £5,000 may join other creditors and petition together, provided the total amount owed to all the petitioners is not less than £5,000. Creditors must pay a deposit to meet the costs of the trustee in bankruptcy and the court fee.

The creditor must usually present the petition at the debtor's local county court hearing centre, as long as it has jurisdiction in bankruptcy matters. The creditor must also arrange for personal service of the petition. This means that instead of merely posting the petition to the debtor, the creditor engages the services of an agent who will hand the petition to the debtor and provide a witness statement confirming that they have done so. If the debtor is avoiding the agent, the creditor can seek to obtain a court order for substituted service, which means that another method of service, for example just posting it through the debtor's letterbox, will be deemed sufficient service.

8.40.2 A debtor's application

If the debtor decides to take the matter into their own hands and apply for their own bankruptcy, they must apply online. An adjudicator, who is an employee of the Insolvency

Service, will decide whether to make a bankruptcy order. The ground for the application is that the debtor is unable to pay their debts. In addition to the fees for the application, the debtor will also need to pay a deposit in respect of the Official Receiver's administration fees.

The adjudicator must make a bankruptcy order, or refuse to make one because the debtor has not proven that they are unable to pay their debts, within 28 days from the application (unless the adjudicator requires further information from the debtor, in which case the decision deadline is extended to 42 days). In practice, the order is almost invariably made within 48 hours.

8.41 The Official Receiver and the trustee in bankruptcy

Once a bankruptcy order has been made, the Official Receiver (OR) acts as the trustee in bankruptcy and takes control of the bankrupt's assets. The OR is employed by the Insolvency Service and is an officer of the court. The OR will ask the debtor for a statement of affairs, detailing their financial position and recent financial transactions. The OR may then make further investigations into the debtor's financial affairs. The OR will also take steps to protect the debtor's property and will dispose of or sell any property which is perishable or decreasing in value (for example, if a sole trader operates a catering business and is storing food).

It is possible for the creditors to appoint a private trustee in bankruptcy, just as with corporate insolvency, but this will only happen when the bankrupt has enough assets to fund the private trustee's fees. Whether the trustee in bankruptcy is the OR or a private trustee in bankruptcy, the bankrupt's estate vests in them automatically from the moment the bankruptcy order is made. The trustee must, where necessary, realise and sell the bankrupt's assets and use the proceeds of sale to pay the creditors. When the trustee has done this, they will apply to be released. The trustee has the power to investigate the bankrupt's affairs, and set aside or challenge transactions which the bankrupt entered into before the bankruptcy order was made, which is effectively part of the realisation of assets process.

8.42 The bankrupt's property

While most of the bankrupt's property forms part of their estate and is therefore vested in the trustee, the bankrupt is permitted to keep some assets which are needed for day-to-day living, such as items they need for work (the 'tools of their trade') and everyday household items such as clothing and furniture. However, if any of these items are of high value, the trustee can sell them and replace them with a cheaper alternative.

Bankrupts are entitled to be paid their salary, but if their salary is more than what is sufficient to meet the reasonable needs of the bankrupt and their family, the trustee can ask the bankrupt to enter into an income payments agreement ('IPA'), which requires the bankrupt to pay some of their salary to the trustee to meet their liabilities. If the bankrupt and the trustee cannot agree on a sum to be paid, the trustee can apply to court for an income payments order ('IPO'), and the court will determine the amount payable. An IPA is enforceable just as an IPO is. The IPA and IPO normally last for a maximum of three years from the date the arrangement or order is made and, therefore, will survive the debtor's discharge from bankruptcy in most cases.

8.43 The bankrupt's home

If the bankrupt is a homeowner, their interest in that home passes to the trustee. If someone else has a legal or equitable interest in the house, or a right of occupation, the bankrupt cannot be evicted straight away and the trustee needs a court order to sell the house. When deciding whether to make an order for sale, the court will weigh up all of the relevant circumstances, including the interests of the creditors, the conduct and needs of a current or former spouse or civil partner and the needs of any children (s 335A IA 1986). After one year of bankruptcy, under s 335A, the creditors' interests outweigh those of anyone else living in the house, unless the circumstances are 'exceptional', and the trustee is therefore likely to be able to obtain an order for sale.

Three years after the bankruptcy order, ownership of the home transfers back to the bankrupt, unless the trustee has:

(a) sold the property;

(b) applied for an order for sale or possession or a charging order over the house; or

(c) entered into an agreement with the bankrupt regarding the home, for example that they may keep their interest in the house in exchange for payment.

8.44 Preserving and increasing the bankrupt's assets

The trustee's primary duty is to the creditors, and they have powers to investigate the bankrupt's affairs and challenge past transactions with a view to increasing the assets available to repay creditors. Following investigation, the trustee can choose to:

(a) disclaim onerous property (s 315 IA 1986);

(b) apply to set aside transactions at an undervalue (s 339 IA 1986);

(c) apply to set aside preferences (s 340 IA 1986);

(d) apply to set aside transactions defrauding creditors (s 423 IA 1986); and

(e) avoid extortionate credit transactions (s 343 IA 1986).

We shall consider each of these options in turn below.

8.45 Disclaiming onerous property

The trustee may disclaim onerous property, for example, unprofitable contracts, land that has the burden of an onerous covenant or a lease which does not have a capital value to be realised for the creditors' benefit. The trustee's disclaimer means that all of the bankrupt's rights and liabilities in respect of the onerous property come to an end and the trustee is discharged from personal responsibility for the property. If anyone suffers loss as a result of the disclaimer (for example, the money they would have earned on an onerous contract), they may prove as an unsecured creditor in the bankruptcy, meaning that they can make a formal claim to be a creditor of the bankrupt.

8.46 Transactions at an undervalue

You will be familiar with this concept from corporate insolvency, although the criteria for a transaction at an undervalue for individuals are slightly different. An undervalue is either a gift or a transaction in which the bankrupt received consideration (in money or money's worth) significantly lower in value than that which they provided. The trustee can investigate transactions during the five years prior to the presentation of the bankruptcy petition.

The trustee does not have to show that the bankrupt was insolvent at the time of the transaction or as a result of the transaction, unless the transaction was more than two years before the petition. If the transaction was with an associate, which essentially means a close relative or business associate (s 435 IA 1986), then even if the transaction was more than two years prior to presentation of the bankruptcy petition, there is a rebuttable presumption that the bankrupt was insolvent at the time of the transaction.

8.47 Preferences

A preference is where an arrangement places a creditor, surety or guarantor in a better position than they would otherwise have been in on bankruptcy, and the debtor intended to do this. An example is repaying a loan to a friend before a loan to the bank, so that the friend does not lose out when the debtor is made bankrupt.

There is a rebuttable presumption of intention to prefer if the preference is in favour of an associate (essentially a close relative or business associate). The trustee can challenge any potential preferences within the six months prior to the presentation of the bankruptcy petition, or within the two years prior to presentation of the petition if the preference is in favour of an associate.

The bankrupt must have been insolvent at the time of the preference, or must have become insolvent as a result of it.

8.48 Transactions defrauding creditors

This action is exactly the same for personal insolvency as it is for corporate insolvency, which you can read about at **8.15**. Again, it is really only used when the time limit for applying to set aside a transaction at an undervalue has expired.

8.49 Extortionate credit transactions

If the bankrupt has obtained any credit in the three years prior to the bankruptcy order, and the terms of the credit are 'extortionate', the trustee can apply to set aside or vary the terms of the credit. 'Extortionate' means that the terms require 'grossly exorbitant' payments or have 'grossly contravened...fair dealing'. There is no substantive reported case law on the use of s 343, despite the fact that sometimes people in financial difficulties resort to taking out loans on very unfavourable terms. This is probably because of the difficulty in showing that the interest rate is 'grossly exorbitant'.

8.50 Distribution of assets

Secured creditors can sell their charged assets, take what they are owed, and pay any surplus to the trustee. If the sale of the charged assets does not realise enough money to pay the secured creditor(s) the entire amount owed to them, the secured creditor(s) will join the unsecured creditors in relation to the outstanding part of the debt.

Once the trustee has finished realising the bankrupt's assets and challenging any of the transactions explained in **8.45–8.49**, the assets will be distributed in the following order, which is set out in the IA 1986:

1. The costs of the bankruptcy. This means all of the expenses incurred as a result of the bankruptcy, which will be mainly the trustee's professional charges and disbursements (eg legal fees).
2. Preferential debts.
3. Ordinary unsecured creditors.
4. Postponed creditors, who are the bankrupt's spouse or civil partner.

Within each category, the creditors will rank and abate equally, meaning that they will share the money available. Each creditor will receive the same percentage of the debt owed to them.

8.51 Preferential debts

Preferential debts rank above the debts of ordinary unsecured creditors. Preferential debts include the wages/salary of employees for work carried out in the four months immediately preceding the date of the bankruptcy of their employer, up to a maximum of £800, plus accrued holiday pay owed to employees. Of course, not all bankrupts will have employees – only those who were sole traders or partners, and even then, they may not necessarily have any employees. As explained in **8.17**, HMRC is now also a secondary preferential creditor.

⭐ *Example – distribution of assets*

Donald is bankrupt. **Table 8.3** *shows the assets that have been vested in his trustee, Donald's liabilities and how the assets will be distributed.*

Table 8.3 Assets, liabilities and distribution of assets of a bankrupt person

Assets	
Proceeds of sale of home, net of mortgage and costs	£50,000
Shares	£15,000
Antique furniture	£33,000
Transaction at an undervalue repayment (sports car sold to brother)	£25,000
Total assets	**£123,000**
Liabilities	
Trustee's fees and expenses	£10,000
Money owed to five employees for the last four months' wages	£4,000
Business creditors	£120,000
HMRC debt	£15,000
Bank loan and overdraft	£50,000

Table 8.3 (*continued*)

Total liabilities	**£199,000**
Distribution of assets	
Assets	£123,000
Less trustee's costs	(£10,000)
Less preferential debts	(£19,000)
Total remaining for unsecured creditors	**£94,000**

> *Donald's assets will be distributed as follows:*
>
> *Unsecured creditors total £170,000. They rank and abate equally, so:*
>
> $$94,000/170,000 = approximately \; £0.55$$
>
> *Unsecured creditors will therefore receive approximately 55p for every £1 they are owed.*

8.52 Discharge

A bankruptcy order is discharged automatically after one year, unless discharge is suspended (see the following paragraph). This means that the bankruptcy ends and the bankrupt is released from most of their previous debts. However, they may still be subject to a bankruptcy restriction order ('BRO') or bankruptcy restriction undertaking ('BRU') (see **8.53.3**).

The property which was vested in the trustee is not returned to the bankrupt, apart from the matrimonial home in some cases (see **8.43**). The trustee may not have realised all of the bankrupt's assets by this point, and the former bankrupt must still assist the trustee with this even once the bankruptcy order has been discharged. Sometimes automatic discharge is suspended if the bankrupt is uncooperative or dishonest during the bankruptcy. Normal practice, however, is to deal with such behaviour by applying for a BRO or entering into a BRU.

8.53 Restrictions on bankrupts

As soon as the bankruptcy order is made, the bankrupt is subject to certain restrictions. There are some restrictions on business activities and personal activities which apply to all bankrupts. Further, 'culpable' bankrupts are subject to further restrictions that last beyond this initial year of bankruptcy.

8.53.1 Business restrictions

Bankrupts are allowed to keep items they need for work (the 'tools of their trade') and a vehicle if it is essential for work. However, it is a criminal offence for a bankrupt to obtain credit of more than £500 without disclosing their bankruptcy. This can make it extremely difficult for the bankrupt to carry on the business. In addition, the bankrupt cannot:

- act as a director of a company (Company Directors Disqualification Act ('CDDA') 1986);

- be involved in the management, promotion or formation of a company, unless the court grants permission (CDDA 1986);

- trade under a different name from the name in which the bankruptcy order was made, without disclosing to anyone they trade with that they are an undischarged bankrupt; or

- continue in partnership, unless the partnership agreement varies the default position in the Partnership Act 1890, which is that the bankrupt will automatically cease to be a partner when they are made bankrupt.

8.53.2 Personal restrictions

Undischarged bankrupts cannot obtain credit of more than £500 without informing the lender that they are an undischarged bankrupt. This means that a bankrupt cannot obtain a credit card or have a normal current account – the bankrupt's bank will probably only allow the bankrupt to have a current account without an overdraft facility. Bankrupts cannot practise as a solicitor without the leave of the Solicitors' Regulation Authority, and there are similar restrictions for other professions.

8.53.3 Bankruptcy restriction orders and undertakings

Bankruptcy restriction orders are designed to protect the public from those bankrupts who are considered to be 'culpable' and to have caused their own bankruptcy by being dishonest, negligent or reckless. They are made by the court and last between two and 15 years. Instead of going through court proceedings, the bankrupt could agree to a bankruptcy restriction undertaking ('BRU') instead, which is an agreement having the same effect as a BRO. Many restrictions apply to a bankrupt subject to a BRO or BRU. The person who is subject to the order cannot act as a company director (or insolvency practitioner or MP) for the length of the order or undertaking, or obtain credit over a certain amount (currently £500) without disclosing the BRO.

8.54 Alternatives to bankruptcy

An individual facing bankruptcy should consider alternatives to bankruptcy before the creditor possibly a winding up petition. The main options open to debtors are an IVA; negotiation with creditors; or a debt relief order (if the debtor has minimal assets and income).

8.54.1 IVAs

An IVA is similar, in many respects to a CVA: it is a binding agreement between unsecured creditors, setting out how much each creditor will receive from the bankrupt in settlement of their debts. The debtor's trustee may seek an IVA during bankruptcy, or the debtor may seek one to avoid the bankruptcy procedure. They will need the professional help of an insolvency practitioner who will effectively formulate the proposals and supervise their implementation if the creditors approve the process. The insolvency practitioner is initially known as the debtor's nominee and will only agree to act if there are sufficient assets to pay their fees. Once the IVA is approved, they are renamed as the supervisor of the arrangement.

8.54.1.2 The IVA procedure

Once the debtor has appointed a nominee to act with them, the debtor must prepare a statement of affairs for the nominee to consider, and should then apply to the court for an interim order to obtain a moratorium. The interim order is usually in force for 14 days. In this period no other proceedings or enforcement action can be taken or continued against the debtor. The nominee then prepares a report for the court stating whether the debtor has put forward any realistic proposals and therefore whether they are prepared to support the calling of a creditors' decision-making process. If such a process takes place, and:

- 75% or more of the creditors in value

- of which at least 50% in value are not associates of the debtor

agree to the proposals, they will be approved. The chair of the meeting (effectively the Insolvency Practitioner) decides if a creditor an associate of the debtor. Every ordinary, unsecured creditor entitled to attend and vote is bound by the decision, even if they did not actually attend the meeting. The IVA is not binding on preferential or secured creditors unless they specifically agree to it.

If the creditors approve the IVA, the nominee, who, as stated earlier, is from that point onwards called a supervisor, implements the proposals. If the debtor does not comply with the arrangement or if it is discovered that the creditors accepted the debtor's proposals based on false or misleading information, the supervisor, or any of the creditors who are party to the IVA, can petition for the debtor's bankruptcy. This is, perhaps, when the debtor has made a transaction at an undervalue or a preference just before entering into the IVA which has not been disclosed. The reason for petitioning for the debtor's bankruptcy in such situations is because supervisors cannot apply to the court to set aside these transactions; only a trustee can.

8.54.1.3 Advantages for the debtor

A debtor who enters into an IVA rather than becoming bankrupt avoids the stigma of bankruptcy and possibly bad publicity. They will possibly avoid a private public examination in court in some cases. They will also avoid the disabilities and disqualifications to which a bankrupt is subject.

8.54.1.4 Advantages for the creditor

The relatively low cost of an IVA compared with bankruptcy, the fact that the whole process is more straightforward, and the fact that the bankrupt will be offering greater returns than would be received in bankruptcy, make it an attractive alternative to bankruptcy for creditors. However, creditors will need to consider whether the bankrupt can be trusted to honour the IVA. If not, the creditor may be able to petition for the debtor's bankruptcy at a later date.

8.54.1.5 The Straightforward Consumer IVA Protocol ('the Protocol')

Many consumers with money problems will have numerous debts, including significant credit card debts. Credit card providers will usually follow the Protocol in relation to these debts, although the Protocol, approved by the British Bankers' Association, is voluntary. The Protocol aims to balance the need for the consumer to be free of debt with the creditors' need to recoup as much as possible. It contains standard terms, including fees for insolvency practitioners and levels of return for creditors.

8.54.2 Negotiation with creditors

From a debtor's perspective, it is always worth talking to creditors if an individual is in financial difficulties. The creditors know that an individual who is heavily in debt will not be able to pay them all they are owed, so it is in creditors' interests to obtain what they can, when they can. An informal arrangement with one or more creditors may enable the individual to avoid bankruptcy. However, because any arrangement would be informal, it would not stop another creditor issuing a bankruptcy petition. So these informal arrangements are sometimes not the answer for debtors. It is partly for this reason that the new breathing space regime was brought in (see **8.54.4** below).

8.54.3 Debt relief orders

Debtors apply online for a debt relief order ('DRO'). Debt relief orders are only for debtors whose assets and liabilities are low in value. They are *not* available if the debtor:

(a) has total unsecured liabilities exceeding £20,000;

(b) has total gross assets exceeding £1,000;

(c) has a car worth £1,000 or more (unless it has been adapted because the debtor has a disability);

(d) has disposable income in excess of £50 per month, after deducting normal household expenditure;

(e) has been subject to a DRO in the preceding six years; or

(f) is subject to another, formal insolvency procedure.

If the application for a DRO is accepted, the OR makes the order. The debtor will then be protected from enforcement action by most of their creditors in the same way as bankruptcy, and will in the vast majority of cases be free of debt at the end of the DRO period, which is 12 months (unless it is extended because of non-cooperation by the debtor).

The debtor must cooperate with the Official Receiver and provide information they request, and is expected to pay their creditors if their financial situation improves. During the time that the debtor is subject to the DRO, the same restrictions apply to them as to a bankrupt (see **8.53**). As with bankruptcy, these restrictions may last up to 15 years if the debtor is dishonest or culpable, and this extra period is obtained by the Official Receiver applying for a Debt Relief Restrictions Order against the debtor.

8.54.4 Debt Respite Scheme ('Breathing Space')

The Debt Respite Scheme (Breathing Space Moratorium and Mental Health Crisis Moratorium) (England and Wales) Regulations 2020 introduced the Debt Respite Scheme ('Breathing Space'). This can give someone in problem debt the right to legal protection from creditor action.

There are two types of breathing space: a standard breathing space and a mental health crisis breathing space. A standard breathing space is available to any client with problem debt, and it gives them legal protection from creditor action for up to 60 days (a moratorium). The protection includes pausing most enforcement action and contact from creditors and freezing most interest and charges on their debts.

A mental health crisis breathing space is only available to a client who is receiving mental health crisis treatment. The mental health crisis breathing space has some stronger protections than the standard breathing space. It lasts as long as the client's mental health crisis treatment, plus 30 days (no matter how long the crisis treatment lasts).

To obtain a breathing space, the debtor must apply to a debt advice provider authorised by the Financial Conduct Authority. To grant the breathing space/moratorium, the debt adviser must be satisfied that the debtor cannot pay some or all of their debt as it falls due. The debtor cannot be an undischarged bankrupt and must not be in an IVA or subject to a debt relief order. The debtor must also not have already had another breathing space in the previous 12 months. The debt must also be a qualifying debt, but nearly all debts will be.

The debt advice providers will use an electronic service provided by the Insolvency Service to contact creditors and maintain a database of debtors who are in a breathing space.

It remains to be seen what effect this new scheme will have on personal insolvency. The second phase of the scheme (a statutory debt repayment scheme) will not be in force until 2023.

8.55 The Corporate Insolvency and Governance Act 2020

CIGA 2020 came into force on 26 June 2020. Some of the provisions have made a permanent change to the law, and these have been referred to earlier in this chapter. Other provisions introduced temporary changes to address the financial problems faced by businesses as a result of the Covid-19 pandemic. These temporary provisions were originally in force until 30 September 2020, but some were then extended. They included a restriction on creditors presenting a winding up petition, unless they had reasonable grounds to believe either that Covid-19 had not had a financial effect on the company or that the company was unable to pay its debts regardless of Covid-19, and a restriction on using statutory demands served between 1 March 2020 and 30 September 2020 as the basis for a winding up petition.

These provisions had all ended by the end of 2021 but it may be useful for you to be aware that they existed when you enter legal practice.

Sample questions

Question 1

Assume that it is 30 January 2023. A company's up-to-date balance sheet shows current assets of £25,000, current liabilities of £16,000 and net assets of £500. On 9 January 2023, a creditor served a statutory demand on the company relating to a debt of £1,500. The debt remains unpaid.

Which of the following best describes whether the company can now be placed into compulsory liquidation?

A   No, because the company is currently solvent on the balance sheet test.

B   No, because the creditor is owed over £750.

C   Yes, because the statutory demand was served 21 days ago and remains unpaid so the creditor will be entitled to petition for the compulsory liquidation of the company.

D   Yes, because the company is currently insolvent on the cash flow test.

E   Yes, because the statutory demand was served 21 days ago and remains unpaid so the company will now automatically go into compulsory liquidation.

Answer

Option C is correct. The fact that the company is solvent on the balance sheet test (option A) is not relevant: under s 123(1)(a) of the Insolvency Act 1986 ('IA 1986'), failure to pay the sum owed within three weeks of service of a statutory demand means that a company is deemed unable to pay its debts so the court can wind up the company. This is not an automatic process: a creditor must issue a winding up petition (s 124 IA 1986), so E is wrong. B is also wrong – it is only where the creditor *is* owed over £750 that they can issue a winding up petition. On the information given, D is wrong too, because the company may well be insolvent on the cash flow test but liquidation does not automatically follow.

Question 2

A client is owed £30,000 by a company in liquidation. The company has assets of £150,000 and liabilities of £325,000. All of its five creditors are unsecured and there are no preferential creditors.

Which of the following best describes how much the client will receive?

A £1

B £0.46

C £2.16

D £13,800

E £64,800

Answer

Option D is correct. You need to divide total assets by total liabilities (150,000/ 325,000 = £0.46). This gives the amount every creditor should receive for each pound they are owed. Then multiply the amount per pound (£0.46) by the amount the client is owed (£0.46 x 30,000) making a total of £13,800.

Question 3

A client has been served with a bankruptcy petition. Her bank has written to her saying that she will lose her home (in which she lives with her two young children) if she does not pay the amounts she owes.

Assuming the bankruptcy order is made and the client's trustee in bankruptcy writes to her stating his intention to seek possession of her home unless she pays her debts and the costs and expenses of bankruptcy, which of the following best describes whether the client will lose her home?

A She will not lose it because the interests of young children outweigh the interests of creditors.

B She will not lose it because a bankrupt is entitled to keep their family home, everyday household items and the tools of their trade, unless the circumstances are exceptional.

C She is likely to be able to stay in the home for a year, after which the creditors' interests outweigh those of any occupants of the house, unless the circumstances are exceptional.

D She will not lose her home if she pays the credit card debt which was the subject of the petition, as that creditor was putting the most pressure on the client.

E She is likely to be able to stay in the home until her youngest child is 18, after which point the creditors' interests outweigh those of any occupants of the house.

Answer

Option C is correct. After one year, creditors' interests will prevail over the interests of any other person living at the property unless exceptional circumstances can be shown (s 335A(3) Insolvency Act 1986). There is nothing in these facts to indicate exceptional circumstances so options A, B and E are wrong. Option D is wrong because insolvency is a class remedy and it is not enough just to pay one creditor and leave others if you want to annul the order and so keep the house. All creditors have to be paid, together with interest in full, and the costs and expenses of the bankruptcy.

9 Income Tax

SQE1 syllabus

Candidates are required to apply relevant core legal principles and rules appropriately and effectively, at the level of a competent newly qualified solicitor in practice, to realistic client-based and ethical problems and situations in the following areas of income tax:

*   chargeable persons/entities (employees, sole traders, partners, shareholders, lenders and debenture holders)
*   basis of charge (types of income/main reliefs and exemptions)
*   the charge to tax: calculation and collection
*   the scope of anti-avoidance provisions.

Learning outcomes

By the end of this chapter you will be able to:

*   understand HMRC's mechanism for charging income tax each year;
*   understand what constitutes income for the purposes of calculating income tax;
*   understand some of the allowable reliefs and allowances available to taxpayers to reduce their tax liability;

- understand how dividend and savings income is taxed;
- carry out an income tax calculation;
- understand how sole traders, partners, employees, directors, lenders and debenture-holders are charged to tax;
- understand income tax payment dates;
- understand the general anti-avoidance rule; and
- understand the National Insurance scheme.

The tax rates set out in this chapter are correct as at the date of publication. Please note that these tax rates may no longer be current at the date of any future SQE assessment.

9.1 Introduction

Income tax produces more revenue for the UK Government than any other tax. The most recent available figures show that in 2020/21, HM Revenue and Customs ('HMRC') collected almost £585 billion in tax, and around a third of this was income tax.

Income tax is an annual tax renewed each year by Act of Parliament. The charging statute for income tax is the Income Tax Act 2007 (ITA 2007) as amended by later Finance Acts. Other important statutes are the Income Tax (Trading and Other Income) Act 2005 (ITTOIA 2005) and the Income Tax (Earnings and Pensions) Act 2003 (ITEPA 2003).

The judiciary plays its part in developing tax law: the meaning of statutory provisions are decided by the court. There are dedicated tax tribunals, from which there is eventually a right of appeal to the Court of Appeal and, with leave, to the Supreme Court.

HM Revenue and Customs also makes official statements, which are important sources of information regarding the meaning and extent of tax legislation. There are several types of statement, but the two most important are extra-statutory concessions and statements of practice. The official statements do not bind the court: they simply give guidance as to the stance HMRC will take in certain circumstances.

9.2 What is income?

There is no statutory or judicial definition of income. Generally, money will be regarded as income if there is an element of recurrence, for example, a salary received every month, or interest received on a bank account. There is no real need for a statutory definition of income because tax legislation lists exactly what is regarded as income, even if it does not provide a generic description.

9.3 Who pays income tax?

Individuals, partners, personal representatives and trustees may have to pay income tax. Charities are generally exempt, and companies instead pay corporation tax (see **Chapter 11**).

9.3.1 Individuals

Individuals who are employed will have to pay income tax if their earnings exceed a certain threshold (and this is usually assessed by their employer and paid directly to HMRC by the employer – see **9.5.1.1**).

Sole traders will also have to pay income tax, based on an assessment of their trading profits. How trading profits are calculated is explained in detail in **Chapter 7**, but in summary:

*   The first step is to ascertain the business's chargeable receipts, which is essentially the money it has received from trading, for example, selling furniture.

*   The next step is to subtract from chargeable receipts any deductible expenditure (such as the cost of buying the furniture in the first place, utility bills and rent) and capital allowances. This resulting figure is trading profit (or loss) and this can be inserted at step 1 of the income tax calculation.

In the examples in this chapter which concern taxation of sole traders, the sole trader's profit has already been calculated, to enable you to focus instead on the principles of taxation.

Individuals may have to pay income tax on other types of income too, for example, income from investments and pensions, interest on bank or building society accounts and dividends received from companies in which they hold shares.

9.3.2 Partners

Partners are responsible for the tax due on their individual share of the partnership profits. The method of calculating trading profit is the same as for sole traders, but the profit will need to be apportioned between the partners in accordance with their shares in the income profits of the partnership. How this is done is explained in **12.13.2**. In the examples in this chapter which concern partnership profits, the partner's profit share has already been calculated so that you can focus on the principles of taxation. Note that if a partner is not an individual but a company, that corporate partner will be liable to pay corporation tax rather than income tax on its share of the profits (see **Chapter 11**).

9.3.3 Personal representatives

Personal representatives pay the deceased's outstanding income tax and income tax chargeable during the administration of the estate.

9.3.4 Trustees

Trustees pay income tax on income produced by the trust.

9.4 The tax year

The tax year runs from 6 April until 5 April the following year. This means that an individual will pay tax on all income earned between these dates. The tax year, also called the year of assessment, is described by reference to the calendar years which it straddles. So the tax year beginning on 6 April 2022 and ending on 5 April 2023 is referred to as the tax year 2022/23. By way of example, a person whose income is in the form of a salary will be charged to tax in the tax year 2022/23 for all salary received between 6 April 2022 and 5 April 2023.

9.5 How to calculate income tax

The rate of tax payable increases as the income of the taxpayer increases. This means that taxpayers with higher incomes pay, on average, higher rates of tax than those on lower incomes.

Tax is payable on taxable income. To work out taxable income, various reliefs and allowances are deducted from the income the individual earns. The allowances and rates depend on the type of income, so when calculating income, it is important to separate out the income into categories so that the types of income can be treated differently. The three categories of income are:

(a) non-savings, non-dividend income ('NSNDI'). This is essentially all sources of income apart from income from savings and income from dividends;

(b) savings income, which is interest from various sources, such as interest on money held in a bank account;

(c) dividend income.

To calculate the income tax payable, you must follow these steps:

Step 1: Calculate total income

Step 2: Deduct any allowable reliefs

The resulting sum is **net income**

Step 3: Deduct any personal allowances

The resulting sum is **taxable income**

Step 4: Separate NSNDI, savings income and dividend income, and calculate the tax on each type of income at the applicable rate(s) (starting rate, basic rate, higher rate and additional rate)

Step 5: Add together the amounts of tax from Step 4 to give the overall **income tax liability**

 Example

To carry out a simple tax calculation, you should follow the five steps outlined above, as illustrated in the example below.

Kim received the following income during the tax year 2022/23:

- *£51,000 share of partnership profits; and*

- *£8,000, after deduction of expenses, from carrying out freelance translation.*

*She is liable to make interest payments of £3,000 per annum on a qualifying loan. The interest payments qualify as an allowable relief. You can read more about allowable reliefs at **9.5.2**.*

Kim is a single person. Kim's income tax may be calculated as follows:

		£
STEP 1	Calculate the total income Partnership profits Translation **TOTAL INCOME**	 51,000 8,000 59,000
STEP 2	Deduct any allowable reliefs (interest) **NET INCOME**	(3,000) 56,000

(continued)

STEP 3	Deduct any personal allowance **TAXABLE INCOME**	(12,570) 43,430
STEP 4	Calculate the tax at the applicable rate(s) £37,700 at 20% <u>£5,730</u> at 40% <u>£43,430</u>	7,540 2,292
STEP 5	Add together the amounts of tax from Step 4 **OVERALL INCOME TAX LIABILITY**	**9,832**

Below we consider each step in more detail.

9.5.1 Step 1: Total income

Step 1 is to calculate total income. To do this, it is important to be aware of what income is charged to income tax under ITTOIA 2005 and ITEPA 2003. The most important sources of income are:

(a) **trading income:** profits of trade, profession or vocation. This applies to sole traders, trading partnerships, sole practitioners and professional partnerships;

(b) **property income:** rents and other receipts from land in the UK;

(c) **savings and investment income:** interest, annuities and dividends;

(d) **employment and pensions income**, including social security payments such as sick pay and maternity pay; and

(e) **certain miscellaneous income** which is beyond the scope of this book.

If the income in question is from one of the sources above, the individual will pay income tax. If the income does not fall into one of the categories of income set out above, the recipient cannot be charged to income tax on this income at all.

Certain income is not chargeable to income tax, including interest on damages for personal injuries or death, interest on savings certificates, certain state benefits, premium bond winnings and income from investment in an individual savings account (ISA).

Income is divided into chargeable sources because the sources of income are treated differently. For example, a landlord may receive income from a rental property, but is permitted to deduct from this expenses such as repairs to the property. Income tax is then charged on the profit, rather than the whole amount of the rent received. Other types of income are not treated in the same way as rental income so need to be calculated separately in the tax calculation.

To work out the taxpayer's total income, you must find out what sources of income the taxpayer has, calculate the income arising under each source and then add all of the sums together. The resulting figure constitutes total income.

Sole traders may suffer a trading loss, for which relief may be available. The examples in this chapter will assume that any sole traders have made a gain, not a loss. For a full explanation of the reliefs available if the sole trader has instead suffered a loss, please see **7.12**.

9.5.1.1 Deductions at source

The taxpayer receives most types of income without any tax having been deducted beforehand. For example, a landlord will receive rental payments in full: the tenant does not deduct a sum to cover the landlord's income tax before paying the rent. This income is referred to as being received 'gross'.

However, the main source of income for most taxpayers will be employment income, that is, their salary. Tax will already have been deducted at source from this income. The payee receives the net amount and not the gross amount, and the employer pays the employee's income tax directly to HMRC at the time the salary is paid through the Pay As You Earn (PAYE) system. The PAYE system also ensures that the personal allowance is deducted. This is relevant because the fact that an employee has already paid income tax must be reflected in the income tax calculation, otherwise the end figure, the tax payable, is inaccurate. Therefore we must 'gross up' any sum received by the employee to find the original sum from which the tax was deducted. We must then enter this gross figure into the calculation of total income.

Grossing up employment income is not a simple task because income tax will be deducted from salary at various rates and national insurance contributions will also be deducted. The position may be complicated further by pension payments or benefits such as health insurance.

9.5.1.2 Savings and dividend income

Interest and dividends are both paid gross. Both savings and dividend income benefit from annual tax-free allowances. Both savings and dividend income form part of total income and must be added to other income at this stage.

9.5.2 Step 2: Allowable reliefs

Total income *less* allowable reliefs = net income

Certain sums, known as allowable reliefs, are deducted from total income to give a figure for net income. The most significant example is interest payments on qualifying loans. Most interest payments, for example, bank overdrafts and credit card interest, must be paid out of taxed income. But in certain cases, tax relief may be available for interest paid on money which the taxpayer has borrowed.

To benefit from this relief, interest must be payable on a 'qualifying loan', including:

- a loan to buy a share in a partnership, or to contribute capital or make a loan to a partnership;
- a loan to invest in a close trading company; and
- a loan to personal representatives to pay inheritance tax.

9.5.3 Step 3: Personal allowances

Everybody is allowed to earn a certain amount of income each year before they start paying income tax. This sum is known as the personal allowance, and it is deducted from net income to obtain the taxpayer's taxable income.

The personal allowance for 2022/23 is £12,570. It can be set against income of any kind but is applied in a certain order:

- firstly, against NSNDI
- if there is surplus, against savings income
- any remaining surplus is applied against dividend income

Any unused personal allowance (for those whose income is less than £12,570) cannot be carried forward for use in future years, unless the marriage allowance applies (see **9.5.3.1**).

Where the taxpayer's income exceeds £100,000, the personal allowance is reduced by £1 for every £2 of income above the £100,000 limit. So a taxpayer earning a net income of £102,000 will benefit from a personal allowance of £11,570 – this is £1,000 less than those earning £100,000, because every £2,000 earned over £100,000 results in a reduction of £1,000 to the personal allowance.

Once a taxpayer's income reaches £125,140, they will not have a personal allowance because their personal allowance will have been reduced to zero by this point.

To calculate the personal allowance for a taxpayer with a net income above £100,000 but below £125,140 you can use the following method:

$$\text{Adjusted Personal Allowance} = £12,570 - \frac{(\text{net income} - £100,000)}{2}$$

The adjusted Personal Allowance is rounded up to the nearest £1.

⭐ *Example 1*

Arpana has a net income of £55,000. She is entitled to deduct the full personal allowance of £12,570 from her net income of £55,000 to obtain a taxable income of £42,430.

⭐ *Example 2*

Margaret has a net income of £120,000. Margaret is not entitled to deduct the full personal allowance as her net income exceeds the £100,000 income limit. Using the above formula, Margaret's adjusted personal allowance can be calculated.

$$£12,570 - \frac{(£120,000 - £100,000)}{2}$$

...which is equivalent to...

$$£12,570 - \frac{£20,000}{2}$$

...which is equivalent to....

*£12,570 – £10,000 = **£2,570***

*Margaret is entitled to deduct **£2,570** from her net income of £120,000 to obtain a taxable income figure of £117,430.*

9.5.3.1 Marriage Allowance

Where a person does not have enough income to use their personal allowance fully for that tax year, they can transfer £1,260 of their personal allowance to their spouse or civil partner. This is not available if the recipient is a higher or additional rate taxpayer.

9.5.3.2 Blind person's allowance

Any taxpayer who is registered blind receives an allowance of £2,600, which is subtracted from net income just like the personal allowance.

9.5.3.3 Property and trading allowances

Allowances for small amounts of property income and trading income are, generally, available to all UK taxpayers. Where individuals are in receipt of gross property income or gross trading income below £1,000, the income will not be subject to income tax and taxpayers are not required to submit a tax return or, where they have other income, declare it in their tax return. Where gross property or trading income is in excess of £1,000, the taxpayer can choose to take the £1,000 allowance as a deduction against gross income instead of deducting actual expenses to arrive at their taxable income figure.

9.5.3.4 Personal savings and dividend allowances

The personal savings and dividend allowances are not to be confused with the personal allowance.

Personal savings allowance (PSA)

The PSA can be set against savings income, so that up to the first £1,000 of savings income will be tax free.

The amount of the PSA to which a taxpayer is entitled depends on whether the taxpayer is a basic or higher rate taxpayer. This is calculated by reference to the taxpayer's taxable income, as calculated at Step 3. (Allowances will be made for allowable pension contributions and gift aid.) Additional rate taxpayers do not receive a PSA.

Table 9.1 sets out the amount of the allowance.

Table 9.1 Personal Savings Allowance

Tax rate	Income band (Taxable income)	Allowance
Basic rate taxpayer	£0–£37,700	£1,000 tax free
Higher rate taxpayer	£37,701–£150,000	£500 tax free
Additional rate taxpayer	£150,001 and above	No allowance

Given how low interest rates are currently, most people will not receive interest of over £500 in any one tax year, so most people will not pay any tax on the interest they receive on money held in a bank or building society account. It is mostly additional rate taxpayers who will be paying tax on interest, because they have no PSA so will pay tax on all the interest they receive.

Examples: taxing savings income and how the PSA works

 Example 1

Miles has a salary of £29,000 and receives interest of £875 a year. He has no relevant allowable reliefs. Miles is a basic rate taxpayer (as all of his taxable income is within the basic rate tax band) and therefore has a PSA of £1,000, which will cover all of his savings income, and so he will not pay any tax on his savings income.

⭐ Example 2

Isabel has a salary of £75,000, so is a higher rate taxpayer. She has no relevant allowable reliefs.

Isabel has a building society savings account and receives £650 annual interest from it. As a higher rate taxpayer, she has a PSA of £500. This is set against her savings income of £650, leaving £150. The £150 will be taxed at the higher rate of 40 per cent.

⭐ Example 3

Elia has a salary of £190,000. Because her taxable income exceeds £150,000, she is an additional rate taxpayer. She has no relevant allowable reliefs.

Elia has a building society savings account and receives £650 annual interest from it. As an additional rate taxpayer, she has no PSA. This means that the whole £650 interest is taxable savings income and will be taxed at 45 per cent.

Dividend allowance

The dividend allowance is £2,000. It means that the first £2,000 of a taxpayer's dividend income will be free from tax. Unlike the personal allowance, all taxpayers (whether basic, higher or additional rate taxpayers) are entitled to the £2,000 allowance. This means that any taxpayer who receives less than £2,000 a year in dividends will pay no tax on their dividends, even if they are higher or additional rate taxpayers.

Nil rate bands

Although the PSA and dividend allowance are described as allowances, HMRC does not regard these as exemptions in the same way as the personal allowance. Instead, the PSA and dividend allowance reduce the rate of tax applied to these types of income to 0% ('nil rate'). The result is that the PSA and dividend allowance are not used at this stage with the personal allowance to reduce taxable income. *Only* the personal allowance is deducted when calculating taxable income. If the PSA and dividend allowance apply, it just means that savings and dividend income will be taxed at 0%. This will become clearer when you consider the calculation in the example at **9.5.9**.

9.5.4 Step 4: Calculate the tax on each type of income and Step 5: add together to give overall income tax liability

The rates of income tax increase as the taxpayer's income increases. In addition, the rates are different for the various types of income. Therefore, before the tax payable can be calculated, the different types of income must be separated from one another.

To find out how much taxable income is comprised of NSNDI and how much of savings and dividend income, the savings and dividend income are deducted from the taxable income figure arrived at in Step 3:

Taxable income *less* savings and dividend income = **taxable NSNDI**

We can then calculate the tax payable on NSNDI.

9.5.5 Order of taxation

Income is taxed in 'slices'. The bottom slice, taxed first, is the NSNDI. The middle slice is the savings income, and the top slice is the dividend income. The tax rates are different for each slice, as shown in **Table 9.2**, and the cut-off point between the rates usually (but not always) changes annually.

Table 9.2 Income tax rates

Top slice (taxed last)	Dividends: taxed at the dividend rates	Dividend ordinary rate: 8.75% Dividend upper rate: 33.75% Dividend additional rate: 39.35%
Middle slice (taxed next)	Interest: taxed at the savings rates	Starting rate for savings: 0% Savings basic rate: 20% Savings higher rate: 40% Savings additional rate: 45%
Bottom slice (taxed first)	NSNDI: taxed at the main rates	Basic rate: 20% Higher rate: 40% Additional rate: 45%

9.5.5.1   NSNDI

First to be taxed is NSNDI. Once you have worked out what NSNDI is, you must tax it at the appropriate rates, shown in **Table 9.2**. You also need to know the tax bands, so that you know at what point a taxpayer will start to pay tax at a higher rate. The income tax bands for NSNDI are:

Rate	Taxable income
Basic rate of 20%	£0–£37,700
Higher rate of 40%	£37,701–£150,000
Additional rate of 45%	over £150,000

The examples below illustrate how to tax the NSNDI.

 Example – how to tax NSNDI

Leo has a taxable income of £200,000, of which £30,000 is savings and dividend income. Leo's NSNDI amounts to:

Taxable income	£200,000
Less savings and dividend income	£30,000
NSNDI	£170,000

Leo's NSNDI will be liable to tax:

(a) at the basic rate of 20% on the first £37,700;

(b) at the higher rate of 40% for income above the basic rate limit of £37,700 but below the higher rate limit of £150,000. For Leo, this means that £112,300 (£150,000 – £37,700) will be taxed at 40%; and

(c) at the additional rate of 45% on the income in excess of the £150,000 limit (£20,000).

The tax liability in respect of his NSNDI will be:

£37,700	@ 20%	£7,540
£112,300	@ 40%	£44,920
£20,000	@ 45%	£9,000
Total NSNDI £170,000		Total tax payable £61,460

The savings and dividend income is calculated separately (not shown).

9.5.5.2 Savings income

Any savings income is taxed next. As explained earlier, the PSA does not operate as an exemption; rather, it reduces the tax rate to nil for the first £1,000 of savings income if you are a basic rate taxpayer and for the first £500 of savings income if you are a higher rate taxpayer. Additional rate taxpayers do not benefit from the PSA.

To tax savings income, the PSA must first be deducted from the savings income figure. This will give the amount of savings income which will be taxed at the savings rates set out below.

Savings income *less* PSA (taxed at 0%) = 'remaining taxable savings income'

The remaining taxable savings income will then be taxed at the savings starting, basic, higher and additional rates. For the tax year 2022/23 the rates are as follows:

Starting rate for savings of 0%	£0–£5,000
Savings basic rate of 20%	£5,001–£37,700
Savings higher rate of 40%	£37,701–£150,000
Savings additional rate of 45%	over £150,000

To work out at what tax rates an individual will pay tax on the remaining taxable savings income, we add their PSA to their taxable NSNDI. Let's say this gives a figure of £36,000 and the individual has remaining taxable savings income of £3,000. The individual will pay tax on £1,700 of the remaining taxable savings income at 20%, and will pay £1,300 at 40% because this portion of the remaining taxable savings income is above the basic rate threshold of £37,700.

Any remaining taxable savings income which falls below the savings starting rate limit of £5,000 is taxed at 0%. If it falls between the savings starting and savings basic rate limits, it is taxed at the basic rate of 20%; if it falls between the savings basic and higher rate limits, it is taxed at the higher rate of 40%. Any excess over the higher rate limit is taxed at the 45% additional rate.

Figure 9.1 illustrates how to calculate income tax rates.

Figure 9.1 Calculating income tax payable

Stage 1: Add PSA to taxable NSNDI
(to establish the relevant rates of tax)

Stage 2: Charge remaining taxable savings income at the appropriate rates

If the taxable NSNDI *plus* PSA is less than £5,000, the Remaining Taxable Savings Income will be taxed at the starting rate for savings. Any Remaining Taxable Savings Income over £5,000 will be taxed at the savings basic rate of 20%.	If the taxable NSNDI *plus* PSA is more than £5,000 but less than £37,700, the Remaining Taxable Savings Income below £37,700 will be taxed at the savings basic rate. Any Remaining Taxable Savings Income over £37,700 will be taxed at the higher rate (or additional rate over £150,000).	If the taxable NSNDI *plus* PSA exceeds £37,700, the Remaining Taxable Savings Income below £150,000 will be taxed at the savings higher rate. Any Remaining Taxable Savings Income over £150,000 will be taxed at the additional rate.	If the taxable NSNDI *plus* PSA exceeds £150,000, the Remaining Taxable Savings Income will be taxed at the savings additional rate.

You can see from the explanation above that adding the PSA to taxable NSNDI just has the effect of pushing the taxpayer closer to a higher tax bracket for taxation of savings income. In many cases this will mean the taxpayer pays more tax than they would have done if the PSA had been taken off at the same point in the tax calculation as the personal allowance.

The following examples illustrate the principles introduced above.

 Example 1

Dafydd has a taxable income (after allowances and reliefs) of £4,990, of which £2,990 is NSNDI and £2,000 is interest. Dafydd is a basic rate taxpayer, and so will be entitled to a PSA of £1,000, which is taxed at 0%. All of his remaining taxable savings income falls within the £5,000 starting rate. He will be liable to tax:

(a) at the basic rate of 20% on the first £2,990 of NSNDI (£598); and

(b) at the savings starting rate of 0% on the remaining 'top slice' of £1,000 of savings income (£0).

 Example 2

Ruth has taxable income (after allowances and reliefs) of £17,300, of which £14,800 is NSNDI and £2,500 is interest. Ruth is a basic rate taxpayer, and so will be entitled to a PSA of £1,000, which is taxed at 0%. All of her Remaining Taxable Savings Income falls within the basic rate (because taxable NSNDI plus PSA = £15,800.) She will be liable to tax:

(a) at the basic rate of 20% on the first £14,800 of NSNDI (£2,960); and

(b) at the savings basic rate of 20% on the remaining 'top slice' of £1,500 of savings income (£300).

⭐ *Example 3*

Charlotte has taxable income (after allowances and reliefs) of £80,000, of which £77,000 is NSNDI and £3,000 is interest. Charlotte is a higher rate taxpayer. She will be entitled to a PSA of £500, which is taxed at 0%. All of her Remaining Taxable Savings Income falls within the savings higher rate band (Taxable NSNDI plus PSA = £77,500.) She will be liable to tax:

(a) *on the NSNDI:*

    (i) *at the basic rate of 20% on the first £37,700 (£7,540); and*

    (ii) *at the higher rate of 40% on the remaining £39,300 (£15,720); and*

(b) *at the savings higher rate of 40% on the remaining 'top slice' of £2,500 of savings income (£1,000).*

⭐ *Example 4*

Colin has taxable income (after allowances and reliefs) of £165,000, of which £148,000 is NSNDI and £17,000 is interest. Colin is an additional rate taxpayer, so he is not entitled to a PSA. He will be liable to tax:

(a) *on the NSNDI:*

    (i) *at the basic rate of 20% on the first £37,700 (£7,540); and*

    (ii) *at the higher rate of 40% on the remaining £110,300 (£44,120); and*

(b) *on the interest:*

    (i) *at the savings higher rate of 40% to the extent that it falls below the higher rate limit of £150,000, so £2,000 (that is, £150,000 – £148,000) will be taxed at 40% (£800); and*

    (ii) *at the savings additional rate of 45% on the remaining £15,000 (£6,750).*

9.5.5.3   Dividend income

To work out the dividend income which will be subject to tax, you must deduct the dividend allowance from the dividend income figure.

Dividend income *less* dividend allowance (taxed at 0%) = '**remaining taxable dividend income**'

The remaining taxable dividend income is taxed at the dividend ordinary rate, upper rate and additional rate. For the tax year 2022/23, the rates are as follows:

Dividend ordinary rate of 8.75%	£0–£37,700
Dividend upper rate of 33.75%	£37,701–£150,000
Dividend additional rate of 39.35%	over £150,000

To ascertain whether the dividends will be taxed at the dividend ordinary, upper or additional rate, you must add the dividend allowance to total taxable NSNDI and total savings income. To the extent that the dividend income falls within the basic rate limit, it will be taxed at 8.75 per cent. To the extent that dividend income falls between the basic rate limit and the higher rate limit, it will be taxed at 33.75 per cent. Any excess over the higher rate limit will be taxed at 39.35 per cent. This is illustrated in **Figure 9.2**.

Figure 9.2   Calculating tax on dividend income

Stage 1: Add dividend allowance to taxable NSNDI plus total savings income (including PSA)

Stage 2: Charge remaining taxable dividend income at the appropriate rates

If the taxable NSNDI *plus* total savings income *plus* the dividend allowance is less than £37,700, the remaining taxable dividend income below £37,700 will be taxed at the dividend ordinary rate (and at the dividend upper and additional rates as appropriate above £37,700).	If the taxable NSNDI *plus* total savings income *plus* the dividend allowance exceeds £37,700, the remaining taxable dividend income below £150,000 will be taxed at the dividend upper rate (and at the dividend additional rate above £150,000).	If the taxable NSNDI *plus* total savings income *plus* the dividend allowance exceeds £150,000, the remaining taxable dividend income will be taxed at the dividend additional rate.

⭐ *Example 1*

Mehmet has taxable income (after allowances and reliefs) of £10,000, of which £6,500 is NSNDI and £3,500 is dividend income. He has no savings income. Mehmet is a basic rate taxpayer. He is entitled to a dividend allowance of £2,000, which is taxed at 0%. All of his remaining taxable dividend income falls within the basic rate, because taxable NSNDI plus dividend allowance = £8,500. He will be liable to tax:

(a) at the basic rate of 20% on the £6,500 of NSNDI (tax payable £1,300); and

(b) at the dividend ordinary rate of 8.75% on the 'top slice' of the remaining taxable dividend income of £1,500 (tax payable £131.25).

⭐ *Example 2*

Rich has taxable income (after allowances and reliefs) of £57,500, of which £42,500 is NSNDI and £15,000 is dividend income. He has no savings income. Rich is a higher rate taxpayer.

Rich is entitled to a dividend allowance of £2,000, which is taxed at 0%. All of his remaining taxable dividend income falls within the higher rate (taxable NSNDI plus dividend allowance = £44,500.) He will be liable to tax:

(a) on the NSNDI:

(i)   at the basic rate of 20% on the first £37,700 (£7,540); and

(ii) at the higher rate of 40% on the remaining £4,800 (£1,920); and

(b) on the remaining 'top slice' of dividend income (£13,000), at the dividend upper rate of 39.35% (£5,115.50).

⭐ *Example 3*

Zara has taxable income (after allowances and reliefs) of £154,000, of which £135,000 is NSNDI and £19,000 is dividend income. Zara is an additional rate taxpayer. She is entitled to a dividend allowance of £2,000, which is taxed at 0%. Part of her remaining taxable dividend income falls within the upper rate and part falls within the additional rate (Taxable NSNDI plus dividend allowance = £137,000, leaving £13,000 of the higher rate available.) She will be liable to tax:

(a) on the NSNDI:

  (i) at the basic rate of 20% on the first £37,700 (£7,540); and

  (ii) at the higher rate of 40% on the remaining £97,300 (£38,920); and

(b) on the remaining dividend income (£17,000)

  (i) at the dividend upper rate of 33.75% to the extent that it falls below the dividend higher rate limit of £150,000, so £13,000 (£150,000 – £137,000) will be taxed at 33.75% (£4,387.50); and

  (ii) at the dividend additional rate of 39.35% on the remaining £4,000 (£1,574).

9.5.6   Taxing both savings and dividend income

So far, we have considered examples where the taxpayer has either savings or dividend income, as well as taxable NSNDI. We will now consider a simple calculation where the taxpayer has both savings and dividend income, in addition to taxable NSNDI.

⭐ Example 1

Fynn has taxable NSNDI of £20,000, savings income of £1,500 and dividend income of £9,000. Fynn is a basic rate taxpayer, so he is entitled to a PSA of £1,000 and a dividend allowance of £2,000.

(a) Fynn will be liable to tax on the NSNDI at the basic rate: £20,000 at 20% (£4,000).

His NSNDI will use up only £20,000 of the basic rate band, leaving £17,700.

(b) The savings income is taxed next. To decide what rate applies to his savings income, the £1,000 PSA is added to his taxable NSNDI and treated as the first slice of his savings income and taxed at 0%. The remaining taxable savings income of £500 all falls within the £37,700 threshold, and is taxed at the savings basic rate: £500 at 20% (£100).

This has used up a further £1,500 of the basic rate band, leaving £16,200.

(c) The dividend income is taxed last. The £2,000 dividend allowance is added as the first slice of Fynn's dividend income, and taxed at 0%. His remaining taxable dividend income all falls below the £37,700 threshold.

Fynn will be liable to tax on the Remaining Taxable Dividend Income at the dividend ordinary rate: £7,000 at 8.75% (£612.50).

The fact that the PSA and dividend allowance are treated as nil rate bands rather than allowances which are subtracted at an earlier point in the tax calculation (like the personal allowance) means that the figure for taxable income remains higher throughout the calculation. The taxpayer will pay more than they would have done were the PSA and dividend allowance treated in the same way as the personal allowance.

⭐ Example 2

Assume now that Fynn has taxable NSNDI of £34,000, savings income of £1,500 and dividend income of £8,000. Fynn is therefore now a higher rate taxpayer and is entitled to a PSA of £500 and a dividend allowance of £2,000.

(a) Fynn will be liable to tax on the NSNDI at the basic rate: £34,000 at 20% (£6,800).

His NSNDI will use up £34,000 of the basic rate band, leaving £3,700.

(b) The savings income is taxed next. To decide what rate applies to his savings income, the £500 PSA is added to his taxable NSNDI and treated as the first slice of his savings income and taxed at 0%. The remaining taxable savings income of £1,000 all falls within the £37,700 threshold, and is taxed at the savings basic rate.

Fynn will be liable to tax on the remaining taxable savings income at the savings basic rate: £1,000 at 20% (£200, as opposed to £100 in Example 1, where Fynn was entitled to a PSA of £1,000).

This has used up a further £1,500 of the basic rate band, leaving £2,200.

(c) The dividend income is taxed last. The £2,000 dividend allowance is added as the first slice of Fynn's dividend income, and taxed at 0%. The dividend allowance has used up all but £200 of the remaining basic rate band. Fynn will be liable to tax at the dividend basic rate on £200 of his dividend income – 8.75% of £200, which is £17.50.

Fynn will be liable to tax on the remaining taxable dividend income at the dividend upper rate: £5,800 at 33.75% (£1,957.50).

9.6 Calculating the tax due

The five steps described above will enable a taxpayer to calculate their overall tax liability for a tax year. Some tax may have been paid already because it was deducted at source. This will need to be reflected at the end of the tax calculation.

9.7 A full income tax calculation

Chris carries on a business in partnership as an environmental consultant and his total income from the partnership's trade for 2022/23 is £52,000. However, to invest in the partnership he took out a loan from the West Kirby Bank, and the interest on that loan is £2,400 per annum.

Chris also has an account at the Waterlooville Building Society on which he received interest of £2,400 in 2022/23. He also owns shares in a company and received dividends of £12,000 in 2022/23.

The following shows how to calculate Chris's tax bill for 2022/23.

Step 1: Calculate total income	
Trade profits	52,000
Interest	2,400
Dividends	12,000
Total income	**66,400**
Step 2: Deduct allowable reliefs	
Loan interest to West Kirby Bank	(2,400)
Net income	**64,000**

(continued)

Step 3: Deduct personal allowances	
Personal allowance	(12,570)
Taxable income	**51,430**
Step 4: Separate NSNDI and savings and dividend income and calculate tax at the applicable rate(s)	
(a) NSNDI	
Taxable income	51,430
Less savings income	(2,400)
Less dividend income	(12,000)
= NSNDI	37,030

This element of Chris's taxable income falls £670 short of the £37,700 basic rate threshold and so is taxed at the basic rate of 20%:

£37,030 @ 20% = £7,406

(b)   *Savings income*

The total of his NSNDI and savings income (£39,430) exceeds the £37,700 basic rate threshold.

As Chris is a higher rate taxpayer (his taxable income exceeds £37,700), he is entitled to a PSA of £500, which is taxed first at 0%.

The remaining savings income after deduction of the PSA (£1,900) all falls within the higher rate band, and so is taxed at 40%.

£500 @ 0% = £0

£1,900 @ 40% = £760

Total tax payable on savings income = £760

(c)   *Dividend income*

The total of his NSNDI, savings and dividend income (£51,430) exceeds the £37,700 basic rate threshold by £13,730.

Chris is entitled to a dividend allowance of £2,000, regardless of whether he is a basic or higher rate taxpayer. This is taxed first at 0%.

None of the remaining dividend income (£10,000) after deduction of the dividend allowance falls within the remaining basic rate band, so it is all taxed at the dividend upper rate of 33.75%.

£2,000 @ 0% = £0

£10,000 @ 33.75% = £3,375

Total tax payable on dividend income = £3,375

Step 5: Add together the amounts of tax from Step 4

Overall income tax liability (£7,406 + £760 + £3,375) £11,541

There are no relevant deductions, as none of Chris's income was deducted at source.

9.8   Taxation of sole traders

Sole traders are almost always subject to income tax, and may also have to pay capital gains tax ('CGT') or inheritance tax ('IHT'), depending on their circumstances and the nature of their trade. Capital gains tax is explained fully in **Chapter 10**, and IHT is covered fully in *Wills and the Administration of Estates*. If they make chargeable supplies exceeding £85,000 in any period of 12 months, sole traders will also be required to register for VAT. See **7.14** for a full explanation of VAT.

9.8.1   Trading profits

Calculating the amount of tax a sole trader must pay requires an understanding of how trading profit is assessed. You read about this in **Chapter 7.** Sole traders determine their trading profits with reference to an accounting period, which is usually 12 months long. The sole trader will choose an accounting period to suit them and their business, and it will not necessarily be the same as the income tax year, which runs from 6 April to 5 April the following year. For this reason, there are rules on how trading profit is assessed for the purposes of income tax. Once you understand these, you will be equipped to carry out an income tax calculation as described in this chapter.

9.8.2   The first tax year

When the business commences, the sole trader will be charged to income tax on the trading profit from date of commencement to the following 5 April. The sole trader must register with HMRC within three months of starting the business.

 Example

Gill, a sole trader, starts her business on 1 November 2022. Her first accounting period runs from 1 November 2022 to 31 October 2023. Gill will be liable for tax on trading profits from 1 November 2022 to 5 April 2023 for the tax year ending on 5 April 2023.

9.8.3   The second tax year

In the second tax year of the trade, income tax will be assessed on trading profit for the whole of the 12-month accounting period which ends in that tax year.

 Example

Going back to the example above, in the tax year ending 5 April 2024, Gill will be liable for tax on trading profits from 1 November 2022 to 1 November 2023.

It can be seen from this example that Gill will be charged to tax twice on trading profits between 1 November 2022 and 5 April 2023. This is called 'overlap profit'. Gill will be able to recoup the tax she has paid twice either when she ceases to trade or if she changes her accounting date to closer to the end of the tax year. However, this could, in the meantime, cause cash flow problems for Gill.

9.8.4   The third and subsequent tax years

After the second tax year in which the sole trader is in business, they will be assessed for income tax based on the trading profits in the 12-month accounting period ending in that tax year.

 Example

In the tax year ending 5 April 2025, Gill will be assessed for tax on trading profits from 1 November 2023 to 1 November 2024.

9.8.5   The final tax year

In the final year of trading, tax will be assessed on trading profits from the end of the last accounting period until cessation of business. From this will be subtracted any overlap profit (unless it has already been recouped by the sole trader changing their accounting period).

9.9   Taxation of partnerships

9.9.1   General rules

Unlike companies, partnerships are not separate legal entities. This means that any tax liability arising from the partnership business is not payable by the partnership but rather by the individual partners, who will pay income tax and/or capital gains tax. Obviously, not all of the income or capital gains made by the business are attributable to one partner; the partners will share capital and profits between them. It is necessary to apportion the profits between the partners. The rules for doing so will be different depending on whether the partnership consists of individuals only or individuals and one or more corporate partners, because companies pay corporation tax rather than income and capital gains tax.

Partners who are individuals may have to pay income tax on trading profits and other income, capital gains tax on capital profits, and inheritance tax. For capital gains tax, please see **Chapter 10**. For inheritance tax, please see *Wills and the Administration of Estates*.

Calculating the income payable by a partner in a partnership comprises the following steps:

1. The partnership's trading profit will be calculated in the same way as trading profit for a sole trader. By way of recap, the formula is:

> Chargeable receipts LESS deductible expenditure
> LESS capital allowances = trading profit/loss

2. The trading profit is then shared between the partners in accordance with their agreement (or, if there is no agreement, the Partnership Act 1890). There are two elements to this: the agreement may well set out what will be paid first, for example salaries, interest on capital, and finally any remaining profit. The agreement should also set out each partner's percentage share of the profits.

3. Each partner will include this figure on their tax return and will be assessed in the ordinary way for income tax, taking account of any applicable reliefs and allowances.

If the partnership makes a trading loss instead, the losses will again be shared between the partners in accordance with their agreement, and the partners can each choose how they will claim any applicable reliefs for their share of the loss.

9.9.2   Change in members of partnership

New partners and retiring partners will be assessed to income tax differently, because for them, the business is either a new one or is coming to an end. New partners are assessed to income tax for their first two tax years on the basis described in **9.8.2** and **9.8.3**.

When a partner is leaving the partnership, they will be assessed to income tax on the basis described in **9.8.5** because it is their final year in business.

In both these scenarios, the existing partners will be assessed for income tax based on the trading profit in the 12-month accounting period ending in that tax year.

Example

Ali, Beatrice and Carina start a business in partnership on 1 January 2019 and prepare accounts based on calendar years. On 1 January 2021, Dhevan joins the partnership. On 30 June 2022, Ali retires. Profits for these four years are:

	£
2019	20,000
2020	27,000
2021	40,000
2022	60,000

(a) *Dhevan's assessments to income tax:*

    (i) *Dhevan's first tax year (2020/21)*

       Dhevan will be assessed to income tax on his share of the £10,000 profits for the (roughly) three-month period 1 January 2021 to 5 April 2021 (this figure being one-quarter of the profit for the full year 2021).

Note: For 2020/21, Ali, Beatrice and Carina will be assessed individually to income tax on their shares of the £27,000 profits made in 2020 (this being the profit for the accounting period which ends in the tax year).

    (ii) *Dhevan's second tax year (2021/22)*

       Dhevan will be assessed to income tax on his share of the £40,000 profits for his first 12 months in the business (this being the profit for 2021).

Note: For 2021/22, Ali, Beatrice and Carina will also be assessed by reference to this period because it is the accounting period which ends in the tax year.

(b) *Ali's assessment to income tax for his final tax year (2022/23).*

    Ali will be assessed to income tax on his share of the profits made from the end of the latest accounting period to be assessed (ie 2021) until the date of his retirement LESS a deduction for his 'overlap profit'. This means that he will be assessed on his share of the £30,000 profits for the six-month period from 1 January 2022 to 30 June 2022 (this figure being one-half of the profit for the full year) LESS a deduction for his share of the £5,000 profits made in the period 1 January to 5 April 2019 which were assessed in both his first and second tax years (2018/19 and 2019/20).

Note: For 2022/23, Beatrice, Carina and Dhevan will be assessed individually on their shares of the £60,000 profits made in 2022 (this being the profit for the accounting period which ends in the tax year).

9.10 Income tax relief on borrowings

If an individual borrows money to buy a share in a partnership or to lend money to a partnership, they can deduct the interest they pay on this borrowing from total income. This loan is a 'qualifying loan'. This encourages individuals to invest in businesses. There is a cap on the amount of tax relief, of the greater of £50,000 or 25% of the taxpayer's total income less allowable pension contributions in the tax year where the relief is claimed. However, the cap only relates to income from sources other than the trade which produced the loss, so its effect is limited.

9.11 Limited liability partnerships

When an LLP is used to carry on a trade or profession, it will be treated for most purposes in the same way as an ordinary partnership as far as income tax is concerned. However, the availability of relief for trading loss is restricted for partners in an LLP in certain conditions.

9.12 Taxation of shareholders

As explained above, shareholders pay tax on dividends. The other possible income tax implications for shareholders are set out below.

9.12.1 Loan to a participator in a close company

When a 'close company' makes a loan to a shareholder, there may be income tax consequences for the shareholder if the close company writes off the loan (see **11.6.1** for a full explanation).

9.12.2 Share buyback

When a shareholder sells their shares back to the company in which they are held, their profit will be the difference between the sale price and the issue price of the shares. This will probably be charged to income tax in the same way as a dividend. However, sometimes the shareholder will pay CGT instead on their profit. The circumstances in which this may happen are explained at **10.17**.

9.12.3 Income tax relief

Tax legislation includes two income tax reliefs for shareholders. The first is relevant when an individual borrows money to purchase ordinary shares in a close company that carries on a trade, or to lend money to a close company that carries on a trade. See **11.6.1** for an explanation of a close company.

The second is income tax relief under the Enterprise Investment Scheme (EIS). It allows the individual to deduct from their income tax liability for the year a sum equal to 30% of the amount they have invested in the ordinary shares of qualifying unquoted companies. The individual can subscribe up to £2 million per tax year in the ordinary shares of qualifying unquoted companies. During the two years before and three years after the share purchase, the taxpayer must not be 'connected with' the company, meaning that the combined shareholdings of the taxpayer and their associates (including spouse and close family) must not exceed 30%.

9.13 Interest received on loans and debentures

Under the ITTOIA 2005, a lender (unless the lender is a company and therefore pays corporation tax) must pay income tax on interest received in relation to a loan. If the lender/debenture-holder is a company, interest received is income, chargeable to corporation tax.

9.14 Taxation of directors and other employees

Salaries, fees and other benefits paid to employees are deductible expenditure when calculating trading profits. Businesses' trading receipts will frequently be reduced to nil or almost nil once salaries have been deducted, because they are one of the most significant types of expenditure for any business. Whilst this will result in the business ultimately paying less tax, the recipients of the salaries or fees will instead pay tax on the income.

Employees, including directors, pay income tax on employment income, pensions income and Social Security income. Here, we will focus on employment income.

Employment income includes 'earnings', which means all benefits received by the employee (or director) which derive from their office or employment as a reward for their services. This is whether they are paid by the employer or by a third party. It is not just salaries which are taxable; non-cash benefits, bonuses and tips are also taxable, but a personal gift would not be because this is not a reward for services. Other payments, such as certain lump sums received at the beginning and end of a person's employment, are chargeable, as are compensation for unfair dismissal and damages for wrongful dismissal (although the dismissed employee receives the first £30,000 of the compensation or damages free of tax).

Note that employees also have to pay National Insurance, which is a tax on earnings and profits of the self-employed. Individuals pay National Insurance to qualify for certain benefits and the state pension. There are different types of National Insurance called classes, and which class an individual is in depends on their employment status and how much they earn. It is deducted from the employee's salary by employers. HMRC produces tables so that employers can check how much an employee should pay.

9.14.1 Non-cash benefits

Non-cash benefits are also taxable. Examples include the use of a company car for private as well as for business use, and private medical insurance. Non-cash benefits are more difficult than salary to tax, because the first step is to work out a cash value. Generally, the value of the benefit is deemed to be the cost incurred by the employer in providing it. So if an employer pays the employee's premium for private medical insurance, the amount of the premiums paid will be taxable. If the employer pays for the employee's gym membership, then the cost of the gym membership will be taxable.

There are certain circumstances in which no tax will be charged to the employee.

9.14.2 Accommodation

Where the benefit is rent-free or low rent accommodation, employees are not charged to tax if:

- it is necessary for the employee to live on the premises in order to perform their duties, for example, certain caretakers; or

- the accommodation is provided so that the employee can perform their duties better and it is customary in that type of employment to have their accommodation provided, for example, a police officer.

9.14.3 Interest-free or low-interest loans

If the employee benefits from special rate loans from the employer, there is no charge to tax when the total amount outstanding on any loans to that employee does not exceed £10,000 at any time in the tax year.

9.14.4 Employer's pension contributions

Directors and other employees are not taxed on the employer's pension contributions if they are paying into an HMRC approved scheme.

9.14.5 Share schemes

Sometimes employers provide non-cash benefits relating to shares in the employer company. Benefits can include a gift of the shares, the sale of the shares at a favourable price or an option to purchase shares in the future. There are possible tax advantages for both parties in using the schemes, but the detail is outside the scope of this book.

9.14.6 Deductible expenditure

An employee can deduct from their income expenditure which is incurred wholly, exclusively and necessarily in the performance of their duties. This is a stricter test than that for deductible expenditure when calculating trading income. The requirement for necessity means that it must be shown that the employee could not perform their duties without the expenditure in question. The strictness of the test means that few items of expenditure will satisfy it, so it is modified in relation to travelling expenses and pension contributions. The employee's contributions to an occupational pension scheme or personal pension scheme are deductible and travelling expenses need not be wholly and exclusively incurred in the performance of their duties. This means that travelling from one place of work to another would generally be deductible, but travelling to work would not, because an employee only commences performing their duties when they arrive at work.

The effect of the rules on deductible expenditure is that any of the employee's expenses which are deductible will be subtracted from total income so that less of the employee's income is charged to tax. The employee is not permitted to deduct any expenditure which has been reimbursed by their employer.

9.15 Collection of income tax and dates for payment

Income tax is collected by HMRC, which is also responsible for collecting other taxes such as corporation tax and VAT.

9.15.1 Collection of income tax: deduction at source

Tax can be collected in two ways: through deduction at source and through the self-assessment regime. Tax on salary, cash and most non-cash benefits is generally deducted at source by the employer.

When tax is deducted at source, the payer of the income acts as a tax collector. They will deduct the correct amount of income tax from the income payment and pay it to HMRC. The taxpayer receives the income net of tax, that is, the tax has already been taken off.

9.15.2 Collection of income tax: self-assessment

Self-assessment is a system HMRC uses to collect income tax. Anyone who receives any income from which the tax has not been deducted at source (eg rental income) must complete a tax return, declaring all their income for the tax year. Any income tax which has been deducted at source should be included on the tax return and the taxpayer's tax liability will be reduced by the amount of income tax that has already been paid.

Unfortunately for HMRC, the self-assessment method carries the risk that the taxpayer will spend the income received before HMRC has been paid, and there will not be enough left to pay HMRC.

9.15.3 The tax return

A taxpayer who has income that is liable to tax is required by law to notify HMRC of this within six months of the end of the relevant tax year. The penalty for default is a fine.

9.15.4 When does tax have to be paid?

There are different tax returns for different types of income and they are issued soon after 5 April each year. Taxpayers are encouraged by HMRC to file an online tax return. The online tax return and any payment must be filed by 31 January following the tax year to which the return relates. If the taxpayer wishes to file a paper return, the submission date is earlier: no later than 31 October.

The taxpayer must make two payments on account towards the income tax due for any tax year, and a final balancing payment to meet any tax still outstanding. The payment dates are:

- first payment on account: by 31 January in the tax year in question;
- second payment on account: by 31 July after the end of the tax year; and
- any balancing payment (calculated once the tax year is over) is due on the next 31 January.

9.15.5 How much are the payments on account?

The first and second payments should each be approximately on half of the taxpayer's tax liability, based on the previous year's accounts. However, the payments are reduced to give credit for any tax deducted at source. The taxpayer does not have to make a payment on account if the amount remaining after giving credit for tax deducted at source is below a certain limit. This is important, because it means that the following people are not required to make payments on account:

- most employees;
- pensioners;
- others who receive most of their income after deduction at source; or
- those who have relatively small tax liabilities.

⭐ *Example*

Mei's income tax liability for 2021/22 came to £20,000, of which £8,000 was deducted at source. Her return for 2022/23 will be issued in April 2023 and a paper return must be submitted to HMRC by 31 October 2023, or an online return by 31 January 2024 at the latest. For 2022/23 she will make interim payments on account of ½ × (£20,000 – £8,000) = £6,000 on 31 January 2023 and 31 July 2023. Her final adjustment for 2022/23 is due on 31 January 2024.

Taxpayers can claim a reduced payment on account or cancellation of the payment on account if they have grounds for believing that if they make payments on account based on the previous year's accounts, this will result in an overpayment of tax in the current tax year.

9.15.6 Penalties for default

HMRC charges interest on any tax unpaid at the due date for payment. This applies to both payments on account and balancing payments. There are also fixed penalties – fines – for late or non-payment.

Taxpayers must maintain adequate records to support the information in their tax return, and there is a penalty for default. HMRC has the power to carry out audits and make enquiries to check whether the tax return is accurate. Taxpayers can appeal against assessments to the First-Tier Tribunal (Tax).

9.16 Tax avoidance

Tax avoidance is using tax law to the taxpayer's benefit to reduce their tax bill, in a way which is arguably lawful but not within the spirit of tax legislation. This is different from tax evasion, which is using illegal methods to reduce tax payments, and which is targeted by domestic legislation and international treaties.

There are many specific legislative measures designed to tackle tax avoidance. This part of the chapter provides an overview of the general anti-avoidance rule ('GAAR'), which was brought into the UK tax system to target abusive tax-avoidance schemes. The GAAR applies to income tax and also applies to the other taxes covered in this book, namely capital gains tax, corporation tax, inheritance tax and National Insurance.

The detail of the GAAR is set out in the Finance Act 2013, the Finance (No.2) Act 2017 and the National Insurance Contributions Act 2014. In addition, HMRC has issued guidance on the GAAR. The general tenor of the GAAR is that tax avoidance is acceptable but abusive arrangements are not.

9.16.1 Abusive tax arrangements

The Finance Act 2013 allows HMRC to make adjustments to a taxpayer's liability to counteract the tax advantages arising from abusive tax arrangements (s 209). The burden is on HMRC to show that the arrangement is abusive.

Section 207 of the Finance Act 2013 defines 'tax arrangement' and 'abusive'. An arrangement is a 'tax arrangement' if, having regard to all the circumstances, it would be reasonable to conclude that the obtaining of a tax advantage was the main purpose, or one of the main purposes, of the arrangement.

A tax arrangement is 'abusive' if entering into or carrying out the arrangement cannot reasonably be regarded as a reasonable course of action in relation to the relevant tax provisions, having regard to all the circumstances. Those circumstances include:

- whether the effect of the arrangement is consistent with the policy objectives of the tax legislation;

- whether the means of achieving those results involves one or more contrived or abnormal steps; and

- whether the arrangements are intended to exploit shortcomings or loopholes in the tax legislation.

If the tax arrangements accord with established practice, and HMRC had indicated its acceptance of that practice before the arrangement was entered into, this might indicate that the arrangement is not abusive.

The 'cannot reasonably be regarded as a reasonable course of action' element of the test for 'abusive' is known as the double reasonableness test, and it allows a wide range of potentially acceptable behaviour on the part of the taxpayer.

9.16.2 Procedure

If HMRC finds that a taxpayer is in breach of the GAAR, it will notify the taxpayer of why it considers that a tax advantage has arisen to the taxpayer from tax arrangements that are abusive, and set out the tax adjustments (or 'counteraction') that the officer considers ought to be taken. The adjustments must be 'just and reasonable', and can be made either by the taxpayer or HMRC. If counteraction is proposed by HMRC, the taxpayer is permitted to make written representations in their defence, and the matter will then be referred to the GAAR advisory panel ('Panel'), who will issue their opinion by way of a notice to the taxpayer and HMRC. HMRC will then, provided that they still agree with the Panel's opinion, give the taxpayer a written notice setting out whether the tax advantage arising from the arrangements is to be counteracted under the GAAR, the adjustments required and the steps that the taxpayer must make to give effect to the adjustment.

Under the Finance (No 2) Act 2017, anyone who enables an abusive tax arrangement may be required to pay a penalty. An enabler is any person who, in the course of their business, enables the abusive tax arrangements that are defeated. This can include individuals, companies or partnerships. Individual employees cannot be enablers because they are not acting in the course of their business. Instead, the firm or company employing them will possibly be liable to a penalty. There is a right of appeal to a tax tribunal. The penalty is equal to the value of the financial or other benefit received by the enabler in return for what the enabler did to facilitate the arrangements.

Summary

- Individuals, partners, PRs and trustees pay income tax.

- There is no statutory definition of income, but 'income' is used to refer to payments and receipts that are recurrent in nature.

- To ascertain if income tax is payable, it must come from one of the sources listed in income tax legislation. If it is not listed there, no income tax is payable. There are also specific exemptions from tax for some types of income.

- Income tax is paid on income received during a tax year, which runs from 6 April to 5 April.

To calculate a taxpayer's income tax liability, there are five steps to follow.

Step 1: Calculate total income

Step 2: Deduct any allowable reliefs to give net income

Step 3: Deduct any personal allowance to give taxable income

Step 4: Calculate the tax at the applicable rate(s)

Step 5: Add together the amounts of tax from Step 4 to give the taxpayer's overall tax liability

Having calculated the taxpayer's overall liability, reduce that liability by any income tax deducted at source (and therefore paid direct to HMRC). The resulting figure is the income tax which the taxpayer is obliged to pay to HMRC.

The taxpayer will submit a tax return to HMRC by 31 January following the tax year to which the return relates. The taxpayer will sometimes make payments on account on 31 January in the tax year in question and on 31 July after the end of tax year in respect of his income tax liability. Any balancing payment must be made by 31 January after the end of the tax year.

Sample questions

Question 1

In one year, a man receives a salary of £21,335 per annum, interest of £75 from a bank savings account, and £2,000 of dividends from shares which he owns in a company.

Assumptions: the personal allowance is £12,570; the personal savings allowance is £1,000 and the dividend allowance is £2,000.

Which of the following best represents his income tax liability for the tax year?

A   £8,765.00

B   £1,753.00

C   £10,840.00

D   £2,168.00

E   £1,153.00

Answer

Option B is correct. NSNDI income is £21,335. Deduct personal allowance (£12,570) to give taxable income of £8,765. This is all taxed at 20% = £1,753. The interest all falls within the PSA (£1,000), which is taxed at 0%, so there is no tax to pay on this. The dividend income all falls within the dividend allowance, which is taxed at 0%, so there is no tax to pay on this either.

Note that the £1,753 represents the man's overall tax *liability* for the tax year. It will be necessary to allow for any tax deducted at source to calculate the amount of tax still owing.

Question 2

A partner joins three friends in a partnership on 6 October 2022, and it is agreed that the four partners will share equally in the partnership's income and capital profits and losses.

Which of the following best describes how the new partner will be assessed to income tax on income from the partnership for the tax year ending 5 April 2023?

A   They will be assessed on a quarter of the partnership's trading profit from 6 April 2022 to 5 April 2023.

B   Their partnership income will not be assessed until 5 April 2024, when they will be assessed on a quarter of the partnership's trading profit from 6 October 2022 to 5 April 2024.

C   They will be assessed on a quarter of the partnership's trading profit from 6 April 2022 to 5 April 2023 but will then receive a rebate for the tax which relates to the period before they became a partner.

D   Their partnership income will not be assessed until 5 April 2024, when they will be assessed on a quarter of the partnership's trading profit from 6 April 2022 to 5 April 2024.

E   They will be assessed on a quarter of the partnership's trading profit from 6 October 2022 to 5 April 2023.

Answer

Option E is correct. They will be assessed on a quarter of the partnership's trading profit because the four partners own the profits in equal shares. The rule is that for the first year, partners are assessed on the trading profit from joining the partnership to the end of the tax year.

Question 3

Following an investigation, a client has been informed by HMRC that they are in breach of the general anti-avoidance rule ('GAAR'). The client does not wish to contest HMRC's finding.

Which of the following best describes the consequences for the client?

A HMRC may sue the client for breach of contract for the amount outstanding.

B HMRC may require the client to pay a fine.

C HMRC may refer the matter to a tax tribunal.

D HMRC may issue a written warning to the client.

E HMRC may request the taxpayer to make just and reasonable adjustments to the amount of tax paid.

Answer

Option E is correct. There is no contract, so option A is wrong. HMRC has the power to order the just and reasonable adjustments – there is no such thing as a written warning (option D is wrong), no power to impose a fine in these circumstances (option B is wrong) and no need to refer the matter to a tribunal (option C is wrong).

10 Capital Gains Tax

SQE1 syllabus

By the end of this chapter, you will be able to apply relevant core legal principles and rules appropriately and effectively, at the level of a competent newly qualified solicitor in practice, to realistic client-based and ethical problems and situations in the following areas of capital gains tax:

*   chargeable persons/entities (sole traders, partners, and shareholders)
*   basis of charge (calculation of gains/allowable deductions/main reliefs and exemptions)
*   the charge to tax: calculation and collection
*   the scope of anti-avoidance provisions
*   business property relief.

Learning outcomes

By the end of this chapter you will be able to:

- understand what constitutes a chargeable asset for the purposes of calculating capital gains tax;

- understand some of the reliefs available to taxpayers to reduce or postpone their capital gains tax liability;

- understand how multiple disposals and part-disposals are taxed;

- understand how losses may be set off against gains;

- carry out a capital gains tax calculation; and

- understand the payment date(s) for capital gains tax.

The tax rates set out in this chapter are correct as at the date of publication. Please note that these tax rates may no longer be current at the date of any future SQE assessment.

10.1 Introduction

Capital gains tax ('CGT') is payable on *chargeable gains* made by a *chargeable person* on the disposal of *chargeable assets* in a tax year, which runs from 6 April one year until 5 April the following year. Capital gains tax is governed by the Taxation of Chargeable Gains Act 1992 ('TCGA 1992').

10.2 What is a chargeable person?

The following are chargeable persons:

- individuals (whether in a personal capacity or as a sole trader);

- personal representatives ('PRs'), when they dispose of the assets of the deceased person;

- partners, when the partners dispose of a chargeable asset. Each partner is charged separately for their proportion of the gain; and

- trustees, on the disposal of a chargeable asset from a trust fund.

Companies do not pay CGT. They pay corporation tax instead (see **Chapter 11**). Charities are also exempt from paying CGT.

10.3 What is a chargeable asset?

'Chargeable asset' includes, under the TCGA 1992, 'all forms of property', including debts, options and incorporeal property (a legal right in property having no physical existence, for example, a patent or a lease). It does not include sterling, so disposal of cash in sterling is not chargeable to CGT.

As with income tax, it is important to follow certain steps to calculate CGT, which are as follows:

Step 1: Disposal of a chargeable asset

Here, you must identify the *disposal of a chargeable asset*, for example the sale of a factory.

Step 2: Calculation of the gain

This is the consideration received for the asset less the cost of the asset, in other words the asset's sale price less its purchase price. Some deductions are allowed, which reduce the gain further, and mean that less tax is ultimately payable (see **10.8**).

Step 3: Consider reliefs

There are various reliefs which may be available to reduce or postpone the tax payable (see **10.9**).

Step 4: Aggregate gains/losses; deduct annual exemption

Gains and losses from all sources must be added together, and the annual exemption of £12,300 is deducted at this stage. The annual exemption is the capital gain every CGT payer can make every year without being taxed on it. The amount usually increases every tax year, and £12,300 is the rate for the current (2022/23) tax year.

Step 5: Apply the correct rate of tax

Capital gains are treated as if they were the top slice of the taxpayer's income for the tax year. There are four rates. The following rates apply to any gains other than residential property or gains which do not qualify for business asset disposal relief:

- If the taxpayer's capital gains and taxable income added together do not exceed the threshold for basic rate income tax (£37,700), the rate of tax payable on the gains is 10%.

- If the taxpayer's capital gains and taxable income added together exceed the basic rate threshold, the rate of tax for any gains up to the basic rate threshold is 10%, and any gains which exceed the basic rate threshold are taxed at a rate of 20%.

10.4 Tax rate for residential property

If the chargeable asset is residential property which is not the taxpayer's main residence, the gains are subject to a surcharge of 8%. This means that any gains which are below the basic rate threshold are taxed at 18% (ie the normal rate of 10% plus the 8% surcharge) and any gains which exceed the basic rate threshold are taxed at 28%, not 20%.

10.5 Tax rate for business asset disposal relief

Any gains which qualify for business asset disposal relief are taxed at 10%, regardless of the taxpayer's income (see **10.9.4**).

Sometimes taxpayers have gains that qualify for business asset disposal relief and other gains that do not qualify. In these cases, the business asset disposal relief gains (taxed at 10%) will be added to their income first, meaning that their other gains will be treated as the top slice of their income and therefore be more likely to be taxed at 20%, or at 28% on residential property.

10.6 Tax rate for trustees and PRs

Gains made by trustees and PRs are all taxed at 20%, or, for residential property, 28%.

 Example CGT calculation

In May, Margaret sells shares for £74,000. The shares cost her £30,000. It is her only disposal during the tax year. Margaret has a taxable income for the tax year of £43,000, which means that all of her gain is taxed at 20%.

Step 1: Identify the disposal

Sale of shares

Step 2: Calculate the gain

Proceeds of disposal	£74,000
Less: Cost	(£30,000)
	£44,000

Step 3: Consider exemptions and reliefs: Nil

Step 4: Deduct annual exemption

Gain	£44,000
Annual exemption	(£12,300)
Chargeable gain	£31,700

Step 5: Calculate the tax payable

20% x £31,700 = £6,340

We will now consider steps 1–3 of the CGT calculation in more detail.

10.7 Step 1: Disposal (sale or gift) of a chargeable asset

There must be a disposal of a chargeable asset. Disposal includes a sale or a gift. If someone makes a gift of a chargeable asset, clearly there is no sale price to use as a basis for calculating the gain. HMRC will use the market value of the asset at the time of the gift, instead of the consideration received, to calculate the gain.

 Example – CGT calculation where the disposal is a gift

In March, Colin makes a gift of an antique watch with a market value of £500,000. He had bought the watch for £313,000. It is his only disposal during the tax year. Colin's taxable income for the tax year is £70,000.

Step 1: Identify the disposal

Gift of antique watch

Step 2: Calculate the gain

Market value of watch	£500,000)
Less: Cost	(£313,000)
Gain	£187,000)

Step 3: Consider exemptions and reliefs: Nil

Step 4: Deduct annual exemption

Gain	£187,000
Deduct annual exemption	(£12,300)
Chargeable gain	£ 174,700)

Step 5: Calculate the tax payable

*20% x £174,700= **£34,940.***

10.7.1 Disposing of part of an asset

Even if the taxpayer only sells or gives away part of an asset, it is still chargeable to CGT (see **10.13**).

10.7.2 The death of the taxpayer

When someone dies, there is no disposal, so no charge to CGT. The PRs are deemed to acquire the deceased's assets at the market value at the date of death (known as the probate value). This means that gains which accrued during the deceased's lifetime are never charged to tax. However, inheritance tax may be payable.

 Example – when the asset owner dies

Sofia dies owning an office building worth £179,000, which she had bought several years earlier for £112,000. There is no charge to CGT on Sofia's death: her PRs acquire the building at the market value as at the date of her death, that is, £179,000. The gain of £67,000 (£179,000 – £112,000) is wiped out and is not charged to tax.

10.8 Step 2: Calculate the gain

The aim is to tax the amount the taxpayer has gained between acquiring and disposing of the asset. To calculate this, start with the consideration for the sale (or the asset's market value if the taxpayer gives away the asset) and subtract any of the following expenditure incurred by the taxpayer.

10.8.1 Initial expenditure

- The cost price of the asset (or its market value or probate value if the asset was given as a gift or the taxpayer inherited it);

- Any incidental costs of acquisition, for example conveyancing fees in relation to the purchase of a property, or other legal fees, valuation fees and stamp duty; and

- Any expenditure wholly and exclusively incurred in providing the asset, for example, the cost of building a property.

10.8.2 Subsequent expenditure

- Expenditure wholly and exclusively incurred in establishing, preserving or defending title to the asset. An example of this would be legal fees incurred to resolve a dispute regarding the title to the property, for example a boundary dispute; and

- Expenditure wholly and exclusively incurred to enhance the value of the asset, which is reflected in the value of the asset at the time of disposal. An example of this would be the cost of building an extension to a house. The cost of normal maintenance, repairs and insurance is not deductible.

10.8.3 Incidental costs of disposal

These include legal fees for the sale and the estate agent's fees or commission.

 *Example – deducting expenditure and incidental costs of disposal*

Sunjeev, whose taxable income for the current tax year is £32,000, sells a small factory for £268,000. He inherited it from his uncle several years ago and it had a market value of £205,000 at the date of his uncle's death. He spent £5,100 on renovations and £8,500 on legal fees in resolving a dispute regarding rights of way. His legal fees for the sale of the factory are £750 and the estate agent charges him £2,700 commission.

Step 1: *Identify the chargeable disposal*

Sale of factory

Step 2: *Calculate the gain*

| Proceeds of disposal | £268,000 |

Less incidental costs of disposal:

Legal fees	(£750)
Estate agent's commission	(£2,700)
Total	(£3,450)
Net proceeds of disposal	£264,550

Less initial expenditure:

Cost	(£205,000)

Less subsequent expenditure:

Cost of legal claim	(£8,500)
Renovations	(£5,100)
Total expenditure	(£218,600)
GAIN	£45,950

Step 3: *Consider exemptions and reliefs: Nil*

Step 4: *Deduct annual exemption*

Gain	£45,950
Annual exemption	(£12,300)
Chargeable gain	£33,650

Step 5: *Calculate the rate of tax*

CGT at 10% on the first £5,700

(the amount of gain below the basic rate threshold, ie £37,700 less taxable income of £32,000) = £570

CGT at 20% on remaining £27,950

(ie amount of gain above the basic rate threshold) = £5,590

Total CGT £6,160

10.8.4 Indexation

When an asset increases in value, the gain cannot all be regarded as profit. Some of the gain will be as a result of inflation, rather than the asset becoming inherently more valuable. Following a period of significant inflation, in 1982 an indexation allowance was introduced to remove the inflationary gains from the CGT calculation, meaning that a smaller gain was charged to tax.

The indexation allowance was used when calculating the gain on an asset which had been owned for any period between 31 March 1982 and 5 April 1998. Indexation was frozen in 1998 for periods of ownership after April 1998, and was removed completely from April 2008.

The allowance is now only relevant where a charge to tax was deferred by using rollover or hold-over reliefs before April 2008. This is because, when the asset is eventually disposed of again and the deferred tax calculated, the calculation must include the indexation allowance, provided that the assets were owned at some point between 31 March 1982 and 5 April 1998.

To calculate the indexation allowance, you need to apply to initial and subsequent expenditure the percentage increase in the Retail Prices Index from the date the expenditure was incurred to the date of disposal of the asset (or, if earlier, April 1998). HMRC publish tables to show this figure as an indexation factor to make the calculation easier for non-mathematicians.

10.8.5 Losses

Sometimes a disposal can result in capital loss, not a gain.

 Example – a capital loss

Aisha bought a holiday cottage for £330,000 three years ago. She paid £400 legal fees, £250 valuation fees and £16,400 stamp duty. This year she sold the cottage for £340,000 and her incidental costs of disposal were legal fees of £500.

Step 1: Identify the disposal

Sale of cottage

Step 2: Calculate the gain/loss

Proceeds of disposal	£340,000
Less: Incidental costs of disposal	
Legal fees	(£500)
Net proceeds of disposal	£339,500
Less: Initial expenditure	
Cost	(£330,000)
Legal fees	(£400)
Valuation fees	(£250)
Stamp duty	(£16,400)
Total expenditure	(£347,050)
LOSS	£7,550

Losses are covered in more detail at **10.12**.

10.9 Step 3: Reliefs

The next step is to apply any available reliefs. Most reliefs are more relevant to smaller businesses, to encourage investment in them. The main reliefs are explained below.

10.9.1 Relief on replacement of business assets ('rollover' relief)

This relief enables sole traders and partners to sell certain assets ('qualifying business assets') without paying CGT, provided the proceeds of sale are invested in other qualifying business assets. The seller will have to pay tax eventually, but the charge to CGT is postponed until the seller disposes of the new asset(s).

10.9.1.1 What are qualifying business assets?

The principal qualifying business assets for the purposes of this relief are land, buildings and goodwill. The asset must be used in the trade of the business rather than being held as an investment. Fixed plant and machinery are qualifying business assets, but their sale usually results in a loss because they are wasting assets. There is no definition of 'fixed', but if the asset is moveable, it is unlikely to be classed as fixed. Company shares are not qualifying assets.

The relief applies when a qualifying asset is disposed of, and the asset is owned by:

- a sole trader, who uses the asset in their trade;

- a partnership, which uses the asset in its trade;

- an individual partner, where the partnership uses the asset in the partnership trade; or

- an individual shareholder, where the asset is used in the trade of the company in which the shareholder owns shares. For this to apply, the company must be their 'personal company', meaning that the shareholder must own at least 5 per cent of the voting shares in the company.

Provided that both the asset disposed of and the asset acquired fall within the definition of qualifying assets, they do not have to be the same type of asset. For example, it is possible to sell qualifying goodwill, and rollover the gain into the purchase of qualifying buildings.

10.9.1.2 Time limits

The taxpayer must acquire the replacement asset within one year before or three years after the disposal of the original asset, unless HMRC allows the taxpayer an extended time period to claim.

⭐ Example – time limits for rollover relief

On 1 May 2022, Edith, a partner in a printing business, sells a building owned by her but used in the partnership's trade. She must acquire (or have acquired) a replacement qualifying business asset between 1 May 2021 and 30 April 2025 if she wishes to claim rollover relief.

10.9.1.3 How is the relief applied?

Firstly, the taxpayer must claim the relief within four years from the end of the tax year in which they acquire the replacement asset (or, if later, within four years from the end of the tax year in which the original asset is sold). The gain is notionally deducted from the acquisition cost of the replacement asset, which gives a lower acquisition cost to use in CGT calculations when the asset is disposed of in the future. This means that a later disposal of the replacement asset is likely to produce a gain that includes both the rolled-over gain and any gain on the replacement asset itself.

Note that the annual exemption cannot be used before the gain is rolled over, so the taxpayer loses the benefit of the annual exemption if they apply for rollover relief.

⭐ *Example – rollover relief on replacement*

On 13 March 2022, Peter sells a workshop that he has owned since 1994 for £77,000. It is his only chargeable disposal in the tax year, and he makes a gain of £33,000. On 1 February 2023, Peter purchases a new, larger workshop for £95,000. Peter claims rollover relief on the replacement of qualifying assets. This means that:

- *Peter will not pay CGT in 2021/22 because the gain on the disposal (the workshop) will be postponed.*

- *The replacement workshop, bought within the three years following the original disposal, will be deemed to have been acquired for £62,000 (£95,000 less the £33,000 gain).*

- *Peter will not be able to use his annual exemption for the 2021/22 tax year.*

Peter sells his new workshop in 2024 for £140,000. The calculation of his gain will be:

Proceeds of disposal	£140,000	
Less		
Adjusted acquisition cost	(£62,000)	(without rollover it would be £95,000)
Gain	£78,000	(without rollover it would be £45,000)

Provided the qualifying conditions were met, the gain from the 2024 sale could also be rolled over.

10.9.2 Rollover relief on incorporation of a business

This is similar to rollover relief on replacement of business assets, in that the charge to CGT is postponed. It applies, subject to certain conditions, when an individual sells their interest in an unincorporated business (ie a sole trader or partner) to a company.

The gain is rolled over into the shares which the seller receives as consideration for the sale of the assets to the company. The CGT is payable when the individual disposes of the shares. This relief encourages people to incorporate and expand their businesses, because if it were not for this relief, often taxpayers would not be able to find the money to pay CGT *and* invest in the new company.

10.9.2.1 Conditions for the relief to apply

- The business must be transferred as a going concern, so after the disposal it must essentially be carried on as the same business but with a different owner.

- The consideration must all be in shares issued by the company. If only part of the consideration was shares, for example, 25% of it, then only that percentage of the gain could be rolled over.

- The business must be transferred with all of its assets, ignoring cash. If the taxpayer retains any of the assets, for example, if they keep the business premises, then the relief does not apply.

10.9.2.2 How is the relief applied?

As with rollover relief on replacement of business assets, the gain is rolled over by notionally deducting it from the cost of acquisition of the new shares.

 Example – rollover relief on incorporation

Hayley runs a successful business as a private dietician and decides that it would be advantageous to run her business as a company. She incorporates a company, HJ Limited, which purchases Hayley's business at its market value of £150,000, in return for 150,000 shares.

If Hayley makes a chargeable gain of £88,000 on the disposal to HJ Limited and she rolls over the gain on incorporation, she will not pay any CGT on the disposal. However, the acquisition cost of her shares in HJ Limited will be deemed to be £62,000 (£150,000 less the gain of £88,000). When, at some point in the future, Hayley disposes of her shares, she will only be able to deduct the shares' notional acquisition cost of £62,000 when calculating her gain on the disposal of the shares.

The taxpayer does not have to apply for this relief. HMRC applies it automatically unless the taxpayer chooses not to use it.

Note that the annual exemption cannot be used before the gain is rolled over, so the taxpayer loses the benefit of the annual exemption if they apply for rollover relief on incorporation.

10.9.3 Hold-over relief on gifts

This relief allows an individual to make a gift of certain types of business asset, or sell them at an undervalue, without paying CGT. If the donee disposes of the asset, the donee will be charged to tax on their own gain and the donor's gain.

10.9.3.1 Conditions for the relief to apply

- It is only available on gifts, or the gift element of a sale at an undervalue.
- Only the part of the gain relating to chargeable business assets qualify for the relief. 'Business assets' include:
  - assets used in the donor's trade, or their interest in such assets, where the donor is a sole trader or a partner whose assets are being used by the partnership;
  - shares in a trading company which are not listed on a recognised stock exchange (AIM is not deemed to be a stock exchange for the purposes of this condition);
  - shares in a *personal* trading company, even if the company is listed on a recognised stock exchange. A 'personal company' is one in which the donor owns at least 5% of the company's voting shares; and
  - assets owned by the shareholder and used by their *personal* trading company.
- If the donee is a company, the relief does not apply to a gift of shares.
- Both the donor and the donee must elect to apply for the relief, because the donee is accepting liability for any CGT payable in relation to the gift when the donee disposes of the asset. The donor and donee must elect for the relief to apply within four years from the end of the tax year of the disposal.

10.9.3.2 How is the relief applied?

The chargeable gain is calculated by taking market value as the consideration for the disposal. The deemed gain is then deducted from the market value of the asset to produce an artificially low 'acquisition cost' for the donee.

When the donee later disposes of the asset, the notional acquisition cost and any qualifying expenditure is deducted from the sale price or the market value (on a gift) to find the donee's gain. The donee's gain will therefore include the held-over gain plus any gain made during their period of ownership of the asset.

Once the donee's chargeable gain has been calculated, reliefs should be considered as usual to attempt to reduce or postpone the donee's tax liability. If the donee dies before disposing of the asset, all of the gains will escape CGT altogether.

Note that the annual exemption cannot be applied before the gain is rolled over.

 Example – hold-over relief on gifts

Gianni gives the family business to his daughter, Laura. At the time, the chargeable assets of the business have a market value of £212,000 and Gianni's gain on those assets is £100,000. Gianni and Laura elect to hold over the capital gain on the disposal.

Three years later, Laura sells the business for £300,000, and makes no other qualifying disposals in that tax year. This means that:

- *Gianni does not pay CGT on the disposal to Laura.*

- *Laura's adjusted acquisition cost is £112,000 (the market value of £212,000 less the capital gain of £100,000)*

- *Gianni's annual exemption for the tax year of the disposal cannot be deducted from the gain.*

- *When Laura sells the business, her gain is:*

	£
Sale price	300,000
Less: adjusted acquisition cost	(112,000)
Gain	188,000

Laura can use her annual exemption for the tax year of the sale to reduce her capital gain.

10.9.4 Business asset disposal relief

Since 6 April 2008, business asset disposal relief (which was called entrepreneurs' relief until April 2020) has been available on gains made by individuals on the disposal (ie sale or gift) of certain assets. If business asset disposal relief applies, the rate of tax will be reduced to a flat rate of 10%.

10.9.4.1 Qualifying business disposal

There must be a 'qualifying business disposal' for the relief to apply. The conditions for each type of interest are set out below:

10.9.4.2 Sole trader or partnership

When a sole trader or individual partner disposes of the whole or part of a business, business asset disposal relief may apply. This includes situations where:

- the business, or part of it, is disposed of as a going concern; or

- assets are disposed of following cessation of the business (provided the assets were used in the business at the time of cessation of business).

To be a qualifying disposal of part or the whole of a business, the interest in the business *as a whole*, not just one or more assets, must have been owned either:

- throughout the period of two years ending with the date of disposal; or
- throughout the period of two years ending with the cessation of the business, provided that the disposal is within three years after cessation of business.

Only assets used for the purposes of the business carried on by the individual or partnership are eligible for relief. Company shares, securities and other assets held as investments are not eligible.

10.9.4.3 Company shares

A disposal of company shares (including securities) may qualify for relief if:

- the company is a trading company; and
- the company is the disponer's 'personal company' (the taxpayer must hold at least 5% of the ordinary share capital in the company and that holding must give them at least 5% of the voting rights in the company), and either or both of the following two conditions are met:
  - the disponer must be beneficially entitled to at least 5% of the profits available for distribution to equity holders and at least 5% of the assets available on a winding up; or
  - the disponer would be beneficially entitled to at least 5% of the proceeds of sale if the whole of the ordinary share capital of the company were disposed of; and
- the disponer is an employee or officer of the company.

The above requirements must have been satisfied throughout the period of two years:

- ending with the date of disposal; or
- ending with the date the company ceased to be a trading company (and the disposal must be within three years of cessation of trading).

To be classed as a 'trading company', the company must not have activities that include 'to a substantial extent activities other than trading activities'. This means that companies which hold substantial cash reserves or investments may fall outside the definition.

⭐ *Example – qualifying business disposal*

Sunil and John each own 50% of the ordinary voting shares in Barnston Electronics Limited, which is a trading company which sells electronic goods. They started the company 11 years ago, and now want to retire and sell all of their shares. Sunil is the managing director, but John started to wind down a year ago, and resigned from the board and his employment then.

Sunil and John then sell their shares to EPL Limited and make a large capital gain.

Sunil's disposal is a qualifying business disposal for the purposes of business asset disposal relief, but John's is not, because he has not been an officer or employee of the company for the whole of the two years prior to the sale.

10.9.4.4 The effect of the relief

If the conditions for business asset disposal relief are met, the taxpayer will pay a flat rate of 10% tax on the gains. This is subject to a lifetime cap of £1 million of qualifying gains. Once the taxpayer has made £1 million of qualifying gains in their lifetime, any gains over and above this amount will not benefit from business asset disposal relief.

Example – lifetime cap

Lena is a higher rate taxpayer and sold her consultancy business as a going concern last year. She made a capital gain of £650,000, which qualified for business asset disposal relief. Yesterday she sold her shares in a food manufacturing business and made a capital gain of £400,000. This gain met the conditions for business asset disposal relief to apply, but only £350,000 of it: the remaining £50,000 takes Lena over the £1 million lifetime threshold for business asset disposal relief. She will pay the 10% business asset disposal relief tax rate on £350,000 of the gain and the normal rate of 20% on the remaining £50,000 (because she is a higher rate taxpayer).

The taxpayer must claim business asset disposal relief on or before the first anniversary of the 31 January following the tax year in which the qualifying disposal was made. So for a disposal made in 2022/23, the claim must be made by 31 January 2025.

10.9.5 Tangible moveable property

Wasting assets are generally exempt from CGT. Wasting assets are assets with a predictable life of less than 50 years. This includes most consumer goods, for example kitchen appliances and televisions.

Not all tangible moveable property constitutes a wasting asset: some assets, such as antiques, will go up in value. These assets are exempt from CGT if the consideration for the disposal is £6,000 or less.

10.9.6 Private residence relief

Any gains made by individuals who dispose of a dwelling house, including grounds of up to half a hectare, are exempt from CGT under private residence relief, provided that they have occupied the dwelling house as their only or main residence through their period of ownership. The last nine months of ownership are ignored.

This enables people to move house without having to pay CGT on the gain.

10.9.7 Damages for personal injury

Damages for personal injury are exempt from CGT, even though recovery of other damages or compensation could constitute the disposal of a chargeable asset.

10.10 Step 4: Aggregate gains/losses; deduct annual exemption

Gains and losses from all sources must be added together, and the annual exemption is deducted from the total gain at this stage. The annual exemption allows the taxpayer to make some capital gains without paying tax. It is a general deduction from the taxpayer's total net gain, but the taxpayer can choose to apply the annual exemption first to the gains that attract the higher tax rates if the taxpayer has gains on more than one disposal which are subject to tax at different rates. The annual exemption for 2022/23 is £12,300.

Any unused part of the exemption cannot be carried forward to the following tax year.

10.10.1 How the reliefs and the annual exemption operate together

Sometimes more than one relief could apply to a particular disposal, meaning that the taxpayer has to choose which relief to claim. In addition, some of the rules regarding the operation of the reliefs effectively restrict when the annual exemption can be used in conjunction with the reliefs. These issues are explained below.

10.10.1.1 Rollover relief on the replacement of qualifying assets and hold-over relief on gifts

Business asset disposal relief cannot apply to any gains which are to be rolled over on the replacement of qualifying assets or held over on the gift of business assets. Further, the annual exemption cannot be first applied to any gains which are to be rolled over or held over under these reliefs.

Rollover relief on the replacement of qualifying assets cannot generally be used in conjunction with hold-over relief (because there is usually no gift) or rollover relief on incorporation (because shares are not qualifying business assets).

10.10.1.2 Rollover relief on the incorporation of a business

If rollover relief on incorporation applies to a transfer of a business, business asset disposal relief and the annual exemption cannot be used. In addition, rollover relief on incorporation cannot be used at the same time as rollover relief on replacement of qualifying assets (because shares are not qualifying business assets) or hold-over relief (because there is usually no gift).

However, if part of the consideration for the sale is cash and part is shares, it is sometimes possible to use rollover relief on incorporation for the part of the gain relating to the part of the business exchanged for shares. Business asset disposal relief and the annual exemption could be used on the part of the gain relating to the part of the business sold for cash.

10.10.1.3 Business asset disposal relief

As we have seen, business asset disposal relief cannot be claimed when using any of the hold-over or rollover reliefs. However, the annual exemption can be used to reduce gains before applying business asset disposal relief.

⭐ *Example – choice of reliefs*

Felicity has run a catering business as a sole trader for 20 years and is a higher rate taxpayer. In April 2022, she gives the business to her daughter, Martha. Felicity takes professional advice and is told that the chargeable gain on the disposal of the business is £175,000. Felicity has made no other chargeable gains in her lifetime.

There are two options.

The first option is to claim hold-over relief for the whole of the £175,000 gain. This means that Felicity will not pay any CGT. This is particularly useful to her because she may not have any money to use to pay the CGT: she has not received any consideration from Martha for the business. However, if Martha and Felicity elect to claim hold-over relief, Felicity will lose the benefit of her annual exemption and cannot apply for business asset disposal relief. It also means that Martha would take over liability for the whole £175,000 gain when she disposes of the business (unless she applied for a relief for herself when she came to dispose of the business).

The second option is to claim business asset disposal relief so that the £175,000 gain is reduced by Felicity's annual exemption of £12,300, leaving a taxable gain of £162,700 to be taxed at 10%. This gives Felicity a tax liability of £16,270.

If Felicity can afford the tax bill of £16,270, she will have a choice of which of the two options to take. Option 1 will mean that Felicity does not have to pay any tax now. Whereas the liability would become Martha's, Martha would only have to pay tax on the gain on the future disposal of the business, and it might be open to her to apply for reliefs at that point so that she would be able to defer payment of tax too.

Option 2 would allow the gain to be reduced by the annual exemption, and would also mean that the business asset disposal rate of 10% tax would be applied. This would mean less tax being paid overall, because Felicity would otherwise be paying 20% tax as she is a higher rate taxpayer and it is a large gain. However, Felicity would have to find the money to pay the tax bill rather than Martha having to pay at some point in the future.

10.10.2 Other reliefs

There are other CGT reliefs, which are outside the scope of this book, such as relief for reinvestment in certain unquoted shares and deferral relief on reinvestment in Enterprise Investment Scheme shares.

10.11 Step 5: Apply the correct rate of tax

This is the final step, and the rate of tax will depend on the nature of the asset and the taxpayer's income.

10.11.1 Categories of chargeable asset

As we have seen, different rates of tax apply to different disposals, depending on the nature of the asset disposed of and the taxpayer's financial position. There are three categories of chargeable asset:

- assets which are not residential property and do not qualify for business asset disposal relief. These are taxed at 10% or 20%, depending on the taxpayer's income;
- assets which qualify for business asset disposal relief, which are taxed at a flat rate of 10%; and
- residential property, which attracts a surcharge of 8% on the normal rates of 10% or 20%.

10.11.2 Calculating CGT when there is more than one disposal

When calculating the tax payable, chargeable assets in different categories must be calculated separately so that the correct rate of tax can be applied.

Any losses and the annual exemption can be deducted from gains in the best way possible for the taxpayer. Losses and the annual exemption should be deducted from gains that would otherwise be subject to higher tax rates. It makes sense, therefore, to deduct them from residential property gains first, then gains on assets which do not qualify for business asset disposal relief and, lastly, gains on assets which do qualify for business asset disposal relief.

⭐ *Example – more than one disposal*

Peggy made the following chargeable disposals in 2022/23:

1. *She sold a set of antique table and chairs for £9,000. She bought the furniture in 2018 for £10,000.*

2. *She sold an investment flat in York city centre for £283,000. She inherited it from her great aunt in 2011, and at the time it had a market value of £175,000.*

3. *She sold her 4% shareholding in Appledore Limited for £25,000. She bought the shares for £10,000 in 2009. She has never been a director of Appledore Limited.*

Peggy's taxable income for the 2022/23 tax year is £38,000.

Table 10.1 illustrates the steps taken to calculate the CGT Peggy needs to pay.

Table 10.1 Calculating CGT where more than one disposal occurs

	Antique furniture	Flat in York	Shares in Appledore Limited
Step 1: Identify the disposal Step 2: Calculate the gain. Proceeds of disposal *Less:* Acquisition expenditure Gain/(Loss) Step 3: Consider exemptions and reliefs	Sale of furniture £9,000 (£10,000) (£1,000) None	Sale of flat in York £283,000 (£175,000) £108,000 None	Sale of shares in Appledore Ltd £25,000 (£10,000) £15,000 None
Step 4: Aggregate net gains/ losses	LOSS	Residential property gain	Non business asset disposal relief gain
		£108,000	£15,000
Deduct current year loss (ie the loss from the sale of the furniture)		(£1,000)	
		£107,000	
Deduct annual exemption		(£12,300)	
Chargeable gains		£94,700	£15,000
Step 5: What are the rates of tax?			
CGT at 20% on £15,000 gain on Appledore shares			£3,000
CGT at 28% on £94,700 gain on investment flat			£26,516
Total CGT			**£29,516**

10.12 Losses

A taxpayer's CGT losses in a tax year may exceed their overall CGT gains. If so, setting the losses against the gains will wipe them out completely and the taxpayer will have no CGT to pay. In such a situation, the setting-off of the current year's losses to wipe out the gains entirely means that the taxpayer loses the use of their annual exemption, which cannot be carried forward to use against gains of future tax years.

If, after setting losses against gains, there are still unabsorbed losses, these may be carried forward to future years and then used to the extent necessary to reduce gains to the limit of the annual exemptions available in those future years. Unabsorbed losses can be carried forward indefinitely. The approach should be:

(a) work out the gain or loss on each disposal made during the tax year;

(b) deduct any losses of the current year from gains;

(c) deduct any losses brought forward from previous years to reduce any remaining gains to the limit of the annual exemption;

(d) deduct the annual exemption from any remaining gains.

Note: As previously stated, the losses and annual exemption should be applied in the most advantageous way for the taxpayer.

⭐ *Example – using previous losses*

In 2021/22, the year before the previous scenario, Peggy made capital gains on disposals totalling £50,000, and capital losses of £85,000. She had no unused losses from previous years.

Gains for the year	£50,000
Less: losses for the year	£85,000
Net loss for the year	£35,000

The £50,000 gain for the 2021/22 tax year is wiped out, and Peggy is not liable for CGT on that gain. The unused loss of £35,000 is carried forward to the next year.

The annual exemption cannot be used for the tax year 2021/22 because there is no net gain. It cannot be carried over to use in future years.

In 2022/23, Peggy's loss of £35,000 carried forward from 2021/22 would be set against the gain on the investment flat in York, because this would otherwise be taxed at the residential property rate of 28%, the highest possible rate of CGT, after deduction of the loss from the sale of the antique furniture. Peggy would apply her annual exemption against the remaining gain on the investment flat for the same reason, as shown in **Table 10.2**, *and would then apply the correct rates of tax, as shown in* **Table 10.3***.*

Table 10.2   Step 4: Aggregate net gains/losses

	Antique furniture	Flat in York	Shares in Appledore Limited
Step 4: Aggregate net gains/losses	Loss	Residential property gain £	Non-business asset disposal relief gain £
		108,000	15,000
Less current year loss		(1,000)	
Less previous year loss		(35,000)	
		72,000	
Deduct annual exemption		(12,300)	
Chargeable gains		59,700	15,000

Table 10.3   Step 5: Apply the correct rates of tax

CGT at 20% on £15,000 gain on Appledore Limited shares	£3,000
CGT at 28% on £59,700 gain on investment flat in York	£16,716
Total CGT	**£19,716**

Using the previous year's losses to reduce the gain has made a significant difference to the CGT payable.

⭐ ***Example – when previous losses are greater than the current year's gains***

*If Peggy had been carrying forward greater losses into the 2022/23 tax year, for example, £200,000, there would be no need to think about the best order in which to apply the losses because £200,000 is greater than Peggy's 2022/23 gains. However, instead of completely wiping out Peggy's 2022/23 gains and carrying forward the reminder of the losses to use in the 2023/24 tax year, the £200,000 losses would be set against the current year's gains until the current year's gains were down to the amount of the annual exemption of £12,300. Then Peggy could use her annual exemption and carry forward the reminder of her losses to the next tax year, illustrated in **Table 10.4**.*

Table 10.4   CGT when previous losses exceed the current year's gains

£	Loss carried forward £	
2021/22 loss	200,000	
2022/23 aggregate net gains/losses		15,000
		108,000
		(1,000)
Use part loss	(109,700)	(109,700)
		12,300
Deduct annual exemption		(12,300)
2021/22 taxable gains		nil
Balance of loss to be carried forward	90,300	

10.13 Part disposals

Where only part of an asset is disposed of, any initial and subsequent expenditure are apportioned when calculating the gain.

⭐ Example – part disposal

In 2009, Isabel bought a plot of commercial property for £200,000. She divided the plot and in October 2022, she sold part of the plot for £100,000. The remaining land is worth £300,000. This is her only disposal in the tax year and her taxable income for the tax year is £40,000.

Identify the disposal: sale of part of commercial property.

Calculation of the gain on the land sold:

Consideration received £100,000.

What is the cost of the land that was sold?

The total value of the two pieces of land is £400,000, comprising the land that was sold for £100,000 and the remaining land, worth £300,000.

The sold land is worth a quarter of the total value of the whole original plot, ie £100,000/ £400,000. Therefore, you must use a quarter of the cost of the original plot (£50,000) as the figure for the acquisition cost of the part of the land that was sold. The CGT calculations are shown in Table 10.5.

Table 10.5 CGT calculation for a part disposal

	£
Proceeds of disposal	100,000
Less:	
Apportioned cost	(50,000)
Gain	50,000
Deduct annual exemption	(12,300)
Chargeable gain	37,700
What is the rate of tax?	
CGT at 20% (because Isabel is a higher rate taxpayer)	£7,540

10.14 Disposals between spouses

When spouses or civil partners are living together, and one makes a disposal of an asset to the other, there is deemed to be no gain or loss. This means that spouses or civil partners can dispose of property to each other without paying CGT. However, when the recipient of the asset disposes of it, they will pay CGT both on any gain they have made and on any gain their spouse or civil partner made during their period of ownership. CGT, then, is only deferred, and not wiped out entirely.

This rule gives spouses the opportunity to save tax by transferring assets to the other person. If the husband or wife wishes to dispose of a chargeable asset but has already used up all of their annual exemption for the tax year, they can transfer the asset to their spouse or civil partner without paying tax. Then the spouse or civil partner can dispose of the asset and use their annual exemption instead so that between them, they have exempt gains of up to £24,600, rather than £12,300.

An inter-spouse transfer would also be beneficial if one spouse paid tax at a higher rate than the other, so that the tax is paid by the spouse or civil partner who pays tax at the lower rate.

⭐ *Example – disposals between spouses*

Assume that for the purposes of this example, Jamila is a higher rate taxpayer throughout and Simon is a basic rate taxpayer throughout.

Jamila bought an antique clock ten years ago for £74,000. Recently she had the clock valued at £115,000. She then gave it to her husband. Jamila will not pay CGT on the disposal.

Usually, when a gift is made, the donee is deemed to receive it at the market value at the time of the gift. However, because the clock was a gift from his wife, Simon is deemed to acquire it for the amount Jamila paid for it, £74,000.

If and when Simon disposes of the asset, he will be taxed on both his own gain and his wife's gain.

Five years later, Simon sells the clock for £130,000. The calculation of his gain will be:

Consideration received	£130,000
Less: Cost	£74,000
Gain	£56,000

If Simon had not acquired the clock from his wife, the normal rules would apply, so the calculation would be:

Consideration received	£130,000
Less: Cost	£115,000
Gain	£15,000

Simon will be liable for more CGT than he would have been on a normal gift, because he acquired the clock from his wife, but Jamila avoided paying CGT at the time of the gift. Further, Simon will pay CGT at 10% as a basic rate taxpayer (we are told that Simon is a basic rate taxpayer throughout), but Jamila would have paid a rate of 20% on all of the gain, as a higher rate taxpayer (we are told that Jamila is a higher rate taxpayer throughout). As a couple, Simon and Jamila have benefited from paying less tax overall.

10.15 Partnerships (of individuals) and CGT

When a chargeable asset owned by a partnership of individuals is disposed of, resulting in a chargeable gain, a charge to CGT will arise just as it would if an individual or sole trader were to sell a chargeable asset.

We have seen that disposal of a chargeable asset includes both a disposal by way of sale and a disposal by way of gift, but it is unlikely that a partnership will make a gift of any partnership assets. The context in which CGT is likely to be relevant for partnerships, then, is the sale of partnership assets, most likely land, premises, goodwill and investments.

When a firm disposes of a chargeable asset, this is treated for CGT purposes as if each partner is making a separate disposal of part of the asset. In other words, each partner pays a proportion of the CGT based on their percentage ownership of the partnership's assets. Sometimes the partners have expressly agreed how they will share the partnership's capital assets. For example, they may have agreed to share capital and capital profits in the same proportion as their initial capital contributions.

 Example

Joan, Kevin and Larry are in partnership, and share capital and capital profits in the following proportions:

Joan – 25%

Kevin – 50%

Larry – 25%

This means that Kevin owns half of each of the partnership's capital assets, and Joan and Larry own a quarter each.

10.15.1 Calculating the gain

Just as each partner will only pay tax on part of the capital gain arising from the sale of the partnership asset, the disposal proceeds and allowable expenditure must also be apportioned among the partners, according to their share of the asset.

 Example

In 2008, Joan, Kevin and Larry from the previous example purchased office premises for £200,000. They have now agreed to sell the office premises for £300,000, making a gain before deductions of £100,000. Kevin owns half of the partnership's assets, so he will be taxed on half of the proceeds of sale of £300,000 (£150,000), less half of the acquisition cost of £200,000 (£100,000) and half of any other allowable expenditure. Joan and Kevin will be taxed on a quarter of the proceeds of sale less a quarter of the acquisition cost and a quarter of any other allowable expenditure.

10.15.2 Business reliefs

Each partner can make their own decision regarding which reliefs, if any, they want to apply for. When disposing of the partnership's business assets, the most common reliefs are:

1. rollover relief on the replacement of qualifying business assets;

2. hold-over relief on gifts of business assets;

3. rollover relief on the incorporation of the business; and

4. business asset disposal relief.

Which relief or reliefs are available will depend on the circumstances. It may be that one partner can claim a relief to which the other partners are not entitled.

10.15.3 Individual disposals

A partner may dispose of their share in the partnership assets even when the firm as a whole is not making a disposal, usually when a partner leaves a partnership. The principles explained above govern how that partner's fractional share of any gain is calculated.

When a new partner joins a partnership, this will involve the other partners disposing of part of their existing share of the asset because the assets are shared amongst more partners.

 Example

Joan, Kevin and Larry each own one third of the assets in their partnership. Mo joins the partnership, and the partners agree that they will share all assets equally. Now that Mo has joined the partnership, Joan, Kevin and Larry each own one quarter of the partnership's assets, rather than a third – a smaller proportion of the partnership assets than they held before Mo joined. This could involve a charge to CGT when Mo buys into the partnership, as Joan, Kevin and Larry will all receive money which is, in effect, payment for the share of the capital assets they are each transferring to Mo.

10.16 Limited liability partnerships

When an LLP is used to carry on a trade or profession, it will be treated for most purposes in the same way as an ordinary partnership as far as CGT is concerned. However, when an LLP ceases to trade, it may be treated as a body corporate rather than a partnership for the purposes of capital gains.

10.17 Buyback of shares and CGT

Usually, when a shareholder sells their shares back to a company, there will be a charge to income tax for the shareholder rather than CGT. The profit represented by the difference between the consideration the shareholder receives and the issue price of the shares will be taxed as a dividend. However, the shareholder's profit sometimes attracts CGT instead. Capital gains tax will be relevant when certain conditions are satisfied:

1. the buyer must be a trading company and its shares must *not* be listed on a recognised stock exchange (AIM is not a recognised stock exchange for the purposes of this test); and

2. the purpose of the buyback must either be to raise cash to pay inheritance tax or be for the benefit of the company's trade (perhaps where there is a rift between shareholders and the company will function more effectively if one of the shareholders sells their shares back to the company); and

3. the seller must have owned the shares they are selling back to the company for at least five years; and

4. the seller must either be selling all of their shares or substantially reducing their percentage shareholding (by at least 25%) to a maximum of 30% of the issued share capital of the company.

If it is difficult to decide whether these conditions are met, the taxpayer can apply to HMRC for advance clearance of their proposed tax treatment of the buyback.

Whether paying income tax or CGT would result in a lower tax liability will depend on the taxpayer's circumstances and how much income they earn. If the taxpayer pays CGT, the availability of reliefs such as business asset disposal relief may significantly reduce their liability to CGT. If the taxpayer is a basic rate income taxpayer, then they are likely to benefit from the ordinary income tax rate for dividends (8.75%) and the dividend allowance.

It is sometime possible to structure the buyback so that the taxpayer obtains the most favourable tax treatment.

10.18 Assessment and payment of CGT

Capital gains tax is paid on all gains in the tax year. Generally it is payable on or before 31 January following the end of the tax year, or 30 days from the making of an assessment, if later. However, a taxpayer is required to submit a provisional calculation of any gains made from the sale of a residential property and pay any tax due within 30 days following completion of the sale.

Payment can be made using HMRC's real-time CGT service, the HMRC property service or by completing a self-assessment tax return in the same way as is required for income tax.

Sometimes (although rarely) payment by ten annual instalments is an option. This is only available where:

• the disposal was a gift;

• the qualifying asset is land, a controlling shareholding in any company or any shareholding (whether controlling or not) in a company whose shares are unquoted; and

• the conditions for hold-over relief to apply must **not** be met.

If payment by instalments is an option, the first payment will be due by 31 January following the end of the tax year in which the disposal was made.

10.19 Tax avoidance

There is a great deal of legislation drafted to combat CGT avoidance, and the legislation focuses on known loopholes or possibilities for tax avoidance in the existing legislation. In addition to these specific measures, the Finance Act 2013 allows HMRC to make adjustments to a taxpayer's liability to counteract the tax advantages arising from abusive tax arrangements. This is known as the general anti-avoidance rule and is explained in detail at **9.16**.

10.20 Inheritance tax ('IHT') and business property relief ('BPR')

There is no charge to CGT on death, because there is deemed to be no disposal of assets and the deceased's personal representatives are deemed to acquire the deceased's assets at their market value at the date of death. However, there are likely to be inheritance tax implications. On death, there is a deemed transfer of value by the deceased of their entire estate immediately before death, and potentially exempt transfers made by the deceased in the seven years preceding their death become chargeable transfers as a result of their death. IHT is explained fully in *Wills and the Administration of Estates*.

Business property relief ('BPR') operates to reduce the value transferred by a transfer of value of relevant business property by a certain percentage. This relief should be considered after applying any spouse/civil partner or charity exemption. It is worth considering it in this chapter even though the subject of this chapter is CGT, because we have covered other business reliefs relevant to the CGT payable on disposal of business property.

A reduction of 100% of the value transferred is allowed for transfers of value where the value transferred is attributable to certain defined types of 'relevant business property' (meaning that there will be no charge to IHT in respect of those assets). Relevant business property means:

- a business or an interest in a business (including a partnership share);

- company shares that are not listed on a recognised stock exchange (AIM is not included in the definition of stock exchange for these purposes). Only the value of the shares attributable to business/trading activities is eligible for the relief.

A reduction of 50% of the value transferred is allowed for transfers of value where the value transferred is attributable to any other relevant business property. They are:

- company shares that are listed on a recognised stock exchange if the transferor had voting control of the company immediately before the transfer;

- land, buildings, machinery or plant owned by the transferor personally but used for business purposes by a partnership of which they are a member, or by a company (whether quoted or unquoted) of which they have voting control (the ability to exercise over 50% of the votes on all resolutions). In assessing whether or not a person has voting control, separate shareholdings of spouses or civil partners can, in certain circumstances, be taken as one, so that if the combined percentage of the votes gives the couple voting control then the test will be satisfied.

To attract the relief, the asset(s) in question:

- must have been owned by the transferor *for at least two years* at the time of the transfer; or

- broadly, must be a replacement for relevant business property where the combined period of ownership is two years. This would include the situation where a sole trader or individual partner incorporated their business – the shares in the company that they received in return would be relevant business property.

If property is inherited from a spouse or civil partner, the surviving spouse/civil partner is deemed to have owned the property from the date it was originally acquired by the deceased spouse/civil partner (but this rule does not apply to lifetime transfers between spouses/civil partners).

Note that:

- For BPR to apply, whether at the rate of 100% or 50%, the transfer does not need to be of the transferor's entire interest in the business or shareholding.

- Where a person has entered into a contract for sale of their business or company shares, their interest is taken to be in the proceeds of sale. So, because cash is not relevant business property, no relief will be available where there is a binding contract for sale (for example, when a shareholders' agreement provides that if a shareholder dies, the shareholder's PRs *will* sell to the remaining shareholders who *will* buy those shares). The problem can be avoided by the use of an *option* to sell or purchase.

⭐ *Example – transfer of a partnership share*

For many years Erin, Fiona and Gupta were partners, sharing profits and losses equally. Erin and Fiona owned the business premises in equal shares as tenants in common. There was no provision in their partnership agreement dealing with the purchase and sale of assets on death. Erin and Fiona were both killed in a workplace accident and their entire estates were inherited by Erin's son and Fiona's daughter respectively.

The interest in the business of each partner qualifies for 100% BPR and also each partner's interest in the premises qualifies for BPR at 50%.

No relief at all would have been available if there was a partnership agreement under which there was a binding contract for the purchase and sale of the partners' interests.

Summary

CGT calculation: steps

Step 1: Identify the disposal (sale or gift) of a chargeable asset (part disposals are apportioned)

Step 2: Calculate the gain – deduct costs of disposal, initial and subsequent expenditure and incidental costs of disposal

Step 3: Consider reliefs. The main ones are:
- Relief on replacement of business assets ('rollover' relief)
- Rollover relief on incorporation of a business
- Hold-over relief on gifts
- Business asset disposal relief

Step 4: Aggregate gains/losses and deduct the annual exemption (deduct the annual exemption from the gains which would be subject to the highest rate of tax). Capital losses carried over from the previous year can be deducted here.

Step 5: Apply the correct rate of tax:
- Standard rate of 10% for basic rate taxpayers and 20% for any gains above the basic rate threshold;
- Residential property rate – apply a surcharge of 8%, meaning that the rates are 18% for basic rate taxpayers and 28% for any gains above the basic rate threshold; or
- Business asset disposal relief rate of 10%, whatever the taxpayer's income.

Sample questions

Question 1

Assume that it is April 2023. In May 2022 a client disposed of her shareholding in a company which specialises in importing and distributing food. The client resigned as a non-executive director of the company in December 2020 but retained her shareholding until May 2022. She sold all of her ordinary shares (6% of the company's issued share capital) for £188,651 on 3 May 2022, having bought them for £133,000 in May 2012, allowing for all relevant costs of acquisition and disposal.

This is the only disposal that the client made in the 2022/23 tax year.

Which of the following best describes whether or not the disposal of the client's shareholding attracts business asset disposal relief?

A   Yes, because the shares were in a trading company and the client held over 5% of the company's shares.

B   Yes, because the client was a director of the company within the two years prior to the disposal and held over 5% of the company's shares.

C   No, because the client was not an officer or employee of the company during the whole of the two years prior to disposal.

D   No, because the client held less than 10% of the company's shares.

E   No, because the company is not a personal company.

Answer

Option C is correct. This is because to benefit from business asset disposal relief, the individual must have:

- held over 5% of the shares in a trading company; and
- been an officer or employee of that trading company; and
- those conditions must have been satisfied for two years prior to disposal of the shares.

The client resigned nearly two years before the disposal so cannot benefit from the relief – she was not an officer or employee for the whole of the two years prior to disposal.

Question 2

Assume that it is April 2023. A client, a higher rate taxpayer, sold his holiday home in the Lake District in February 2023 for £450,000. He purchased it in 2010 for £300,000. The initial expenditure (legal fees, valuation fees and stamp duty) amounted to £17,000 and the incidental costs of disposal were £3,000.

He has made no other disposals in the tax year and has no losses to carry forward from previous tax years.

Assumptions: the annual exemption for capital gains tax for individuals and personal representatives is £12,300, whereas for trustees it is £6,150.

Which of the following CORRECTLY states the sole trader's liability for capital gains tax for the tax year?

A   £11,770

B   £150,000

C   £130,000

D   £32,956

E   £23,540

Answer

Option D is correct.

Disposal value	450,000
Costs of disposal	(3,000)
Acquisition Value	(300,000)
Initial expenditure	(17,000)
Chargeable gain	(130,000)

Chargeable gain (£130,000) less the annual exemption of £12,300 = £117,700.

If the chargeable asset is residential property which is not the taxpayer's main residence (here, the client is selling his holiday home), the gains are subject to a surcharge of 8%. As the client is a higher rate taxpayer, he will pay CGT at the rate of 28%.

£117,700 x 28% = **£32,956**

Question 3

A client, who was a basic rate taxpayer, dies owning a small office building worth £290,000. The office building was given to her as a gift by her mother several years ago, and she used it as an artist's studio. At the time of the gift, the office building had a market value of £100,000.

Which of the following best describes the client's CGT position with respect to the office building?

A   The client will pay CGT on the gain of £190,000 (subject to any initial expenditure and costs of disposal).

B   The client's personal representatives will pay CGT on the gain of £190,000 (subject to any initial expenditure and costs of disposal).

C   The client's personal representatives will pay CGT on the building's market value of £290,000.

D   The client will not pay any CGT and her personal representatives will acquire the building at a deemed value of £100,000 as at the date of the client's death.

E   The client will not pay any CGT and her personal representatives will acquire the building at market value as at the date of the client's death.

Answer

Option E is correct. There is no charge to CGT on the death of a taxpayer, so option A is wrong. The taxpayer's personal representatives acquire the property at market value (here, £290,000) as at the date of the taxpayer's death, so options B, C and D are wrong. The capital gain is therefore wiped out (although there may be inheritance tax implications).

11

Corporation Tax

SQE1 syllabus

Candidates are required to apply relevant core legal principles and rules appropriately and effectively, at the level of a competent newly qualified solicitor in practice, to realistic client-based and ethical problems and situations in the following areas of corporation tax:

- basis of charge

- calculation, payment and collection of tax

- tax treatment of company distributions or deemed distributions to shareholders

- outline of anti-avoidance legislation

Learning outcomes

By the end of this chapter you will be able to:

- understand the steps required to carry out a corporation tax calculation;

- understand when companies are entitled to capital allowances, including the annual investment allowance;

- understand some of the reliefs and exemptions available to companies to reduce or postpone their corporation tax liability;

- carry out a corporation tax calculation;

- understand corporation tax payment dates.

The tax rates set out in this chapter are correct as at the date of publication. Please note that these tax rates may no longer be current at the date of any future SQE assessment.

11.1 Introduction

As we have seen, companies do not pay income tax or capital gains tax ('CGT'). Instead, they pay corporation tax. However, this does not mean that you have to understand a completely unfamiliar set of principles to carry out a corporation tax calculation. This is because, putting it simply, corporation tax consists of tax on income profits and tax on capital gains, both of which are calculated in a very similar way to income tax and CGT for individuals. The key statutes governing corporation tax are the Corporation Tax Act 2009 and the Corporation Tax Act 2010.

The corporation tax financial year runs from 1 April to 31 March (which may differ from the company's financial year, which can start at any time of year). Financial years are described by reference to the period in which they commence, so the corporation tax year running from 1 April 2022 to 31 March 2023 is 'Financial Year 2022'. For Financial Year 2022, the corporation tax rate is 19%, although other rates do still exist for certain specific activities.

A corporation tax calculation consists of the following steps:

Step 1: Calculate income profits

Step 2: Calculate chargeable gains

Step 3: Calculate total profits and apply any available reliefs against total profits

Step 4: Calculate tax at the appropriate rates

We will now consider each of the steps in more detail.

11.2 Steps in a corporation tax calculation

11.2.1 Step 1: Calculate income profits

The most common type of income which is chargeable to corporation tax is trading profit. In this chapter, we will concentrate on trading profit, but it is worth highlighting that property income and certain income associated with loans are also chargeable to corporation tax. **Chapter 7** explains how to calculate trading profit for all of the types of business covered in this book, and you should now refer back to **Chapter 7** for a full explanation of the calculation. Once you have calculated trading profit, you can move on to Step 2 of the corporation tax calculation.

Note that dividends paid to shareholders and a company's payments to shareholders for shares bought back by the company are not deductible expenditure when calculating a company's trading profits.

11.2.2 Step 2: Calculate chargeable gains

The next step in the corporation tax calculation is to calculate chargeable gains. These are calculated in a similar way to CGT, but there are some differences. The stages to calculate the chargeable gain within Step 2 are as follows:

Stage 1: Identify a chargeable disposal

Stage 2: Calculate the gain (or loss)

Stage 3: Apply reliefs

Stage 4: Aggregate remaining gains or losses.

11.2.2.1 Stage 1: Identify a chargeable disposal

At this stage of the calculation, you must identify any disposal of chargeable assets. The disposal can be by way of sale or by gift.

Chargeable assets

Chargeable assets for the purposes of corporation tax are defined in almost exactly the same way as for CGT. The most likely chargeable assets will be land, buildings, and shares in other companies. However, they must not form part of the company's income stream, otherwise they will be classed as income profits rather than chargeable gains. In addition, different rules apply for the disposal of goodwill and intellectual property (see **11.5**).

Plant and machinery

In practice, plant and machinery are unlikely to increase in value and so a chargeable capital gain is unlikely to arise. The details of the interaction between capital allowances and capital gains is outside the scope of this book.

11.2.2.2 Stage 2: Calculate the gain (or loss)

To calculate the gain (or loss) on a chargeable disposal, you should follow the calculation set out below.

Proceeds of disposal (or market value in the case of a gift or sale at an undervalue)

LESS

Costs of disposal

= Net proceeds of disposal

LESS

Other allowable expenditure (initial and subsequent expenditure)

= Gain (before indexation) or loss

LESS

Indexation allowance

= Gain (after indexation)

What is a sale at an undervalue?

If the company sells an asset below market value, this may just be a bad bargain, in which case, the actual sale price will be used as the figure for proceeds of disposal. However, if there was a gift element to the sale at an undervalue, the market value of the asset will be used as the figure for proceeds of disposal. If the sale was to a 'connected person', it will be deemed to have taken place at market value instead. A person is a 'connected person' if that person controls the company, either alone or with others connected to them. A company is connected to another company if they are both controlled by the same person, or by a combination of that person and others connected with them.

If disposing of the asset results in a loss and not a gain, the loss can be deducted from the company's chargeable gains for the accounting period, but not from its income profits. Any unused loss can be carried forward to subsequent accounting periods to be deducted from the first available chargeable gains made by the company.

The indexation allowance

When an asset increases in value, the gain cannot all be regarded as profit. Some of the gain will be as a result of inflation, rather than the asset becoming inherently more valuable. Following a period of significant inflation, on 31 March 1982 an indexation allowance was introduced to remove the inflationary gains from the corporation tax calculation, meaning that a smaller gain is charged to tax.

To calculate the indexation allowance, you need to apply to initial and subsequent expenditure (but not costs of disposal) the percentage increase in the Retail Prices Index from the date the expenditure was incurred to the date of disposal of the asset (or, if earlier, 31

December 2017 – see below). HMRC publishes tables to show this figure as an indexation factor to make the calculation easier. After calculating the allowance, you must deduct it from the gain (before indexation) to give the gain (after indexation).

The indexation allowance is used when calculating the gain on an asset owned for any period from 31 March 1982. If various items of expenditure were incurred at different times, different indexation factors will need to be used for each item of expenditure. Indexation was frozen on 31 December 2017, meaning that no indexation allowance is applied to any initial and subsequent expenditure from December 2017 onwards.

Since the concept of indexation was not introduced until 31 March 1982, the indexation allowance for assets owned on 31 March 1982 is based on the market value of the assets on 31 March 1982, not actual cost.

Note that the indexation allowance cannot be used to create or increase a loss.

⭐ *Example – indexation*

Queensbury Limited ('Queensbury') acquired some land for £120,000 in February 2005. The incidental costs of acquisition were solicitors' fees of £2,000 and surveyor's fees of £1,000.

Queensbury spent £10,000 on legal fees in June 2017, defending the title to the land.

Queensbury sold the land in April 2022 for £285,000. The incidental costs of disposal were £2,000 (comprised of legal and estate agent's fees).

*For the calculations shown in **Table 11.1**, assume the indexation factor for February 2005 is 0.467 and that for June 2017 it is 0.021.*

Table 11.1 Calculating the gain after indexation

	£	£
Proceeds of disposal		285,000
Less incidental costs of disposal		(2,000)
= Net proceeds of disposal		283,000
Less initial expenditure:		
Acquisition cost	120,000	
Incidental costs of acquisition	3,000	(123,000)
Less subsequent expenditure		(10,000)
= Gain (before indexation)		150,000
Less indexation allowance:		
On initial expenditure	(123,000 x 0.467)	(57,441)
On subsequent expenditure	(10,000 x 0.021)	(210)
= Gain (after indexation)		**£92,349**

11.2.2.3 Stage 3: Apply reliefs

There are fewer reliefs available to companies than to individuals. The main reliefs available are described below.

Rollover relief on the replacement of qualifying business assets

This relief allows companies to postpone the payment of corporation tax following the disposal of a qualifying asset, when the consideration received for the qualifying asset is used to acquire another qualifying asset.

What is a qualifying asset?

The main qualifying assets are land and buildings, although other more unusual assets, such as ships, also qualify. The company must use the asset in its trade: assets held by way of an investment are not qualifying assets.

Note that:

- company shares are *not* qualifying assets;

- the relief does not apply to goodwill and other intellectual property, which are subject to a separate rollover relief (see **11.5**);

- fixed plant and machinery are qualifying assets, but selling such assets will rarely produce a gain because they usually depreciate in value. Further, rollover relief in relation to such assets will be restricted if they are wasting assets. There is no statutory definition of fixed plant and machinery, but if the item is movable, and intended to be movable so that the layout of the workplace can change, it will not be classed as fixed.

For the relief to apply, the asset disposed of and the asset acquired with the proceeds of sale do not need to be the same type of asset. They both just need to fall within the definition of qualifying asset.

Time limits

The company must acquire (or have acquired) the replacement asset within one year before or within three years after it disposes of the original asset, unless HMRC allows the company to have an extended period to acquire the replacement asset.

 Example – time limits for rollover relief

Queensbury disposes of an asset on 1 May 2022. If the board wants Queensbury to benefit from rollover relief on replacement of a qualifying business asset, Queensbury would need to acquire the replacement qualifying business asset between 1 May 2021 and 30 April 2025.

The effect of the relief

If the company disposes of a qualifying asset, and purchases another qualifying asset to be used in the company's trade within the time limits set out above, the company's liability to corporation tax arising from the disposal can be postponed by rolling over the gain on the disposal of the original asset into the acquisition cost of the replacement asset.

The gain is notionally deducted from the acquisition cost of the replacement asset. This gives a lower acquisition cost to use in the corporation tax calculation when the replacement asset is sold. In essence, when the replacement asset is sold, it will be deemed to have a lower acquisition cost than it actually had. This will mean that the difference between the initial acquisition cost of the replacement asset and its sale price will be greater, and more corporation tax will be paid overall, to account for the gain on the original asset. If only part of the consideration received on the disposal of the original asset is used to purchase the new asset, there will be restrictions on the availability of rollover relief.

Example – rollover relief on the replacement of qualifying business assets

On 13 June 2022, Newton Limited buys a new factory for £200,000. Two months later, it sells a factory that it has owned for several years. The sale price was £175,000 and Newton Limited made a gain on the sale, after indexation, of £40,000.

If Newton Limited claims rollover relief on the replacement of qualifying assets:

- *it will not pay corporation tax on the gain made on the disposal of the original factory; and*

- *the replacement factory (it is classed as a replacement even though it was purchased before the original premises were sold) will be treated as having been acquired for £160,000, ie the acquisition cost less the rolled over gain of £40,000.*

If Newton Limited sells the new factory two years later for £235,000, its gain will be calculated as follows:

Proceeds of disposal	£235,000
Less *adjusted* acquisition cost	£160,000
Gain (before indexation)	£75,000

Without rollover relief, the gain would only be £35,000 (ie proceeds of disposal of £235,000 less actual, not adjusted, acquisition cost of £200,000).

The gain from this sale could again be rolled over if the qualifying conditions were met.

11.2.3 Step 3: Calculate total profits and apply any available reliefs against total profits

In Step 3, you must add together the company's income profits and capital gains. The resulting figure is the company's total profits for the accounting period. By this point, certain reliefs have already been applied, but at Step 3 those reliefs which are applied against total profits must be considered.

Certain trading loss reliefs are deducted from total profits, namely carry-across/carry-back relief, terminal carry-back relief and carry-forward relief. These reliefs are covered in detail at **11.4**.

Certain qualifying donations to charity are also deductible from total profits.

11.2.4 Step 4: Calculate the tax

Steps 1 to 3 establish the company's taxable profit for the accounting period. At Step 4, the appropriate tax rate is applied to taxable profit, to calculate tax payable.

The corporation tax financial year runs from 1 April to 31 March. If the company's accounting period – its financial year – is different from the corporation tax financial year, and the corporation tax rate changes from one corporation tax year to the next, the company will have to pay tax at one rate on a proportion of its profits and at the new rate on the rest of its profits for the financial year.

11.3 A corporation tax calculation

Your firm acts for ELF Limited, which manufactures toys. Total sales in the accounting period were £2,250,000. During the accounting period, the company incurred the following costs:

- purchase of second-hand machinery for £226,000

- stock for £435,000

- salaries of £340,000

- utility bills of £110,000

- rent of £25,000

- insurance of £7,000

The company sold a factory in May 2022 for £510,000. It had purchased the factory in January 2007 for £360,000, and paid incidental costs of £12,000 at the time. Its costs of disposal were £21,000. The company's existing pool of plant and machinery had a written-down value of £460,000 at the start of the accounting period. Assume that for a disposal in May 2022 the indexation factor from January 2007 is 0.298.

Table 11.2 Calculating corporation tax

Step 1: Calculate income profits	£	£
Trading income		
Chargeable receipts		2,250,000
Less deductible expenses (income in nature; wholly and exclusively for the purpose of the trade; not statute barred)		
Stock	435,000	
Salaries	340,000	
Utility bills	110,000	
Rent	25,000	
Insurance	7,000	(917,000)
		1,333,000
Less Capital allowances		
The company qualifies for AIA (no super-deduction because the plant and machinery was not brand new)	226,000	
Existing pool of plant and machinery 460,000 x 18%	82,800	(308,800)
Total trading (and income) profits		1,024,200

(continued)

Table 11.2 (*continued*)

Step 2: Calculate chargeable gains		
Premises		
Disposal proceeds		510,000
Less incidental costs of disposal		(21,000)
Net proceeds of disposal		489,000
Less initial expenditure		
acquisition cost	360,000	
incidental costs of acquisition	12,000	
		(372,000)
Gain before indexation		117,000
Less indexation		
Acquisition cost 360,000 x 0.298	107,280	
Costs of acquisition 12,000 x 0.298	3,576	
		(110,856)
Gains after indexation		6,144
Reliefs None on the facts		
Step 3: Calculate total profits and apply any available reliefs against total profits		
Income profits		1,024,200
Chargeable gains		6,144
Total profits		1,030,344
No reliefs available against total profits		
Taxable profits		**1,030,344**
Step 4: Calculate tax at the appropriate rates		
1,030,344 @ 19%	**Corporation tax due**	195,765.36

11.4 Relief for a trading loss

Sometimes, the calculation of trading income results in a loss rather than a profit. The company may be able to claim tax relief for this loss. The reliefs available for a trading loss are set out below and summarised at the end of this section in **Table 11.3**. Where the company is eligible for more than one relief, the company may choose which to claim. If applying a particular relief does not absorb all of the company's losses, the company can claim as much relief as is available under one relief and then claim relief for the balance of its loss under any other available relief. Companies cannot claim for the same loss twice.

Often companies claim relief under whichever provision is best for cash flow: out of the reliefs described below, carry-across/carry-back relief and terminal carry-back relief may lead to a refund of tax already paid. Carry-forward relief reduces the amount of corporation tax that the company will have to pay in the future.

11.4.1 Carry-across/carry-back relief for trading losses

Companies may carry across their trading loss for an accounting period and set it against total profits for the same accounting period. This is carry-across relief. If, after setting the losses against total profits, there are still some losses remaining, the remaining losses can then be carried back and set against total profits from the accounting period(s) falling in the 12 months prior to the accounting period of the loss, on condition that the company was then carrying on the same trade. This is carry-back relief.

If there are no profits at all for a particular accounting period, carry-back relief allows the company to set its losses for the current accounting period against total profits from the accounting period(s) falling in the 12 months prior to the accounting period of the loss, on condition that the company was then carrying on the same trade.

Applying these reliefs often leads to companies receiving a rebate of corporation tax they have already paid.

 Example – carry-across and carry-back relief

Grange Limited makes a trading loss in its accounting period ending 31 December 2022. It can 'carry across' these losses and set them against any other profits it has made during the accounting period, for example investment income. Any remaining losses can be carried back to set against all profits in the previous accounting period, ending 31 December 2021.

In response to the Covid-19 pandemic, the Government introduced a temporary measure allowing trading losses to be carried back three years instead of one. This measure has now ended.

11.4.2 Terminal carry-back relief for trading losses

When a company ceases to trade, it can carry back any trading losses and set them against the company's total profits from any accounting period(s) falling in the three years before the start of that final 12 months, taking later periods first.

 Example – terminal carry-back relief

LBJ Limited makes a trading loss in 2022. Its accounting period ends on 31 December and it ceases trading on 31 December 2022. It can set its 2022 losses against any profits it has made in 2022, and, if it still has losses remaining, it can set them against profits from 2021, 2020 and 2019. It cannot go back further than 2019 because the relief only allows it to set losses against total profits from any accounting period falling in the three years before the start of its final 12 months (ie 1 January 2022).

Claims for carry-across, carry-back or terminal carry-back relief must be made within two years from the end of the accounting period in which the loss was incurred.

11.4.3 Carry-forward relief for trading losses

A company may carry forward its trading loss for an accounting period and set it against subsequent profits in the next accounting period. In order to benefit from this relief, the company must continue to trade and certain other conditions must be met. Any remaining loss can be carried forward again and set against total profits in subsequent years.

A claim for carry-forward relief must usually be made within two years of the end of the accounting period in which the company will apply the losses to reduce total profits. The maximum amount that can be claimed under this allowance is £5 million, plus 50% of remaining total profits after deduction of the allowance. Note that this relief changed on 1 April 2017 – before that date, the relief could only be used against profits of the same trade; since that date, companies have been able to set the losses against total profits.

If the company does not meet the conditions to set the loss against total profits, it can still carry forward the loss and instead set it against profits of the same trade.

⭐ *Example – carry-forward relief*

Ennerdale Limited makes a trading loss in the accounting period ending 31 March 2022, but makes a profit the following year. Under carry-forward relief, it can deduct its 2021/22 losses from its total profit for the accounting period ending 31 March 2023. If there are any losses remaining, it can carry these forward to the accounting period ending 31 March 2024, and so on, until the losses are exhausted.

Table 11.3 Summary of corporation tax reliefs

Name of relief	When loss occurred	Losses set against	Relevant accounting periods
Carry-across/ carry-back relief	Any time	The company's total profits	The accounting period of the loss and the accounting period(s) falling in the previous 12 months.
Terminal carry-back relief	The final 12 months of trading	The company's total profits	The accounting period(s) of the loss and the accounting period(s) falling in the three years previous to the final 12 months of trading, taking later periods first
Carry-forward relief	Any time	The company's total profits Subsequent profits of the same trade if the conditions for setting against total profits are not met (at Step 1 of the tax calculation)	Subsequent accounting periods until the loss is absorbed

11.5 Corporation tax on goodwill and intellectual property

Goodwill and intellectual property (eg trademarks, patents, design rights and copyright) are intangible fixed assets. They are capital in nature but receipts from transactions in intangible fixed assets are treated as income receipts for the purposes of the company's corporation tax calculation.

Expenditure on intangible fixed assets is generally deductible when calculating the company's income profits. When an intangible fixed asset is disposed of, and provided the conditions are met, any profit can be rolled over into the acquisition of replacement intangible fixed assets. This means that the corporation tax in relation to the profit from that disposal is deferred.

11.6 Groups and close companies

Provisions exist within tax legislation to make sure that there is no significant advantage or disadvantage, from a tax point of view, to trading as a company rather than as a sole trader or partnership. We will now consider some of those provisions in so far as they relate to close companies and to groups of companies.

11.6.1 Close companies

A close company is a company either:

- controlled by five or fewer participators; or
- controlled by participators (any number of them) who are directors or shadow directors.

A participator is a person who owns shares in the company, or has the right to acquire shares in the company. To ascertain whether the participators 'control' the company, the test is whether the participators own more than half of the shares in the company or have more than half of the voting power in the company, or have the right to acquire more than half of the shares in the company.

When a close company loans money to a participator or their associate (broadly, 'associate' means a close relative or business partner), the company must pay to HMRC an amount of money equivalent to 33.75% of the loan. The payment is akin to a deposit: payment will be refunded to the company if and when the participator/associate repays the loan or if the loan is written off. No tax is payable if:

- the loan is made in the ordinary course of a money-lending business, for example, a bank loan by a bank to a shareholder; or
- if the loan (added to any other such loan made to the same person) is no more than £15,000 *and* the borrower works full-time for the company *and* owns no more than 5% of the company's ordinary shares.

The borrower does not have to pay any tax in relation to the loan, unless the company writes off the debt.

The reason for these provisions is to prevent tax avoidance. If these provisions did not exist, directors or shareholders could borrow money from the company, instead of receiving it as taxable income or dividend, and arrange for the company not to enforce the obligation to repay for many years, if at all. The loan would then be almost akin to a salary, but tax-free.

Shareholders of a close company who take out a loan to purchase shares in the company or to lend money to the close company may be able to claim income tax relief on the interest payable on the loan.

11.6.2 Groups of companies

Organising a business by separating it into different companies is a useful way of operating, because it minimises risk, allows the business to run a number of different operations in a more organised way and streamlines management structure. Given that each company in a group of companies is a separate legal entity, each company will be charged to tax separately. However, tax legislation exists to try to ensure that operating as a group of companies is tax neutral; that is, it is no more or less advantageous from a tax point of view than trading as a single company.

11.6.2.1 Group relief

This relief allows the company to transfer certain losses and expenses to another company within the same qualifying group. The transferee will then use the loss or expense to reduce its taxable profit. Both companies must fit the definition of a group in order for this relief to be used.

11.6.2.2 What is a group for the purposes of group relief?

One company must be the 75% subsidiary of the other, or both companies must be 75% subsidiaries of a third company. The test for being a 75% subsidiary essentially means that the holding company must own, directly or indirectly, 75% or more of the subsidiary's ordinary shares.

 Example

A

↓

80%

B

↓

80%

C

A and B are in the same group, and so are B and C. A and C are not in the same group because A does not own, directly or indirectly, 75% or more of C's ordinary shares. A has an indirect shareholding of 64% in C (80% x 80% = 64%).

11.6.2.3 How does group relief work?

Once it has been established that two companies are in the same group, one company (the transferor) can surrender certain items, including trading losses and management expenses, to the other company (the transferee). The loss or expense must have been incurred in an accounting period that overlaps with the accounting period of the transferee (who will be using the loss or expense from the other company to reduce its profits in that accounting period).

There are some restrictions on the application of the relief when the transferor has other profits, or the transferee has losses of its own. In addition, group relief does not apply to capital losses, only income losses.

11.6.2.4 Chargeable disposals

Sometimes companies in a group can arrange for the company that will benefit most from a tax perspective to dispose of a chargeable asset owned by another company in the group.

11.6.2.5 What is a group for the purposes of chargeable gains?

For this relief, the group consists of a company, its direct 75% subsidiaries and the direct 75% subsidiaries of those subsidiaries, and so on. All of the subsidiaries in the group must be effective 51% subsidiaries of the principal company. This means that the principal company must be beneficially entitled to more than 50% of the available profits and assets of the subsidiary. The group is only permitted to have one principal company.

 Example

A

↓

80%

B

↓

80%

C

↓

75%

D

A, B and C are in the same group for the purposes of chargeable gains, because A owns at least 75% of B and B owns at least 75% of C, and A effectively owns 64% of C (80% x 80% = 64%), satisfying the 'effective 51%' test. However, D does not form part of the group because A has an indirect shareholding of only 48% in D (80% x 80% x 75% = 48%), which means that D is not an effective 51% subsidiary of A.

11.6.2.6 How does relief for chargeable gains work?

Once it has been established that the two companies are within a group for chargeable gains purposes, one of the companies can transfer a chargeable asset to the other on a tax neutral basis. This means that the disposal is treated as giving rise to neither a gain nor a loss by the transferor. The transferee can then use the loss to reduce its own chargeable gains, so, as a group, the companies will pay less tax overall.

11.6.3 Rollover relief

When a company is in a group for chargeable gains purposes and it disposes of a chargeable asset outside the group, it can roll over its gain into qualifying assets that it acquires (provided it satisfies the criteria for rollover relief – see **11.2.2.3**). As an alternative, it can roll over its gain into qualifying assets acquired by another company in the same group.

Group relief under chargeable gains provisions are subject to certain anti-avoidance provisions. These are designed to stop companies using the rules to their benefit when they join or leave a group. These provisions are outside the scope of this book.

11.6.4 Groups, VAT and stamp duty

It is now worth mentioning two other tax implications of belonging to a group of companies, even though they are not connected to corporation tax.

Firstly, stamp duty and stamp duty land tax will not be charged on transfers of assets between companies which are in a qualifying group, provided that certain conditions are met.

Secondly, in terms of VAT, a group of companies may be able to register for VAT as a group under a single registration. See **7.14** for a full explanation of VAT.

11.7 Corporation tax on distributions

11.7.1 Dividends

When a company receives dividends from shares it has in another UK company, in principle they are taken into account when calculating its corporation tax liability. However, there are a number of exceptions whose effect is to exempt most dividends from corporation tax, preventing double taxation. Double taxation would otherwise arise on distributing profits that have already been assessed to tax on the company which paid the dividends.

11.7.2 Profit for the seller on a buyback of shares

When a company sells shares back to the company in which the shares are held, it must work out how any profit on the sale will be treated in its corporation tax calculation. If the buyback satisfies the CGT rules (the test for which is set out at **10.17**), the profit will be taxed as part of the selling company's chargeable gains. If not, it will be taxed as income.

11.8 Notification to HMRC

A company must inform HMRC in writing of the beginning of its first accounting period, and must do so within three months of the start of that accounting period. After that, every year HMRC will issue a notice to the company requiring it to deliver a self-assessment corporation tax return.

11.9 Payment

The deadline for filing the self-assessment return with HMRC is 12 months from the end of the relevant accounting period. For most companies, corporation tax is payable within nine months and one day from the end of the relevant accounting period. This means that the company is required to pay corporation tax to HMRC before it is required to file its tax return. Therefore companies will make a payment based on their anticipated corporation tax liability for the period, and will make a balancing payment (or receive a rebate) once the final figure for corporation tax has been established.

Large companies, meaning those with annual taxable profits of £1,500,000 or more, usually (depending on the company's overall corporation tax liability) have to pay tax in four instalments on the following dates:

1. Six months and 13 days after the start of the accounting period;
2. Three months from the first instalment due date;
3. Three months from the second instalment due date; and
4. Three months and 14 days after the end of the accounting period.

⭐ *Example – corporation tax payment dates for large companies*

Newton Limited's taxable profits for the financial year are £4,000,000, and it must pay corporation tax by instalments for its accounting period ending 30 June 2022. These instalments will be due on 14 January 2023, 14 April 2023, 14 July 2023 and 14 October 2023.

Very large companies, which means those with annual taxable profits of over £20,000,000, have to pay the tax in four instalments during the accounting period. The due dates are:

1. Two months and 13 days after the start of the accounting period;
2. Three months from the first instalment due date;
3. Three months from the second instalment due date; and
4. Three months from the third instalment due date.

11.10 Tax avoidance

There is a great deal of legislation drafted to combat corporation tax avoidance, and the legislation focuses on known loopholes or possibilities for tax avoidance in the existing legislation. In addition to these specific measures, the Finance Act 2013 allows HMRC to make adjustments to a taxpayer's liability to counteract the tax advantages arising from abusive tax arrangements. This is known as the general anti-avoidance rule and is explained in detail at **9.16**.

Sample questions

Question 1

A private limited company made income profits of £600,000 in its accounting period ending 31 March 2023. In the same accounting period, it also made a chargeable gain of £1 million. It is not entitled to any tax reliefs or exemptions.

Which of the following statements best describes the company's tax position for the accounting period ending March 2023?

A   It will have a capital gains tax liability of £200,000.

B   It will have a corporation tax liability of £304,000.

C   It can reduce its liability to tax on the chargeable gain by deducting an annual exemption of £12,300.

D   It is a company and so not required to pay any tax in respect of capital gains.

E   It will pay income tax on its trading profits and capital gains tax on its chargeable gains.

Answer

Option B is correct. Companies pay corporation tax on their gains, not CGT or income tax (meaning that options A, D and E are wrong) on their gains and do not benefit from an annual exemption (meaning that option C is also wrong). It is necessary to add income profits and chargeable gains together in order to ascertain total profits and the appropriate rate of tax. This company has total profits of £1,600,000, and pays corporation tax of 19% on these profits, giving a tax liability of £304,000.

Question 2

A company's income in the accounting periods from 1 April 2020 to 31 March 2023 is set out below. The company's accounting reference date is 31 March.

Year	Trading profit (£)	Rental income (£)
2020/21	25,000	20,000
2021/22	15,000	20,000
2022/23	(10,000)	20,000

Assume that it is now late 2023 and the client is still trading but anticipates making a loss again for the financial year 2023/24. Its rental properties are empty and the company is receiving no rent for them. If the company continues to trade, which of the following best describes the tax relief(s) the client should claim for its losses in the 2022/23 accounting period?

A   Terminal carry-back relief, because the company has stopped making trading profits.

B   Carry-forward relief, so that the losses can be set against future profits of the same trade.

C   Carry-across relief, so that total profit for 2022/23 is reduced to £10,000.

D   Carry-back relief, so that trading profit for 2021/22 is reduced to £5,000.

E   Carry-across or carry-back relief, to reduce total profit for 2021/22 or 2022/23 by £10,000.

Answer

Option E is correct. The requirements for terminal carry-back relief have not been met: the company was clearly not in its final 12 months of trading in 2022/23 (option A is therefore wrong). Carry-forward relief is risky as the company may not make future profits (so option B is wrong). The client can choose between carry-back and carry-across relief to reduce total profits from one of those years by £10,000. The fact that it can choose which relief to use means that options C and D are wrong in stipulating that the company has only one available form of relief to claim.

12 Partnerships and Companies: Accounts and Regulation

SQE1 syllabus

Candidates are required to apply relevant core legal principles and rules appropriately and effectively, at the level of a competent newly qualified solicitor in practice, to realistic client-based and ethical problems and situations in the following areas:

- finance: financial records, information and accounting requirements
- corporate governance and compliance: documentary, record-keeping, statutory filing and disclosure requirements

Learning outcomes

By the end of this chapter you will be able to:

- understand the principle of double entry bookkeeping;
- understand the purpose of final accounts;

- understand how to interpret a profit and loss account and balance sheet;
- understand the accruals basis of preparing final accounts;
- understand how partnership accounts are compiled and arranged;
- understand the differences between company accounts and those of an unincorporated business;
- understand the domestic and international accounting standards and principles which dictate how a company's accounts are prepared and presented; and
- understand the documents that form a company's reports and accounts.

12.1 Introduction

The focus of **Chapter 7** was calculating trading profit. In this chapter, we turn to business accounts in general: how they are prepared and what they can tell us. Then, we consider the regulatory framework governing company accounts, and the domestic and international accounting standards which dictate how company accounts are prepared and presented. This will mean that in practice, you will be familiar with the presentation of and terminology in any accounts that you examine.

12.2 Business accounts

We will now turn to business accounts, and start by considering record-keeping. Just as individuals have bank statements and bills to help them to keep track of their financial position, business owners need information to monitor the finances of their business. This is the purpose of accounts: the business owner (or a bookkeeper) will use all of the business's financial records – statements, invoices, receipts – to prepare the business's accounts. The accounts provide a useful summary of the business's financial position.

There are two common meanings of the word 'accounts'. The first is the day-to-day records of the business's transactions, and the second is the accounting year end summary (Final Accounts).

12.3 Who will look at accounts?

Business owners will need accounts to assess the financial state of the business and plan for the future. There are many other people who will need to see a business's accounts. For example, bankers will ask to see business accounts when they are deciding whether to lend money to the business, and solicitors will want access to a business's accounts if their client is buying the business. HMRC will need a copy of the business's accounts to assess tax, and companies usually have to send a copy of their accounts to Companies House every year.

12.4 The role of accountants

Almost all businesses will have a firm of accountants which they use to help them to prepare the financial records they need to keep, and advise them on taxation. Accountants will produce accounts which follow the rules on how financial information is recorded. It is important that this information is standardised to enable those who are viewing accounts to understand the information they contain quickly and easily, and to enable them to compare accounts for the same business across different accounting periods, or to compare the accounts of different businesses. Most companies have to file audited accounts at Companies House, and these must be examined by a registered auditor, who will provide their opinion as to whether the accounts give a true and fair view of the affairs of the business. Accountants also advise on tax matters such as reliefs and exemptions.

12.5 Taxation

A business's accounts are a starting point for assessing tax liability. Businesses that employ staff must keep Pay As You Earn ('PAYE') and National Insurance records, which HMRC will want to see, and VAT records.

12.6 Accounting standards

It is impossible to compare accounts unless the accounts have been prepared on a standard basis. The accounting profession has strived to ensure uniformity and the UK Financial Reporting Council has produced the Financial Reporting Standards, which describe accounting methods which should be applied to all financial accounts. Their aim is to give a true and fair view of the business's finances. These standards are not legally binding, but failure to adhere to them can lead to disciplinary action by the governing body of the professional in question. In addition to domestic standards, there is an international standard set by the International Accounting Standards Board.

12.7 What information do accounts provide?

Businesses need to be able to calculate their profits. To do this, they need to know how much income they have received in an accounting period, and what expenses they have incurred. They also need to know what their assets and liabilities are, so that they can ascertain what the business is worth. Understanding these four categories – income, expenses, assets and liabilities – is key to understanding bookkeeping and accounts.

Income is what the business earns from trading or offering its services, for example, money received for the sale of furniture in a furniture shop, or money paid for legal services supplied by a law firm.

Expenses are items the business has paid for, and which it will benefit from for a short time. Examples include, the price paid for gas, electricity, petrol, or stock bought for resale – those sums it needs to incur in order for the business to operate.

Assets are essentially what the business owns, or has a right to own. For example, its business premises, if it owns them; machinery; vehicles; cash and debtors (because it has a right to the money owed to it by its debtors, and, in theory, it will receive this money when the debtor pays). Whereas expenses will benefit a business for a short time, assets tend to provide a longer-term benefit to a business.

Liabilities are what the business owes. Examples are money outstanding on a bank loan, or money owed to creditors.

12.8 Double entry bookkeeping

Businesses must keep records of every financial transaction, otherwise they will not be able to work out how much they have spent or earned. They need to record their day-to-day financial transactions in order to prepare accurate accounts. The recording of a business's financial transactions is known as bookkeeping. All businesses use the double entry bookkeeping system. This was developed over 600 years ago and is used all over the world. It is based on the principle that there are two aspects to every transaction – for example, if a business buys premises, it both acquires premises and has less cash. If a business receives payment for an outstanding invoice, it has more cash and loses the debt owed to it. The two aspects of every transaction are recorded in the business's books, which have a left-hand column and a right-hand column. The left-hand column is called the debit column (shortened to DR) and the right-hand column is called the credit column (shortened to CR).

Under the double entry system, the business has separate accounts for each aspect of the business. For example, it will have one for cash, one for each type of expense, and one for each debtor. Every single transaction is recorded as it occurs.

Bookkeepers check the accuracy of the books at regular intervals, perhaps daily or monthly, perhaps weekly. They will also check the business's books at the end of its accounting period, which is usually one year. They will add all the DR balances and all the CR balances on the accounts. If there are no errors in the books, the two figures should be the same. This process of adding together all the DR and CR entries is called preparing the trial balance. An example trial balance is set out below.

 Example – trial balance

Last month, Niamh started her own business as a surveyor. She contributed £15,000 capital to the business. She paid £800 in rent for her office, and paid £750 to her receptionist as wages. Then she sent out her first bill to Mrs Jones for a surveyor's report (£600).

This is how those figures would appear on a trial balance:

Trial Balance	DR	CR
	£	£
Capital		15,000
Cash	13,450	
Wages	750	
Rent	800	
Profit Costs		600
Debtors (Mrs Jones)	600	
	15,600	15,600

You will see that the DR and CR balances are the same. Also note that the capital contribution is shown on the DR column as being split between cash, wages and rent: this is how the capital of £15,000 has been used in the business.

Preparing a trial balance is the first step in preparing the business's final accounts, which are its year-end summary accounts. Further explanation of the double entry book system is beyond the scope of this book, but it is important to understand that it exists and why it is the basis for preparing the trial balance and then the final accounts. You will encounter double entry bookkeeping in more detail when you study solicitors' accounts.

12.9 Final accounts

We will now consider how a trial balance can be translated into final accounts.

12.9.1 The purpose of final accounts

Businesses need and want to know how well their business is performing financially, and what it is worth. The final accounts, which comprise the profit and loss account and the balance sheet, give them this information.

The profit and loss account shows how profitable the business is, that is, how successful it is in its day-to-day operations, whether those operations are trading or providing services.

The balance sheet shows what the business is worth, taking into account all of its assets and all of its liabilities.

All of the information in the profit and loss account and balance sheet are from the trial balance, but the information is presented in such a way that it is easy to understand the business's profitability and worth from looking at the final accounts. The final accounts are prepared once a year, at the end of the business's accounting period.

We will now consider the profit and loss account and balance sheet in more detail.

12.9.2 The profit and loss account

The profit and loss account tells us how profitable a business is, through a simple calculation:

Income – Expenses = Profit

If the business's income exceeds its expenses, the business has made a profit. If the business's expenses exceed its income, the business has made a loss.

Only those items which are classified as income and expenses will appear on the profit and loss account. It is important to identify income and expenses accurately, and not to confuse them with the business's assets and liabilities (which will instead appear on the balance sheet). There is no place for assets and liabilities on the profit and loss account – knowing, for example, the value of the business's fixed assets does not tell you anything about how successful the business is in its day-to-day trading.

On the profit and loss account, all of the income figures are grouped together, followed by the expenses. Then the expenses are deducted from total income to calculate profit. The items are set out vertically, so the layout of the profit and loss account is:

Income

–

Expenses

=

Profit

Example – how a trial balance becomes a profit and loss account

Alice is an accountant with her own practice. The extract below is from her trial balance for the accounting period which has just ended.

Extract from Trial Balance	DR	CR
Profit Costs		200,000
Interest Received		30,000
General Expenses	17,000	
Wages	45,000	

Alice's profit and loss account will show the same figures, but they will be presented in a different way:

Profit and Loss Account [for year ended x]	£	£
Income		
Profit Costs	200,000	
Interest Received	30,000	
		230,000
Expenses		
Wages	45,000	
General Expenses	17,000	
		(£62,000)
NET PROFIT		168,000

The columns on the profit and loss account are different from the columns on the trial balance. The convention on the profit and loss account is to show workings in column(s) to the left and carry the main figures across to the right-hand column. There are no DR or CR columns. You will remember from **Chapter 7** that brackets are used to show that a figure is to be deducted or that it is a minus figure. In the example above, we have a net profit. If Alice's expenses had exceeded her income, the final figure in the profit and loss account would be a net loss.

Business owners can use the profit and loss account to assess how profitable the business is. There are two ways of increasing profits: reducing expenses or increasing income. Businesses can increase income by selling more, perhaps because they are creating different or better products or marketing them better, or by increasing their prices. Businesses can decrease expenses by, for example, buying cheaper stock or raw materials, reducing the number of employees, or renting cheaper premises.

12.9.3 Trading accounts

Businesses which buy and sell goods have a preliminary account called a trading account, in addition to their profit and loss account. Businesses engaged in the provision of professional services, like law firms, do not need a trading account.

The trading account shows gross profit by subtracting the cost of sales (the cost of buying trading stock) from the income received from sales. This figure is the business's gross profit. The gross profit is then transferred to the profit and loss account. Any other income, and other expenses such as utility bills, will also be added to the profit and loss account and factored into the calculation of net profit.

Having a trading account as well as a profit and loss account means that businesses can see where the problem lies if they are not satisfied with their net profits. The trading account will enable them to assess whether their business is buying stock at too high a price or whether it is its other expenses, shown on the profit and loss account, which are reducing its net profit by so much.

12.9.4 Balance sheet

We now turn from the profit and loss account to the balance sheet, which is the other element to the final accounts. The balance sheet shows the worth or value of the business by listing its assets and liabilities on the last day of the accounting period. It must be headed with the date of preparation. It is often described as a snapshot of the business, because it shows how much the business is worth on the day of preparation, and this could change the very next day. For example, a balance sheet showing as one of the business's assets a debtor who owes £100,000 will not be worth as much as it seems if the very next day it becomes clear that the debtor is insolvent and there is no money left to pay its debts.

The calculation which the balance sheet essentially shows is:

Assets – Liabilities = Net worth of the business

The balance sheet does not just show assets in one section and liabilities in the other. It has two sections, one showing the value of the assets less liabilities owed to third parties and the other showing the amount owed to the proprietor as capital. These two amounts will be the same. It might help you to think of the top half as showing you where the money is – tied up in fixed assets, used to buy stock, in the business's bank account, for example – and the bottom half as showing you where the money came from – the owner's initial capital contribution and profits earned since trading began, for example:

Employment of capital = where the money is *now*

Capital employed = where the money originally came from

As with the profit and loss account, the balance sheet calculation (Assets – Liabilities = Net Worth) is shown vertically. In the example set out below, you will see that the first part of the calculation (Assets – Liabilities) is followed by the value to the proprietor, and the sections are labelled 'Employment of Capital' and 'Capital Employed' respectively.

Example – a balance sheet

Balance Sheet as at [date]

	£	£	£
EMPLOYMENT OF CAPITAL			
Fixed Assets			
Premises		167,000	
Machinery		<u>88,000</u>	
			255,000
Current Assets			
Stock	4,000		
Debtors	3,000		
Cash	<u>90,000</u>	97,000	
Less Current Liabilities			
Creditors	3,000		
Bank overdraft	<u>5,000</u>	(8,000)	
Net Current Assets			<u>89,000</u>
Less Long-term Liabilities			
Loan from Bank (9 year)			<u>(75,000)</u>
Net Assets			**<u>269,000</u>**
CAPITAL EMPLOYED			
Capital			
Opening balance*		100,000	
Net profit**		309,000	
Drawings***		(140,000)	
			<u>269,000</u>

*opening balance is the money the business owner paid into the business when they started the business, so that the business could use it to start operating – for buying stock, renting premises, paying employees etc.

**net profit is the money the business has made since it started trading.

***drawings refers to the money the business owner has taken out of the business since it started trading. This figure has brackets round it because it needs to be subtracted – it has been taken out of the business, which reduces the business's value.

You will see from the balance sheet that assets and liabilities are also sub-divided.

12.9.4.1 Assets

Assets are split into fixed assets and current assets. Fixed assets are used in the business to enable it to run effectively. Examples are business premises and machinery. Current assets are short-term assets. Examples are stock, debts and cash.

12.9.4.2 Liabilities

Liabilities are divided into current and long-term liabilities. Current liabilities are liabilities which are repayable in 12 months or less from the date of the balance sheet, for example, a bank overdraft or an invoice owed to a supplier. Long-term liabilities are liabilities which are repayable more than 12 months from the date of the balance sheet. The most obvious example is a bank loan.

Assets appear on the balance sheet in increasing order of liquidity, that is, how easy it should be to turn the business's assets into cash, to meet its short-term liabilities. So fixed assets are at the top with current assets underneath. This means that any premises will always be at the very top of the balance sheet, at the top of fixed assets, and cash will always be at the bottom of current assets.

Net current assets is a key figure for a business. It shows the difference between current assets and current liabilities and it is an important figure because it shows the business's liquidity.

Net assets is another key figure, and is calculated by subtracting short-term and long-term liabilities from fixed and current assets. This figure will always be equal to the amount owing to the business owner as capital at the end of the year.

The 'Capital Employed' section shows the value of the business to the owner. It consists of the balance on the capital account (which represents the amount put into the business by the owner(s)), and also the net profit from the profit and loss account (which represents the money the business has made over the year). Sometimes the business owner(s) will have withdrawn money over the year, and this will be shown on the drawings account. The balance on the drawings account is deducted from the other figures in the Capital Employed section.

Understanding the balance sheet is crucial for a business owner, because it enables them to analyse the health of the business. If the business's liabilities exceed its assets, it is clearly in financial difficulty. Even if it has a high assets figure, it may have little cash to pay invoices, and may risk insolvency proceedings if it cannot pay a creditor.

12.10 Adjustments

So far, we have considered financial transactions as they occur. This gives a distorted view of the business's books. It means that bills which have been received but not paid will not appear in the accounts, so the business will look as if it is better off financially than it really is. For this reason, final accounts are prepared using the accruals basis, meaning that income and expenses are recorded in the period to which they relate instead of in the period when payment or receipt occurs. Final accounts must include all expenses relating to the accounting period, even if a bill has not yet been received. When final accounts are prepared, there will have to be some adjustments to the trial balance to ensure that the final accounts are prepared on the accruals basis. Some common types of adjustments are discussed below.

12.10.1 Outstanding expenses

Expenses will be entered in a trial balance when they are paid. The profit and loss account and balance sheet will show expenses which have been paid, for example, a utilities bill.

However, when preparing final accounts, additional, unpaid bills will also need to be included as an adjustment. They will appear in the profit and loss account as an expense, and in the balance sheet as an additional current liability, under 'accruals'.

12.10.2 Prepayments

Prepayments are the opposite of outstanding expenses. A prepayment is a payment which the business has made in advance. Perhaps the business has bought something this year to use in the next financial year, or perhaps it is required to pay for something in advance, which it will not benefit from until the next financial year, for example, rent. Prepayments are added to the balance sheet as current assets, labelled 'Prepayments'. A prepayment will also reduce the value of the prepaid item in the expenses section of the profit and loss account.

12.10.3 Work in progress

Work which solicitors have carried out but for which they have not submitted a bill is called work in progress. Law firms try to ensure that they issue bills as quickly as possible to reduce outstanding work in progress, but there will almost always be some work in progress from the current year carried over to the next financial year. This is classed as an asset, because once it is billed to the client, it should result in the business receiving a cash payment. It will appear as additional income (known as profit costs) in the profit and loss account for the current year and as an additional current asset on the balance sheet.

12.10.4 Closing stock

Unless they are in their first year of trading, businesses will begin their accounting year with some stock already in their warehouse, which they did not sell during the previous accounting period. They will then purchase stock during the accounting period, and there will undoubtedly be stock remaining at the end of that accounting period. This stock is called closing stock.

Closing stock will be an additional item in the current assets section of the balance sheet, to show that the business will be starting the next accounting year with some stock already purchased.

12.10.5 Bad and doubtful debts

A figure for debtors will appear in the balance sheet. Debtors are classed as a current asset, but not every debtor will pay. They may be insolvent, or may refuse to pay, and the business may not think it is worth the time and money to pursue the debt. The business should review its debts on a regular basis, and include those which it believes will never be paid (so-called 'bad debts') in the profit and loss as an expense. The effect of 'writing off' the debt in this way is that the debt will no longer be shown on the balance sheet: it will be deducted from the debtors figure.

Doubtful debtors – those who may not pay – are entered in the expenses section of the profit and loss account as 'provision for doubtful debts' and are also subtracted from the debtors figure on the balance sheet.

12.10.6 Depreciation and revaluation

Most assets depreciate over time. After several years, they will be worth nothing, or almost nothing. For example, a car or piece of machinery will usually be worth more when it is new than when it is five or ten years old. This is called depreciation, which is shown in the profit and loss account as an expense item which reduces net profit. Usually the directors will determine the amount of depreciation as a percentage of the value of the asset.

Some assets do not tend to depreciate, and they will appear in the accounts at the acquisition value. This figure will become less accurate the longer the asset is owned. Business owners may, in these cases, have assets revalued, and show the up-to-date value in the accounts. An example is property. Property tends to increase in value over time, and a property valuation from ten years previously gives an inaccurate picture of business assets, as it will almost undoubtedly have increased substantially in value over the course of ten years.

12.10.7 Disposing of assets

If a business disposes of a fixed asset, it will usually receive cash by way of consideration. Therefore its total assets do not change, but its balance sheet will. The fixed assets figure will reduce, and the cash figure will increase. Usually, however, assets do not sell for exactly the value at which they are recorded in the accounts. If the asset is sold for more than the figure recorded in the accounts ('book value'), it will be shown in the profit and loss account as profit. If it sells for less than its book value, it will be recorded in the profit and loss account as a reduction of net profit.

⭐ *Example – Final accounts, showing adjustments*

Note the following adjustments, explained at 12.10, which make the accounts more complicated than the ones you have encountered so far in this chapter:

- *opening and closing stock – opening stock is valued at £20,000 in the balance sheet and closing stock is valued at £15,000 in the balance sheet;*

- *bad debts – there is a figure of £500 in the balance sheet for bad debts;*

- *provision for doubtful debts – valued at £3,000 in the balance sheet;*

- *depreciation on cars – valued at £4,100 in the balance sheet;*

- *prepayments – valued at £1,500 in the balance sheet;*

- *accruals – valued at £1,000 in the balance sheet.*

Trading and Profit and Loss Account Year Ended [date]			
Income	£	£	£
Sales			577,000
Less: Cost of Goods Sold			
Purchases		205,000	
Opening Stock		20,000	
Closing Stock		(15,000)	
			(210,000)
GROSS PROFIT			367,000
Less: Expenses			
General (£80,000 + £1,000*)		(81,000)	

(continued)

(continued)

Trading and Profit and Loss Account Year Ended [date]			
Income	£	£	£
Rent Paid (£3,000 – £1,500)		(1,500)	
Bad Debts		(500)	
Provision for Doubtful Debts		(3,000)	
Depreciation on cars		(4,100)	
			(90,100)
Net Profit			276,900
Balance Sheet as at [date]			
EMPLOYMENT OF CAPITAL			
Fixed Assets			
Premises Office Furniture		280,000 18,600	
Vehicles	40,000		
Depreciation	(4,100)		
		35,900	
			334,500
Current Assets			
Closing stock		15,000	
Debtors	15,000		
Less provision for doubtful debts	(3,000)		
		12,000	
Cash at bank		1,900	
Prepayments		1,500	
		30,400	

(continued)

Trading and Profit and Loss Account Year Ended [date]			
Income	£	£	£
Current Liabilities			
Creditors	7,000		
Accruals*	1,000		
		(8,000)	
NET CURRENT ASSETS			22,400
NET ASSETS			356,900
CAPITAL EMPLOYED			
Capital	100,000		
Drawings	(20,000)		
Profit	276,900		
			356,900

*the figure of £1,000 represents expenses that the business is required to pay at some point in the future – the liability has already been incurred – but it has not paid them yet (see **12.10.1** for an explanation).

12.11 Analysing accounts

Now that you have a good understanding of how accounts are presented, we will consider how to analyse the accounts to understand a business's financial situation.

Looking at accounts alone can be misleading, because they show what has already happened and do not necessarily reveal much about the future. In addition, they only give financial information. They do not tell us about other matters which will affect how well the business performs, such as a declining market, a poor reputation, an up-and-coming competitor or internal conflict. However, accounts are still a very important factor in assessing a business's value and prospects.

12.11.1 Understanding the wider context

There are some steps you can take when analysing accounts to help you to understand the wider context, including:

1. **Checking the date of the balance sheet**. Is it up to date, and therefore showing an up-to-date financial position? Has it been distorted by a recent seasonal boost in sales, resulting, for example, in a high cash balance and lots of debtors?

2. **Look at the business's accounts from previous years**. This will help to show whether the business is growing and becoming more profitable, or in decline.

3. **Check how valuations have been carried out, and how recently**. Freehold premises almost always increase in value over time, and if they have not been valued recently, the business may well be worth more than it appears. Fixed assets, such as machinery, can be valued in different ways, so you need to check how this was done and think about whether this is an accurate reflection of value. Finally, it is really important, in a trading business, to check how closing stock is valued. Closing stock is the stock remaining at the end of the financial year. Stock may appear on the balance sheet at cost price, but on closer investigation the stock is obsolete or damaged, so will never realise this amount if it were sold.

4. **Analyse the debtors figure**. Debtors are classed as assets, because when they pay the outstanding debt to the business, the business will have more cash. However, sometimes debtors do not pay.

5. **Is there a bank overdraft?** This is classed as a current liability, because it is repayable on demand. It will reduce the current assets figure and make it look as if the business may have difficulty paying its debts in the short-term. However, in reality banks will not demand repayment of an overdraft unless the business is in financial difficulties, so a large overdraft may not be a problem.

6. **Look for exceptional items, which may distort the accounts for that year**. For example, perhaps the business has made a major investment in machinery, which will increase profits in the long run, but which has not happened yet.

12.11.2 General considerations

The main reasons for reading a business's accounts are to ascertain whether the business is profitable and whether it can pay its debts.

12.11.2.1 Profitability

The profit and loss account shows whether the business has made a profit. This does not mean, however, that the business has cash in the bank or can pay its debts. To understand this, consider how the profit and loss account is compiled. It will show how much the business has sold or how much it has charged for services, and this will be part of the calculation of profit. But the business may not have received payment. Looking at the balance sheet may reveal a high figure for debtors and no cash in the bank. Alternatively, perhaps the business has made a large profit but used the cash received to buy expensive equipment, so there is no cash in the bank.

Profitability, then, does not mean that the business can pay its debts (although, of course, a profitable business is still more likely to be able to pay its debts than an unprofitable one).

12.11.2.2 Can the business pay its debts?

The balance sheet shows whether a business can pay its debts.

Liquidity is the availability of liquid assets to a business. A liquid asset is an asset that can easily be converted into cash in a short amount of time. In the context of a balance sheet, this means current assets. An extremely valuable factory and office premises are of no use to a business if it needs cash within the next fortnight: it cannot sell a factory and office premises in two weeks, so owning these valuable assets will not help it to pay its debts as they fall due. Businesses can only feasibly use current assets to meet their liabilities. Therefore, it is important that the business does not run short of current assets.

If a company is unable to pay its debts as they fall due, or if its liabilities exceed its assets, a company will be deemed to be insolvent. Please see **Chapter 8** for a full explanation of how to assess whether a company is insolvent.

12.11.2.3 What assets are liquid?

Cash is the most liquid current asset, because it can be directly used to pay a debt. Debts are also reasonably liquid because they are likely to be paid, in cash. If not, businesses can sell debts on to a debt factor, whose business it is to purchase other people's debts from them for less than the amount of the debt. The debt factor then collects the debts when they are due, and makes a profit because they can collect the full amount of the debt although they only paid a percentage of the amount of the debt to the seller. Stock is not as liquid as cash or debts, because it might be difficult to sell the stock quickly, or for a good price, or it may be seasonal, damaged or obsolete stock.

12.12 Accounting formats and principles

You now have a good understanding of how businesses keep accounts and how final accounts are compiled and interpreted, but the examples in this chapter have so far focused on the accounts of the simplest form of business, that of a sole trader. We now turn to specific formats and accounting principles which relate to partnerships and companies.

12.13 Partnership accounts

The fact that partnerships have two or more owners means that partnership accounts will need to show more information than the accounts of sole traders. Partnership capital is contributed by partners and the firm's profit is owed to those partners. The partnership will need to keep separate records for each partner, showing how much capital they contributed, how much profit is owed to them, and how much they have withdrawn during the year.

Each partner will also have an account in their own name, called a capital account, which shows the amount contributed by each partner.

12.13.1 Share of profits

Partners will share profits and losses in accordance with their partnership agreement (or, if there is no agreement, in equal shares (Partnership Act (PA) 1890 or the LLP Regulations 2001). Sometimes one or more partners may receive a salary to reflect the fact that they carry out more work for the business, or they may receive interest on capital contributions. Any remaining profit will then be divided between partners in the proportions set out in the partnership agreement, PA 1890 or LLP Regulations 2001. It is important to remember that salary and interest in this context are not separate from profit; partners are not employees and so 'salary' in this context just means that some partners are entitled to a certain amount of the profits before the profits are divided up between the partners, and awarding interest is just a way of awarding a greater share of the profit to those who have contributed more capital.

12.13.2 The appropriation account

Partnership and LLP profit and loss accounts are prepared in the same way as the profit and loss accounts of sole traders, but there will also be an appropriation account showing how net profit is divided between the partners.

 Example – the appropriation account

Marianne and Lindsey are in partnership. When the partnership was set up, Marianne contributed £20,000 and Lindsey contributed £10,000. The firm's net profit for the year is £33,000. Under the partnership agreement, both partners receive interest on their capital contributions, of 8% per annum. Marianne also receives a salary of £5,000 per annum. The remaining profits are split equally between Marianne and Lindsey.

Extract Profit and Loss Account for year ended ...

	£	£	£
Net Profit			33,000
Appropriations	**Marianne**	**Lindsey**	
Interest on Capital	1,600	800	2,400
Salary	5,000	-	5,000
Profits	12,800	12,800	25,600
	19,400	13,600	33,000

The column on the right is a running total of how the profits have been allocated.

12.13.3 Current account

The net profit is owed to the proprietors of the business. Where there is only one proprietor, the profit is usually credited directly to the capital account. In the case of a partnership, it is usual to have a separate current account for each partner to which the appropriation of net profit (including salary and interest) is added and from which drawings are deducted. The reason for separating capital and current accounts is that, as we have seen, partners are often entitled to interest on capital contributed. It is therefore desirable to keep the original capital contribution of each partner readily identifiable and unaffected by subsequent appropriations of profits and drawings.

12.13.4 The balance sheet

The capital and current account balances of each partner are shown separately on the balance sheet in the capital employed section. The partnership's balance sheet would be very complicated if it included full details of salaries, interest on capital, profit shares and drawings. Usually, then, an appendix is provided to show movements on current accounts, and just the balance of the current account is inserted on the balance sheet.

Example – the separation of capital and current account balances

(Extract) Balance Sheet at ...

Capital Employed	£	£
Capital		
Partner A	20,000	
Partner B	80,000	
Current		
Partner A	15,000	
Partner B	12,000	
		127,000

12.13.5 Changes in partners

If a partner leaves or joins part-way through an accounting period, the net profit for that year will be apportioned between the period before and the period after the change. Two appropriation accounts will be prepared. The first will show the allocation of profit earned before the change in membership, in accordance with the partnership agreement before the change. The second will show the allocation of profit earned after the change, in accordance with the shares set out in the partnership agreement in force after the change in membership.

12.13.6 Taxation of partnerships

Partners submit their own tax returns, claiming their own personal allowances.

12.14 Company accounts

A company's accounts are prepared on the same basis as the accounts of a sole trader or partnership. Companies use the double entry system, and will prepare a trial balance leading to the preparation of annual final accounts. However, company accounts will still look slightly different from the accounts of a sole trader or partnership, firstly because a company is a separate legal entity, and secondly because companies are more closely regulated by statue and accountancy rules than sole traders and partnerships.

It is important to remember that the accounts are still showing the same information that sole traders and partnerships show in their final accounts.

12.14.1 Shares

The most obvious difference between unincorporated businesses and companies is that companies have shares. Below we consider the impact this has on the company's accounts.

12.14.2 Issuing shares

Shareholders finance the company by paying money in return for shares. Whereas in unincorporated businesses, the introduction of money is recorded in a capital account for each contributor, with companies, the payment of money in return for shares is recorded in a share capital account. The share capital account records all of the shareholders' contributions, rather than having an account for each shareholder, which could become complicated and unwieldy.

The section of the balance sheet which shows how much the shareholders have contributed is often headed 'capital and reserves', but is sometimes headed 'Financed by' or 'Equity'.

Shares are either issued at par value – meaning that, for example, a shareholder will pay £1 for an ordinary £1 share – or the shareholder will pay a premium to reflect the fact that the company is profitable and its shares are now worth more than their £1 nominal value. The premium will be shown separately, in the share premium account.

Companies may have more than one type of shares, for example, ordinary and preference shares. They will be shown separately on the balance sheet.

Example – how shares are recorded

(Extract) Balance Sheet for Y Ltd as at 31 December Year 1

Net Assets	**500,000**
Capital and Reserves	
Preference Shares	100,000
Ordinary Shares	300,000
Share Premium Account	100,000
	500,000

12.15 Maintenance of capital

It is a general principle of company law that the company's capital, which includes the money the shareholders have paid for their shares, must be maintained. However, as we saw in **Chapter 4**, companies can in certain circumstances buy back their own shares from shareholders. If this occurs, the shares are cancelled and the issued share capital is reduced by the nominal amount of the shares. Shareholders can usually (depending on the company's articles) sell their shares to third parties, but this will not be shown in the final accounts: it is a personal transaction between the shareholder and a third party.

12.16 A company profit and loss account

A company's profit and loss account will look very similar to the accounts of a sole trader. It will show trading income and expenses and the figures are calculated using the same accounting principles. However, there are some small differences in the way expenses are shown on a company's profit and loss account. In a company, the owners (shareholders) and directors are a separate legal person from the company, so when the company pays its directors a salary, it is a company expense and will appear as an expense on the profit and loss account. Contrast this with a partnership, where the partners might receive a salary, but the salary is just a name given to an arrangement where the partner receives some of the partnership's profits before the profits are divided between the partners: a salary in this sense is just a name given to the way the profits are allocated to the partners.

12.17 Appropriation of profit

A company's net profit is used for particular purposes, and for a company, the main purposes are taxation, dividends and retention of profits.

12.17.1 Taxation

Tax is not shown in the accounts of unincorporated businesses because the businesses themselves do not have a tax liability. It is the sole trader or partners who have a personal liability for income tax or CGT. Companies have their own liability to corporation tax, and this is shown in the accounts.

Unless they are large companies, which pay two of their instalments of corporation tax during the accounting period to which the tax relates, companies do not have to pay corporation tax until nine months after the end of the accounting period. This means that when the final accounts are prepared, at the end of an accounting period, the company will not yet have paid any tax on its profits from the accounting period. The profit and loss account will show that a certain sum is needed to pay the company's corporation tax bill. It will do this by showing the company's profits before and after tax.

Example – showing profits before and after tax

In its first year of trading, a company has income of £100,000 and expenses of £50,000. It estimates that corporation tax of £9,500 will be payable.

(Extract) Profit and Loss Account for the year ending ...

Net Profit before tax	<u>50,000</u>
Tax	<u>(9,500)</u>
Post Tax Profit	40,500

The tax due to HMRC will appear on the balance sheet as a current liability.

Example – provision for tax		
(Extract) Balance Sheet as at ...		
Current Assets		
Cash	15,000	
Current Liabilities		
Creditors	(2,000)	
Provision for Tax	(9,500)	
Net Current Assets		**3,500**

When the tax is paid, the 'provision for tax' will disappear from the current liabilities section and cash will decrease in the current assets section, to reflect the fact that the company has used cash to pay its tax bill.

12.17.2 Dividends

As we saw in **2.8.4**, companies are only permitted to pay dividends from profits (although they could be paid from previous years' accumulated profits, rather than the current year). However, companies are unlikely to distribute all of their net profit. This is partly because they need money to pay expenses and run the business. Secondly, much of the company's profit may not be in the form of cash. Debtors are counted as an asset, so will be factored into the net profit calculation in the profit and loss account, but they do not produce any cash for the company until they pay. Or perhaps the company used some of the money it made during its accounting period to buy a fixed asset. If this is the case, the profit will be shown in the profit and loss account, but will not be represented by cash sitting in the company's bank account; instead, it has been ploughed into a fixed asset. Dividends as such will not be included as an item in the profit and loss account but, once paid, the cash figure will be reduced accordingly.

12.17.3 Retained profit

The balance of the net profit, after tax and dividends, is retained in the business. These retained profits are generally known as the profit and loss reserve. Because the profit and loss reserve consists of profit the business has made while trading, it does not form part of the capital of the company. This means that it can be distributed to shareholders if the directors decide to recommend a dividend. Contrast this with share capital, which forms part of the capital of the company because it derives from the money shareholders have paid for shares. It is not usually available to shareholders because of the principle of maintenance of capital.

12.18 A company balance sheet

12.18.1 Capital and reserves

The main feature of a company balance sheet which differs from an unincorporated business is in the 'Capital Employed' section, which is often called the 'Capital and Reserves' section in company accounts. You have already considered the capital section of the balance sheet, and now we consider the 'reserves' part.

Example – capital and reserves

(Extract) Balance Sheet as at ...

NET ASSETS £177,000

CAPITAL AND RESERVES

Share Capital £100,000

Debenture Redemption Reserve £25,000

Profit and Loss Reserve £52,000

SHAREHOLDERS' FUNDS £177,000

The reserves part of a balance sheet shows what the company 'owes' to its shareholders – the money shown in here would be paid to shareholders (after payment of any outstanding debts of the company) if the company were wound up. There are different types of reserve, the main difference being between revenue reserves and capital reserves. Most reserves are revenue reserves, which can in theory be distributed to the shareholders, for example through the payment of a dividend, even if the company decides not to do so. Capital reserves cannot be distributed to shareholders.

The profit and loss reserve is the most significant revenue reserve. It consists of the company's profits, after tax and after payment of any dividends the company has decided to pay. If the company makes a profit every year, and there is still some left after payment of tax and dividends, it will be added to the profit and loss reserve. This means that over time, the figure in the profit and loss reserve will increase unless it is spent.

It is common for the different reserves to be 'labelled' in the accounts, to show why the profits have been retained rather than paid to shareholders by way of dividend. An example of a label is the 'debenture redemption reserve', shown in the balance sheet extract above, which will indicate that some of the profits have been retained to repay a debenture in the future. It is important to remember that this is just a label – the money is still retained profit, but the label tells anyone looking at the accounts how much the company is planning to use to repay the debenture.

Capital reserves are not available for distribution to shareholders because they are part of the long-term capital of the company. An example of a capital reserve is the share premium account. When shares are issued at a premium, the company must record the surplus over the nominal value of the shares on the share premium account. The surplus is part of the capital of the company.

12.18.2 Consolidated accounts

Parent companies must normally produce a consolidated profit and loss account and balance sheet showing the group's profits or losses, assets and liabilities. This requirement reflects the commercial reality that the group is a single unit and it enables shareholders to assess the performance of their company within the context of the whole group.

Each individual company in the group still has to prepare its own final accounts in addition to the parent company preparing the consolidated accounts.

12.18.3 Regulation

Regulation is a way of making sure that accounts are all prepared in a uniform way, so that they are more transparent and can be easily understood and interpreted. It enables direct comparisons to be made between businesses.

12.18.4 Statutory regulation

Companies are subject to a great deal of statutory regulation, most of which is set out in the CA 2006 (Part 15). For companies classed as micro companies, small companies and medium-sized companies, the requirements are less onerous. Please see **2.5.5** for a definition of a small company and a micro-entity. A medium-sized company is defined as a company with a balance sheet total of not more than £18 million, a turnover of not more than £36 million, and no more than 250 employees in a particular financial year (s 465 CA 2006).

Under the CA 2006, companies must keep 'adequate accounting records' and prepare accounts for the company for every financial year. Directors must not approve accounts unless they are satisfied that they give a true and fair view of the assets, liabilities and financial position of the company. Directors can incur civil and criminal liability for untrue or misleading statements in the company's accounts (see **3.22.6**).

As we saw in **3.22.6**, companies must file their annual accounts with the Registrar of Companies and send a copy of their annual accounts and reports for each financial year to shareholders, debenture holders and anyone else who is entitled to receive notice of general meetings. The final accounts of public companies must be put before the members in a general meeting.

Companies must usually have their accounts audited. Many small companies and dormant companies are exempt from this requirement, but shareholders holding 10% or more of the nominal issued share capital may require the company to have its accounts audited.

12.18.5 Accounting principles

Whilst companies have long been subject to statutory regulation, more recently the professional bodies of the accounting profession have worked together to produce uniform accounting principles.

The latest statement of best practice is FRS 102, The Financial Reporting Standard, and it is applicable in the UK and Republic of Ireland. It is aimed at achieving consistency in the preparation of accounts and is sometimes referred to as 'UK GAAP' or 'New UK GAAP', to distinguish it from the similar systems of other jurisdictions. It specifies certain methods of calculation and sets out detail which must appear on the profit and loss account and balance sheet.

The International Accounting Standards Board (IASB) issues its own International Financial Reporting Standards (IFRS), which can be adopted in different jurisdictions. The IFRS have different rules from FR102, but cover the same points as FR102.

We will now consider how statute and UK and international regulation determine the form and content of accounts.

12.18.6 UK format

The CA 2006 requires companies to prepare either 'Companies Act Individual Accounts' or 'International Accounting Standards Individual Accounts', which essentially comply with FRS 102 and the IFRS respectively. Note that both require the preceding financial year's figures to be shown alongside the equivalent figures for the current financial year, which enables comparisons to be made between financial years so that directors can spot changes and patterns emerging in the accounts. This aspect of the accounts has been omitted in the examples that follow, for the sake of simplicity.

12.18.6.1 The Companies Act Individual Accounts

The CA 2006 provides that Companies Act Individual Accounts must include a profit and loss account and a balance sheet, and must comply with any relevant regulations. The main regulations which cover company accounts formats are the Large and Medium-sized Companies and Groups (Accounts and Reports) Regulations 2008 (SI 2008/410) and their equivalent for small companies, SI 2008/409 (together, 'the Regulations'). The Regulations contain templates showing the way the profit and loss account and balance sheets must be drawn up. Some variation is permitted, so you will encounter slightly different formats in practice.

12.18.6.2 Profit and loss account

The following is a simple profit and loss account, also known as an income statement.

Example – profit and loss account in the UK format		
Profit and Loss Account for the Year ended ...		
	£000	£000
TURNOVER	250,000	
Cost of Sales	100,000	
GROSS PROFIT		150,000
Distribution costs	15,000	
Administrative costs	20,000	
		(35,000)
OPERATING PROFIT		115,000
Interest Receivable		5,000
PROFIT BEFORE INTEREST		120,000
Interest Payable		(2,000)
PROFIT BEFORE TAXATION		118,000
Tax		(25,000)
PROFIT FOR THE FINANCIAL YEAR		93,000

The first point to note is that company profit and loss accounts separate income, expenses and profit generated by their trading/operating activities from other items such as finance costs. This enables them to see immediately how well they are performing in terms of trading activities.

The profit and loss account for a company does not itemise every expense; rather, it groups them together into categories such as 'Administration Expenses'. This stops the profit and loss account from being too complicated to interpret quickly. There will be notes accompanying the accounts, which give a more detailed breakdown and explanation of the figures. The names of the categories of expenses are dictated by accounting standards. You will also note some differences in terminology. An example is that sales are usually called 'turnover'. Finally, the company's corporation tax liability will be shown at the end of the profit and loss account.

The following is an example of a simple balance sheet, also known as a statement of financial position.

Example – balance sheet in the UK format			
Balance Sheet as at ...			
	£000	£000	£000
ASSETS			
FIXED ASSETS			
Tangible Assets			200,000
CURRENT ASSETS			
Stock	50,000		
Debtors	50,000		
Cash	45,000		
		145,000	
Amounts Falling Due within 1 Year			
Creditors	20,000		
Provision for Tax	25,000		
		(45,000)	
Net Current Assets			100,000
Total Assets less Current Liabilities			300,000
Amounts Falling Due after more than 1 year			
Bank Loan			(20,000)
NET ASSETS			280,000

(*continued*)

CAPITAL AND RESERVES			
Share Capital			200,000
Profit and Loss Reserve			80,000
SHAREHOLDERS' FUNDS			280,000

The first point to note is that the first section is headed 'Assets' rather than employment of capital, as on a balance sheet for a sole trader or partnership. Secondly, current and long-term liabilities are instead categorised as amounts falling due within one year and more than one year respectively. A provision for tax has been included, which is due within one year, but usually has not been calculated by the time the balance sheet is prepared.

Finally, there is an additional figure representing 'Total Assets less Current Liabilities', which shows the value of the business before accounting for long-term liabilities.

12.18.7 International format

Instead of providing templates, the IFRS usually just set out minimum requirements for the information which must appear in the accounts. The profit and loss account (income statement) is very similar in format to the profit and loss account in the UK format, the main difference being that sales/turnover is labelled 'Revenue'. The international format of the balance sheet, or statement of financial position, seems very different from the UK format, but the differences are mainly just terminology. For example, 'non-current assets' and 'non-current liabilities' are used instead of 'fixed assets' and 'long-term liabilities'. 'Debtors' and 'creditors' are instead 'receivables' and 'payables'. Closing stock is labelled 'inventories' and 'debentures' as 'loan notes'. FRS 102 itself also adopts this international terminology.

12.18.8 Annual reports and accounts

The CA 2006, FRS 102 and IFRS require additional reports and financial statements to be produced, in addition to the balance sheet and profit and loss account. The documents are known collectively as the 'Reports and Accounts', and what is required depends on the size and type of company. The additional documents include the following:

12.18.8.1 Strategic Report

This contains a review of the company's business, designed to enable the performance of the company to be measured and assessed. This report is required under the CA 2006, but small companies are exempt.

12.18.8.2 Chair's Report

A Chair's Report is often produced by quoted companies, but it is not a strict requirement for any company to prepare one. It explains what has happened to the company over the course of the financial year, and cannot be relied upon as an objective assessment of the company's fortunes because the Chair is likely to present the company in the best light possible.

12.18.8.3 Directors' Report

The Directors' Report contains factual information about the company and a review of the company's business, as well as confirmation that the auditors (where relevant) have been given all relevant information. The requirements of a Directors' Report are set out in s 416 CA 2006. Failure to comply with those requirements is a criminal offence (s 418 CA 2006). Small companies do not need to include some of the statutory information.

12.18.8.4 Auditors' Report

This report is prepared by the company's auditors, and in it, the auditors are required to state whether, in their opinion, the accounts give a true and fair view of the financial state of the business.

12.18.8.5 Notes

The FRS 102 and the IFRS require the accounts to be accompanied by a set of explanatory notes. They expand on the information in the profit and loss account and balance sheet and are usually several pages long.

Summary

Business accounts

Businesses keep detailed daily records using the double entry bookkeeping system. These records are used to produce a trial balance.

1. At the end of the accounting period, the trial balance is used to prepare the final accounts, which consist of the profit and loss account and the balance sheet.

2. The profit and loss account is based on the calculation

    Income – expenses = profit

3. The balance sheet shows the net worth of the business and is based on the calculation:

    Assets – liabilities = net worth of the business

The top half of the balance sheet shows employment of capital which, putting it simply, means *where the money is now*. The bottom half of the balance sheet shows capital employed, which is *where the money originally came from.*

Partnership accounts

1. Partnership profit and loss accounts have an appropriation account, to show how profits have been divided between the partners. There will also be a separate capital account and current account for each partner.

Company accounts

1. Company accounts differ from those of a sole trader or partnership because companies have a separate legal identity from the shareholders (owners) and directors.

2. Companies' net profits are:

   (a) used to pay tax;

   (b) paid to shareholders as dividends; or

   (c) retained within the company.

3. Parent companies must produce consolidated accounts which show the financial position of all of the companies in the group and therefore the group as a whole.

4. Companies are regulated by statute and UK and international accounting standards, which ensure that accounts are prepared using uniform accounting principles so that they are easy to understand.

Sample questions

Question 1

The following information is from the accounts of a business:

• Sales	150,000
• Fixed assets	100,000
• Cost of sales	50,000
• Current assets	22,000
• Current liabilities	10,000
• Long-term liabilities	53,000
• Capital employed	59,000

Which of the following best describes the value of the business's net current assets and net assets?

A   The business's net current assets are 12,000 and its net assets are 59,000.

B   The business's net current assets are 12,000 and its net assets are 118,000.

C   The business's net current assets are 112,000 and its net assets are 118,000.

D   The business's net current assets are 122,000 and its net assets are 12,000.

E   The business's net current assets are 40,000 and its net assets are 59,000.

Answer

Option A is correct. Net current assets are calculated by subtracting current liabilities from current assets, so the calculation is 22,000 – 10,000, resulting in a figure of £12,000 for net current assets. Net assets are calculated by subtracting both current and long-term liabilities from fixed and current assets. The calculation is (100,000 + 22,000) less (10,000 + 53,000), that is, 122,000 – 63,000, resulting in a net assets figure of 59,000.

Question 2

A client, which is a partnership, gives you the following information about its business over the course of the financial year:

(a) It has a trading profit of £200,000; and

(b) The client has received an electricity bill for £500 but has not yet paid it.

Which of the following best describes where the figures listed in (a) and (b) above will appear on the client's balance sheet and/or profit and loss account?

A   Item (a) will appear on both the profit and loss account and on the balance sheet, and item (b) will appear on the balance sheet as an accrual.

B   Item (a) will appear on both the profit and loss account and on the balance sheet, and item (b) will appear on the balance sheet as a prepayment.

C   Item (a) will appear on the balance sheet as income, and item (b) will appear on the profit and loss account as an expense.

D   Item (a) will appear on the balance sheet as income, and item (b) will appear on the balance sheet as an expense.

E   Both items will appear on both the profit and loss account and balance sheet.

Answer

Option A is correct. Trading profit is shown at the end of the profit and loss account – this is what the profit and loss account is designed to calculate. It is also shown on the balance sheet under 'capital employed'. The bill will be shown as an accrual on the balance sheet because it has been received but not yet paid.

Appendix 1: Table of key Companies House forms

AA01	Change accounting reference date
AD01	Change registered office address
AD02	Register a single alternative inspection location (SAIL)
AD03	Move the company's records to the SAIL
AD04	Move the company's records to the registered office
AP01	Appoint a director
AP02	Appoint a corporate director
AP03	Appoint a secretary
AP04	Appoint a corporate secretary
CH01	Change the details of a director
CH02	Change the details of a corporate director
CH03	Change the details of a secretary
CH04	Change the details of a corporate secretary
CS01	Confirmation statement
IN01	Register a private or public company
MR01	Register particulars of a charge
NM01	Change a company name
PSC01	Give notice of an individual person with significant control
PSC02	Give notice of a relevant legal entity with significant control
PSC04	Give notice of change of details for a person with significant control
PSC05	Give notice of change of details for a relevant legal entity with significant control
PSC07	Give notice of ceasing to be a person with significant control
RR01	Re-register private company as a plc
SH01	Return of allotment of shares
SH03	Notify a purchase of own shares
SH50	Apply for trading certificate for a public company
TM01	Terminate an appointment of a director
TM02	Terminate an appointment of a company secretary

Appendix 2: Summary of key shareholders' resolutions under the Companies Act 2006 and the Model Articles

Shareholders' ordinary resolutions	
To approve a long-term service contract	Section 188 CA 2006
To ratify a director's breach of duty	Section 239 CA 2006
To appoint a director	MA 17
To remove a director	Section 168 CA 2006
To appoint an auditor	Section 485 CA 2006
To remove an auditor	Section 510 CA 2006
To authorise a substantial property transaction	Section 190 CA 2006
To temporarily suspend MA 14	MA 14(3)
To authorise a loan to a director	Section 197 CA 2006
To authorise a payment for loss of office	Section 217 CA 2006
To 'activate' s550 CA 2006	Section 550 CA 2006 and transitional regulations
To authorise directors to allot shares	Section 551 CA 2006
To remove the authorised share capital clause in the company's articles	Transitional regulations passed under the CA 2006
To authorise a buyback contract	Section 694 CA 2006

Shareholders' special resolutions	
To change the name of the company	Section 77 CA 2006
To amend the company's articles of association	Section 21 CA 2006
To disapply pre-emption rights	Section 569 – 571 CA 2006
To approve the re-registration of a private company as a public company	Section 90 CA 2006
To approve a payment out of capital	Section 716 CA 2006

INDEX

Bold page numbers indicate figures, *italic* numbers indicate tables.